The European Community and the Challenge of the Future

THE EUROPEAN COMMUNITY AND THE CHALLENGE OF THE FUTURE

Edited by Juliet Lodge

St. Martin's Press, New York

First published in the United States of America in 1989
Reprinted 1990

Printed in Great Britain

ISBN 0–312–03181–5 cloth
ISBN 0–312–03238–2 paper

Library of Congress Cataloging-in-Publication Data

The European Community and the challenge of the future / edited by
Juliet Lodge.

    p.   cm.
Bibliography: p.
Includes index.
ISBN 0–312–03181–5 : $45.00 — ISBN 0–312–03238–2 (pbk) : $19.95
  1. European Economic Community.   2. Europe—Economic integration.
I. Lodge, Juliet.
HC241.2.E83412   1989
337.1'42—dc20
                                              89–30460
                                                CIP

Contents

IV. Future Perspectives

Abbreviations

ACP	African, Caribbean and Pacific members of Lome
Bull.EC	Bulletin of the European Communities
CAP	Common Agricultural Policy
CEN	European Committee for Standardization
CENELEC	European Committee for Electrotechnical standardization
CMLR	Common Market Law Review
COM	Commission Document
COMECON	Council for Mutual Economic Assistance
COMETT	Community in Education and Training for Technology
COREPER	Committee of Permanent Representatives
CSCE	Conference on Security and Cooperation in Europe
CSP	Confederation of Socialist Parties
D-G	Directorate-General
EAGGF	European Agricultural Guidance and Guarantee Fund
EC	European Community
ECJ	European Court of Justice
ECU	European Currency Unit
EDC	European Defence Community
EEC	European Economic Community
EEIG	European Economic Interest Grouping
ELR	European Law Review
EMS	European Monetary System
EMU	Economic and Monetary Union
EP	European Parliament
EPP	European People's Party
ERASMUS	European Community Action Scheme for Mobility of University Students
EPC	European Political Cooperation
ERDF	European Regional Development Fund
ESC	Economic and Social Committee
ESF	European Social Fund
ESPRIT	European Strategic Programme for Research and Development in Information Technology
ETUC	European Trade Union Confederation
EURATOM	European Atomic Energy Authority
EUREKA	European Research Coordination Agency
EUT	Draft Treaty establishing the European Union
FRG	Federal Republic of Germany
GATT	General Agreement on Tariffs and Trade
GDP	Gross Domestic Product
IMP	Integrated Mediterranean Programme
JCMS	Journal of Common Market Studies
JEI	Journal of European Integration
JET	Joint European Torus

MECU	Million ECUs
MEP	Member of the European Parliament
MP	Member of Parliament
MTN	Multilateral Trade Negotiation
NATO	North Atlantic Treaty Organization
NIC	Newly Industrializing Country
NTB	Non-tariff Barrier
OECD	Organization for Economic Cooperation and Development
OJ	Official Journal
SEA	Single European Act
SEM	Single European Market
The Six(EC6)	The founding six members of the EC (France, Italy, FRG, Belgium, Netherlands and Luxembourg
The Nine (EC9)	The Six plus Denmark, Ireland and the UK
The Ten (EC10)	EC Nine plus Greece
The Twelve	EC10 plus Spain and Portugal
US	United States of America
USSR	Union of Soviet Socialist Republics
UK	United Kingdom
VAT	Value Added Tax
VER	Voluntary Export Restraint
WEU	Western European Union

Contributors

Harvey Armstrong is Senior Lecturer in Economics, Lancaster University.

Gordon Daniels is Reader in Modern Japanese History, Sheffield University.

Scott Davidson is Lecturer in Law and Director of Legal Research, European Community Research Unit, Hull University.

Kevin Featherstone is Lecturer in the Department of European Studies, Bradford University.

Roy H. Ginsberg is Assistant Professor of Government at Skidmore College, Saratoga Springs, New York.

Adrian Hewitt is a member of the Overseas Development Institute, London.

Juliet Lodge is Reader in European Community Politics and Director of the European Community Research Unit, Hull University.

John S. Marsh is Professor and Head of the Agricultural Economics Department and Dean of the Faculty of Agriculture and Food, Reading University.

John Pinder, OBE, is Professor at the College of Europe, Bruges, Senior Fellow at the Policy Studies Institute, London and President of the Union of European Federalists.

Michael Shackleton works in the secretariat of the Committee on Budgets of the European Parliament.

Margaret Sharp is Senior Research Fellow at the Science Policy Research Unit, Sussex University.

Panos Tsakaloyannis teaches European politics at Athens University.

Paul Taylor is Senior Lecturer in International Relations, London School of Economics.

Preface

The 1980s have been a decade of upheaval for the European Community and its member states. Internal and external factors have made rapid change imperative. The member states have seen themselves to be under threat from outside competition which has impelled them to seek closer cooperation over an ever-increasing range of issues. A deep-seated uneasiness persists, however, over both the EC's capacity to cope with the new demands on it and over the appropriateness and capability of its institutional arrangements.

The question that remains to be adequately confronted concerns not simply the EC's institutional balance but the furtherance of liberal, representative democracy in a regional organization committed to promoting an ever-increasing union among its peoples without simultaneously forcing the withering away of its component nation states. This tension is often expressed in the debate over European Union and national sovereignty. However, the discussion about appropriate mechanisms for managing, controlling and overseeing policy processes whose effects escape one agency – be it a supranational or a national authority – will be sharpened over the next decade. This is because the Single European Act amendments to the Rome Treaty have both extended the actual scope of European integration and rendered the intended field of action envisaged by the framers of the Rome Treaty more tangible and visible.

If EC goals are to be advanced and old and new policies fully implemented then far more, by way of integrated policy-solving and oversight is implied than has been recognized so far. While it may be necessary, in the absence of other mechanisms, to restrict constitution-making to *ad hoc* agreements reached by member governments (who still refuse to accede to the European Parliament's wish that it perform a constituent role for the EC), awareness has grown of the need for measures to ensure that some democratic control be exercised over the expanding role of executives.

The commitment to realize the Single European Market has prompted action in a number of areas essential to the functioning of a common market which have been hitherto neglected. The SEM has made explicit what was implicit in many of the EC's original goals. As the EC advances into the 1990s, it has to deal with these and with the fears they engender, not least among national governments used to exercising their authority over many areas (that they have traditionally seen as their preserve) relatively unfettered by outside interference. The 1990s will change this.

Whatever new initiatives and developments may occur during the 1990s, the starting point is the *acquis communautaire* and the body of experience gleaned over the past thirty years. While villified as an ossified organization, in historical perspective the EC seems to have been rather dynamic. Of course states and the EC have made mistakes and failed to grapple with sensitive issues (like agricultural fraud) with sufficient diligence. Sometimes they have been too relaxed about implementing goals to which they are theoretically committed. Yet during the 1980s major shifts in states' policymaking processes and perceptions have occurred (though not of course simply as a result of EC membership) and the Euro-dimension in them is increasingly dominant.

This book has modest aims. It seeks to describe some of the developments that have fashioned the EC so far. Individual chapters try to outline how some key policy sectors have evolved and adapted, and which existing and 'new' issues are likely to receive increasing attention during the 1990s as the EC seeks an integrated approach to policymaking and problem resolution both internally and externally. Space constraints and the sheer extent of EC activity make coverage of all issue areas impossible. The book, therefore, addresses some key questions and policy areas likely to interest new students of the EC. It examines some policy areas that illustrate the type of problems that occur, notably in respect of redistributive policy goals.

It is divided into three main sections. The first considers the political and institutional context within which EC policymaking occurs. The interplay between major national governments is examined as well as key policymaking EC institutions. The second section examines a number of 'internal' policy issues and sectors. A brief overview of aspects of the context within which internal policies unfold is followed by an appraisal of the dynamics behind the Single European Market. Some major areas are examined along with the constraints imposed by the budget. The third section focuses on European Political Cooperation, the EC's 'external image' and aspects of the EC's 'external' policies. Particular attention is paid to relations with the United States, the African, Caribbean and Pacific countries and to the Pacific Basin. A final short section sketches future challenges presented by the expansive logic of Social Europe and the environmental policy.

This book looks at some of the issues and priorities confronting the EC and its member states. We have selected those of immediate and continuing concern to our students. We aim to provide a basic introduction to the EC and some of its major policies. More technical and specialized issues have been necessarily omitted to enable us to focus on key issues having a more general interest and relevance. Space constraints have also impelled us to refer mostly to readily accessible English language sources. However, we strongly recommend a reading of primary source documents and the official publications of the EC.

Part I Institutional perspectives

1 The New Dynamics of EC integration in the 1980s

Paul Taylor

In the late 1980s, it looked as if the pace of European Community integration had once more begun to accelerate following turbulence in the early 1980s. This chapter examines the reasons for this. The main changes in the relationship between the state and regional organization in Western Europe, which they imply, are discussed. And the question of where the new balance is to be found between integration and autonomy is considered.

The main events in this phase are well known. They include the settlement in 1984 of the British complaint about excessive budgetary contributions, a former source of considerable animosity between Mrs Thatcher's government and, in particular, that of President Mitterrand (Denton, 1984: 117-40); the initiation of a campaign for the strengthening of the powers of the EC's institutions that led to the 1984 Draft Treaty on European Union (EUT) (Commission, 1984: 7-28); the agreement on the Single European Act at Luxembourg in December 1985, and the instigation of a new programme for the achievement of a Europe without frontiers by 1992 (Lodge, 1986: 203-223; European Parliament, 1985); and the agreement about a package of budgetary measures on 11-12 February 1988 which increased the scale of resources available to the Communities, imposed restraints upon CAP spending, doubled the size of the funds, and introduced new procedures for exercising financial discipline (European Council, 1988).

In the mid-1980s President Mitterrand realized that expressions of support for a higher level of integration, such as that proposed by the EUT, were a very good strategy for putting pressure on the British to accept a compromise in the settlement of their budgetary grievance. Kohl's government in the FRG partly in response to the French, and partly on its own initiative, acted in ways which gave credence to this strategy. Its effectiveness rested upon the vulnerability of the UK government, particularly a Conservative one, to the apparent threat to move a core of original members to a higher level of integration, if necessary without Britain. A Conservative government had ignored comparable threats to its cost in the late 1950s, when the EEC had been formed without Britain (Camps, 1964). British diplomacy, therefore, now had to balance two objectives: satisfying specific interests and staying in the game. A measure of compromise in the former had become necessary to achieve the latter.

Various EC developments since 1984 are discussed primarily from the British perspective because the British determined the pace of integration, as the French had from 1958 until the mid to late 1960s and the West Germans from then until the late 1970s. Progress depended primarily upon solving British problems and finding ways of exerting pressure upon Britain. Two closely interrelated arguments are developed: the key to further integration was getting the British to move and the perception of the need to do this, particularly in the calculations of the French, was itself a crucial factor in placing high on the EC's agenda items extending the scope of integration and strengthening the central institutions.

A curious symbiosis has emerged between national interest and the Community: regional processes and systems are seen to be reaching the point at which increasingly frequently the former can ironically only be satisfied by making real concessions to the latter as Mrs Thatcher's Bruges speech scorning the idea of European unification showed. These arguments are developed in three interrelated contexts below. In the next section, the diplomacy about the UK budgetary rebate in 1984 is considered. Then the causes and character of the SEA in 1985-6 are discussed. In a final section, the budgetary problems in 1987-8 and the budgetary settlement of February 1988 are considered. It is shown that patterns of diplomacy may be identified in 1984 which dominated the whole period under discussion.

The budgetary rebate

The Thatcher government and the rest had been quarrelling since the 1979 Dublin Summit about the interrelated issues of the allegedly excessive net British contribution to the EC budget, the question of the permanent adjustment of the budgetary mechanism and the CAP's reform. Relations moved towards crisis point just before the outbreak of the Falklands War in 1982, but then on 24 May a short-term solution was hastily cobbled together (Stephens, 1982). In 1983, however, Britain raised the scale of diplomatic pressure, but despite valiant, though perhaps not very well-managed, efforts by the Greeks during their presidency, the Athens Summit in December 1983 ended in deadlock. When the French took over the presidency for the first six months of 1984 there was a general sense that now was the time for a massive diplomatic effort to get the British problem out of the way once and for all, which the French government skilfully orchestrated. In this context the failure of the March 1984 European Council in Brussels was particularly disastrous.

For a few hours after its breakdown the two chief protagonists, Mrs Thatcher and President Mitterrand, with his foreign minister, Claude Cheysson, behaved as if they had looked into the abyss, and were shocked into an awareness of the desperate need to hold themselves back. The French initially spoke of excluding the British from various meetings of EC states set up to discuss new initiatives, while the British cabinet actively discussed ways of unilaterally, and probably illegally, holding back payments to the EC (*Financial Times*, 22 March, 1984). Quite quickly the two leaders changed their tone: the need for quiet reflection and further patient diplomacy was asserted. But when agreement was eventually reached at Fontainebleau in June 1984, the deal was only marginally different from that rejected in March, and all sorts of loose ends were left which would not have been tolerated earlier.

Though the UK government, one suspects deliberately, made it difficult for some weeks after the settlement to judge the Fontainebleau agreement – they were very slow to produce any detailed accounts – diplomacy between March and June had achieved very little. But that attitude of British leaders, particularly senior foreign policy officers and Mrs Thatcher, had changed. The latter had even turned up at Fontainebleau with a *billet doux* called *Europe: The Future* in which she claimed that 'periodic expressions of pessimism about the future of the Community have never turned out to be justified'. 'Progress that has been made is unlikely to be reversed' (*Europe – The Future*, 1984). This letter was described as having been given to the EC Heads of Government by the Prime Minister as 'a contribution to discussion at the European Council held at Fontainebleau 25/26 June 1984'. Mrs Thatcher had decided on a softer line.

The flavour of failure in March and the measure of achievement on Fontainebleau in June 1984 can only be appreciated in the light of a closer look at the details (Wyles, 1984: 24). At Brussels a deal was tantalizingly close. There had been broad agreement to introduce quotas on milk production – though the Irish had held out for special treatment – and to impose a greater degree of financial control of CAP spending. There had been agreement to increase the ceiling on EC VAT resources from 1 per cent to 1.4 per cent though this was conditional, on German insistence, upon enlargement to include Spain and Portugal. France and the others had accepted the principle of the so-called 'formula' which they had strongly resisted in earlier years that allowed for a permanent adjustment in the budgetary arrangement to ensure a fair return to Britain; and the UK conceded that in calculating the scale of the return only payments out of VAT would be taken into account. The latter concession reduced the agreed scale of the UK deficit – called the GAP – from almost 2 bn ECUs to 1.6 bn ECUs (1 ECU = approximately 0.6 of a £ sterling). Disagreement remained over how much of the UK contribution to the EC budget was to be returned to them. This was a vital issue since the proportion would apply, according to the 'formula', for the next few years, and since the members insisted that agreement on this was the condition of acceptance of the whole package.

These negotiations from late on the nineteenth to late on the twentieth of March 1984 were extraordinary for the leaders' obduracy over relatively trivial sums, and for the light they threw on Mrs Thatcher's negotiating style. The French had conceded that they thought around one bn ECUs should be restored; Mrs Thatcher's first bid was for 1.35 bn ECUs out of the GAP of 1.6 bn ECUs. In bilateral discussions with the British on the afternoon of 20 May, President Mitterrand said that they would accept 1.1 bn. Mrs Thatcher declined to compromise. The others resisted her claim with increasing irritability. It was her against the Nine. Eventually Chancellor Kohl said that the UK would get back not a penny more than 1 bn ECUs that year without the formula. He rose and indicated that he was about to leave. At this point Mrs Thatcher said she would take 1.25 bn ECUs but by then it was too late.

The acrimonious meeting broke up without agreement (Jenkins, 1984: 17). The difference between the highest offer by the French and Mrs Thatcher's late bid was 150 m ECUs, around £86 million at the current sterling rate. For this sum, paltry by the standards of national budgetary expenditure in even the smallest developed states, the EC had been taken to the brink of disaster. This was probably the lowest point in relations between the British and the others, especially the French, of the 1970s and 1980s. It follows, of course, that this meeting also marked the beginning of an improvement.

In some ways Fontainebleau represented a stepping back from the brink. It was agreed that the British should get a single payment of £600 million in 1985 and that afterwards the sum returned would be 66 per cent of the gap between

Britain's VAT contribution and the EC's share of expenditure in Britain. The arrangement was to apply only while the own resources ceiling remained at 1.4 per cent of VAT: if the resources level changed, as it did in February 1988, the scale of the rebate was open to renegotiation. For 1983 this formula produced a return to the UK of 107 bn ECUs, about £631m. The British gained no significant improvement over what would have been within fairly easy reach in March had they conducted themselves differently. But the atmosphere was different and Mrs Thatcher's letter to the other heads of government suggested a more positive spirit on her part. A number of elements were added to the Brussels package to strengthen the EC's identity in the minds of the European people, and an Ad Hoc Committee on Institutional Affairs was set up to consider ways of strengthening EC institutions, something slipped in by the French. The British accepted it, as it were, before they could catch their breath (Cheeseright, 1984).

By late 1984 and early 1985, the EC had moved into calmer waters, despite, rather than because of, British diplomacy. Quite a number of squall clouds were still visible, however, not the least of which was that the EC was still under severe financial pressure. Special contributions from member states outside the legal budgetary framework were required in late 1984. The EP refused to release the rebate agreed for 1984 until the extra sums had been provided (*The Guardian*, 5 October 1984). The Council also proposed a budget for 1985 which covered only ten months of the year, and which made no allowance for the UK rebate: this the EP rejected. Negotiations with Spain and Portugal ran into difficulties raising doubts about their accession in January 1986, and the West Germans continued to insist that unless this happened there could be no increase of the VAT ceiling to 1.4 per cent.

In early 1985 the EC was in a financial mess. It was desperately short of money, dependent on uncertain handouts from governments, and no one knew from where the much fought-over British rebate would come. The striking thing was that there was now a measure of confidence, in the absence of any hard evidence, that it would turn out more or less all right in the end. The conclusion was hard to resist that the one concrete achievement of those who conducted British diplomacy towards the EC in 1984 was to frighten themselves into a more conciliatory attitude. Certainly any substantive gains from this investment of diplomatic energy were very hard to detect.

What explains this change of tone, which was particularly marked between the Brussels and Fontainebleau meetings, was in part that the French government was no longer benefiting from the operation of the CAP to the same degree as it had previously, and the accession of Spain and Portugal could probably have the effect of turning France, among others, into a net contributor to the EC budget. The French were, therefore, more prepared to compromise with the British than they had been earlier. Nonetheless, the settlement was possible because the British, and not the French, had changed their positions though the Thatcher government tried to conceal this. This change needs to be explained. The key point was that at the March meeting the strategy of implying support for higher levels of integration, from which the UK could be excluded, occurred to the French president as a way of dealing with the British problem. This strategy could rest on the seeming reality of the special relationship with Germany, a central element in Franco–British relations from then into 1988, and a crucial factor in shaping the SEA and the February 1988 budgetary agreement.

The strategy probably emerged accidently in the few hours immediately following the breakdown of the March 1984 Brussels European Council. Mitterrand could hardly help perceiving a link between his initial reaction of calling for a conference of those in the EC who would 'stand up and be counted' (Wyles, 1984) – which amounted to keeping the UK out of discussions about ways of taking the EC forward – and the UK rapid retreat. On 24 May 1984 – after Brussels and before Fontainebleau – Mitterrand spoke to the EC and supported the EUT. Indeed, he explicitly called for a *new* treaty and suggested a conference of governments to negotiate it (Commission, 1985a: 1). The idea of a new treaty, included in the EP's original proposals, was itself seen by the British as a threat. It meant that those governments which agreed with its terms would not be subject to the veto of dissenting members, as is the case with the amendment procedures of the Treaty of Rome as laid down in Article 236. It opened up the prospect of a more supranational inner core, which the UK could only join at the expense of its sovereignty.

Mitterrand was prepared to sharpen further the horns of the dilemma for the UK, and to do so in a manner which completely escaped the notice of the British press at the time. No doubt Mrs Thatcher's 'letter of conciliation' was welcomed, but the arrangements at Fontainebleau were carefully orchestrated to get the message home. Thus, the act of beginning the negotiations, of getting down to business, was delayed for several hours while Mitterrand informally confessed what *The Times* (27 June 1985) described in scoffing tones as his 'dreams of Europe'. These included acceptable things, like a Europe with no customs barriers, but also slightly 'wild' things like a European flag, a European anthem, TV station, and so on. Mitterrand was using the arts of high diplomacy: he was letting Mrs Thatcher see the future. The British press paused only to pour a little cold water on the agreement to set up the Adonnino Committee on a *People's Europe*. Very little attention was given to the decision, to which the United Kingdom reluctantly assented, to set up an *ad hoc* committee on institutional reform.

Kohl generally supported France. He invariably tried to patch up disagreements with the French whenever they occurred, as had happened before the Milan summit in June 1985. At Milan the UK reaction was one that by then had become typical; and there was the implication that the FRG had somehow sacrificed its true interests, which would have led it to side with the British, in order to butter up the French (*The Times*, 29 June, 1985). The Franco–German Treaty of Friendship of January 1963 had, however, been given a new lease of life with an extension of the consultative procedures on political cooperation between the two states. Measures were also taken to ease Franco–German trade relations ahead of the practice of the others, and there were reports of Franco–German efforts to create a 'core' of more integrated states. Kohl was also prepared to make sympathetic noises about the EUT. In the 1984 EP elections, the EUT was probably higher on the agenda in FRG than in any other state. The CDU/CSU government's views towards France, and a more united Europe, were ambiguous, but from the UK point of view it was significant that Kohl was prepared to express his attachment to both ahead of immediate calculations of interest. When the latter got in the way, as they sometimes did, efforts were made to recover the situation.

In one particular respect, Kohl was arguably decisive. When he rose from the table in anger at 6.30 p.m. on 20 March 1984 in Brussels, he revealed a carelessness about UK reactions which carried an unmistakable and ominous warning for the latter. They could, as it were, 'take it or leave it'. Kohl's action was decisive in revealing the flaw in the British diplomatic armament – that they were prepared to make sacrifices in order to avoid being excluded from the inner sanctum – and more than any other single act it changed the direction of movement of the tide of European integration in the mid-1980s. Perhaps this was the underlying reason for Mrs Thatcher's publicly acknowledged dislike of Kohl, a sentiment which was obviously reciprocated.

Britain and the Single European Act

The SEA's character may be explained in terms of judgements and interests derived directly from Fontainebleau. The British found themselves under pressure to make concessions towards European Union, and to EC policies about which they had serious misgivings, in order to stay in the game, and to attain their own specific goals that were of equal and vital importance.

The British wanted no truck with any of the several variations of future development in the EC then being discussed – except one (Wallace, 1985; Langeheine and Weinstock, 1985). They abhorred a two-tier Europe. One reason for this was that it would reduce their ability to exercise influence in the EPC framework which they very strongly supported. They also disliked strongly Europe *à la carte* or the idea of graduated integration; the existing example of this, the EMS arrangement, and the proposal to reactivate West European Union, were to be regarded as exceptions to the rule. Britain wanted everyone to go forward at the same gentle pace, one ideally suited to UK capacities and inclinations.

One problem for the UK was that by early 1985 various items on the agenda of integration – completion of the Common Market, the strengthening of EPC and the rather ambitious proposals for institutional reform – had been refined and increasingly firmly linked together in a single package. Britain had tried to prevent this. In the Ad Hoc Committee for Institutional Affairs (known as the Dooge Committee, after its Irish chairman) the pattern was set. It established a 'convergence of priorities' in the particular sense that the need for a 'homogeneous internal economic area', the 'promotion of common values of civilisation' and the 'search for an external identity' was spelled out, and made conditional upon the achievement of 'efficient and democratic institutions', meaning 'a strengthened Commission', the extension of the EP's powers and the ECJ's reform. A method for obtaining these goals was recommended in the Report: it was held that a 'conference of the representatives of the governments of the member states should be convened in the near future to negotiate a draft European Union Treaty based on the *acquis communautaire*, the present document, and the Stuttgart Solemn Declaration on European Union, and guided by the spirit and method of the [EUT]'. Mitterrand approved this general line by appointing a known Euro-enthusiast, Maurice Faure, as his member of the committee (Ad Hoc Committee, 1985: 33). An explicit and detailed programme for action leading to a new treaty was clear.

All the UK representative, Malcolm Rifkind, could do was to enter a number of reservations which were noted in footnotes. With his Greek and Danish colleagues he held that the proposals should be the 'subject of consultations between the governments before the June European Council', and opposed the idea of the conference of government representatives which looked suspiciously like the constituent assembly of a federal union. Rifkind alone entered reservations on proposals to strengthen the EP – at most it should 'make more use of its right to put forward proposals for community action', and there should be improvement and extension of the conciliation procedure; he opposed the proposal that the incoming Commission president should nominate his own team of Commissioners for government approval (Ad Hoc Committee, 1985: 28). Governments should continue as at present to nominate and approve unanimously what Mrs Thatcher now frequently referred to as 'our Commissioner(s)' in flat defiance of the stipulations of the Rome Treaty. And with Greek and Danish representatives he insisted that the January 1966 Luxembourg Accord, which required that there should be consensus voting in the Council of Ministers if a state held that a matter concerned its vital national interest, should continue to operate. No reservations on the policy objectives were entered.

This pattern of doubts on the proposals for institutional reform, and support for the policies, remained the British position until the June 1985 Milan European Council. It had, however, by then been somewhat refined in that the need for a state to justify in detail its wish to invoke the Luxembourg Accord was asserted by the UK government, and the contradictory appeal was addressed to the others that majority voting should be used more frequently in the Council of Ministers' decision-making. But UK reluctance to accept that institutional arrangements mattered was a problem: British exhortations to better behaviour in the use of the veto had little appeal (Wallace, W., 1985).

By the June Summit, a further element had been introduced into the package with UK agreement which further increased the difficulties for the British of steering a way between either accepting the package as a whole or risking stronger pressures towards a two-tier Europe. This was the attachment to the package of an explicit time constraint, namely, the achievement of a Europe without frontiers by a specified date, 1992. This meant that agreement about the institutional changes, as well as programme details, had to be reached soon – procrastination offered Britain no escape.

The first mention of the 1992 deadline was in the Commission president's statement to the EP on 14 January 1985. Speaking of the next European Council, he said: 'now that some Heads of State and Government have decided to set an example ... it may not be over-optimistic to announce a decision to eliminate all frontiers within Europe by 1992 and to implement it' (Commission, 1985b: 6). This ambition was approved by the Brussels European Council on 29-30 March 1985. The governments' response then was to ask the Commission to draw up a detailed programme with a specific timetable for its meeting in June. The result was the preparation of the much discussed *White Paper on Completing the Internal Market* presented at Milan.

On 1 July 1985 it was reported in Britain that the Milan Summit had been 'extremely bad-tempered' and that Mrs Thatcher's 'anger and frustration', even 'undisguised fury', had shown through (*The Times*, 1 July 1985). When viewed in the longer perspective, the dice can be seen to have been loaded against a favourable outcome. The French strategy, the refinement of the proposals for Europe without frontiers in the White Paper, and the pressure of deadlines, meant that the British would now have to accept an intergovernmental conference with the amendment of EC decision-making on its agenda. Only the

Greeks and the Danes joined Britain in voting against Mitterrand's proposal for a conference. Again, Kohl attracted Mrs Thatcher's particular wrath by supporting the French. Mitterrand said that the outcome had 'sorted out those in favour of a strong united Europe from those who were hanging back'. *The Times* said disingenuously that his comments had 'rekindled speculation about a two-tier Europe' (*The Times*, 1 July 1985). Precisely so! From the British point of view the awful irony was that making the concessions demanded of them on institutional reform had by now become a way of keeping such speculation alive. The more they conceded, the more the supranational tendency would be fed and the greater the demands which could be made upon them.

In the House of Commons' subsequent discussion of the outcome of the Milan Summit, Jonathan Aitken MP mischievously asked Mrs Thatcher if the time had come to consider Mitterrand's proposal for a two-tier Europe (*The Times* 3 July 1985). The answer was short and simple: she disagreed. The obvious concession, therefore, had to be made. At a meeting of the General Affairs Council of Foreign Ministers, 22-23 July 1985, Britain went along with the others in agreeing to the convening of an intergovernmental conference by the Luxembourg presidency, in office in the second half of 1985, which was explicitly asked to consider the 'revision of the Rome Treaty' and the drafting of a treaty on political cooperation and European security (Commission, 1985a: 2). The British had at least gained the important concession that there would not be a new treaty. Early on in the discussions of the intergovernmental committee, some governments, especially the Italians, the Belgians and the Dutch, pressurized Britain by speaking explicitly of the possibility that some of the Ten could go ahead of the others. It was, therefore, perhaps not surprising that in early October British Foreign Secretary, Sir Geoffrey Howe, gave the 'first indications that Britain would accept treaty amendments on a pragmatic basis' (Corbett, 1987: 242).

The underlying dynamics of the SEA negotiations are now clear. On the one hand were a group (including the French, the Italians, the Dutch, Belgians, Luxemburgers and the Germans) which inclined to a more ambitious set of changes for the EC institutions, though probably no member actually wanted to give the EP the sole right both to initiate and approve legislation (Butler, 1986: 156). The French by this time did not need to lead this faction at all stages: the Italians in practice in 1985-6 usually carried the Euro-banner. The Germans sometimes dragged their feet but generally and eventually inclined to this group to UK annoyance: for example at the Kohl–Thatcher meeting in November 1985 they agreed to exclude economic and monetary union as a goal in the SEA. Kohl changed his mind when the French and Italians liberalized their exchange control provisions and these goals were eventually included in the Agreement's Preamble.

The British headed a group of doubters which included Greece and Denmark. It was vital to realize, however, that the outcome of the negotiations between this group and the others cannot be completely explained by reference to the specific interests and exchanges on particular policies. Longer-term dynamics meant that the British group was necessarily and invariably on the defensive, particularly on institutional questions. They had to make specific concessions to avoid incurring non-specific and longer term costs and fight a rear-guard battle to prevent fundamental alterations in the EC's structure. Thanks to the Mitterrand strategy, success in this depended paradoxically upon making concessions on precisely those questions, while at the same time struggling to make them as small as possible. The SEA's character was largely explicable in terms of the outcome of this struggle and this feature was captured in Mrs Thatcher's extraordinarily arrogant remark to the Commons on 5 December, 1985, on her return from Luxembourg: 'Part of our task the whole time has been to diminish their expectations and draw them down from the clouds to practical matters' (*The Times*, 6 December, 1985). The reader should consider the likely reactions of Kohl, Mitterrand *et. al.* on reading about this comment.

There is a sense in which the SEA was a considerable achievement for British negotiators. A way had been found to make what appeared to be major concessions to those who wanted stronger EC institutions, while at the same time introducing qualifications to significantly mitigate their implications. Much depended upon the discussions at Luxembourg between the heads of government: they took twenty-one hours over settling the main questions, eleven more than had been planned. As a result, the British could comfort themselves, for the time being at least, that what they had wanted all along had been achieved: a system which depended for its success upon the convergent interests and political goodwill of governments rather than upon some constitutional relocation of the metaphysical bases of power. This judgement does not need to rest upon the assumption that the UK took the lead in positively seeking and obtaining outcomes in all cases where they benefited. In some cases, indeed, British advantage was a product, gratefully accepted, of negotiations led by others.

Much depended upon the nature of the EP's new powers and upon the implications of majority voting in the Council of Ministers, and the policy areas to which these changes were to apply. The proposal to introduce co-decision making for the EP with the Council – in effect to give each of the partners a veto – was successfully resisted. Instead, a cooperation procedure was introduced (See chapter 3). In the ten areas to which this new procedure was to apply, the governments could as a last resort veto Council attempts to overcome the EP's wishes. The most important area, covered in the new Article 100a, under which the Council was to take decisions by majority vote, on its first reading, to implement the establishment and functioning of the internal market – Europe without frontiers. If the members had the will to work for this, it might be assumed that as a matter of good sense, and to avoid unnecessary delays, they would not use what amounted to a veto by inaction. But the arrangement, nevertheless, meant that states *in extremis* could stop the EP from getting what it wanted.

In view of British appeals to the others to rely more upon majority voting in the Council, it might seem odd that Mrs Thatcher should have made it clear that 'the Luxembourg compromise [allowing a national veto] was unaffected'. She also said that there had been 'no transfer of powers from Parliament to the Assembly'. She even avoided using the term 'European Parliament', which the SEA had formally accepted.

The apparent inconsistency in the British position may be discussed with reference to Article 69 of the Treaty of Rome on the liberalization of capital movements. This was not subject to the cooperation procedure, though according to the Treaty such movements were to be taken by a majority vote after the first two transitional stages. Article 69 carried an important implication for the UK 'the liberalisation of banking and insurance services connected with movements of capital shall be effected in step with progressive liberalisation of movements of capital'. Banking and insurance services were also to be liberalized, as the Rome Treaty intended, by majority vote, without EP involvement. What seemed to be revealed was a British strategy for attempting to disarm those states, such as Greece, Spain and FRG, which might have wished to place difficulties in the way of liberalizing banking and insurance, by appealing for their acceptance of majority voting, at the same time retaining the right to invoke the Luxembourg Accord if necessary to protect their own interests. Paradoxically, the British now saw majority voting as a means of national leverage to stop the others from preventing Britain from getting what it wanted, rather than a mechanism for facilitating the easier definition of a European interest as was believed by some Euro-enthusiasts.

It was also in the UK interest that 1992 was not to be a legally binding deadline, but more of a date for measuring the achievement. This is not to deny that there was an ambition to move significantly forward by then – UK Commissioner Lord Cockfield had been placed in charge of the programme. But the state of UK industry, though its improving condition had created an increased confidence by late 1985, was not such as to justify the removal of a safety net. Indeed, allowing the EP to use the cooperation procedure with regard to Article 100a decisions could be seen as one strand in such a net: it was a way of working which would inevitably slow the process down. Article 100b provided other strands. In effect, the remaining detractions from the internal market were to be listed by the Commission in 1992, and decisions about their equivalents in the various member states, and about their removal if there were no equivalents, were then to be taken on the basis of majority decision in the Council (first reading) and the cooperation procedure. Recalcitrant states would thereby have ample opportunity for protracting the process of achieving a Europe without frontiers if this were then deemed necessary.

Other aspects of the SEA illustrate Britain's wish to minimize concessions to the European centre, while avoiding accentuating centripetal tendencies in other members, and obtaining specific ends. Many relate to a broad disagreement between those inclined to include in the SEA explicitly what was thought necessary to complete the internal market, and those who wished to move forward in a more pragmatic fashion by only accepting the general principle to begin with, and making further adjustments in the light of experience. The UK had the latter pole position among group. The former included the Commission, Italy, France and the Benelux countries, usually with German support. The list of exclusions from the range of specific goals linked with the completion of the internal market and monetary union reflected interests. In Article 6, 'policy on credit and savings, medicines and drugs' was carefully excluded from the cooperation procedure. Similarly, in Article 18, according to paragraph 2 of the agreed new Article 100a on the approximation by the EC of laws, regulations and administrative actions in member states to achieve 'the establishment and functioning of the Common Market' – a process which was also to involve the cooperation procedure – 'fiscal provisions, and those relating to the free movement of persons' and the 'rights and interests of employed persons', were to be excluded. The latter was, of course, sensitive in Britain as the free movement of persons would have involved removing boundary controls which Home Secretary Douglas Hurd in May 1988 insisted were necessary to control terrorism. On this the UK was the most resistant of the Twelve. In any case, such concessions to the idea of a united Europe were likely to be highly contentious in the Conservative party in the 1980s. They might also have eased the movement of political undesirables.

Article 17 may also be seen as being essentially a British compromise in that it held that Article 99 should be modified, seemingly as little as possible, solely to allow the EP to be *consulted* about provisions for the harmonization of legislation concerning turn-over taxes, excise duties and other forms of indirect taxation. It is hard to understand why such a miniscule adjustment should have been necessary, except to force the British to make some kind of concession, to which they reacted by attempting to draw a line over which they would not step. The question of standard rates of VAT – encompassed in the Article 99 reference to turn-over taxes – had become politically sensitive in Britain in the mid-late 1980s. Politicians on both sides of the political divide were determined to resist attempts to introduce VAT on a number of items including children's clothes, food and books, partly because there was some public feeling against it, though no doubt this could have been mitigated by politicians had they been so minded, and partly because some British politicians would regard such a step as undermining the fundamental and ancient right of Parliament to levy taxes. So the cooperation procedure was excluded from the new Article 99 and as before the Council would act 'unanimously on a proposal from the Commission'.

From the UK point of view the new arrangements on cooperation in economic and monetary policy had advantages. A new section on these matters was introduced into the Rome Treaty which meant that the Commission now had responsibilities in the operation of the EMS. This could be seen as a further consolidation of EC arrangements since previously EMS mechanisms had formally not been a part of these. On the other hand Article 102a explicitly required that 'in so far as further development in the field of economic and monetary policy necessitates institutional changes the provisions of Article 236 shall be applicable'. Proposals for new EMS institutional arrangements for the EMS would, therefore, from then on be subject to the amendment procedures of the Rome Treaty, and could be vetoed by dissenting states, even those, such as the British which had not yet joined the EMS. Thus the UK acquired the means of preventing the others from creating a two-tier European monetary policy, a significant development in view of Mrs Thatcher's opposition to UK membership in the EMS, and her hostility to a Franco–German initiative in 1988 in favour of moving towards a European central bank (Palmer, 1988); this last proposal was also criticized by the Bundesbank.

On some matters it is not difficult to become cynical about the attitude of UK diplomats during the negotiations. On the environment, for instance, they agreed that the 'polluter should pay' and that the EC was to have a role in protecting the 'quality of the environment', 'the protection of human health' and 'the prudent and rational utilisation of natural resources' (Article 25 SEA; new Treaty of Rome Article 130r). But, having made that gesture, the reservation was entered (New Article 130s) that any EC action should be decided by Council unanimity. This may be judged as no more than commercial caution; it became a matter of bad taste, even moral error, when set beside Britain's major failure to control emissions producing acid rain and other pollutants, widely accepted as gravely damaging German and Scandinavian forests and the generally obstructive attitude of the Government towards legislation on environmental and analogous questions. In late September 1988, Thatcher's speech advocating new global efforts to solve environmental problems met with astonishment.

Britain also agreed to an EC effort to strengthen the 'scientific and technological basis of European industry', but insisted (with German support) that the Multi-annual Framework Programme in which it was to be embodied, be subject to unanimity in Council. However, only months later the UK refused anything other than a minimum budget, and, limited their participation in the European space programme. The general British posture seemed to be to encourage technological innovation and the use of venture capital, but not at the European level and not out of the public purse. They seemed prepared to enter into commitments at the European level which they had no intention of honouring to ensure that they could be more easily frustrated. One illustration of this was the British behaviour regarding the financing of the Horizon 2000 project of the European Space Agency which was described by Lord Shackleton, a respected Labour Lord as constituting 'appalling bad manners and arrogance' (*Independent*, 5 October 1988: 2). The British had procrastinated about the level of finance for the agency, and were refusing to endorse a 5 per cent increase in the budget to support Horizon 2000, which represented a core science programme. The UK alone opposed the rise, but held a veto as the decision, according to the SEA, was subject to Council unanimity.

Thus, the SEA can be judged a considerable British achievement. In its details it reflected UK interests in a nuanced and comprehensive way. On the other hand, the British, and, of course, the varying coalitions of states with which they were involved, had had to make concessions. They wanted the completion of the internal market but even in this there was an element of ambiguity: they were pushed onto the band-wagon because of the others' apparent willingness to go on ahead. The few areas where there was unambiguous enthusiasm were the liberalization of the capital market, and of the related arrangements for banking and insurance and the EPC. In these areas, however, the UK's preferred method was one of low-key negotiations among governments leading to specific commitments with no immediate implications for institutional change.

Despite its modest immediate effects, the SEA stands as a symbol of the constraints which had now been placed upon those governments which preferred a minimalist approach to Europe. The question arises of whether the concessions would, despite the conscious intentions of these states, further strengthen those constraints, and it is with this question that the next section of this chapter is concerned. Now we must evaluate the extent to which the constraints upon British action, deriving from the regional system, were evolving in the longer term.

Integration constraints

In 1987-8 four interrelated issues rose to the top of the diplomatic agenda. They were the questions of controlling CAP spending; budgetary discipline; changing procedures for revenue raising so that new sums could be found to cover expanding expenses and increasing regional aid to the new Mediterranean states. These matters were discussed in particular at three meetings of the

European Council: at Brussels in June 1987, which ended in great acrimony; at Copenhagen, 4-5 December 1987, at which no settlement was reached, but which, much to everybody's surprise, was remarkably good tempered; and at a special meeting planned at Copenhagen, at Brussels on 10-12 February 1988, which produced a settlement. As before the battle lines were drawn between the British – in occasional alliance with one or more other members but in increasing danger of being isolated – on the one side, and a larger group, led by France and the FRG.

The immediate appearance of the February 1988 outcome was that Britain had conceded. 'Against all expectations, and in defiance of the Prime Minister's most deeply entrenched instincts, the Summit had ended in success' (*The Observer*, 14 February 1988). On each of the major items on the agenda there was either 'no change' or a major British concession, compared, say, with the Copenhagen Summit. The outcome represented a triumph of the 'Mitterrand strategy'. Hugo Young qualified this interpretation, however, when he wrote:

the Brussels agreement ... may come to be seen as the most momentous retreat of Mrs Thatcher's career ... Where all earlier encounters have been represented as a matter of total victory or defeat ... a different perspective is necessary to explain the kind of fudge Mrs Thatcher was defending in the Commons yesterday ... There really is no alternative but for Europe's senior statesperson at last to show that she belongs to the continent in which we live. [*The Guardian* 16 February, 1988]

Though Mrs Thatcher had compromised she had, in Young's view, yet to realize where she stood in the world.

The compromise must be seen in the light of the constraints discussed earlier in this chapter and the hierarchy of issues they suggest. Most analysts explained it as an outcome of diplomacy about an explicit, visible agenda, and there is naturally scope for so doing (see below). A second kind of explanation concerns diplomacy about a disguised, yet implicit agenda. The 1987-8 negotiations had implications for the pattern of the future development of the EC's structure and the British gained concessions in this area which at the time were not fully appreciated by the others, but which nevertheless encouraged the UK to make concessions on the visible agenda. There was a hidden trade-off between items on the two agendas which obviously had not been possible at Luxembourg in December 1985 because all items then, structural/constitutional and specific, had been placed on the visible agenda. A third level of diplomacy concerned items on an emerging agenda: this included the longer-term implications of the agreements about specifics, which were being realized and accepted at a relatively gradual but uneven pace by governments. They included adjustments in the scope of integration, necessary to the internal market's completion, such as the adoption of stronger monetary arrangements, and strengthening the mechanisms for managing the business cycle in common. These three levels of diplomacy and the links between them will now be considered.

CAP spending had pride of place on the visible agenda. The British, initially with Dutch support, wanted in particular a ceiling of 155 million tonnes on EC cereal production, coupled with rather severe penalties for farmers who exceeded that target. The UK also insisted that the rate of increase in CAP spending be limited to 60 per cent of the EC's national output growth, while the FRG argued for 70-80 per cent and France 100 per cent. France also wanted a higher cereal ceiling initially at 165 million tonnes, and weaker stabilizers in the event of over-production. At an Anglo-German summit in London in January 1988, Mrs Thatcher rejected even 160 million tonnes a year.

Yet in the early hours of 13 February 'this was precisely the figure she presented to the doubting journalists as evidence of peace in our time'. Details of the agreement also revealed that the UK had accepted 'an annual growth rate of EAGGF guarantee expenditure of 80% of GNP', [Presidency, 1988] and a relatively soft system of stabilizers. In each marketing year an additional co-responsibility levy of 3 per cent above the intervention price would be paid by the first buyer, refunded if production was at or below the agreed ceiling. If above the ceiling, this levy would not be refunded, and the intervention price for the following year would be cut by 3 per cent. This amounted to a modest disincentive on over-production. In addition, a set-aside programme was agreed according to which producers would be induced to take 'at least 20% of arable land used for cultivating products covered by the Common Market organisations' out of production. A formula for compensating farmers for income lost provided for payments of a minimum 100 ECUs to a maximum of 600 ECUs per hectare (Presidency, 1988: 38-9).

Greater discipline in spending on the CAP intervention system was agreed. States were obliged to provide more detailed information about spending 'within each marketing organisation so as to ensure that the rate at which appropriations in each chapter are used is known with precision one month after expenditure has taken place' (European Council, 1988, Section 2, 6). The Commission would then compensate states for actual expenditure on agricultural support within eight weeks. This represented an extension of the payment period compared with the earlier practice by one half-a-month. In this way the Commission could be more confident that states could not in future profit by claiming amounts above what they had actually paid. Other measures for increased control over CAP spending were also introduced. The balance of the agreement on agriculture was closer to that supported by France and the FRG, and rather distant from the UK position.

As to the structural funds, the pattern of support and opposition to increases in allocated resources varied somewhat from that on CAP spending. But for most of the negotiations Britain appeared to be the most adamant in resisting increases above 50 per cent by 1992. France gave some support to this position for a while though the FRG wanted more. When negotiations seemed deadlocked for the third time running, on 12 February Mrs Thatcher struck a deal with Spanish Prime Minister Gonzales, whereby the British would make concessions on the funds' financing which were particularly beneficial to the southern countries, in return for their support on the agricultural side. This deal broke down when Britain failed to get its way on agriculture. In the event, Britain eventually conceded most ground. It was agreed that 'commitment appropriations for structural funds will be doubled in 1993 by comparison with 1987' (European Council, 1988, p.2).

In view of these various retreats when compared with earlier positions, it was surprising that Britain also accepted largely without alteration the Commission's original proposals on how to increase the scale of own resources. The UK had earlier insisted that any increase should be tied to a significant tightening of controls on farm intervention, 'the problem which has faced us for eight years' (*The Times* 13 February 1988). Relative failure in this area did not, as might have been expected, lead to increased opposition to the budgetary changes, and, in the agreement a fourth resource, which would ensure that own resources for commitments would increase to 1.3 per cent of GNP by 1992 was accepted (Commission, 1987). The three other 'resources' remained unchanged. The implications of a range of further steps to achieve discipline with regard to both regulated and non-regulated expenditure (See chapter 7 on the Budget), in other words, the budget as a whole, are considered shortly, though it was striking that these received relatively little attention either in the initial reporting of the agreement in Britain or in Mrs Thatcher's preliminary announcements. The 'hot' items were CAP spending and the structural funds.

Why did the British make such a significant range of concessions on items on the visible agenda even though rather late in the day? On 11 December 1987 *The Times* carried a singularly bellicose leader warning of the dangers of giving way on the various matters which were to be negotiated, and that afternoon British officials seemed to be prepared for failure. By late Friday, however, the British had back-peddled enough to allow a settlement. It seems likely that responsibility for the change of position rested firmly with Mrs Thatcher and a relatively small group of her closest advisers. A key period may have been mid-afternoon on 12 February, when according to officials, Mrs Thatcher did something which for her was quite extraordinary: during the conference she retreated by herself to a room for an hour's solitary contemplation. Afterwards her position was conciliatory.

One reason for the change of mind could be that during the previous week, and during the Brussels conference itself, the UK had become progressively more isolated. This had not mattered on previous occasions: Britain had cherished its singularity. At Copenhagen, however, UK officials for the first time went out of their way to express their delight that Mrs Thatcher had 'succeeded in avoiding the impression given at the last Summit that she was isolated in an 11-1 minority' (*The Times*, 7 December 1987). But confidence that rather more balanced diplomatic groupings, varying with regard to specific issues, could emerge gradually, disappeared in early 1988. The Germans once more veered towards the French, as, for instance, at a meeting of agricultural ministers in January, and when there were signs that the Dutch were moving to join the majority leaving Mrs Thatcher isolated. The Dutch had previously supported the British line on the ceiling on agricultural production. The apparent failure of the attempted Spanish deal confirmed this isolation, and the reaction of French and German diplomats to Mrs Thatcher's personal style must have sharpened UK appreciation of the dangers of being alone. At one point French Prime Minister Chirac allegedly uttered 'an enormous obscenity' in comment upon Mrs Thatcher's behaviour (*Observer*, 14 February 1988). The significance of psychological factors should not be underestimated.

Another part of the explanation of UK behaviour was the more obvious one that there was a risk of losing all or part of the UK rebate. The Commission had argued in 1987 that the scale of the rebate should be related solely to imbalances arising from the CAP's operation. Governments had refrained from raising the question of the UK rebate at Copenhagen, though according to the terms of the June 1984 agreement, this was formally a possibility as the level of 'own resources' was now to be adjusted. This possibility was held as a kind of 'sword of Damocles' over Britain as the February 1988 summit approached. France was expected to press for a phasing out of the compensation to the British (*Financial*

Times, 10 February 1988). Mrs Thatcher pointed out 'triumphantly' at her press conference on 13 February that the rebate had saved £3bn for the British taxpayer over the preceding three years.

It seemed fair to conclude, therefore, that

> what determined her to settle at the last minute was a negotiator's judgement, which could only be made on the spot. It was that any further delay, postponing the decision to the Hanover summit in June, would have imperilled what Britain cares about even more than farm surpluses, namely the Fontainebleau agreement on the British rebate. [Young, *The Guardian*, 16 February 1988]

Accordingly, it was agreed, with some minor adjustments that the June 1984 European Council conclusions on the correction of budgetary imbalances remained applicable for as long as the new decision on own resources remained in force. A postponement until the Hanover summit might also have interrupted progress towards 1992, and this also pushed the UK towards a settlement. It was a package of agreements about specific interests which reflected UK determination to avoid raising the question, in any form, of whether Britain was in the game.

Yet these various gains and losses about specifics still fall short of a fully convincing explanation of the British retreat. Another element needs to be added: namely that Mrs Thatcher gained concessions in the particular area of budgetary discipline as a result of diplomacy of 1987-8, and the decision taken at the February 1988 Summit with regard to this discipline carried major implications for the EC's future development which were not fully appreciated by the negotiating partners. As Nicoll has pointed out, concern with budgetary discipline became prominent on the agenda relatively late in 1984 at a time of renewed movement towards strengthening the EC (Nicoll, 1986). This coincidence suggests UK realization that the matter of budgetary discipline had structural implications. It also coincided with German realization that budgetary discipline could be used to cut CAP spending, without launching a full-scale attack on the German farming lobby which would have been electorally damaging for the CDU–CSU–FDP coalition.

It should be added, however, that the question of budgetary discipline had entered into the pattern of relations between major contributing states and the international institutions of which they were members in at least one other major context at the same time. The US had, after the Kassebaum amendment, also stressed the need for budgetary discipline in the central system of the United Nations, and also with regard to the Special Agencies (Taylor, 1988). In this case, as with the British and the EC, the apparent objective was to use resources more efficiently, to relate decisions about finance more directly to decisions about policy and to place responsibility for decisions about new tunes more firmly into the hands of those who paid the piper. Yet, certainly with regard to the UN, and arguably the EC, the issue was also used to try to get a grip on the pattern of the future development of the organization. There was a disguised agenda. Linkage between approaches to such analogous issues within governments is highly likely.

A significant implication of budgetary discipline, and the reason for its popularity with those opposed to strengthening Europe, was that it allowed prior judgements about finance to constrain the choice of policy, rather than the other way round. If policy led there would be steady pressure towards the expansion of the budget in the light of new proposals which had integrative implications. If finance led pro-integration policies could be more easily constrained. Efficient resources use, if taken as a conscious primary goal, was to be seen as the enemy of integration.

The cornerstone of budgetary discipline was the laying down of an overall own resources ceiling and annual ceilings for payment appropriations, that is those sums actually to be paid in each year, until 1992. These were to grow annually from 1.20 per cent of GNP in 1988 to 1.30 per cent of GNP in 1992. Ceilings for commitment appropriations, that is the sum of promises made for future payments, were also to be agreed, maintaining a 'strict relationship' with appropriations for payments; there were to be increases, which were required to be regular, until 1992 (Presidency, 1988, p.3). Decisions about the sums to be allocated were to be made before each financial year according to a 'medium-term financial perspective'; implications for the particular year were to be submitted for approval to the Council and EP not later than 15 February. It was stressed that 'the Communities' annual budget for the financial years 1988-92 shall be kept within the ceilings' (European Council, 1988, Section 2, p.3).

A wide range of new procedures were adopted to help achieve these goals. The much more careful distinction between payments for appropriations and payments for commitments was one of these (See chapter 7), but this distinction should be understood in the context of a further change, namely an insistence upon what were called 'transparency' and 'annuality'. The specific implication of the application of these principles was that carry-overs of differentiated appropriations would no longer be automatic.

These changes produced a more complete – and transparent – annual statement of finances and, therefore, mitigated the problem of not being able to see at any point what sums in the budget were a carry-over from the previous year, for what sums the EC was liable at any particular point in time 'and which *must* be paid' and those sums which could *perhaps* be paid. This problem had allowed the Council to agree to policies which involving expenditure which could not be covered without agreeing to new money, precisely because there was uncertainty about how much was in the kitty. Conversely, there was no system by which the Council could be required to pay for expenditure to which it was committed. Lack of clarity about the 'certainty' of existing commitments made this worse. Hence, there were continuing threats of incipient bankruptcy in the 1980s which were solved by creative accountancy such as the 'negative overdraft'. This actually meant not paying for policies which had been agreed. The EP concluded that the permanent and growing imbalance in the EC budget was essentially a product of Council decisions and agreed that therefore budgetary discipline was absolutely necessary.

Uncertainty about the budget also made it more likely that the Council would adopt policies requiring a bigger budget, but the new arrangements also meant that after 1992 a brake could be applied to future expansion, though a means of controlled acceleration was needed until then. From now on no policy with budgetary implications could be agreed unless a decision about revenue was taken at the same time. This significantly strengthened the hand of the anti-integrationists such as the British. The EC had been delivered into the hands of the accountants.

The genuine complaints about agriculture opened up the opportunity to do something about budgetary discipline in general which, as the EP recognized, also threatened to limit its own small capacity to increase the budget in the area of non-regulated finance. Indeed, Mrs Thatcher's team must have been somewhat encouraged by their success in keeping the Commission's support, and by the seeming preparedness of the Commission to attach blame to the EP in this area, with allegations of Parliament's 'over allocation in many budgetary headings, resulting from over-estimates of spending capacity' (Commission, 1987, p.10). The EP refuted this by pointing out that the Commission's own estimates in the area of non-regulated finance had usually been higher than its own (EP, 1987: 14-15). Nevertheless, it was clear that non-compulsory expenditure would be subject to the new ceilings, though it was argued by Commission and EP representatives that in this area tighter budgetary management was largely a matter of presentation. The amount of waste was negligible compared with the average national administration. The British, as well as the Germans, deliberately and grossly exaggerated the problems in controlling EC expenditure, for instance, with regard to the research budget.

The EP could be forgiven the cynical view that 'it is by no means certain that Council's political commitment to implementation of the [SEA] ... would prevail over the temptation to oppose any increase in the maximum rate particularly in cases where additional resources would have to be found for the EAGGF guarantee section (EP, 1987, p.14, para. 25).

The SEA could in principle involve more expenditure under the non-compulsory heading, and the maximum rate referred to the pace of increase in that context. The EP complained that this amounted to an illegal amendment to the Treaty of Rome. Despite some concessions by the governments on consultations about the necessary sums, and an explicit commitment to find sums necessary to carry out the terms of the SEA, the EP's budgetary role seemed weakened by the new arrangements. There was some evidence that the Commission had moved into a more critical stance on the EP's budgetary powers and this must have given further encouragement to those who wished to find in budgetary discipline a measure of compensation for the concessions made on specifics.

The budgetary discipline agreements were implicitly about the EC's future structure and boosted those who preferred an intergovernmental rather than a more supranational approach. Not only were governments now to be brought more rapidly in the Council to a realization of the budgetary implications of their choice of policies, a good recipe for a minimalist approach, but the hand of those who wished to place a cap upon EC spending by 1992 was strengthened. Nothing much about the growth of the budget could be done until then. The integrative strategy implied, for instance, by the MacDougal Report back in 1977 which involved a steady expansion of the EC budget with a slow accretion correspondingly of EP powers was again not taken up (Commission, 1977). Of course, the effectiveness of this approach remained to be seen, but a UK government could not but have been encouraged by the new arrangements. These gains on the disguised agenda facilitated the surprising concessions on the visible one.

A distinction has to be made between the diplomacy of the time and what could be called the emerging agenda. Items on the latter were touched obliquely and were not a part of the currency consciously used at the negotiations. Mrs

Thatcher could have concluded that she had on balance gained adequate concessions at the February 1988 special meeting of the European Council when both the visible and disguised agenda were taken into account, though the fact that she could not explain the nature of her victory implied that there was also a sense in which she had failed. The need to claw back surreptitiously some of the assets of the supranational tendency was itself an admission of the continuing strength of the latter. A more overt approach risked placing Britain in the position of having to go even further in the direction it disliked. Indeed, any direct discussion of the EC's structure now necessarily raised the spectre of a two-tier Europe, a danger evident since 1984.

It should not be forgotten that finding a way forward in the EC was crucially dependent upon the building of successful coalitions. This had become a more complex process as the number of members increased and as some of these gathered into formal groups – a southern group, a northern group, etc. Successful coalitions need to attract the support of the smaller states. Their behaviour also showed underlying tendencies, or a sense of role, which had to be reckoned with in specific contexts. The Dutch and Belgians had to steer a careful course between a natural sympathy for Britain (a product of history) and a general support for advanced forms of supranationalism. On occasions, therefore, these two governments tried to mediate. More usually they tried to use their special relationship to present the case for stronger central institutions to the UK in a sympathetic way. The Danes and the Greeks formed a second group which generally supported UK preferences for weak EC institutions; the Danes in particular resisted any concessions to supranationalism, and sometimes were more fundamentalist in this than the UK. A third group of weaker states included Spain and Portugal, which seemed to take a pragmatic line on the underlying constitutional issues, preferring for the time being to place primary stress on obtaining specific economic returns from the EC. The way in which the coalitions were formed depended primarily upon the pattern of diplomacy between the big four, and the UK was the litmus test of the chances of future integration. Stress is, therefore, once again placed upon developments in Britain.

Hugo Young wrote that 'Mrs Thatcher's concessions on the [EC] budget were concessions to the idea of Europe. They were made in order to sustain the very notion of the Community' (*The Guardian*, 16 February 1988). There was, however, considerable doubt about whether she and her senior advisers intended this to happen, but concessions had become progressively more difficult to avoid. Despite UK intentions, UK concessions on the visible agenda sustained the very notion of the EC. In the longer term, the United Kingdom's political relationship with Europe was progressively consolidated. There had been a sea-change in UK thinking about where it stood in the world: that it was a European state was increasingly hard to dispute, and a gradual alignment of its interests with those of the continental states was evident. The decision to complete the internal market by 1992 also carried with it major implications for both the level and scope of regional arrangements in Europe. If the UK wanted the first, the pressures to accept the latter would inevitably grow.

Within Britain this underlying trend was recognized. Within her Cabinet there was evidence of Mrs Thatcher's increasing isolation on her doubts about Europe. The Foreign Secretary and the Chancellor of the Exchequer both openly disagreed with her about the need to join the EMS. The Home Secretary, though prepared to drag his feet on some matters, such as easing restrictions on the movement of people, as at a meeting of the Trevi Group in June 1988, was also inclined to support closer links with Europe. In the Labour Party, too, change was evident. The new party document referred to the need to stay in Europe. The regime of the Communities' system was on the way to being consolidated in Britain.

These developments were linked with a noticeable alteration in the tone of the public debate about Europe. The need to plan for the new internal market was necessarily accompanied by a public relations' strategy directed at business by the government. The visibility of Europe increased. But there was also evidence of a growing realization that there was an insistent tendency towards stronger European arrangements such as a European monetary authority, or even a kind of European central bank as proposed by Kohl and Mitterrand. There may have been startled reactions and hostility to the prospect of, say, closer Franco–German military cooperation, but UK reactions were now more generally not, as they used to be, that this was rather a silly irrelevance, but rather anxiety that this was yet another game which they would now need to join. Increasingly, the others went ahead, but Britain had to tag along behind.

Mrs Thatcher made a major speech about the future of Europe at the College of Europe in Bruges on 20 September 1988. It was sharply criticized as 'unrelentingly negative' by those in the Commission who favoured a more supranational Europe, and by states such as Italy and the Netherlands but enthusiastically welcomed by opponents of a stronger Europe. It was, however, also an excellent illustration of the major theme of this chapter: that in the 1980s a new balance between the autonomy of the states and EC integration had been struck. It was particularly revealing to find this balance in the remarks of someone who was the most forthright and indeed nationalistic of European leaders.

The speech contained clear indications of the perception that the extension of the scope of integration was necessary in order to promote the wellbeing of the various separate nation states: the latter had a symbiotic relationship with the former. Therefore 'willing and active co-operation between independent sovereign states is the best way to build a successful European Community', and 'Europe will be stronger precisely because it has France as France, Spain as Spain, Britain as Britain, each with its own customs, traditions and identity. It would be folly to fit them into some sort of Identikit European personality'. The states were to be served by the achievement at the European level of a wide range of policies which 'encourage enterprise' – 'if Europe is to flourish and create the jobs of the future, enterprise is the key'. The *acquis communautaire* and the various EC initiatives of the mid-1980s were, therefore, necessary and important, but not in Mrs Thatcher's view because of their contribution to strengthening regional arrangements, but because of their reinforcement of the distinctive life of the separate states.

Accordingly the EC was definitely not to be a framework within which new regional administrative and governmental arrangements were to be nurtured. Mrs Thatcher's image of Europe was of a kind of macro-enterprise zone, free of regulations which could increase the cost of labour and impede the movement of capital, and equally of the kind of centralized supervision which could be the product of 'arcane institutional debates'. Mrs Thatcher justified her opposition to a European central bank (this was not 'the key issue'). Those who wished to see stronger institutions were derided: 'We have not successfully rolled back the frontiers of the state in Britain only to see them reimposed at a European level with a European superstate exercising a new dominance from Brussels'.

Yet even Mrs Thatcher's view implied that regional arrangements had to be strengthened and the balance between integration and autonomy restruck. If the goal of a Europe without frontiers was to be achieved a major extension of the scope of integration would necessarily follow. Business organizations in the various member states were to be permitted and encouraged to operate in the Common Market as a whole as if it were their own domestic market: hence the major effort to remove the range of restrictions and barriers which had previously discouraged this. What was being contemplated even by the most ardent intergovernmentalists went far beyond the traditional practice of international co-operation between states: it amounted to the creation of a single economic space. A further range of interdependencies would inevitably follow. Mutual trade would be increased to levels closer to those within the US and a new range of transnational organizations and connections would emerge. The balance could be said to have changed even if only the scope of integration were taken into account.

The more interesting question, however, is about the implications of these developments for the level of integration, for the powers of the central institutions. Mrs Thatcher denied that there were any such implications. The Commission president Jacques Delors differed. He said that over the next few years the EC would be responsible for some 80 per cent of all legislation in the Twelve, during which time an embryo European government might emerge. The truth probably lies closer to the latter view than the former. There was certainly an increase in the powers of the central institutions in the 1980s, in the form of the cooperation procedure, majority voting in the Council and also an extension of the Commission's executive powers. Pressure in favour of further increases in these powers continued, and even increased, and it is difficult to see how the new European economic space could be managed without further transfers. The alternative, an attempt at cooperative management by governments of the full range of complex and urgent matters which would arise, would be inefficient and liable to failure.

Mrs Thatcher's speech reflects the increasing pressures in favour of increasing the level of integration. It suggests a sense of having been overtaken by the new dynamics of European integration, at the same time seeking to slow down processes which could not be halted, and salvage whatever could be salvaged for national sovereignty. The Mitterrand strategy gave at least a significant push to these processes, but they also acquired momentum because of dynamics recognized in the mid-1960s by the neofunctionalist theorists. Any explanation of the continuing high position of the issue of the EMS's development on the European agenda would need to include elements of neofunctionalism; spill-over from 'Europe without frontiers' was one cause of increasing interest in many quarters in a European central bank, and regardless of Mrs Thatcher's intentions, such interest will continue. It is increasingly likely that such a bank will be created and that Britain will be a member.

The student of the EC in the 1980s therefore needs to return to the writings of a group of scholars – the neofunctionalists – whose writings have for many years been unfashionable. They provide the essential context of theory in which to place the practice of diplomacy and even the speeches of Prime Ministers so that they may be better understood. This chapter has noted a variation on the old themes: in the 1980s an underlying dynamic was evident that had less likelihood of appearing when the EC had fewer members. It is that diplomatic relations can emerge between core and peripheral states in such a way that all are subject to greater incentives to integrate.

References

Ad Hoc Committee for Institutional Affairs (1985), *Report to the European Council*, SN/1187/85 Brussels, 29-30 March.

Butler, Sir Michael (1986), *Europe: More than a Continent*, London, William Heinemann, p.156.

Camps, Miriam (1964), *Britain and the European Community*, Princeton, Princeton University Press.

Cheeseright, Paul (1984), *Financial Times*, 28 June.

Commission of the European Communities (1977), *The Role of the Public Finance in European Integration*, (MacDougal Report), Brussels, April.

— (1984), 'Draft Treaty Establishing the European Union', *Bulletin of the European Communities*, 17, no.2, pp.7-28.

— (1985a), *The Inter-governmental Conference: Background and Issues*, London, p.1.

— (1985b), 'The thrust of Commission Policy', *Bulletin of the European Communities*, *Supplement 1/85*, 14 and 15 January.

— (1985c), *Completing the Internal Market: White Paper from the Commission to the European Council*, Luxembourg, Office for Official Publications, June.

— (1986), 'Single European Act', Title II, Section 1, especially articles 6 and 7 *Bulletin of the European Communities, Supplement 2/86*, Luxembourg, Office for Official Publications.

— (1987), *Communication on Budgetary Discipline*, Com(87) 430, Final, Brussels, August, p.3.

Corbett, Richard (1987), 'The Intergovernmental Conference and the Single European Act' in Roy Pryce, (ed.), *The Dynamics of European Union*, London and New York, Croom Helm, p.242.

Denton, Geoffrey (1984), 'Restructuring the EC Budget: Implications of the Fontainebleau Agreement', *Journal of Common Market Studies*, XXIII, no.2, pp.117-14.

Europe – the future (1984), para. 26, unpublished, dated 25-26 June.

European Council (1988), *Texts of Agreement reached at European Council*, 11-12 February 1988, including documents SN517/88 and SN461/88, p.7.

European Parliament (1985), *A New phase in European Union*, Luxembourg, General Secretariat.

European Parliament (1987), Session Documents, Series A, Document A 2-200/87/Part B, 7 November, p.5.

Financial Times, (1984), 'Cabinet Debates block on EEC payments', 22 March.

Financial Times (1985), 4 December.

Hartley, T.C. (1981), *The Foundations of European Community Law*, Oxford, Clarendon Press.

Jenkins, Peter (1984), 'Behind the Lines at the Battle of Brussels', *The Guardian*, 22 March.

Langeheine, Bernd, and Weinstock, Ulrich (1985), 'Graduated Integration: A Modest Path Towards Progress', *Journal of Common Market Studies*, 23.

Lodge, Juliet (1986), 'The Single European Act: Towards a New Euro-Dynamism?' *Journal of Common Market Studies*, 24, 203-23.

Nicoll, William (1986), 'From Rejection to Repudiation: EC Budgetary Affairs in 1985',

Journal of Common Market Studies, 25.

Palmer, John (1988), 'Hard Pounding for the EMS', *The Guardian*, 18 May.

Presidency (1988), *Making a Success of the Single European Act: A Note*, SN 461/1/88, Brussels, p.3.

Schmuck, Otto (1987), 'The European Parliament's Draft Treaty Establishing the European Union (1979-84)'.

Stephens, Robert (1982), 'Britain's Other War', *The Observer*, 23 May.

Taylor, Paul (1988), 'Reforming the System: Getting the Money to Talk', in Paul Taylor and A.J.R. Groom, (eds), *International Institutions at Work*, London, Pinter pp.220-36.

The Sunday Times (1985), 'Super-EEC Plan Leaves Britain in the Cold', 3 March.

The Times (1985a), 27 June.

The Times (1985b), 1 July.

Wallace, Helen (1985), 'Europe: the Challenge of Diversity, London, Routledge and Kegan Paul for the Royal Institute of International Affairs, 1985, pp.29-49

Wallace, William (1985), in *The Times*, 2 July.

Wyles, John (1984), 'So Near and Yet So Far', *Financial Times*, 22 March, p.24.

2 EC Policymaking: institutional considerations

Juliet Lodge

Introduction

Traditionally, it has been commonplace to speak of a 'decisionmaking' rather than a 'legislative process' in the European Community (EC) and wrongly to depict EC 'decisionmaking' outcomes as 'decisions' that are of a lower order to 'superior' domestic legislation and laws. States have seen the EC as being 'out there' rather than as an internalized and intrinsic part of the regular broader arena in which they operate. The 1980s made the changeover to viewing the EC in the latter light imperative. Some states adapted quickly. Others, even on the eve of the 1990s, still cling to outmoded concepts of national sovereignty which Jean Monnet in 1943 warned were inimical to peace, economic prosperity and social progress (Monnet, 1978).

Such divisions cannot be dismissed as mere expressions of ideological differences. They have serious implications for the formulation, adoption and implementation of decisions taken within the EC setting. Their impact extends beyond the machinations of the member states among themselves at the EC level to affect the whole of the supranational-level legislative process. They also permeate myriad aspects of government and public and private-sector policymaking within the member states from the national level downwards. The EC has become a central frame of reference for an incalculable number of actors most of whom will hope to influence and/or gain from the eventual outputs of the EC's decisionmaking process. Space limits preclude a wider discussion of this here, where the aim is to sketch how the pattern of interactions between the EC's key decisionmaking institutions feeds into the debate of where the EC is going and what kind of organization it is.

Originally, the EC could lay claim to being unique among international organizations primarily because it had a decisionmaking process whose outputs were both binding upon its members and took precedence over national legislation where EC and national legislation were in conflict; and it had accepted the legitimacy of a supranational authority to legislate with the active consent of the member states on behalf of the Community as a whole. The EC can still claim to be unique, but the debate today is not so much about its uniqueness among international organizations but about its goal: is it transforming itself into something that is recognizable as a federal state?

The recurrent argument about the distribution of political authority among the EC's institutions is often seen to be an important clue as to the direction of European integration. This means that analysis has concentrated on supranational-level patterns of actor interaction. Relatively little attention has been paid to the ways in which, and the relative pace at which, domestic

26

political authorities have reacted to European integration. Arguably, the 1990s will exhibit further sub-national-level clues to the direction of European integration. However, this section seeks merely to point out some features of EC policymaking which have been influential in the assessment of European integration and which help to show why the EC now faces a crisis of political authority.

Traditionally, EC decisionmaking outcomes have been depicted as the outcome of a Commission–Council dialogue. Accordingly, policy has been seen as the product of a supranational Commission proposing legislation to a Council that deliberates and decides upon its adoption (Henig, 1983). Into this dialogue, the European Parliament (EP) has inserted itself with increasing effect (notably since the first direct elections in 1979) although the EP has not been portrayed as a legislature *per se* until recently. Nor did all the member states accept its right to call itself a 'Parliament' as opposed to an 'Assembly' until 1987 when the former was accepted in the Single European Act (SEA). An almost irrelevant adjunct to the dialogue has been the Economic and Social Committee (ESC). Finally, as chief judicial arbitrator and interpreter of EC legislation there is the European Court of Justice (ECJ); as political arbitrator, the relatively 'young' European Council; and as financial overseer, the Court of Auditors. These institutions, along with the European Investment Bank, have been portrayed as the key institutions of a unique supranational European polity where pluralism held sway (Lindberg and Scheingold, 1970). Indeed, economic and political pluralism has been held to be the *sine qua non* of European integration: only those states having a West European conception of liberal democracy broadly conceived may become EC members.

In this scenario, the extent of European integration has been measured crudely with reference both to a variety of different indicators and to the different strategies thought necessary to attain a posited 'end state' of integration. While the indicators isolate certain changes which are said to typify one of the following – functionalism, neo-functionalism, confederalism, new neo-functionalism, federalism and neo-federalism – all implicitly rely on changes in EC-level institutional interaction to confirm a posited trend. Accordingly, integration has been measured with reference to shifts in loyalties of elites from national to supranational settings (Mitrany 1966, 1975; Haas, 1964; Lodge, 1975); increased cross-border trade flows within the EC (Deutsch 1966; Nau, 1979); the spillover of supranational action from one policy sector to another (Lindberg 1963, Haas, Lindberg and Scheingold, 1971); parallel actions; the movement up a supposed hierarchy of policy issues from the allegedly minimally sensitive, economic sectors to the highly sensitive, high-political sectors at the core of national sovereignty (Groom and Taylor, (1975).[1]

Finally, the pace and direction of integration has been assessed using an implicit linear scheme whereby integration begins on a functionalist level, progresses through neo-functionalism ultimately to federalism (Friedrich, 1968). Central to this is an evaluation of the changing balance of power between the three key institutions in the policymaking process: the Council, the Commission and the EP. Accordingly, sharp distinctions have been drawn between different integrative phases in the EC. Depicted as discrete, the overlap and different features said to typify one co-exist with others and/or reassert their distinguishing characteristics as the policy agenda and political personnel change. On the one hand, the extent to which the Commission has been able to expand the scope of its competences and jurisdiction over a widening range of policy sectors and, on the other hand, the extent to which the Council (or specific governments – the French in the 1960s, the British in the 1980s) has reined in the expanding scope of the EC's policy agenda and outputs have been used as impressionistic measures of the progress of European integration.

The 1950s were portrayed as the era of High Authority and Commission supremacy: the age of functionalism when integration was given direction by a High Authority and Commission relatively free from government restraint. The 1960s saw the growth of supranational pressure-group activity and the demands of Gaullism (Caporaso, 1974; Harrison, 1974; Heathcote, 1966). In that neo-functional era, economic prosperity added fuel to the integrative process in a way not completely dissimilar to the 1992 movements of the 1980s. Yet this phase too was checked by intergovernmentalism and the apparent upstaging of the Commission by the Council, trends which spilled over into the 1970s (Puchala, 1968, 1972). Observers variously characterized this as a time of confederalism (Taylor 1975) and growing interdependence (Keohane and Nye 1977) with the EC falling short of federation but beyond a regime (Wallace 1983) as member governments stubbornly refused to cede (formally at least) policymaking authority and sovereignty to supranational institutions and reclaimed instead a pivotal, directing role for themselves. This image was reflected institutionally in decisionmaking deadlocks, the seemingly indefinite postponement of majority voting in the Council, the introduction of EC summits (later called European Councils and kept on an intergovernmental, non-EC rather than a supranational organizational footing – a situation only loosely altered by the SEA), growing political recognition of the Committee of Permanent Representatives' importance and the establishment – outside the formal EC system – of European Political Cooperation (EPC).

Though easily interpreted as signs of governments' ultimate ability to limit the pooling of sovereignty and to 'control' the pace of integration, such developments underscored their commitment to its expansion, no matter the contrary rhetoric. The public political presentation of such initiatives as being sponsored by the member states rather than the Commission or the EP was crucial. Even in the 1980s, while President Mitterrand could claim much credit for France's more visionary quest for greater integration, the evolution of the strategy to attain it was the product of the critically timed Spinelli initiative on European Union and Spinelli's careful encouragement of France. The member governments tend to follow rather than initiate such integration; until now, they have also tended to try and contain it given the importance attached to the maintenance of national sovereignty. Through public political gesture they can legitimize something that is already underway.

Integration theorists may be tempted to see this as a means by which governments can contain their citizens' attachment to the state and curb any inclination to switch loyalties to 'outside' bodies affecting their socio-economic progress. Governments can certainly erase any idea that the supranational authorities are uniquely responsible for such progress and so inhibit any (rather fanciful) threat of zero-sum switches leading to the ultimate withering away of the nation-state. Alternatively, such tactics can be construed as signs of the continued relevance of power politics. Whatever theoretical construct is placed on such developments, it is clear that institutional innovation and evolution do illuminate integration's dynamics and provide an indicator of how integration can become locked-in early on: the beneficiaries of integrative policies support them; the disgruntled seek their alteration to benefit themselves. Change and adaptation typify integration. Conflict between the states and among the EC's institutions is almost always integrative. The EC's importance as a frame of reference for an ever-expanding scope of policy activities formerly consigned to 'domestic' ministries and for a range of cultural and sporting events continues to grow and this is seen as confirming the trend towards decentralized federalism. Institutional change itself spurs this process on.

By the 1970s, no sooner had the 'new' actors been set up than pressure for greater institutional (and implicitly political and economic) integration grew. The outlet for such pressures was to be the European Councils. Successive summit declarations reinforced integration and the commitment of the founding Six, then Nine and Ten to European Union throughout the 1970s. Yet none of the new members was to be as pro-integrative as the new Iberian entrants in the late 1980s. High points were the declarations of the 1969 Hague summit; that in Paris in 1972, in Copenhagen in 1973; declarations in 1974; the commitment to Euro-elections and the Tindemans Report of 1975; the Genscher–Colombo proposals for a European Act in 1980 – later transformed into the July 1983 Solemn Declaration on European Union – and the overtly federalist Draft Treaty establishing the European Union of 1984. Finally, at the end of 1985 on the eve of the EC's third enlargement, agreement was reached on the Single European Act. While the SEA is not a federalist document, it has been depicted as part of a federalist phase in European integration associated with the 1980s. Institutionally this is reflected in the EP's growing power, the re-alignment of the inter-institutional balance to the Council's possible disadvantage, the codification of EPC and by the federal role of the ECJ.

While useful as a heuristic device to depict EC decisionmaking as something that occurs between a set of supranational-level institutions, it is misleading to assume that this is 'all there is'. EC policymaking is a far more complex phenomenon and the absence of consensus over what the EC is becoming sharpens the importance of inter-institutional issues and begs an answer to the problem of the EC's looming crisis of political authority. Before briefly describing some of the main attributes of the EC's policymaking institutions, it may help to comment upon some of the issues and the wider institutional context within which EC policymaking unfurls at the supranational level.

The issues: *executives v. parliaments*

Different ways of conceptualizing the EC lead observers to focus on different aspects of the policymaking processes. When examining the interactions between public legislative and executive authorities, EC decisionmaking can be conceptualized as a pyramidal hierarchy at the apex of which stand EC institutions. National governments form the middle stratum and sub-national/ regional and local administrative actors the base. The various strata can be analysed in terms of horizontal and vertical interactions. Such analyses can be illuminating but they necessarily oversimplify complex interactions, omit assessment of the impact of private actors and often unintentionally create a misleading impression that EC policymaking can be managed in a systematic and rational way; that it is a rational process; that rational, 'good' and 'optimum' policy outputs are the goal and are invariably attained; and that the policymaking process is clearly regulated and coordinated both horizontally and vertically when, in practice, the degrees of regulation and coordination vary considerably from sector to sector, state to state, agency to agency. Moreover, the various strata are not as stable or nearly as impermeable as this model suggests. Nor are policy outputs the products of a neat, rational policymaking process.

Flow charts of EC policymaking highlight interactions between bureaucratic and (to a lesser extent) government actors. Indirectly, they can contribute to the idea that EC policymaking follows fairly standard procedures, routes and patterns of actor interaction. Indeed, the EEC treaties themselves prescribe certain functions for certain institutions. The fact that EC policymaking necessarily relies on interaction between the national and EC bureaucracies has led to the accusation that the EC is run by a monolithic, unaccountable technocracy. Technocratic politics are a feature of EC policymaking, but the problems of technocracy seem less acute as the EC enters the 1990s than those associated with the distribution of political authority between and among the EC institutions responsible for legislative outputs that affect everyone in the Community.

EC policymaking processes are largely dominated by bureaucracies and governments that provide little scope for parliamentary institutions (whether national parliaments or the EP) to intervene and to exercise roles traditionally believed to be the hallmarks of legislatures in liberal democratic polities (see below under EP). Moreover, the institution that does take decisions on the adoption of Commission legislative proposals, the Council, is often seen as being preoccupied with the defence of national interests against the encroachment of a common EC interest. This experience detracts markedly from the ideals of upgrading common interests to the benefit of all and from the idea that states join the EC because it is believed to be in their long-term national interest to be a member of the Community. It also means that governments have a major stake in ensuring that as much decisionmaking as possible is susceptible to their influence and control. Anything that inhibits this is rightly or wrongly construed as detrimental to them. The price paid has been stagnation, decisionmaking blockages, institutional paralysis and a significant constraint on the EC's capacity to respond effectively and efficiently to outside pressures. As the EC enters the 1990s, these problems cannot be dealt with (often on an *ad hoc* basis) simply by augmenting governments' roles in EC policymaking through the medium of the European Council, EPC, EPC's new secretariat the CPR, or the various Councils. Not only is it clear that various coalitions of states may seek to dominate and manipulate the policy agenda but the question of who – which state(s), which insitution(s) (EC or national) – is ultimately responsible and accountable for decisions taken has to be faced. The current lack of consensus over this makes for a crisis of political authority in the EC that is often hidden by the recurrent concern expressed over the democratic legitimacy of the European Parliament.

Power politics: states v. the EC

The concentration on bureaucratic horizontal and vertical interaction seems warranted by the reality of deficient parliamentary participation and by the marginalization of the role of citizens. While 'direct democracy' is seen to be unworkable within the member states and at the supranational level, and while citizens themselves might be believed to have only a peripheral role *vis-à-vis* EC policymaking processes, the evolution of EC decisionmaking and the continuation of its democratic deficit has important lessons for the member states.

EC decisionmaking has not evolved as a technocratic process (sometimes disingenuously believed to be devoid of bureaucratic politics itself) whose goal has been the production of rational and maximally optimum outcomes. Instead, it has been mediated by the vagaries of power politics between member states and their political leaders; by states jostling for position and comparative advantage; by statesmen having a long-term vision of Europe's future; and by those blinded by short-term calculations. Some have actively courted allies and partners within the EC that have withstood short-term changes of personnel and policy disagreements. Such relationships have gone beyond the idea of coalition-building tactics typical of interactions around one or more shorter-term policy issues.

Worthwhile as all this may be, the question of democracy has meanwhile been ignored. The cynic would say deliberately so because the decline of legislatures' power enhances the ability of the executive to proceed without parliamentary encumbrance. This has been a feature of the years during which the EC was formed, grew, prospered and expanded.

The two are not necessarily causally related. But member governments' unwillingness to rectify the EC's democratic deficit highlights how convenient the decline has been. It may, indeed, have been necessary to limit the role that national parliaments could play in a supranational policymaking process. It might even have been politically expedient to restrict the role given initially to the 'Assembly'. However, the future offers no such excuses. National parliaments' and governments' fears about the erosion of sovereignty seem almost trivial compared to the greater erosion of democratic controls by executives that will inevitably result from continued refusal to redress the deficit. It is not so much that anxiety over sovereignty is completely unfounded, or that it is a mere smokescreen, an expression of wishful thinking for pre-1945 days. Rather, it legitimizes a process of unfettered executive dominance and allows legislatures to wither on the vine by default.

The tussles between the EC's institutions representing the member governments (notably the Council of Ministers) and those representing 'Europe' (notably the Commission but more pertinently now the EP) are a source of continuing interest. They are instructive because they reveal how the balance shifts from one to the other. Any erosions of Council supremacy, any indicators of it being called publicly to account, of it being subject to some 'outside' (sic) control are interpreted as indicators both of integrative trends – towards federalism or intergovernmentalism crudely speaking – and of the extent to which integration has broadly positive or negative outcomes. Governments' consent to greater integration is mediated by their expectations and the realities of EC redistributive policies on their own states. National and sometimes selfish considerations are ever-present.

Inter-institutional tussles are shorthand for the battles member governments have to wage on several fronts in order to assert their legitimate interests in EC policymaking. (See below on the Council.) The Commission, the ECJ and the EP as well as majority voting in the Council itself are formidable 'opponents' to a government that for whatever reason decides that a proposed policy is not in its interest and must be radically altered and resisted. In the ensuing 'confrontation' the psychological mind-sets of 'them' and 'us' become persuasive.

The 'them' versus 'us' psychological predisposition is not restricted to a battle between those epitomizing supranational and national standpoints. It is not necessarily only a battle between the member states on the one side and the Commission and EP on the other. Rather, the need for coalition formation within the Council – among the states – gives rise to other 'set piece' dichotomies: north versus south, rich versus poor, centre versus periphery, the big versus the rest, and so on. However, the fact that coalition building among the states is essential in the Council when matters are to be decided by majority vote accentuates the impression that a 'them – us' confrontation between the member states and the Commission is the rule. Moreover, the Commission's prerogative to initiate legislation that is then presented to the Council and the EP contributes to the impression: the Council is on the receiving end of a process of devising policy that is, formally at least, conducted elsewhere. Inevitably, the Council's members are liable to react defensively.

The reality of EC decisionmaking shows, however, that while confrontation is a normal part of the legislative process, such confrontation is not destructive. It is about facing and trying to reconcile different views on a mutually acceptable basis. Governments differ in the bargaining tactics they adopt. A lot of posturing occurs. For some, quiet diplomacy is the rule. For others, strident assertion of (already Europeanized) national interests becomes an integral part of negotiation within the EC. All, however, are committed to maximizing their own potential: the EC is a forum which none can do without, but whose true significance to their own well-being some deliberately underplay in the domestic public arena. The UK is a striking example of the latter. Yet many others are chary of developments that suggest a curtailment of national autonomy, supremacy and independence. That is why changes in the EC's institutional balance are so often perceived as threatening and become the most obvious arena of the 'them versus us', the EC versus states, dispute. Sovereignty was pooled long ago. Governments remain afraid to acknowledge this and to admit it to themselves as much as to their citizens.

If this suggests that many, if not all, EC member governments have not psychologically adapted to being inside the EC, it is not surprising that they should resist any changes – especially institutional changes – that explicitly confirm the ascendancy of supranational EC institutions over which they have little control. However, the demands of 1992 mean that psychological agility will be prized. If 'Social Europe' becomes a reality, many of the current idiosyncrasies regarding worker participation, employees' rights to information in companies, minimum health and safety standards, individuals' rights and obligations (including the right to vote in Euro- and local elections) will have to be contemplated seriously by governments who, until now, have seen these areas as their exclusive preserve. Some harmonization is inevitable. Pressure for a Euro-Bill of Rights is bound to grow. The problem for member states is that the dispute over 'Social Europe's' provisions cannot be contained. Nor can it easily be presented in terms of the 'states versus the EC' chimera. On the contrary, in states where there is little if any consensus among the major political parties over socio-economic matters, national governments can expect to see their opponents lobbying against them at EC level as well as within the state itself. There can be little doubt that EC policymaking will be played out against a background of growing Council – EP interaction and struggle, and that the question of accountability will greatly exercise those anxious to contain the undoubted national trend towards government by executives. Steps to redress the balance at the EC level may well spill down over the longer term to the national level.

The EP, almost alone among parliaments within the EC, is increasing its power at a time when national parliaments' roles appear to be largely trivialized or receding. In confronting the issue of the EC's democratic deficit, moreover, the EP will be likely to use whatever opportunities come its way. At the very least, this will mean a full and thorough exploitation of the cooperation procedure and of its own Rules of Procedure. Unless member governments can control or contain 'their' nationals in the EP, parliamentarians denied an effective role in either national or EC policymaking processes may well begin to construe one of their roles as being to oppose the Council. Becoming 'the Opposition' to 'the Government' (viz Council even though it does not have the power to initiate legislation) may seem both necessary and desirable once the heady success of exercising limited influence through the cooperation procedure wanes.

The corollary to this would be governments seeking greater corporate unity (within the Council) and greater cohesion and coherence of purpose at the domestic level within the bureaucracies and with other interested parties. Achieving such cohesion and consensus will be far from easy, but will be necessary.

The institutional parameters for policymaking therefore present enormous challenges at the supranational and national levels of policymaking. Moreover, as the effects of 1992 spill down to the local level, the number of actors involved in vertical and horizontal interactions will grow exponentially. They will make their own demands on a system that is, in many respects, overextended and adapting quickly to change. If they find that any of the supranational actors are, as a result, insufficiently responsive, there can be little doubt that they will seek the ear of those ready to listen. Lobbying of the EP continues to grow apace because even if MEPs at present have relatively limited ability to influence policy outcomes, they do have the ability to embarrass the Council. This power could be more effectively realized in the future.

Above all, the policy demands on the system over the next decade or so are likely to be such that the key institutions themselves will wish to avoid confrontation. They will be drawn into more regulated contact. This will be particularly true of the Council and the EP. They will have to seek constructive dialogue and ways of integrating, using and developing policy networks and of managing a policymaking process that MEPs will insist be subject to parliamentary influence and control. We now focus on the Commission and Council and briefly look at the European Council and ESC before examining the EC's putative legislature in more detail.

The actors

The Commission

There is a grain of truth in the old cliché: 'The Commission proposes and the Council disposes'. It is certainly true that the Commission is entrusted with functions that have led to it being called the 'motor of European integration'. Based in Brussels[2] the Commission has information offices throughout the member states and around the world. Its delegations are accredited to other states (sometimes amid much public political debate over diplomatic proprieties concerning the Commission's role – as in the case of Australia) and it receives foreign accreditations and plays a prominent role in the EC's external relations.

Organization

The Commission is a Eurocracy headed by seventeen political appointees (until 1989 all men!) nominated and appointed by common accord of the EC's twelve member governments. In practice, the big states have two commissioners apiece and the others one each. These seventeen are supported by a bureaucracy (known as a secretariat and headed usually by an influential and experienced bureaucrat). This bureaucracy is sub-divided into directorate-generals (DGs) that broadly mirror administrative responsibilities for given policy areas. The Commission's size has been much villified even though it is smaller than the local authorities of many EC cities. Its secretariat consists of nearly 12,000 officials, translators and interpreters (to deal with the EC's nine official languages) mainly based in the Berlaymont building in Brussels and usually recruited by means of competitive examination. National officials can also be seconded to the Commission (with different effects depending on the national origins of the official, her/his career perspectives and the prestige, or lack of it, attaching to such secondments) (Feld and Wildgen, 1975).

EC enlargements have always caused problems within the Commission's secretariat as established officials (or Eurocrats as they are often called) have had to make way for a quota of civil servants from the new entrants. In so doing, senior positions have been forfeited, mismatches between skills and functions have ensued with consequent negative effects on efficient policymaking. The calibre of personnel in different DGs can be so uneven as to lead to some DGs being seen as distinctly 'minor' and even second class. These problems are compounded by Commission recruitment practices which, in addition to exacerbating problems of morale and mobility within the civil service, have adversely affected Commission effectiveness and the development of an élite corps (Wallace, 1983:58). Investigations have led to internal reforms and improvements (see Spierenberg; Three Wise Men). Nevertheless, it remains true that problems encountered by the Commission's staff may, on occasion, be aggravated by the Commission's multinational composition and concomitant diversity of administrative styles (Michelmann, 1977), traditions, practices and ambitions Commissioners and their staff have both for different policy sectors and for their own careers. The effects may be integrative or malintegrative and may so inhibit organizational cohesion and efficiency that the Commission's ability to adapt its style of policy management and execution to fast changing situations is impaired. Government expectations of 'their' nationals in the Commission have undermined the ideal of the Commission as a collegiate body promoting the EC's 'collective interest', and recruitment and appointment practices reinforce this.

Appointment

The process of selecting the seventeen Commissioners is often protracted and highly political. That of selecting the Commission President has been likened to a 'papal chimney-smoke' (Budd, 1987:31). The Commission President serves a renewable two-year term of office (usually four in all), but the renewal itself is often plagued by political sensitivities, especially when major political initiatives are in the offing or underway, as in the case of the Delors Presidency. The way in which a Commission President exercises his role can also give rise to problems if national leaders feel that he is overstepping the mark and/or usurping their pre-eminence on the European and international stage, as was the case when de Gaulle vetoed the re-appointment of Commission President Hallstein. More recently, Mrs Thatcher's attempt to ridicule President Delors' vision of a united Europe served to highlight how difficult many political leaders find an independent, politically minded Commission President. It is up to the Commission President to decide whether he will adopt a technocractic, political or presidential style of managing and giving direction to the Commission's and to the EC's work.

The Commission President's style and willingness to adopt a high political profile are affected by many factors, including the degree of support he commands from major states for his role conception and vision of future EC integration. Governments can weaken and constrain any grandiose role the Commission may harbour for itself (for example, as a putative EC government with a directly elected president) by various means. For instance, they could appoint as president someone lacking a high international profile (so minimizing his ability but possibly raising that of the Council president to be an influential speaker on the EC's behalf in international dealings). This tactic does not commend itself in the 1990s. However, there can be little doubt that governments do weigh up many considerations when nominating the Commission President. Moreover, if the President does increase his role in the appointment of Commissioners, and if the EP's influence too becomes meaningful, then the political weight of the Commission will indeed increase. It is not without reason that the EUT strengthened the Commission's role and that the EP continues to affirm the EUT's principles for a future EC constitution.

Problems can arise too if one or more governments suspect that a presidential nominee is biased towards more Europeanism than they find palatable, or if his experience in the European Community arena is exceptionally deep. Gaston Thorn was president of all three major EC institutions – the Commission, the Council and the EP (not simultaneously, of course) – but this experience gave him particular insights into the workings of the three bodies. Had he been a national of one of the big states, it seems unlikely that he would have been elected EP president after his earlier posts. Delors' experience and vision makes him a formidable Commission President bent on shaping the EC's future.

The Commission has six vice-presidents drawn from different member states. Like the President and the other Commissioners, they have responsibility for different policy sectors. Which Commissioner assumes responsibility for what portfolio is subject to great debate among the governments and is but one factor in determining the composition of the Commission. The Commission serves a four-year term of office and the appointment of Commissioners is beset by national sensitivities. One of the first problems for member governments is to decide which of their nationals they are going to put forward as candidates to be considered by their colleagues. The big states with two Commissioners apiece are in a position to ensure the nomination of those whose political allegiance lies with the governing party (or governing coalition parties, as in the FRG's case, for example). Traditionally, one of the UK's Commissioners has been drawn from the major opposition party. Any deviation from this practice invariably leads to a public political row. Moreover, the big states tend (in the case of the UK recently) to ensure that one of their nominees is seen as 'senior' to the other, and will even refuse to renew the term of office of an outgoing Commissioner to enable them to put two new inexperienced people in the Commission, one of whom is depicted as senior and implicitly deserving a more important portfolio (for example Brittan and Millan).

The Commission broadly reflects a national and a political balance. Its make-up does not (yet) mirror the political spread of the EC's electorate or the EP's majority tendence, partly because the terms of office of the two institutions do not yet neatly coincide, and partly because the idea of the Commission representing a particular ideological leaning is unacceptable to most governments (and contrary to the ideal role originally prescribed for it). Yet MEPs increasingly demand that there should be some correspondence between the EP's ideological majority and the composition of the Commission (and have devised means for attempting to effect this). MEPs' demands for a voice in the appointment of the Commission President and the Commissioners have not yielded much in terms of formal rights in the appointment process, even though the EP is now consulted after the governments have made their choice of President. However, by amending its Rules of Procedure, the EP invested itself with a right to hold a vote of confidence on the Commission by means of a vote of investiture when it assumes office and announces its programme to Parliament. Delors certainly seems to value the added authority EP endorsement of the Commission's programme gives the Commission. This right is seen as a partial corollary right to the EP's power to sack the Commission *en bloc* by a motion of censure passed by a two-thirds majority of MEPs. Individual Commissioners can be removed and compulsorily retired, on application to the ECJ, for misconduct (see Merger Treaty Art.19). On taking up their office, Commissioners swear their independence and Euro-allegiance in front of the ECJ.

The Commission takes decisions on a collegiate basis, but individual members assume responsibility for one or more portfolios, the distribution of which engenders intense rivalry between the member governments. Portfolios can be made up on a pick-and-mix basis to pacify 'injured' parties or to ensure that each Commissioner has at least something important to supervise. Nationality, political allegiance, relationship to socio-economic groups, previous experience, prestige and goals (especially when renewing or denying appointment) and the portfolios that particular governments covet for domestic political reasons all affect the appointments and distribution of responsibilities. Thus, states with major agricultural interests normally seek to hold the agricultural portfolio and to colonize the relevant DGs. The sheer importance of the CAP also adds prestige to a small state if it acquires agriculture. (Ireland's Ray MacSharry currently is responsible for the CAP and rural development.)

France has traditionally had a strong hold on overseas development portfolios. The new Commission's make-up similarly shows how some responsibilities have been given to Commissioners from states with a particular national interest in a policy sector: Abel Matutes and Manul Marin (Spain) are responsible for relations with Latin America, Mediterranean Policy and fishing, respectively; a British Commissioner has responsibility for competition policy and financial institutions; Jean Dondelinger (Luxembourg) is in charge of a Citizen's Europe, broadcasting policy, audio-visual and communication policies; and Delors and Christiane Scrivener hold the portfolios central to progressing economic and monetary integration. States engage in horse-trading, not always discreet, to manoeuvre their nominees into favoured positions, often with little regard for the effects of a 'successful' bid on their own internal management of EC issues. Domestic civil services face numerous problems as a result.

Each Commissioner has a 'cabinet', a small personal staff not part of the Commission's bureaucracy or part of the DGs, but which plays a crucial role in the internal political management and external links of the Commission (Wessels, 87); wields considerable influence, as filter between the Commissioner and the DGs (Henig, 1983:12), and performs information and intelligence functions for her/him. Yet, Commissioners are rarely good at operating outside their own domaine (or DG) even though 'cabinet' task forces and special groups of Commissioners sit to examine related policy clusters. Policy planning across the DGs remains fraught. This has serious implications for policy development, management, execution and implementation. These are not entirely specific to the Commission in its performance of its bureaucratic functions (Wallace, 1983). The Commission also performs major political functions but the parameters of the policy formation process and organizational problems are inhibiting factors.

Commission powers and functions

The Rome Treaty reserves almost exclusively for the Commission the power to initiate legislation. Hence, its denomination as 'the motor of integration'. The Commission exercises this power in complete independence. It may not seek or follow instructions from individual member governments or other interests on the content of its proposals. These must, instead, reflect the 'common good' and 'common interest' (as it is perceived by the Commission) of the EC. The Commission is enjoined to draft legislative proposals accordingly. To safeguard Commissioners' independence, national governments undertake to respect that independence and to desist from trying to influence them in the performance of their tasks.

In theory, Commissioners are autonomous and give a solemn undertaking, during a special session of the ECJ, to remain above national politics and the advancement of national interests. In practice, this independence is less than absolute (Van Miert, 1975). While national governments cannot remove or sack Commissioners whose policies they dislike during the Commission's normal term of office, they can refuse to re-appoint such a member. This is a powerful hidden weapon at national governments' disposal in contrast to the EP's power to sack the whole Commission – so far never achieved (see below). In practice, national governments do expect, though rarely obtain, unwavering 'loyalty' from their Commission appointees. If a Commissioner diverges too much from what his national government sees as reasonable, or if he is seen as insufficiently diligent on its behalf, then he is unlikely to be re-appointed. Mrs Thatcher used this weapon in order to try and decelerate the integrative momentum of Lord Cockfield's proposals on completing the single market.

Increases in the Commission's political clout inevitably mean a rise in disputes with member governments, and notably with those known to be in a minority. Such a result can prove productive as the Delors Presidency has shown. Indeed, the careful timing of the presentation of Commission initiatives and legislative proposals assumes even greater importance. While in the normal course of events, the Commission does have an eye to tabling proposals at favourable times, it is clear that major and somewhat controversial initiatives can expect a better reception if introduced to coincide with a run of Council Presidencies known to support them. A premium exists on coordinated planning between the Commission (especially the President) and Council counterparts. Increasingly, the EP will grow in importance in this respect.

While the Commission does possess many of the attributes of bureaucracies and while it is committed to impartiality and remaining *au dessus de la mêlée*, it cannot advance integration unless it does have a political vision of the possible and a realistic view of the medium-term goals of European integration. In exercising its functions, it no longer simply executes the Rome Treaty. It interprets the spirit of the Treaty in a far bolder manner. This is necessary given the changing international political economy within which the EC must operate in as coherent and cohesive a manner as possible. At the more routine internal level, the Commission must also display political acumen. Its legislative role again shows how it is more than a bureaucracy. Astute politicking can make the difference between success and failure. Awareness of an overall goal can also bolster the attempt to give direction to EC integration. The problem for the Commission is, however, that in exercising its political and executive functions, insufficient coordination within the Commission can produce contradictory and inadequate legislative outcomes. Nevertheless, the legislative process itself has tended to 'lock-in' integration. Proposals may lie on the table for years (since outright rejection is rare) before being adopted in modified form. The cooperation procedure (see p.71) may lead to proposals being dropped if they do not get anywhere within twelve to eighteen months, but the bureaucratized nature of EC decisionmaking does have an integrative effect on the whole. Legislative proposals are rapidly enmeshed as they are referred to the plethora of working parties under the Commission, national bureaucracies, the Committee of Permanent Representatives (see below), the EP and the Council of Ministers. Integration proceeds incrementally even without grand designs to guide it and since EC law takes precedence over national law in the event of conflict, ECJ rulings too are seen as locking-in integration.

Commission proposals

Commission proposals are not fashioned out of thin air. Rather they represent the culmination of an extensive process of consultation with leading representatives of Euro-level interest groups, national experts, senior civil servants and politicians (where appropriate). While a Commissioner assumes general responsibility for a given policy sector, the proposals cannot be advanced without the approval of the whole Commission. Each proposal is carefully elaborated with the help of the various departments within DGs. The *chef de cabinet* (see below) will have first prepared the ground and *ad hoc* groups of Commissioners most concerned by a particular proposal usually work together on complex issues. Only routine matters are delegated to individual Commissioners who are then empowered to act within the confines of a very narrow remit on the Commission's behalf. Recurrent agricultural regulations are adopted under this arrangement, some 11,450 being adopted this way in 1987 (Noel, 1987:42).

Given the technical nature of much of the Commission's work and the range of issues that it must address, it has procedures which allow it to pass on to the weekly Commission meetings only the most important or sensitive ones. Highly sensitive issues may be examined by the Commission alone together with the Secretary-General rather than, in the usual course of events, with the relevant Commission officials. Decisions are often reached only when the Commission is unanimous, although mainly by a majority vote which also binds the minority. Straightforward and routine matters are dealt with by 'written procedure' whereby the Commissioners are sent the dossier and draft proposal. If they do not submit reservations or rejections within a specific period (usually a week), the proposal is deemed adopted (Noel, 1987:42).

Depending on their aim, Commission proposals take different forms. There are several types of official EC acts, including policy programmes, earmarked policy 'years' (for example, the Year of the Environment) and international programmes. For the purposes of this discussion of the actors in the legislative process, the most important Commission proposals take the form of legislative proposals: regulations, directives and decisions. Commission recommendations and opinions are not binding on those to whom they are addressed.

Regulations are the most important means of promoting precise legislative uniformity. Regulations are binding in their entirety and are directly applicable in all the member states. They confer obligations and entitlements directly upon natural and legal persons in the member states. They have 'direct effect' (Mathijsen, 1986; Parry and Dinnage, 1981). Once published in the *Official Journal* a regulation must be enforced and complied with (Ziller, 49). Also important and in some respects a preferred means of advancing Commission goals in difficult areas are directives. *Directives* are binding with regard to the goal to be achieved and may be addressed to some or all member states. Member states are free to decide how to enact the directive. They also confer entitlements on natural and legal persons. Directives are often misleadingly referred to as 'secondary' legislation. Governments prefer directives to regulations because of the leeway for delay that they allow by permitting the governments to determine how to give effect to the goal that they prescribe. *Decisions* are binding in their entirety on the member states to whom they are addressed. They are rulings applicable to individual cases and are addressed to individuals or states.

The task of *initiating* legislation is clearly one of the Commission's most vital and most political functions. While it also exercises *wide-ranging rule-making, supervisory, executive, managerial* and *bureaucratic* functions, it performs other political functions in the course of giving effect to Treaty provisions. It is responsible for ensuring 'the proper functioning and development of the common market', thus becoming the EC's '*watchdog*': it ensures that the Treaty's provisions and legislation are applied and, if necessary, refers infringements to the ECJ. It is *guardian* of the Treaty. It can also formulate recommendations or deliver opinions on matters covered by the Treaty in instances where directed to do so and where it considers them necessary. This gives the Commission the right to exercise a good deal of political discretion which it can use to expand the scope of integration.

It exercises political discretion in its dealings with the other key institutions. It can sound out opinions before making proposals formally. In this pre-decisional phase, inter-institutional dialogue can help to define the parameters of what is likely to constitute a proposal that is broadly acceptable to the member states and therefore likely to stand a chance of being adopted. The Commission has a power of decision and participates in the shaping of measures taken by the Council and the EP's committees. Indeed, this practice has led to it being dubbed the Council's 'thirteenth' member.

The Commission does not simply perform a *mediative* function at the pre-decisional stage on formal and informal bases. Rather, this is part and parcel of its exercise of legislative authority in the EC. By eliciting information from and consulting national bureaucracies, the EP, European and national interest groups and other parties both at the pre-decisional stage of formulating a proposal and thereafter as it begins its passage through the institutions, it acts as *honest-broker* and works towards the production of acceptable compromises. This is an extremely important political role. The fact that only the Commission has the right to amend formally legislative proposals being discussed underlines the power invested in it. This is only partly compromised by the more complicated decisionmaking procedure involving two rather than a single reading under the 'cooperation procedure'.

The interaction between Commission officials and civil servants from national bureaucracies, whether from the Committee of Permanent Representatives (COREPER) or on a more informal basis, has resulted in the growth of 'bureaucratic interpenetration' or *engrenage* – the intermingling and enmeshing of civil servants at all levels and across the ever-widening range of EC decisionmaking. This is not limited to the policy formation phase as more agencies become involved later when EC legislation is implemented. The impact of this intermingling has affected EC, national- and regional-level administrations differently. Each of the member states has developed different means of managing and overseeing internal decisionmaking on EC issues (see page 79 for full reference to Wallace, 1973). EC issues, once regarded as 'foreign affairs', are now part of the daily cut and thrust of national bureaucratic politics. They have become internalized and their internalization has brought a series of further problems (ranging from difficulties in administrative coordination of overlapping policy areas to the politicization of troublesome issues at the highest levels) in their wake. Moreover, misunderstanding over the cooperation procedure has caused problems among domestic ministries whose views have diverged over the pursuit of their interests. This was sharply highlighted in the row over the 'Smoking causes Cancer' directive in Britain.

Engrenage has been portrayed as a technocratic conspiracy whereby bureaucrats seek to mystify Council members and national politicians by the technicalities and Euro-jargon of their proposals in the expectation that this will encourage them to delegate decisions to civil servants – notably those in COREPER. However, *engrenage* is not a conspiracy. Rather it is desirable and necessary to the EC's legislative process.

The Commission does not give a policy proposal its shape and direction in isolation: the proposal that is eventually submitted to the Council is the product of much deliberation and consultation with member governments and outside interests (both client groups and newcomers find the Commission comparatively accessible). This places a premium on its mediative and bargaining capacities which come under even greater pressure when a proposal reaches the Council. Package deals, horse-trading and the less publicly visible alterations of the wording and content of proposals cannot proceed without Commission complicity and help given in the course of it performing its role as honest-broker between competing national and other interests. The result inevitably is bureaucracy and compromise. The idea of upgrading the common interest in the pursuit of integration seemed to be largely forgotten until SEA amendments to complete the internal market by a given deadline placed a premium on 'a Euro-interest' in specific sectors (such as Euro-standards) that would rise above the lowest common denominator.

There are, moreover, numerous policy sectors (notable among them being agriculture) where the Commission assumes executive and managerial responsibility for implementing and administering decisions. Examples include the administration of EC finances (including the European Social Fund, European Regional Development Fund, and so on) and the implementation of the CAP, fixing levies, export refunds, etc. In such cases and in other cases where the Commission exercises delegated powers from the Council, the nature of the policymaking process can vary substantially from sector to sector. There are a plethora of committees in which the Commission assumes a key role either as participant, mediator or consultative partner. Management committees, for example, may be chaired by a non-voting Commission member but comprise member governments' representatives. There are numerous consultative committees, and committees for the implementation of regulations. The precise rules governing the Commission's role *vis-à-vis* the various committees became acutely controversial following the SEA and the Council's decision to curb Commission autonomy (see below). That the Council should have been worried by the Commission underlines the fact that the Commission plays a pivotal role in the legislative process and a role that is becoming increasingly politicized.

During the 1970s the vogue was to argue that the Commission had degenerated from a supranational Eurocracy to no more than the Council's secretariat (Sasse, 1975 and 1977). This caricature of the Commission illustrated how national governments could seriously limit its ability to advance integration. The mechanisms through which member states promote their interests will be considered briefly below. However, it is important to realize that the picture that a given Commission projects of itself depends on the charisma of its president, the personalities of its members and on the political climate in which it operates. If member governments are committed to the attainment of 'integrative' goals by specific, highly visible deadlines like 1992 then the Commission can project a more dynamic image especially if it enjoys member governments' confidence.

Its credibility would be tarnished were it to fail to initiate the requisite legislation rendering governments unable to deliver on their commitments. Mutual interdependence between the Commission and the Council is mediated by political factors. A strong Commission President and convinced Commissioners are vital to securing integrative outcomes in negotiations with sometimes formidable political opponents. The personalities of Council members and the political environment surrounding Council deliberations are equally but differently important for member governments.

The Council of Ministers

Typically the Council is portrayed as the 'brake' on EC integration. Its chief role is to adopt legislative proposals initiated and submitted by the Commission. In so doing, it performs a legislative function: it is the EC's actual legislature. This role is both vital to and a potential liability for successful EC policymaking since the member governments are called upon to perform contradictory functions (see below). Yet, the Council is usually depicted as a supreme body united in protecting national interests and sovereignty against supranational incursions. But governments are not monolithic. They cannot hope to negotiate EC decisionmaking except by constantly seeking and forging alliances with other member states, with factions within governing coalitions, government departments and with bureaucratic, political and economic elites within and across national boundaries, within the EC and the Commission. This is no easy matter. Indeed, the Commission's problems of policy coordination and so on seem relatively minor by comparison. However, it must also be remembered that internal organizational constraints on rational decisionmaking besiege both bodies, and that many of the external limits on the Council affect both it and the Commission. Before considering the Council's role in the EC's legislative process, some of these constraints must be outlined.

A key constraint lies in its composition and in government expectations of the roles and duties of individual members. The Council comprises representatives (usually ministers accompanied by officials) of the twelve member states. Its actual composition is determined by the policy sector under discussion. Ministers of Agriculture attend Council meetings dealing with the CAP, for example, Ministers of Foreign Affairs attend 'General Councils' and ministers from other departments attend those Council meetings that fall under their competence.

The Council is not a collegiate body. It has several, and often twelve, competing opinions as to what constitutes an acceptable compromise on a draft Commission proposal. Moreover, its members' views are often informed by extraneous considerations. Decisions will be deferred or accelerated depending on whether a given state expects to gain or lose something in the course of bargaining in the event of an election in another member state bringing different personnel and a government with different political convictions to later Council meetings, for example.

Electoral uncertainty, crises and general elections can seriously frustrate EC decision-making. It is extremely unusual for a politician to be in power for the full duration of the Commission's term without facing interim elections. Even if a government survives, cabinet changes may mean that the face of the person responsible for agricultural or technological issues, for instance, changes at critical points in the bargaining process. In 1981 there were elections in six of the ten member states which led to socialist victories in France and Greece and coalition changes in Ireland and the Netherlands (Fitzmaurice, 1983:2). Different demands of different coalition parties within member governments do affect governments' positions within EC bargaining, and affect different policy sectors differently. Similarly, heads of state and/or governments may agree to major policy initiatives only to find that within months of the summit (now known as a European Council) most of them have been ousted from office. Elections at other levels (local, municipal etc), domestic party constraints and internal rifts may also divert national governments' attention from EC issues or may lead them to procrastinate at critical junctures. External factors can and do affect member governments differently. The Falklands in 1982 showed how preoccupation in one arena led the UK to a high-risk EC bargaining strategy and to finding itself outvoted on an agricultural issue amid great controversy.

The potential for negative consequences arising out of the instability and lack of continuity in the organs in which member states are represented should not be exaggerated. Continuity in personnel is not always a source of strength, if the person(s) involved are not committed to acting in a positive manner in EC affairs and seek largely the advancement of their particularistic or national interest. Greater continuity in the sectoral Councils may, however, be advantageous. It must also be remembered that the appearance of instability at the political level is not mirrored at the bureaucratic levels where much of the hard negotiations take place.

Organization of the Council
The actual organization of the Council outwardly appears to accentuate its inherent instability. Council meetings are chaired by a President-in-Office. The Council Presidency rotates every six months among the member states according to the alphabetical order of the names of the states as written in their own language. Like the Commission President, the Council President has an important role to play on the international scene and the member states are jealous of the Council President's right to represent EC views *vis-à-vis* other states. It is clearly important that in international forums, coherence exists between the view presented by the Commission President and the Council President who, under something known as the 'Rome formula', become twin pivots of a 'bicephalous Presidency'. Broadly speaking, the Commission President negotiates on behalf of the EC as such on all issues within its competence while the Council President represents the member states.

Under European Political Cooperation arrangements, the Council President's role is even greater (see chapter 12). The Presidency functions as the Twelve's external representative. The Council President has acted as spokesman for the Twelve in a range of forums from the Conference on Security and Cooperation in Europe and the Euro–Arab dialogue to among others the UN General Assembly (Edwards, 1987:40). One of the more important tasks is to liaise with and inform the US (notably on EPC developments which are discussed by the member states' representatives as a group in Washington before the state holding the presidency communicates them to US officials via the local diplomat) (Taylor, 1980).

To enable a Council President effectively to articulate the EC as opposed to his/her own national view, the practice has arisen whereby Council Presidents do not usually also have to represent their member state's views (which may be at variance with the agreed EC line). At a minimum, it is normal for a Council President to differentiate statements in terms of whether she/he is speaking as Council President or as national spokesperson/Foreign Minister (Edwards and Wallace, 1977: O'Nuallain, 1985). Moreover, disquiet is often expressed as to the precise extent of Community competence over the continued and residual competence in international negotiations and forums of the member states (Edwards, 1987, 39; De Vree *et al.*, 1987; Ifestos, 1987).

At a more mundane and routine level, the Council Presidency assumes a managerial function (including voting); it may engineer political initiatives; it acts as an honest-broker and mediator in Council bargaining; and communicates and liaises (with differing degrees of commitment, intention and effectiveness) with the other key institutions. Its managerial function is of utmost importance. How this function is exercized depends on many factors. The UK acquired the reputation for a somewhat introverted and restrictive style of management following the issue of a now notorious set of instructions designed to limit the amount of information made available to the EP. Routinely governments may issue directions to their ministries on how to relate to other EC institutions and this inevitably affects their overall style of managing the Council while occupying the Presidency. Some states have a clear conception of the kind of stamp they wish to imprint on the Council; others seem to project national styles into the EC arena; others seek to alter inter-institutional relations in a positive way.

National considerations inevitably intervene so that particular states gain a reputation for a certain style of management. Some cultivate close links with the Commission and, to a lesser but growing extent, with the EP. Others may try and use the Presidency to advance issues central to their national interests – with greater caution than in the past. All find that their effectiveness in the Presidency is assisted if their own national administrative departments liaise well and coordinate their efforts. Those who have developed longer-term coalitions and alliances with other EC states (either within the context of triumvirate initiatives – the troika arrangements involve the past, present and immediate future Presidencies working together – or through bilateral accords (for example France and Germany) or discussions) may also use these to their advantage. All now indicate upon assuming the Presidency what their priority goals are for their period in office and endeavour to leave it with a decent record of achievement. This is a 'Europeanizing' imperative since the relatively short term of office concentrates Presidents' minds on what is feasible and likely to be acceptable to twelve rather than six states.

The managerial function demands further that the Presidency give direction to the Council's activities. This may mirror the broad interests of certain groups of states. Recent example shows that when Greece took over the Presidency from the FRG in July 1988, the emphasis switched – as expected – to internal market issues that had largely been neglected by the earlier preoccupation with the need to demolish barriers to trade and the free flow of capital. Hence the emphasis on the 'Social Europe' dimension to 1992. The Presidency is assisted by the Council's secretariat and by the Commission, whose representatives are present at its meetings.

The President is responsible for convening or not convening meetings of the Council and its working groups and committees. She/he must also try and persuade the relevant ministers from all states to attend if it is intended to call a vote. (A minister may send a non-voting 'substitute' to a meeting, and may depute another minister to vote on his/her behalf.) Tactical absences do occur. Leaving aside the meetings of actual ministers, it has been calculated (Edwards, 1987:36) that within a six-month period 150 working groups may need to meet either regularly or sporadically. COREPER, set up to assist the Council, meets at least twice a week.

Already, it is clear that the Council is underpinned by an important (but not overly large) bureaucracy that maintains as much continuity as possible between the different Presidencies and which does much of the 'donkey-work'. Bureaucratization of the Council's work is inevitable partly for reasons associated with the volume of work and its often technical nature. Numerous specialized committees report directly to the Council (the Monetary Committee, the Budget Policy Committee, medium- and short-term economic committees and others). Bureaucratization is also necessary because the Council does not meet in permanent session. Its members are first and foremost ministers in national governments and for many their EC workload is of less immediate political concern and perhaps also of less interest than their national workload. The compartmentalization of EC and national issues and the growth of the former makes the artificial distinction between the two increasingly difficult to sustain. Many states appointed 'EC Ministers' to create some coherence in their overall approach to EC questions, to form a political gatekeeper between COREPER and senior officials at home and to try and minimize contradictory lines being adopted by ministers drawn from different ministries. This is all the more necessary given the rarity of joint Councils (for example between Agriculture and Finance Ministers who might and do pursue diametrically opposed policies), the unwieldy nature of Jumbo Councils and the fact that decisional practices and Council procedures may vary significantly according to the sector in question. Moreover, the Council is fragmented at the ministerial level alone into the Council of Foreign Ministers (or General Council), numerous Technical Councils for specific sectors; and the European Council. Preparatory work devolves on the secretariat, COREPER and other often highly influential committees such as the Special Committee on Agriculture (SCA) (Wallace, 1983:64). In addition, ministerial meetings take place on a bilateral basis, and multilaterally on the periphery of Council meetings (for example 'fireside chats', the Conference of Finance Ministers, the Conference of Foreign Ministers for Political Cooperation). Generally, the Council President plays an important and influential role as coordinator of, and honest-broker between, divergent national interests. The process of conciliating national interests is undertaken both by direct bilateral diplomacy, especially on the eve of important Councils and European Councils (see below) and, on a daily basis, by the COREPER.

COREPER: honest-broker or clandestine Council?
COREPER has been described as the gate-keeper between the supranational and national systems since its members may represent the EC view to domestic officials and the national view to their counterparts and to the Commission. COREPER has existed since 1958 but was only legally recognized as an organ playing a role in the EC in 1965 (article 4 of the Merger Treaty). Its contemporary role seems to be as an advocate of national viewpoints, mediator and conciliator between and coordinator of emergent coalitions around policy issues.

COREPER's meetings are attended by the Commission. COREPER consists of Permanent Representatives (government representatives of ambassadorial rank). It has its own burgeoning network of working groups and committees comprising civil servants drawn from national bureaucracies. It is divided into COREPER I (for technical matters dealt with by deputies from each permanent representation) and COREPER II – the Permanent Representatives themselves. COREPER's President rotates in parallel with the Council Presidency.

Commission proposals are referred to COREPER for scrutiny. It may pass technical issues under the 'A' points procedure, avoiding further discussion by the Council. The Council then automatically approves them; they are drafted in the EC's official languages; adopted usually at the next Council meeting, are signed by the president and published or forwarded to whom they are addressed. Should COREPER fail to reach agreement on an issue, outstanding points are referred to the Council if possible with options that improve the chances of agreement in Council. To this end, COREPER meets both formally and informally. Formally, the officials have to abide by their governments' instructions. Informally, they can explore all manner of solutions which ministers may themselves explore informally over lunch with their counterparts on the first day of a Council meeting (Butler, 1987:30). Thus, COREPER, like the Council, has potentially incompatible roles to fulfil. Its members formally represent their governments *vis-à-vis* the Commission and in COREPER and its subordinate bodies; they act on the individual instructions of their governments. Collectively, however, they seek to prepare and engineer solutions acceptable to the Twelve. COREPER can be likened to a permanent conference simultaneously negotiating numerous issues and seeking compromises and side-payments as expedient. It has also been likened to a legislature with power exceeding that of the institution purporting to exercise legislative functions. But its main role has been more often seen as being akin to that of a senior board of directors taking daily decisions on EC policies (Butler, 1987:30). The Council cannot function without it. Indeed, it may refer issues back to COREPER when it is deadlocked: both COREPER and the Council Presidency are looked to as the source of potential compromises. Since there is such a premium on the elaboration of consensus and compromise (even forgetting for a moment the 'Luxembourg compromise'), the tendency has been for talks to continue, almost indefinitely, with the result that Council Presidents have delayed putting questions to the vote even when they might have been passed by a majority. This has resulted in protracted negotiations, bottlenecks and stagnation.

There can be little doubt that the Council is in some respects ill-equipped to perform the complicated legislative functions ascribed to it. It does possess its own bureaucracy. It is assisted by COREPER, and it has developed ways of giving direction (through the Presidency) to its work. Two major sources of Council weakness, however, lie in its policymaking deficits and in its contradictory role.

It is ironic that a system of decisionmaking that depends so heavily on the production of consensus should lack the kind of coordinating mechanisms necessary to ensure coherence in the distillation of a position, either in the Council or the Commission. Structural attributes of both account in part for this. In the Council's case, the result is a policy environment that is both 'disaggregated and competitive' (Wallace, 1983:65). As Wallace argues, accepted channels for the authoritative resolution of conflicts or arbitration among competing interests is wanting. Weaknesses in policy coordination at the national level, in the Council and in the Commission compound each other. Since internal reform seems so difficult to achieve, the likelihood is that EP pressure in the context of the cooperation procedure will impel greater internal coordination on the part of the Council and the Commission. The EP's potential for undermining laboriously arrived at compromises in both will demand that they improve their internal organizations.

The Council's contradictory role

The Council performs a contradictory role in the EC. Comprising member states' representatives, it is a body that articulates and concerns itself with national interests. Imbued by the Rome Treaty with the power to pass legislation, it acts as the EC's legislature. The EP has pretensions to this role, but it has only recently acquired a more generalized – but still fairly limited – right of co-decision with the Council. While the future may dictate a different role for the Council – and many advocate it sharing legislative power on at least a co-equal basis with the EP – for the time being it is jealous of its power and extremely reluctant to share or cede a portion of it to the EP. Many have suggested that its proper role be that of an upper chamber specifically charged with representing states' interests (and perhaps modelled on the Bundesrat (Herman and Lodge, 1978)) and having a qualified rather than almost absolute right to decide whether or not draft legislation be adopted.

For the present it retains its traditional image as an almost omnipotent legislative body that curbs the integrative momentum set in motion by the Commission and dictates the pace of integration according to the speed at which the least enthusiastic state wishes to progress. 1992 has certainly been upset by this picture in that some states have (possibly simply to underscore their conviction in the European ideal and their impatience with those dragging their feet) called for more EC action in a two- or three-speed Europe (also known as *abgestüfte* Integration (Grabitz, 1984)) and have advocated greater resort to variable geometry (Wallace with Ridley, 1985). The advantages of *abgestüfte* Integration are believed to lie in the imperative it would place on the determination of the EC's medium- to long-term objectives and on the sanctity of 'core' EC commitments such as the CAP and the customs union, however the latter may be defined.

Traditionally the answer to breaking Council deadlock was seen to lie in reform of its voting procedures. It was argued that the resort to majority voting (even wholesale qualified or weighted majority voting where fifty-four votes out of seventy-six are needed) would democratize and accelerate the legislative process. In itself this would neither end voting by unanimity (since unanimity is prescribed in several places by the Rome Treaty) nor necessarily threaten the 'national veto'. Nor would it safeguard the interests of those states in a minority of less than three states. It would, however, mean that providing an issue had been put to the vote the chances of it being adopted sooner rather than later should increase. This is, however, a major proviso given the Council's tendency to negotiate away disagreement wherever possible – even if the process takes over a decade to accomplish (on average two to five years elapse between the submission of a Commission proposal and the emission of a Council decision) – or to postpone taking a decision at all on a contentious piece of legislation. The Council has always had the right to reject a Commission proposal, but to do so it must be unanimous: unanimity on rejection has been far harder to secure than the adoption of a less than rational let alone optimum proposal. Not surprisingly, once a proposal is adopted, it is exceedingly difficult to revise it. States seek to keep any advantages they have secured or minimize any compromises.

Majority voting underlines the essential incongruity in the Council between its role as the EC's legislature and its members' preoccupations. Council decisions are taken on the basis of winning coalitions of states. No decisions, for example, can be taken without the accord of at least one of the big states. When votes are weighted, the distribution is: ten each to the UK, France, the FRG and Italy; eight to Spain, five to Belgium, the Netherlands, Greece and Portugal; three to Denmark and Ireland and two to Luxembourg.

The amendments to the Treaty of Rome introduced through the SEA meant that some areas formerly subject to unanimity became subject to majority voting. In theory, this should mean that decisionmaking will be accelerated. In practice, it has to be set against the fragility of coalitions. Under the cooperation procedure, in particular, the production of a minority winning coalition to block the qualified majority is crucial (see below). Moreover, in the past majority voting was practised when one or two Council members were tactically absent for a vote, or abstained (or temporarily withheld agreement) lest a positive vote for the item on hand prove politically sensitive at home. Note how governments still 'blame' the Commission for all manner of EC decisions which they have themselves endorsed but which they feel the public will dislike acutely.

Until majority voting (even possibly simple majority voting) becomes the norm rather than the exception, it will be easy to attribute EC deadlock to inadequacies in Council voting procedures rather than to the inadequacies that permeate the whole legislative process, to the absence of clear objectives and commitments to certain policies and EC values and the absence of politico-economic coherence and effective medium- and long-term economic strategies. Moreover, criticism against the Council will magnify its incongruous tasks. It acts as a legislature but always meets in camera – a practice rightly criticized as 'undemocratic' – making precise and public identification of individual states' positions difficult irrespective of 'informed leaks'.

As the cooperation procedure begins to bite, it will be increasingly implausible for governments to justify the Council rather than the directly elected EP having the final say over whether a draft legislative proposal is passed or not. It is unlikely that publics will be satisfied with the argument that ultimately heads of state and government can, through the European Council, take decisions when the Council defaults. Even they are unhappy with being used as a court of appeal or arbitration. Furthermore, the EP has since the early 1980s seized the initiative itself and prodded the European Council into confirming the need for major new initiatives over a range of areas. The Council and the European Council are not genuine initiators. They respond and provide the political approval for further action. The locus of a vision for the EC's future has shifted into the parliamentary arena. As the EP becomes proactive, so even the Commission finds itself having either to incorporate parts of EP 'own initiatives' into its own proposals, or to associate itself with initiatives it endorses (though not usually fully, as it would be unpolitic to do so) rather than fronting them. The EP is, to a lesser extent than the Council, on the offensive in an inter-institutional battle which will result in the EP and Commission effectively asserting themselves and securing Council accountability that has for so long eluded them.

The Strategic role of the Euro-Council
The European Council originated as summit meetings of the heads of government and/or state. (The French President is the only head of state to

attend and since 1985, the French head of government also attends.) Cynics saw the regularization of summitry in 1974 (on the initiative of French President Giscard d'Estaing) as inimical to European integration, as a crude device by heads of government keen to 'get in on the act' and to grasp a role for themselves in EC affairs before integration eclipsed them as well as the states. Some saw Euro-Councils as reminiscent of the Fouchet plan to insert a political, intergovernmental directorate over the supranational bodies. Others, saw it as potentially integrative (Haas, 1976: Lodge, 1975) in that it was a body that could give direction (hopefully) when the usual institutional dialogue became blocked. Indeed, meeting three times a year (twice per annum since 1987) the European Council soon became a referee in disputes among the member states, between different sectoral Councils, and the Commission. It also was seen as a court of arbitration when the Council had failed to reach a decision. This role sat uneasily with the more grandiose expectations of what it would deliver. Sorting out Council deadlocks detracted from the idea that it was the supreme authority in the EC and from the politically charged business of summitry. Yet, this function almost more than anything served to create the impression that it was an important body in the EC.

Not until the SEA was there any reference to the European Council in the EC treaties. Its existence outside the supranational framework increased suspicion of governments' motives and, of course, suited governments keen on a flexible, non-binding arrangement. The intergovernmental nature of the European Council is reinforced by its composition; by the extensive bilateral links between member states (some of which, such as the Franco–German treaty are equally formalized) that precede European Councils; and by the European Council's linkage to European Political Cooperation (EPC) (see chapter 12). It is no coincidence that the European Councils assumed mid-stage in the 1970s with the revival of the idea of the EC being guided by a political triumvirate (Schmidt for the FRG, Giscard d'Estaing for France and the UK Prime Minister) and with the growth of EPC. Moreover, a series of summits had been responsible since the Hague summit of 1969 for relaunching European integration and permitting the EC's first enlargement. Summit communiqués had been bold and ambitious (for example Paris, 1972) in charting future goals such as Economic and Monetary Union; and a Citizens' Europe (Copenhagen, 1973). The Benelux scotched any ideas of an Anglo–Franco–German axis leading the EC and the European Councils became institutionalized as a parallel arrangement to the existing set-up. Even if they have secured consensus for issues which the Council had failed to resolve, actual decisions have generally been left to the Council of Ministers (Wessels, 1987:41).

From 1974 the European Councils have assumed a 'motor' role in integration. They have launched their own initiatives when a powerful coalition of some states (always including France and the FRG have nudged them along (Simonian, 1985)). They have responded to or taken up those launched elsewhere (notably on institutional reform and European Union) and have sanctioned cooperation over a range of areas not necessarily strictly within the EC's competence. Foreign policy is one such area (as distinct from external relations which is the Commission's responsibility as it proceeds from trade). In other sectors, the European Council may simply have sanctioned politically developments occurring in the private sector (for example) whose progress depended on a visible and tangible EC-level commitment. This is true of the internal market and even now major companies are vying with each other to produce the successor to the Cockfield Whitepaper for the late 1990s.

The European Council's 'motor' role is perhaps less an expression of heads of governments' intention to be seen as the supreme source of authority in the EC than of the reality of contemporary European integration. The EC has become the prime site for promoting cooperation among the Twelve. It is not a question any more of national policy goals being 'Europeanized' to improve their chances of attainment. Rather, the EC is the reference arena for national goals: the question is whether or not they can be met better, more cheaply or more efficiently and effectively by EC cooperation than by individual (often competitive) unilateral national action alone. The 're-nationalization' of some aspects of EC policies may occur through the back-door or as part of a deliberate strategy (Taylor, 1983), but states compare policies that are costly to them with advantages they obtain from other sectors. Side-payments clearly matter but are not the overriding consideration. There has been an important shift towards the EC arena over the past decade and this will intensify.

Economic and Social Committee

The ESC has 189 members from the twelve states appointed from lists drawn up by member governments. Each state has a national quota of members (the big four have twenty-four apiece; Spain twenty-one; Belgium, Greece, Portugal and the Netherlands twelve each; Ireland and Denmark nine each; and Luxembourg six). They are drawn from three very broad groups: employers (Group I), workers (Group II) and 'various' (Group III) – that is agriculture, SMEs, the professions, consumers and so on. The ESC is a microcosm of national and Euro-interest groups to some extent. However, there is neither consensus among the Twelve over which major national groups should have seats, nor do the umbrella Euro-pressure groups have seats. Once appointed, the members serve in a personal capacity. They are independent of member governments but act once again as links between them and the EC and channels of communication to national groups. This role is important given the possibility that a member government's line on a particular proposal may diverge from that of one or more interest groups from the same state.

The ESC has a consultative, advisory role. It issues opinions on draft legislation. It divides its work into plenary and specialist group sessions. It has a right of initiative which enables it to bring matters to the attention of the Commission, the EP and the Council, but legislation occurs only if ESC views are taken up by the Commission (ESC, 1981). ESC expertise is valued by MEPs and by the Commission. It lacks direct power of amendment but, on highly technical matters, its specialist inputs can lead the Commission to make technical changes that may be critical to the industries and interests involved. The Council, by contrast, tends to ignore the ESC. Various proposals for changing its role have been advanced. These range from: making it into a third chamber of an EC legislature; or an expression of corporatism in the EC; to abolishing it (Lodge and Herman, 1980). In general, it seems to be a weak institution in terms of its formal powers. Yet, it is valued, increasingly, as a forum within which ideas can be exchanged between national counterparts. As 'Social Europe' takes off, the ESC may become a more visible vehicle for the expression of interest groups' views. Even so, it is unlikely to become the most important or influential body for interest group action.

Apart from all the ESC's own study groups and the multitude of other working groups and committees established in connection with the Commission and Council, there are other committees with specific roles involving interest groups (for example joint committees – labour and management committees for certain industries such as textiles and construction – and advisory committees on socio-economic matters and related issues, including transport and the approximation of laws on foodstuffs, etc). In addition, there is the Standing Committee on Employment and the Tripartite Conference within which the 'social partners' (representatives from employers and employees) and 'decisionmakers' (representatives of the Commission, Council and member states) seek to concert their efforts and promote consensus on broad economic and social guidelines both at EC level and at the national level towards national public authorities and private interests. So far, the results have been mixed.

The 'social dialogue' was revived in 1985 in the framework of the Val Duchesse dialogue. The SEA commits the Commission to 'try to develop the social dialogue between social partners at European level which could result, should the social partners consider it desirable, in contractual relations'. Collective European framework conventions are being discussed and there is growing interest in the idea of a European social charter to define a set of basic social rights which could form the starting point for further negotiations between the social partners. The Commission Vice-President for Social Affairs M. Marin presented a position paper in February 1988 which discussed social policy with reference to the internal market. Social policy is broadly conceived and does not connote the limited ideas associated with social security provision in the UK. His position paper makes it clear that 1992 will demand far greater constructive interaction between the social partners than has been the case hitherto. In addition, the demands of evolving European company law (which itself necessitates a constructive dialogue and information flow between social partners at all levels) and the Commission's interest in the establishment of a standard work contract covering all workers (including part-time and flexi-time workers) mean that greater involvement of interest groups at the pre-decisional and policy formulation stages will become the norm.

This in turn requires rapid inter- and intra-organizational changes among and between the social partners at sectoral, regional, national and EC levels. 'Social Europe' demands not only concerted action on a host of social policy (not just employment-related) issues but requires consultation on policy proposals designed to promote economic and social cohesion. The drive for the SEM and the creation of a 'European social space' might strengthen corporatist features of EC policy implementation, and increasingly, formulation. While it is often argued that this will weaken still further pluralism in the EC, the renewed and vigorous campaign to promote parliamentary democracy and to rein in executive and administrative power will be a significant countervailing force.

Pressure Groups

EP plenaries attract over 200 lobbyists covering all manner of issues and economic interests. Pressure groups themselves are organized at a supranational level in European umbrella pressure groups. These enjoy ready access to EC decisionmakers, to each other and to other important actors. Most are based in Brussels. It has been estimated that well over 700 Euro-pressure groups direct their energies toward the EC (ESC, 1980a). The Commission has regular contact with the most important and keeps a list of those it officially recognizes. Indeed, such contacts (primarily with representatives of 'capital/industry' rather than 'labour') have been fostered by the Commission and have been seen as especially important to developing two-way communication between the groups and the Commission. The growth of such groups' activities has also been seen as an indicator of spill-over and further integration. It has led to concern that corporatist policymaking might be encouraged by the Commission.

While there are some corporatist features in the EC, these pertain primarily to policy implementation rather than policy formulation. There have been some notable exceptions to this more recently where the formation of an EC-level group was the precondition of successful lobbying. Photocopier manufacturers led by Rank Xerox and Olivetti were so worried at Japanese penetration of the EC market (over 80 per cent) that they formed a Eurogroup CECOM and complained to the Commission about EC pricing policy. Their joint action was critical in securing Commission support for their argument. The result was the imposition of a compensatory levy on EC imports of Japanese photocopiers (Butt Philip, 1987:82-3).

The growing importance attached by international organizations, foreign corporations, national pressure groups and economic and industrial producers to being informed about the EC and being in a position to lobby on a discreet personal basis early on has led to representatives being appointed to Brussels to mingle with all the relevant EC elites and interests. Over 130 states are represented by ambassadors to the EC, and the EC has trade and aid agreements with over 100 countries. They also lobby the appropriate Commission DGs along with indigenous EC members' representatives and groups. Disparate regional branches of major national groups can concert EC action via their national representatives in Brussels and may do so irrespective of what the Euro-umbrella organization's tactic (if any) may be.

In most cases, the Euro-organization is a clearing-house for different national interests. It is a place where views can be exchanged and any common cause outlined in working parties. However, the reluctance of national component groups to give the Euro-organization independent powers (with all that entails in terms of administrative apparatus and personnel) means that only a few are able to pursue common causes (Butt Philip, 1983). Most act as clearing-houses and information transmission belts for their component members. Fewer still influence the content and direction of EC legislation. Even so, there are a plethora of advisory and consultative committees and bodies (derided as Euro-quangos) which involve interest groups (ESC, 1980b). Sectoral policy committees, in particular, consume a vast amount of detailed material from them, and the style of interest intermediation in the EC has developed certain corporatist features notably in the agricultural and social policy areas (Sargeant, 1985:240).

Most Euro-quangos are advisory. Two invest policymaking powers in national representatives of labour and capital – the European Centre for the Development of Vocational Training and the European Foundation for the Improvement of Living and Working Conditions in the EC – but so far have not dealt with significant issues or, more accurately perhaps, become embroiled in political battles over redistributive policies in the EC. By contrast, the Advisory Committee on the European Social Fund is supposed to have no more than a limited role in offering advice to the Commission on ESF applications, but has in practice influenced the actual distribution of the monies available.

The relatively weak capacity of Euro-pressure groups to aggregate, present, articulate and pursue a common line is due to many factors and cannot be simply ascribed to inadequate central organization. The domestic structure, personnel, constitutions and role of the component groups significantly impair the Euro-groups' ability to influence policy. If necessary, the Commission has bypassed the Euro-groups and dealt directly with national groups or has developed corporatist arrangements with individual companies (for example ESPRIT) (Chapter 11; Sargeant, 1985:244). Ironically, while the Commission may wish to encourage more corporatist arrangements, representatives of 'capital' have been wary and unions, by contrast, positive. The push to 1992 is likely to affect the development of a 'partnership' between capital/industry and labour and the Commission. EC competition laws have already helped to dismantle corporatist arrangements in the UK (Sargeant, 1985:250).

The 1980s' upsurge in national de-regulation has already begun to be coupled with demands (notably from those in dominant positions) for Euro-level re-regulation. The Commission itself is becoming more active in respect of company mergers (where it used to exercise its powers less expansively). The 1990s are very likely, therefore, to increase interest group involvement and influence at the policy formulation stage. New sectoral Euro-groups may become necessary, and national interests that have so far been able to avoid much EC-engagement are likely to be drawn in. At present, however, the extent of Euro and national interest group participation is policy-led. Major EC policy areas have associated Euro-groups that differ in their capacity to organize themselves and influence policy outcomes, but which are seen as important.

The most important Euro-pressure groups include: the Committee of Professional Agricultural Organisations (COPA), the Union of Industries of the EC (UNICE) and the European Trade Union Confederation (ETUC). There are also relatively well-organized and influential Euro-pressure groups dealing with savings banks (GCECEE), textiles (COMITEXTIL), insurance (CEA) and a range of other interests which are consolidated in 'bureaux' (for example the European Environmental Bureau (EEB), the European Bureau of Consumers' Unions (BEUC), 'permanent conferences' (for example of Chambers of Commerce and Industry, small- and medium-sized industrial enterprises; and the European Centre of Public Enterprises (CEEP) (Kirchner and Schwaiger, 1981).

There is a heavy concentration of interest groups in certain sectors. Of the officially recognized groups in 1980, 40 per cent represented industrial employer interests; a third were from the food and agriculture sectors and the rest covered a variety of areas (Butt Philip, 1987: 76). The strength of the agri-food interest corresponds to the position of the CAP (itself moulded by the Commission and such groups in the 1960s) within the EC.

It is clearly vital for interest groups to be sensitive to Commission developments and to have the ear of the Commission. However, information exchange and lobbying are not focused exclusively on the Commission, Council (and its off-shoots) and the EP. Interest groups have an additional institutional link into the policymaking process via the Economic and Social Committee. The fact that some sectoral policy demands extend beyond the EC's confines means that action is pursued in other organizations such as GATT, OECD and the International Labour Organization. Moreover, many Euro-pressure groups include as associate or full members representatives from non-EC states. Pressure groups and others quickly responded to the cooperation procedure in anticipation both of the EP's increasing role as a supranational legislature and of the need to adapt to the acceleration of the internal market.

From 1 July 1989, cross-frontier cooperation by firms will be facilitated by the new legal instrument of the European Economic Interest Grouping (EEIG). Its aim is to promote cross-frontier economic cooperation, economic growth and integration (*European File*, 6/89).

The Court of Justice

While outside the scope of this discussion, it must be remembered that the European Court of Justice is an important EC institution. Its rulings are binding. It has the right to rule on the validity of EC law and, more importantly, to interpret EC law which itself assumes precedence over national law that may conflict with it (see Usher 1981). It clearly is a federal court and is likely to expand in the future. Moreover, it has tended to interpret EC law in an expansive way that has been useful to the Commission and the European Parliament (Freestone, 1983; Mathijsen, 1986; Easson, 1987). Increasingly, the ECJ is called on to give preliminary rulings on questions referred to it by national courts. A court of first instance is being set up. There can be no doubt that EC and national law are becoming intricately intermeshed with a concomitant Europeanizing effect on national law and pressure on the ECJ to build up a consistent body of EC case-law (Noel, 1987:38).

The Court of Auditors

Set up by the treaty of 22 July 1975, the Court of Auditors held its first meeting on 25 October 1977. It has twelve members (chosen from especially qualified people of those who belong or have belonged to external audit bodies) appointed for six-year renewable terms by the Council acting unanimously after consulting the EP. Like the Commission, the Court is a collegiate body whose members are independent and pursue the EC's general interest. Its members enjoy the same privileges and immunities as ECJ members.

As the EC's external 'financial conscience', it is responsible for the audit of the legality, regularity and sound management of EC finances (internal auditing remains a matter for each institution's financial controller) (Noel, 1987:39). Its roles include assisting the EC's Budgetary Authority (the EP and Council) in controlling the implementation of the budget. So far, the Court has not shied away from criticizing the EP on occasions (for example in 1982), from intervening on its own initiative and commenting at any time on issues or at the request of another EC institution. It has on several occasions condemned the lack of a single seat for the EC's main institutions and criticized the costs arising from this. It has the right also to conduct direct investigations on the spot within

EC institutions and also within the member states in liaison with national bodies. Its annual report is published in the EC's *Official Journal*. The EP has made full use of the opportunities opened by the Court's investigatory powers, opinions and annual report to strengthen its own control over EC expenditure and to lend weight to its annual decisions granting a discharge on the implementation of the EC budget. It has refused to do the latter in the recent past and clearly sees the Court as an important moral and political ally in the struggle to alter expenditure in accordance with its own priorities.

Note

1. For a detailed list of work on integration theory see Chapter 1 in J. Lodge (ed)(1983), *The European Community: Bibliographical Excursions*, London, Pinter.

References

Brugmans, H. (1970), *L'Idée Européenne*, Bruges, De Tempel.

Budd, S. (1987), *The EEC: A Guide Through the Maze*, London, Kogan Page.

Bulmer, S. and Wessels, W. (1987), *The European Council*. London, Macmillan.

Butler, Sir Michael, (1987), *Europe: More than a Continent*, London, Heinemann.

Butt, Philip, A. (1983), 'Pressure Groups and Policy-Making in the European Community' in J. Lodge (ed), *Institutions and Policies of the European Community*, Pinter, London.

Butt, Philip, A. (1987), 'Pressure Groups in the European Community and Informal Institutional Arrangements' in R. Beuter and P. Taskaloyannis, *Experiences in Regional Cooperation*, EIPA, Maastricht.

Caporaso, J. (1974), *The Structure and Function of European Integration*, Calif. Goodyear.

Claude, I. (1956), *Swords into Ploughshares*, New York, Random House.

Commission of the EC (1989), The EEIG, European File 6/89 Luxembourg, Office for Official Publications.

Deutsch, K.W. (1966), *Nationalism and Social Communications*, Cambridge, Harvard University Press.

De Vree, J., Coffey, P., Lauwaars, R.H. (eds) (1987), *Towards a European Foreign Policy*, Dordrecht, Martinus Nijhoff.

Easson, A. (1987), 'The Court of Justice of the European Communities: Jurisprudence during 1986', *Journal of European Integration* 11, 63-75.

Economic and Social Committee (1980a), *European Interest Groups and Their Relationships with the Economic and Social Committee*, Farnborough, Saxon House.

Edwards, G. (1987), 'The Presidency and the Role of Summits: Some Pointers for ASEAN' in R. Beuter and P. Tsakaloyannis (eds), *Experiences in Regional Cooperation*, Maastricht, EIPA.

Edwards, G., and Wallace H. (1977), *The Council of Ministers and the President in Office*, London, Federal Trust.

Ehlermann, C. D. (1984), 'How flexible is Community Law? An unusual approach to the concept of "two speeds" ', *Michigan Law Review*, 82,1274-93.

ESC (1980b), *Community Advisory Committees for the Representation of Socio-Economic Interests*, Farnborough, Gower.

ESC (1981), *The Right of Initiative of the Economic and Social Committee of the European Communities*, Brussels, Delta.

Etzioni, A. (1966), *Political Unification*, New York, Holt, Reinhart.

Feld, W. and Wildgen, J. (1975), 'National Administrative Elites and European Integration: Saboteurs at Work?' *Journal of Common Market Studies*, 13,244-65.

Fitzmaurice, J. (1983), 'European Community Decisionmaking: the National Dimension' in J. Lodge (ed.), *Institutions and Policies of the European Community*, Pinter, London, 1-8.

Friedrich, C.J. (1968), *Trends of Federalism in Theory and Practice*, New York, Praeger.

— (1969), *Europe: An Emergent Nation*, New York, Harper and Row.

Freestone, D, (1983), 'The European Court of Justice', in J. Lodge (ed.), *Institutions and Policies of the European Community*, London, Pinter, 42-53.

Grabitz, E. (ed.) (1984), *Abgestüfte Integration: eine Alternative zum herkömmlichen Integrationskonzept*, Kehl, Engel.

Groom, A.J.R. and Taylor, P. (eds.) (1975), *Functionalism*, London, London University Press.

Haas, E.B. (1958), *The Uniting of Europe*, London, Stevens.

— (1964), *Beyond the Nation State*, Stanford, Stanford University Press.

— (1976), *The Obsolescence of Regional Integration Theory*, Berkeley, Berkeley University Press.

Harrison, R.J. (1974), *Europe in Question*, London, Allen & Unwin.

Heathcote, N. (1966), 'The Crisis of European Supranationality', *Journal of Common Market Studies* 5,140-71.

Henig, S. (1983), 'The European Community's Bicephalous Political Authority' in J. Lodge (ed.), *Institutions and Policies of the European Community*, London, Pinter, 9-20.

Herman, V. and Hagger, M. (eds) (1980), *The Legislation of Direct Elections to the European Parliament*, Farnborough, Gower.

Ifestos, P. (1987), *European Political Cooperation*, Aldershot, Avebury.

Kaiser, R. (1972), 'Towards the Copernican Phase of Regional Integration', *Journal of Common Market Studies*, 10,207-32.

Keohane, R. and Nye, J. (eds)(1972), *Transnational Relations and World Politics*, Cambridge, Harvard University Press.

— (1977), *Power and Interdependence*, Boston, Little Brown.

Kirchner, E. and Schwaiger, K. (1981), *The Role of Interest Groups in the European Community*, Farnborough, Gower.

Jacqué, J.-P. (1983), 'Conquêtes et révendications: l'évolution des pouvoirs législatifs et budgétaires du Parlement européen depuis 1979', *Journal of European Integration* 6,155-82.

Lehmbruch, G. and Schmitter, P. (eds)(1982), *Patterns of Corporatist Policymaking*, London, Sage.

Lindberg, L. (1963), *The Political Dynamics of European Economic Integration*, Stanford, Stanford University Press.

Lindberg, L. and Scheingold, S. (1970), *Europe's Would-be Polity*, Englewood Cliffs, Prentice Hall.

— (eds) (1971), *Regional Integration*, Cambridge, Harvard University Press and Special Issue of *International Organisation*, 24.

Lodge, J. (1975), 'Towards the European Political Community: EEC Summits and European Integration', *Orbis*, 19, 626-51.

— (1978), 'Loyalty and the EEC: The Limitations of the Functionalist Approach', *Political Studies*, 26:232-48.

Lodge, J. (1982), 'The European Parliament after Direct Elections: Talking Shop or Putative Legislature?' *Journal of European Integration* 5, 259-84.

Lodge, J. (1983), *The European Community: Bibliographical Excursions*, London, Pinter.

Lodge, J. (1987), 'The Single European Act and the new legislative cooperation procedure: a critical analysis', *Journal of European Integration* 11,5-28.

Lodge, J. and Herman, V. (1978), The European Parliament and The European Community, London, Macmillan.

Lodge, J. and Herman, V. (1980), 'The Economic and Social Committee in EEC decisionmaking', *International Organization* 34,265-84.

Mackay, R.Q.G. (1940), *Federal Europe*, London, Michael Joseph.

Mathijsen, P.S.R.F., (1986), *A Guide to European Community Law*, London, Sweet & Maxwell.

Michelmann, H -J. (1977), *Organizational Effectiveness in a Multinational Bureaucracy*, Farnborough, Saxon House.

Miert, K. van (1975), 'The appointment of the President and Members of the European Commission,' CMLR, *12* 257-73.

Mitrany, D. (1966), *A Working Peace System*, Chicago, Quadrangle.

— (1975), *The Functional Theory of Politics*, London, Martin Robertson.

Monnet, J. (1978), *Memoirs*, translated by R. Mayne, London, Collins.

— (1955), *Les Etats-Unis d'Europe ont commencé*, Paris, Laffert.

Nau, H.R. (1979), 'From Integration to Interdependence', *International Organization*, 33,119-47.

Nicoll, W. (1986a), La procédure de concertation entre le Parlement européen et le Conseil, *Revue du Marché commun*, no.293, 3-10.

Nicoll, W. (1986b), Les procédures Luns-Westerterp pour l'information du Parlement européen, *Revue du Marché commun*, no.300, 475-6.

Noel, E. (1987), *Working Together*, Luxembourg Office of the ECs.

O'Nuallain, C. (ed.) (1985), *The Presidency of the Council of Ministers*, London, Croom Helm.

Palmer, M. (1983), 'The Development of the European Parliament's Institutional Role within the European Community, 1974-83', *Journal of European Integration*, 6,183-202.

Pelkmans, J. and Winters, A. (1988), *Europe's Domestic Market*, London, Routledge, Kegan Paul.

Pentland, C. (1973), *International Theory and European Integration*, London, Faber.

Puchala, D. (1968), 'The Pattern of Contemporary Regional Integration', *International Studies Quarterly*, 12,38-64.

— (1972), 'Of Blind Men, Elephants and International Integration'. *Journal of Common Market Studies*, 10,732-63.

Sargeant, J. (1985), 'Corporatism and the European Community' in W. Grant (ed.), *The Political Economy of Corporatism*, London, Macmillan, 229-54.

Sasse, C. (1975), 'The Commission and the Council: Functional Partners or Constitutional Rivals?' in P. Dagtoglou (ed.), *Basic Problems of the European Community*, Oxford, Blackwell, 89-109.

Sasse, C., Poullet, E., Coombes, D. and Deprez, G. (1977), *Decisionmaking in the European Community: A Reappraisal*, New York, Praeger.

Simonian, H. (1985), *The Privileged Partnership*, Oxford, Clarendon.

Taylor, P. (1975), 'The Politics of the European Communities: The Confederal Phase', *World Politics*, 27,336-60.

— (1980), 'Political Cooperation Among the EC Member States' Embassies in Washington', *Journal of European Integration*, 4,29-42.

— (1983), *The Limits of European Integration*, London, Croom Helm.

Wallace, H. with Ridley, A. (1985), *Europe: The Challenge of Diversity*, London, Routledge, Kegan Paul.

Wessels, W. (1987), 'Decision-Making in the European Community' in R. Beuter and P. Tsakaloyannis (eds), *Experiences in Regional Cooperation*, Maastricht, EIPA.

Ziller, J. (1987), 'The European Community as a Legal Entity', in R. Beuter and P. Tsakaloyannis, op. cit.

3 The European Parliament – from 'assembly' to co-legislature: changing the institutional dynamics

Juliet Lodge

Introduction

The European Parliament, unlike national parliaments in the EC, is an institution dedicated to increasing its powers. Parliaments are said to be everywhere in decline, to be a relic of a bygone age. Modern societies are said to be too complex to be managed in traditional ways; technocratic and executive-dominated government (even if overloaded) is seen as more capable (however imperfectly) of meeting demands. Such arguments deny the hardwon roles and rights of elected bodies to hold those who govern responsible and accountable for what they do in the name of their citizens. Parliaments make the management of modern societies more difficult. But that is no excuse for allowing them to be systematically denuded of power and for a vacuum in political control over the executive to develop unchecked. In the EP's case much agonizing has arisen over suspicions as to what integration, symbolized by an elected parliament with legislative aspirations, means for national sovereignty. Direct parallels between the EC and national systems cannot be drawn: the EC is not a state, for example. But, the federal idea of dual citizenship is pertinent to the debate about European Union and the role of an elected EP in it. The idea that collective identity is realized through its parliamentary expression remains potent.

The EP is considered to be the most disruptive of EC institutions as it is the one most dissatisfied with the distribution of authority and the one most associated with pressure to reform the EC and to advance European Union through supranational-level parliamentary democracy. Moreover, its conception of European Union is one that most nearly resembles the federal view of citizens having obligations, rights and responsibilities as members of their states and as members of the Union (Bieber *et al.*, 1985; Lodge, 1986). The creation of a sense of European identity among citizens is something that will be on the agenda over the coming decade. Enfranchising citizens for Euro-elections is but one step in a process designed to set out what EC citizenship means. Whether or not this will go rapidly beyond steps to encourage labour mobility (such as the mutual recognition of professional qualifications, ERASMUS, Euro-driving licences, etc.) and electoral rights remains to be seen. However, the pressure for a European Bill of Rights will continue along with the rise in petitions to the EP.

The EP realizes that its goal to become the EC's legislature cannot be effectively justified to the public or attained while it remains largely invisible to the public or while it has the damaging image of being a 'yuppy' tourist club or 'gravy train'. The question of its own public image, its visibility and the extent of its powers are separate but linked issues. Efficient decisionmaking cannot occur, MEPs rightly claim, when the EP lacks a permanent seat (in Brussels alongside the Commission, the Council, COREPER, the Economic and Social Committee and major interest groups). In default of member governments agreeing to fix Brussels as the seat for the EP, MEPs have to travel between Brussels for committee meetings; Strasbourg for plenaries, known as 'part-sessions', and occurring for five days each month (except August) and sometimes twice a month, and occasionally Luxembourg, a pre-election base and now home to part of the EP's Secretariat. Competition among the governments concerned to base the EP in one of these cities has been intense, has resulted in court cases and spectacular building programmes to attract the EP to Luxembourg, Strasbourg and now Brussels. This reflects the fact that the EC's founders were unable and unwilling to designate a seat of government for the EC – an EC capital – a highly sensitive (even subversive) issue. MEPs and governments today are split over a base for the EP. Yet, the necessity of centralizing in one city the work of at least those institutions that perform a governing role is pressing. Disruptions, delays and inefficiency consequent upon dispersal are not conducive to effective decisionmaking. Other institutions including, the Court and the new court, the Court of Auditors, the European Investment Bank, the Patent Office and so on may be scattered throughout the Twelve to smooth political feathers. The 1990s will see Brussels confirmed as the seat of the EC's governing bodies. Before looking at the EC's legislative process and cooperation procedure in more detail, the EP's history, composition and organization will be sketched in briefly.

Origins

The EP originated as the Common Assembly of the ECSC. Even then it was seen as an appendix to the decisionmaking powerhouse of the High Authority (the rough equivalent of the Commission). Even the Council of Ministers was an afterthought and did not figure in the original plans of Monnet and Schuman but was established at the request of the Benelux countries. When the EP was established in 1958, as an institution like the ECJ, common to the three communities – ECSC, EEC and Euratom – it was called 'the Assembly'. In 1962, its members decided to refer to the Assembly as the European Parliament. For political reasons, governments did not follow suit until over a decade later (and Mrs Thatcher still denigrates it on occasions as 'the Assembly').

The name is important because 'assembly' connotes a talking chamber, a weak institution with minimal authority *vis-à-vis* the executive. By contrast, 'parliament' connotes a legislature. Like its predecessor, the EP was given a consultative role in EC decisionmaking, a role that governments and others justified in all manner of ways. Often it was argued that the poor calibre of MEPs militated against it being given important powers. The EP retorted that the calibre of its MEPs would only improve if it were directly elected and given a legislative role. The chicken and egg argument of whether or not its powers should be extended before or after its members were directly elected by EC voters in accordance with treaty provisions rambled on for years and delayed an increase in its authority.

Direct elections

Member governments proved extremely reluctant to permit the EP's direct election. Instead, MEPs were appointed from the membership of national parliaments and the spread of political opinions in the member states was not reflected. Until the late 1960s, neither the Italian nor the French Communist parties were represented in the EP, for example. Some years were to elapse after the PCI and PCF (Italian Communist Party and the French Communist Party) had decided that participation in the EP was not incompatible with communism before their members entered the EP. A later EP boycott occurred following UK entry when Labour MEPs (nominated members) refused to take up their seats until after the 1975 referendum on the terms of entry (Lodge, 1975; Butler and Kitzinger, 1976). Their arrival in the EP coincided with the climax of the EP's efforts to secure direct elections. Ironically, many of the Six had supported British entry to boost the 'democratization' of the EC through the EP's quest for direct election and power. The 'mother of parliaments' was found seriously wanting.

In 1975, following the acquisition of limited budgetary co-decision powers with the Council, the EP's politically expedient argument that direct elections were warranted and would not result in a major increase in its power (because elected members would wish to exploit fully existing powers) persuaded governments to agree to such elections being held. In January 1975 it adopted a Convention on its direct election. In September 1976 the Council adopted the Act on the election of the EP by direct universal suffrage. Direct elections were supposed to be held in 1978, but the enabling legislation in the member states was delayed and the elections postponed for one year. Contrary to the EEC treaty's provision under Art. 138 for a uniform electoral procedure (drafted by the EP and still to be adopted by the governments) each member state introduced its own method of election. Some had five per cent hurdles which had to be passed to win a seat, others had far higher (masked) hurdles over 15 per cent (as in the UK) and the Euro-elections were held on different days spread over a four-day period. As a result, while the elected EP could claim to be 'more representative' of the spread of public political preferences than it's predecessors, serious distortions arose (Lodge and Herman, 1982). These remain and are chiefly due to Britain electing seventy-eight MEPs on a single-member constituency, 'first past the post' majority system rather than on the basis of proportional representation (PR) favoured by Northern Ireland and by all other EC members using either multi-member national or regional constituencies (Lodge, 1986; Herman and Hagger, 1980; van den Berghe, 1982).

The 1989 Euro-elections will be the first with all twelve states electing MEPs within a four-day period. Complicated rules have been developed to cope with the refusal of the governments to adopt the EP's draft common electoral procedure (for PR in multi-member constituencies); and to permit the elections to occur on the same day. Different rules regarding state funding (in addition to EC funding of Euro-elections), opinion polls, advertising, the broadcasting of results, eligibility criteria for candidates and voters have all helped to distort the results and to de-Europeanize, indeed to nationalize, what is a European event by definition (Lodge, 1986).

Big differences in turnout (ranging from under 33 per cent in Britain to over

80 per cent in Italy and Belgium, for example) have been attributed to many factors. These include: lack of a uniform electoral procedure, compulsory voting in some states, the degree of electioneering undertaken by government leaders, pro- or anti-Europeanism, absence of conflict among national parties over EC membership and competing national, regional or local elections (Luxembourg's general election is held on the same day as the Euro-election and often all its six MEPs, having been elected, then switch to national politics). Additional contributing factors are rules on advertising, the acceptability or otherwise of the dual mandate (as in the UK whereby MEPs may opt to sit in the EP and national parliament), media coverage, public awareness, electoral fatigue, public apathy and/or disillusionment with the EC. It was also argued that turnout was influenced by the type and extent of EC-wide transnational party inputs. Only the major tendencies initially were able to group themselves into such transnational 'parties': the Socialists – Confederation of Socialist Parties; the Christian Democrats – the European People's Party; and the various liberal parties – the Federation of European Liberals and Democrats. The ability of such parties to form these transnational alliances for electoral purposes underlined cleavages within other parties that were nominally sister parties (as in the case of the Communists, for example). By 1984, the Greens too were able to produce a semblance of electoral unity and were later to form the Rainbow Group in the EP. For all, the elections highlighted EP party group fragmentation. Ideological affinity was often an unconvincing veneer. These factors in turn helped to account for the EP's poor image and relative invisibility. T. e European election information programmes mounted for 1978/9 did little to overcome public ignorance. The EP's work record remained largely incomprehensible (Lodge, 1986; Lodge and Herman, 1982; Reif, 1984). Such criticisms, however, must be seen against an average turnout across the EC of over 60 per cent. This compared favourably with US Presidential election turnouts and is not that poor for a unique electoral event to a relatively unknown and widely misunderstood 'parliament'.

Euro-elections retain a rather negative image. This has suited many politicians anxious about the EP's potential. In 1977-8 few seemed dismayed by the possibility of the first elections being postponed. Why? First, the logistics of drafting and enacting the enabling legislation in the Nine was far from simple. Opponents made political capital out of delaying parliamentary approval of the legislation (Herman and Hagger, 1980). Second, anxiety over the EP's ambitions was sufficiently widespread to lessen any sense of urgency: article 138(EEC) had been ignored for nearly twenty years. This masked persistent concern over the meaning of direct elections for national sovereignty. Seen since the 1948 Hague Congress as a milestone *en route* to a federal Europe, the elections dispelled the illusion that the EC would remain an apolitical, functionally specific organization devoid of serious on-going constitutional implications for the exercise of power by national governments.

Yet, through its direct election, the EP was said to become the repository of popular sovereignty. Since sovereignty was seen as indivisible (notably in UK circles), it was inferred that such elections meant a zero-sum loss of sovereignty for the member states' parliaments. While experience has proved otherwise, this political fiction is paraded by anti-marketeers. Perhaps more germane to some governments' fears on this score was private recognition of how these elections are linked with the greater issue of the rectification of the EC's democratic deficit through the EP exercising both a genuine legislative role in the EC, and political control over the governments (in the Council of Ministers) which have escaped national parliaments' control and effective supervision.

Calibre of MEPs

The extent to which the EP at any one time presses for an increase in its legislative authority and role depends partly on majority support and the commitment to this goal among its membership. In 1979 it was falsely thought that most MEPs would not wish to seek to expand the EP's role and powers. Within two years, this illusion was shattered. MEPs had come of age. Some used the EP as a stepping stone or springboard to faster national career advancement; some rounded off often illustrious years in national politics; others became 'Euro–MPs' first and foremost and many had matching legislative ambitions for the EP. Whatever the role conception of MEPs – whether they see themselves as the advocates and protectors of national interests, or the promoters of European ideals and policy solutions according to their own particular ideological leanings – the history of the EP since the first direct elections in 1979 has been one of a quest to fill a vacuum of political control in the EC. The EP's new power under the cooperation procedure is merely a first step in filling this vacuum.

Composition and Organization

The EP has 518 MEPs. Each state is given a 'quota' which roughly corresponds to its population size although Luxembourg is over-represented and the FRG under-represented. The distribution is: eighty-one each to France, the FRG, Italy and the UK; twenty-four each to Belgium, Greece and Portugal; Spain, sixty; Netherlands, twenty-five; Denmark, sixteen; Ireland, fifteen and Luxembourg six. The majority of MEPs are members of the EP's supranational party groups whose strength is given in brackets: Socialist Group (165); the Christian Democratic, European People's Party (114); European Democratic Group (66) – including UK Conservatives; Communist and Allies (48); Liberal and Democratic Reformist Group (45); European Democratic Alliance (29); Rainbow Group (20) – Greens and Ecology parties; European Right (16). Fifteen MEPs are 'non-attached'.

Set up on the initiative of MEPs are also over forty 'inter-groups' that cross party boundaries and seek to promote causes and action on specific areas: for example the influential Kangaroo Group that has agitated for the realization of the internal market; the Federalist Intergroup for European Union; and others on the EP's seat (one pro-Strasbourg, the other pro-Brussels); the media, disarmament, the young, South Africa, and so on. These do not have the powers or rights enjoyed by the official party groups.

Rules stipulate what criteria have to be met for a group of MEPs to gain official status as a party group. These set out minimum size and national make-up. Party Group status is important as the Groups plan the EP's work. The Groups' leaders are members of the EP's Enlarged Bureau and draft plenary agenda, and allocate the all important committee chairpersonships, rapporteurships and tasks. Competition for such positions within and between national contingents of MEPs in the same group can be as intense as it is between the Groups themselves.

Of particular interest is the allocation of positions on the EP's permanent committees whose responsibilities broadly mirror those of the Commission's DGs. (A Commission member now usually attends EP committee meetings and a Council minister or minister-of-state may also attend important committees twice or more during a Council presidency.) The committees have a key role to play in the legislative process (see below). After scrutinizing draft legislation, their views may be adopted by plenaries as a motion for resolution constituting the EP's formal opinion. They also have the power to: draw on outside expertise; use the EP's research facilities and personnel; send MEPs on fact-finding missions in and outside the EC; hold public hearings (outside Brussels on occasion – the Institutional Affairs Committee came to London in 1987); and, as necessary, set up sub-committees and committees of inquiry (such as that on the Situation of Women established during the 1979-84 term and the more recent one on agricultural stocks). The EP's control of its own budget is useful as the EP decides on the extra staff it needs (but bids for funding at the appropriate time). The EP also has a wide range of inter-parliamentary links with parliaments throughout the world. Such contacts are regularly maintained, and the most important are cultivated by the EP and their opposite numbers, as in the US case, for instance. The EP has learnt from US experience and has tried to combat its own lack of specialized knowledge by setting up an experimental project in Scientific and Technical Options inspired by the US Congress's Office of Technology Assessment.

Party considerations also influence the appointment of MEPs to serve on particular committees and as rapporteurs for given issues. MEPs wishing to sit on a given committee indicate their preference to their party chairperson and party bureau (which reflects the national make-up of the EP party group). Specialist expertise and political considerations affect the chances of gaining a committee seat.

Intra and inter-party rivalry is intense but cross-party voting is common, especially where issues of national interest unite MEPs from a given state. National party considerations intrude into EP party politics for political and technical reasons (such as the filling of vacant seats – either by the 'revolving seats' and tourniquet (EPWD1-1078/82) favoured by some in the past; by the next on the list taking the vacated seat or by bye-election as in Britain). National parties and governments may try to determine the line 'their' MEPs take but MEPs have an independent mandate. Many both resent and defy national interference. The EP's party groups are increasingly independent from sister parties at home and national contingents (even from governing parties) do oppose their own national government on occasions to the chagrin of the latter. They play a major role in electing the EP's officers, allocating resources and organizing the EP's work.

The intense bargaining typifying the selection of MEPs for committee posts is more public when the EP President is elected, if necessary in several ballots, for half the EP's five-year term. The President delegates duties to Vice-Presidents (who reflect the EP's party composition) and constitute the Bureau which meets as the more powerful Enlarged Bureau when the EP's parties' chairpersons or deputies attend. There is also a College of Quaestors to deal with working conditions, etc.

The EP – talking-shop or legislature?

Until the 1980s the EP lacked many of the attributes typical of modern legislatures in West European liberal democracies (Loewenberg, 1971). Its legislative, control and budgetary powers were very limited and its ability to perform information, education, communication, legitimation and representation functions was circumscribed (Herman and Lodge, 1978). However, its true influence extended beyond its constitutional powers, and it has repeatedly expanded its scope of action and field of influence irrespective of formal limits on its powers. If anything, these have served to reinforce its desire to circumvent them and to influence the EC's policy and decisionmaking environment.

The EP has exploited its right to set its own agenda to discuss all manner of international, EC and domestic issues and to perform a 'grand forum' role. In so doing, it has come to be the EC's conscience (a role formerly attributed to the Commission). Its topical and urgent debates can shape and reflect political opinion (and encourage the Commission, for example, to allocate emergency aid swiftly to disasters before the EP's next plenary). However, the EP can rarely enforce its preferred policies (outside the cooperation procedure).

The EP is also the EC's grand stage for visiting statesmen and women. Indeed, outside the EC, the EP is held in far higher regard than it is inside, and its foreign policy and external relations' role is seen as significant if limited (Lodge, 1987a). The fact that foreign statesmen use the EP as a platform is of mutual benefit: it improves the EP's image and visibility and affords statesmen access to a wide European audience and media. Third-country missions frequently attend plenaries. The political importance of the EP's agenda-setting right should not be under-estimated: national parliaments by and large find their agendas set for them by government.

Originally, the EP was invested with consultative, 'advisory and supervisory' powers by the treaties. Accordingly, it has the right to issue Opinions on draft legislation. These are not binding on either the Commission or the Council in areas outside the cooperation procedure. By amending its Rules of Procedure in 1981, the EP tried partly to remedy this: it gave its scrutiny committees a quasi-second-reading role and a power of delay (Lodge, 1982). The legality of this was confirmed by the Court ruling in the isoglucose case: a piece of draft legislation was struck down as illegal because the Council had passed it without first obtaining the EP's Opinion in an area where it was mandated to do so by the EEC Treaty (Cases 138/79 and 139/79; Palmer, 1983). This delaying power affected its relations with the Commission and the Council, making the former somewhat more receptive to its views and encouraging it to enter into early discussions with the relevant EP committee to avert later delay, and heightening Council appreciation of the need to honour the letter of the treaty in respect of consulting the EP. However, this delaying tactic is no substitute for real power. It has proved weak (the Council can circumvent it by taking decisions 'in principle' or 'subject to the EP's opinion') and the EP has used it infrequently.

The EP has limited control powers. It has the right to sack the Commission if it can muster a two-thirds majority in favour of a motion of censure to this effect – something tabled only four times and voted (unsuccessfully) twice in 1976 and 1977. As a form of political protest, threatened and actual motions of censure are weak and none have been tabled since 1977. The weakness of this 'power' (inspite of its political importance as an expression of parliamentary power to 'unseat rulers') is underlined by the fact that, in theory, governments could reappoint a sacked Commission. A vicious circle of sacking–reappointment could ensue although some believe that some Commission nominees would not wish to take up their posts under such circumstances. Denied a right in the nomination of the Commission, the EP has acquired some role in the process. Under the 1983 Solemn Declaration on European Union, the EP gained the opportunity to debate and vote on a new Commission's programme presented to it. Also, the president of the member states' representatives seeks the EP's Enlarged Bureau's opinion on the Commission President nominee. The EP gave itself the right to take a formal vote ratifying and expressing confidence in the Commission (first used for the Thorn and Delors (Mark I) Commissions). The Delors Commission deferred taking its oath until after it had got the EP's vote of confidence. The issue was fudged with the Thorn Commission.

Except on specific areas of budgetary control, EP committees do not exercise oversight powers over the executive. The EP acquired the right to exercise some control over the EC's budget in 1970 and 1975: a power that bolstered its claim to direct election through reference to the principle of 'no taxation without representation'. It can veto the whole budget and may alter expenditure, within rigid margins, on 'non-compulsory' sections of the budget. But it lacks effective power over the greater part of spending earmarked for 'compulsory' expenditure. The 'conciliation procedure' has not greatly helped the EP to assert itself and acrimonious budgetary exchanges have dominated proceedings even after inter-institutional agreements (between the presidents of the Council, Commission and EP) have been endorsed (Chap. 7); Jacqué, 1983).

One of its more powerful 'weapons' lies with its right to adopt the budget; it is the threat of non-adoption which has some force. Even then, governments may not prove conciliatory unless they are extremely keen to see immediate expenditure on items of particular interest to them for the year in question. Since 1975 the EP has sole right to grant the discharge for the EC's budget. The 'discharge weapon' is not without force since the Financial regulation requires the institutions to take all appropriate steps to take action on the comments in the decisions giving discharge. This at least impels the Commission to attend to EP budgetary scrutiny. It is doubtful whether it has the same desired effect on the Council, which tended to set aside EP criticism of for instance, the depreciation of agricultural stocks in 1983 and 1985 until the threat of insolvency forced the issue upon the European Council in 1988. However, Pinder points out that some of the committees used by Council to control the Commission's execution of EC legislation have undermined the efficient use of EC funds, and 'many have the effect of strangling necessary executive initiative' (Pinder, 1988). This highlights the importance of the 'commitology' issue which led to an EP appeal to the ECJ. Whether the EP will be able to regain a degree of influence by cutting budget appropriations for committees that obstruct measures enjoying EP approval, as Holt suggests, remains to be seen (Holt, 1988). In the meantime, the EP will have to both continue to examine creatively all legislation with financial implications, budgetary issues and the Court of Auditors Annual Report, and exploit the conciliation procedure.

The EP has used its limited budgetary powers both discreetly to influence outcomes or in highly politically visible ways to defeat or pressurize the Commission on the implementation of policies on 'non-obligatory' spending where it can place an item (the budget-line) into reserve (Chapter 100). Through this, it has prevented direct reimbursements to the UK Treasury of UK refunds until agreement on the refunds being used on infra-structure programmes decided by the EP.

The EP's largely deliberative and negligible powers have been augmented over the years by MEPs testing procedures to increase their authority by side-stepping the hurdle of formal treaty amendment under Art. 236 (and the attendant risk of immediate failure owing to the requirement that amendments be ratified by national parliaments following their unanimous approval by governments). MEPs have followed a dual-pronged strategy. The first 'incremental' or 'minimalist' approach (dominant during the 1970s (Palmer, 1983)) commits them to gradually exploiting existing powers and to operating on the basis that anything not explicitly denied the EP by the treaties is permissible. EP actions can, after all, be challenged in the ECJ (Art. 173). The minimalist approach has also been used to introduce practices from national parliaments and to arrange EP business in ways that enhance its advisory and supervisory role; that establish politically useful precedents in inter-institutional relations; and crucially that give it a power of legislative initiative. Astute interpretation of the Treaty and its Own Rules allowed the EP to find, for itself, a right of legislative initiative. Through the device of 'own initiative reports', the EP made clear its views (albeit in a sometimes less than well-drafted manner) on what legislation – over a wide array of policy sectors – should become the subject of formal Commission proposals. Its initiatives on unemployment (through the Social Fund), education and food aid (Hunger in the World) proved influential. This seemingly simple device when handled shrewdly by MEPs of conviction was to prove extremely useful: it was the basis of the draft Treaty establishing the European Union in 1984. It was also a useful vehicle for increasing formal EP-Commission contact on a future legislative agenda.

The 'natural alliance' of the EP and Commission has also been bolstered through this. In January 1977 new Commission President Jenkins assured the EP that the Commission would not introduce proposals unlikely in its view to win EP majority support. In February 1986, Delors said the Commission would do all it could to advance proposals made in EP 'own initiative' reports and Resolutions. The EP has not always fully exploited such useful undertakings and it is difficult to identify the extent to which EP resolutions have led to Commission action. It is calculated that 20 per cent lead to executive action but only in spectacular instances is it clear that the Commission has built on EP resolutions (for example in respect of the European Technological Community (Sharp and Shearman, 1987) bolstered by the EP exhibition on information technology (IT) in Strasbourg). Usually, it stresses resolution points that coincide with its current activities and ignores the rest. Moreover, the Commission rarely looks more than once at such resolutions. Their effectiveness in influencing policy is hard to measure and MEPs use them for different purposes. Some aim at introducing new executive policies or actions or changing a policy's emphasis. Others simply try to extract more information from or to pressurize the Commission and Council who, in turn, use them as a source of ideas.

The EP has been adept at capitalizing on parliamentary procedures to enhance its control and supervisory powers. An early example of this was the introduction and extension of questions. The EP may table written and oral questions with or without debate, or for question time, to the Commission (Art. 140, EEC). The right to table questions is an individual right except for oral questions with debate which devolve to the parties and committees. The Council and the Council of Foreign Ministers have agreed also to answer such questions (1972 and 1975 respectively) although they are not obliged to do so and their answers are notoriously evasive compared to the Commission's (usually) more informative replies. More recently, Council Presidents – including prime ministers – have addressed the EP on the programme of work for their Presidency and on the outcome of European Councils. Question time has a symbolic importance that is greater than its actual effect. It is poorly attended and many MEPs use it to gain domestic publicity for themselves. Similarly in early 1988, UK MEPs abused the 'explanation of the vote' procedure to make domestic points by reading out excerpts from '*Spycatcher*', the book banned in the UK. The EP has also capitalized on treaty articles rarely used (for example in 1982 using Art. 175 to take the Council to task for failure to act on transport policy). It has amended its own Rules of Procedure to increase its scope to intervene in the legislative process and to call the Commission and the Council to account.

The minimalist strategy has been coupled since 1980 with a 'maximalist' frontal assault on the EP's powers. The late Altiero Spinelli was instrumental in this approach which started from the premise that the unattainability of consensus among governments and MEPs for a major revision and extension of the EP's formal powers need not make the quest for real legislative power unrealistic. This demand has withstood the test of time. From the outset it was carefully couched in insistence on the desperate and immediate need for both policy and institutional reform in the EC. Through the Spinelli-led Crocodile initiative (Lodge, 1986; Bieber, 1985), the EP successfully challenged conventional wisdom that anything requiring unanimous approval by governments would fail. It did so firstly by exploiting its own powers; secondly by placing its quest within the broader context of the crises facing the EC; and thirdly by trying (somewhat less successfully) to mobilize national elite and public opinion in favour of change in the EC (not just in the EP's powers, an angle that, if stressed would have been counter-productive in some states).

It accomplished this by using its existing authority to decide its agenda and to set up committees as it saw fit. The EP can put items onto the EC agenda by using a role its Rules give it to draft 'own initiative' reports to draft proposals for EC action (and hopefully legislation to be tabled by the Commission which, in any event, reports in writing every six months on its action on such reports). This was used to push Euro–Union. Between 1980-2, the Political Affairs Committee's (PAC) subcommittee on institutional questions delivered eight reports on the EP's relations with the Council (EPWD1-216/81); Commission (1-71/80); ESC (1-226/81); European Council (1-739/81); EPC (1-335/81) and national parliaments (1-206/81) and on its legislative role (1-207/81) and role in the negotiation and ratification of treaties of accession and EC agreements with third countries (1-685/81). A PAC report covered the EP's seat (1-333/81). Two other reports broached the highly sensitive issue of security cooperation (1-946/82) and arms procurement. Several suggestions from these reports became practice. For example, the Council quickly accepted the idea of the Council President-in-Office making a programme speech to the EP during each Presidency; and of the Council Presidents of the technical Councils appearing before EP committees from time to time to improve Council–EP consultation

(Palmer, 1983). The reports also fed into the process leading to the Draft Treaty establishing the European Union, adopted by the EP in February 1984 (Cardozo and Corbett, 1986).

The EP accomplished its aim secondly by setting up a permanent committee on institutional questions (in practice charged with drafting treaty amendments in view of European Union), the Institutional Affairs Committee (IAC). It and the Crocodile Club capitalized on the EP's tendency towards cross-national and cross-party voting. Thirdly, Spinelli and other IAC members lobbied national government members as well as national parliaments. There was impressive support for the EUT outside the EP. It became clear that with the right organization (a critical consideration) the EP could wield influence and play an interesting agitational role. While the EUT did not feature as a major issue across all the member states during the 1984 elections, the idea that institutional reform – and specifically the role of the European Parliament in the EC – could be put to the people (the EC's voters) gained credence and resulted in the call for a Euro-referendum on the EP assuming a constituent role. Without the EUT and the constant pressure from the EP it is doubtful that the SEA would have seen daylight.

However, recent successes have not dispelled the idea that the EP is essentially a weak institution whose role, some argue, should be curtailed. The political context within which the EP has successfully used both the minimalist and maximalist strategies to advance its quest for legislative power has been important. Key points in the early 1980s were the first Euro-elections six months earlier; the talk about European Union (after inaction on Tindemans), that is the Genscher–Colombo proposals for a Draft European Act (Bull.EC 11-1981; Weiler, 1983) and the Commission's May 1980 Mandate; the political imperatives of EC enlargement; the economic imperatives of stagnation and competition from the United States, Japan and the NICs; its reports on the internal market and 'non-Europe'[1] and to a lesser extent the fact that within the national setting, EC issues were becoming part of daily political discourse and some Europeanization of political debate was occurring. The EP is a sometimes reviled institution and an easy scapegoat for national governments fearful of its challenges to their supremacy. It will and must go on seeking an increase in EC competences, efficiency and democracy. The EP has become very much the EC's conscience and the guardian of European Union and democratic ideals.

The EP's chances of exercising a recognizable legislative role depend on the recently established cooperation procedure. Important as 'own initiative' reports are for establishing the principle that the EP should and can 'initiate' legislation, their symbolic significance exceeds their actual effect. Indeed, the EP itself acted to weed out ill-prepared 'own initiative' reports. It streamlined the management of its own business to enhance the potential impact of its legislative actions on the Commission and the Council. Ultimately, however, there is no substitute for genuine entrenched power. The cooperation procedure is a small step in the right direction.

The Cooperation Procedure

The cooperation procedure applies to only ten articles of the Rome Treaty: Articles 7: prohibition of discrimination on grounds of nationality; 49:

progressive realization of freedom of movement for workers; 54(2): abolition of existing restrictions on freedom of establishment; 56(2): coordination of provisions on special treatment for foreign nationals on grounds of public policy, public security or public health; 57: mutual recognition of diplomas etc., to facilitate work by the self-employed; 100A and 100B: approximation of provisions having as their object the establishment and functioning of the internal market; 118A: social policy – working environment, health and safety of workers; 130E: economic and social cohesion; and 130(Q): research and technological development. Two-thirds of the proposals in the Commission's 1985 White Paper on the internal market fall under the cooperation procedure.

The cooperation procedure is designed to allow the EP to play an effective but qualified role in the legislative process. To enable it to play such a role, the EP swiftly reformed its internal organization and streamlined its often cumbersome procedures. This was essential to facilitating the mobilization of the 260 MEPs needed to pass amendments under the cooperation procedure, and to enhancing interaction with the Commission from the outset.

To realize its legislative ambitions the EP must exploit the cooperation procedure since the SEA otherwise provides for only a modest accretion of its power. The EP's assent to enlargement (Articles 99 and 237) and to association agreements (Article 238) is required, but the scope for an EP input is limited although the financial protocols attached to such agreements offer scope for argument (Nicoll, 1986a) and the exercise of influence both under and outside the Luns–Westerterp procedures (Nicoll, 1986b:300; Lodge, 1987a). The EP in March 1988 blocked agreement on three protocols to the EC–Israel agreement partly because it objected to Israel's discretion over the implementation of sections dealing with Palestinian access to the EC market (EPWD A2-144/88: A-2-145/88; A1-146/88). The EP can postpone giving its assent to agreements involving financial protocols for as long as it sees fit: it controls its agenda and decides when items should be discussed. As early as December 1987, the EP demonstrated its intention to insist on its views being accommodated whenever new financial measures are foreseen and during the annual review of financial protocols attached to agreements with third countries. Logically, the EP should try to influence the Commission's negotiating mandate prior to the start of agreement talks. Budgetization of the European Development Fund under Lomé IV is another area in which the EP wants co-decision. Moreover, it may well make its assent to further EC enlargement conditional on further institutional reforms.

The biggest constraints on the EP becoming a co-legislator under the cooperation procedure arise out of the Council's behaviour. Moreover, the SEA did not abolish the veto. However, while the Commission made it clear that it would treat the EP as a co-legislator, the Council adopted a minimalist position which the EP challenged repeatedly (to good effect). The Commission capitalized on the EP's control of its own agenda and timetable. It accepted that the Commission and the EP's Enlarged Bureau should agree on an annual legislative programme. The political significance of this should not be underestimated. The cooperation procedure and '1992' put a premium on keeping up the momentum. Legislative planning is now accepted between the EP, Commission and Council. Subject to rolling forecasts, it heightens mutual awareness of legislative priorities and opens the door to rational policy planning.

What does the cooperation procedure entail? It sets up a system of two readings tied to deadlines (an innovation) to deter rolling non-decisions and deliberations extending over many years that typified traditional decisionmaking. Under the cooperation procedure, the legislative process begins with the submission of a Commission proposal to the EP. The Council may begin deliberating but may not *act* until after the EP has made its view known. If the Council were to have parallel discussions at this point, its tendency to develop and stand by its own compromises would necessarily make it less receptive to making changes in its own first reading in order to accommodate EP amendments.

In the all-important first reading, the EP may reject or amend the proposal, withhold or emit its Opinion. It may persuade the Commission to amend the proposal to accord with its wishes or to withdraw it before a vote is taken. This is a useful tactical weapon should the EP suspect that a majority for the proposal cannot be found or that its majority views are being overlooked. Should the Commission refuse, the EP may delay the legislative process by referring the proposal back to its committee(s). It thereby holds up the Council which may not act (even if it has reached a view, 'the common position') pending the announcement of the EP's Opinion. The Commission could sabotage EP tactics by withdrawing the proposal altogether but risking the charge that it had ill-prepared it in the first place.

If the EP emits its Opinion, the proposal goes, with the Commission's view on the EP's Opinion, to the Council. The Council then adopts a 'common position' by qualified majority vote and transmits it to the EP. Both the Council and Commission are obliged to inform the EP fully of the reasons which led to their decisions, though the EP President has had to push the Council for proper information. Unless the EP gets full information, it can say that it has not received the common position and delay progress.

The EP has three months within which to approve (starting by the receipt of) the common position. If it does do, or if it fails to express a view on the common position, the Council adopts the proposal according to the common position. EP silence is interpreted as assent at this stage. It is unlikely that the EP would remain silent, but the precise parameters of the three-month deadline can be critical to averting misunderstanding or, more vitally, to allowing the EP by absolute majority (260) either to propose amendments to the common position (for details see Lodge, 1987b:13) or to reject it.

Should the EP reject the common position, the Council can overrule if unanimous on a second reading. The unanimity provision gives the EP another chance to influence the outcome by persuading one government to thwart the attainment of unanimity pending accommodation of EP wishes. However, this may backfire, if governments used the opportunity to stall or to exercise a disguised veto by hiding behind a seemingly *communautaire* facade of backing the EP. The Commission can also inject transparency into the process by discreetly informing the EP as to the identity of 'awkward' Council members. It can also give the impression of either pushing the Council and/or siding with the EP by requesting the Council to vote by simple majority to proceed to a vote.

Should the EP amend the common position, the proposal reverts to the Commission which, within a deadline of one month, may revise its proposal (that is the one on which the Council has issued a common position) before sending it back to the Council for a second reading. The Commission may, at this stage, send to Council any EP amendments that it has not accepted together with its view of them.

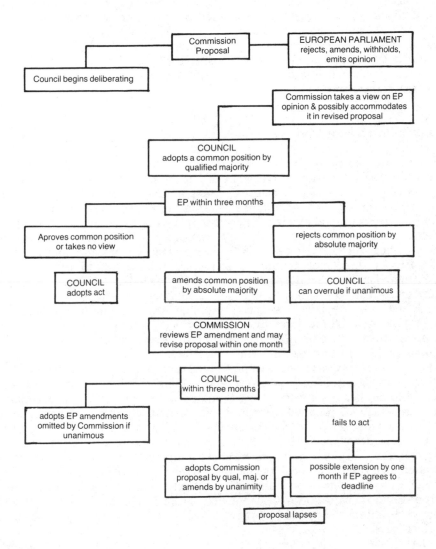

Figure 3.1 The cooperation procedure.

In the second reading, the Council has three months within which to take a number of courses of action. If unanimous, it may overrule the Commission and incorporate the excluded EP amendments. By qualified majority, it may adopt the Commission's re-examined proposal. If unanimous, it may amend it. With EP agreement, it may delay a decision for a further month to allow more time for consideration. Or, it may fail to act in which case the proposal – contrary to Commission and EP wishes – lapses (and does not remain 'on the table' for years, as is the traditional practice). Again, disguised use of the veto may encourage some governments to seek inaction, and the attendant risk of proceedings before the ECJ by the EP against the Council. However, the hope is that the proposals in question will be of sufficient interest to a number of states to prevent this happening.

Implications for inter-institutional relations

The cooperation procedure demands systematic inter-institutional cooperation between the Commission, Council and EP at the pre-legislative as well as first and second reading stages. Informal but politically significant contacts now occur between the three institutions at various levels but most critically at the level of presidents and officials. There is ample scope for early EP intervention at the pre-legislative stage because the *precise legal base* of a proposal is critical to determining whether it proceeds under the cooperation procedure (of interest to the EP) or under the traditional procedure (of interest to the Council). Confrontation has already occurred. The EP amended its Rules so that a committee named as responsible for scrutinizing a proposal under the traditional, one-reading procedure is obliged to examine the validity or appropriateness of the legal base. The EP has secured close Commission cooperation on this. Upon the SEA's entry into force, it sent the EP ahead of the Council a list of 145 proposals whose legal base would be amended. The EP agreed with all but nine and got the Commission to accept its view on two of them. The EP agreed to regard as a 'first reading' the opinions it had already delivered on them except for twelve opinions given before 1979. In examining the legal base of proposals afresh, it also concluded that ten international agreements now fell under the assent procedure and that this would have to be concluded before the Council could finalize the agreements. At the time of writing, the majority of issues now subject to the cooperation procedure were drafted under the traditional, one-reading system. The delay until July 1987 of the SEA's entry into force meant that further re-examination of existing proposals' legal bases had to be conducted. From July, however, the legal base was reviewed on a proposal-by-proposal basis. No second readings took place before the end of 1987.

The process of determining the legal base of a proposal is far from simple. Redistributive policy goals cannot be implemented without reference to both structural funds – subject to the budget procedure – and to the more focused aims of the economic and social cohesion (convergence) programmes – subject to the cooperation procedure (SEA Title II and OJ C70 25.3.86). Moreover, proposals may be examined to see whether they should come under articles prescribing Council unanimity (for example article 130S on environmental matters) or article 100a, requiring Council action by qualified majority and the use of the cooperation procedure. The EP has an interest in ensuring that as many proposals as possible are tabled under articles relating to the completion of the internal market. Where proposals cross policy sectors falling partly under the traditional decisionmaking (single-reading) system and partly under the cooperation procedure, the aim is to make them subject to the latter. The EP is not always successful in this. Both the Commission and the Council have chosen legal bases to exclude the EP. After Chernobyl, the Commission used article 31 (Euratom) to fix maximum permitted radio-activity levels for foodstuffs to guard against market fragmentation. This article provided merely for the EP's consultation. The EP failed to get the legal base changed (OJ C 125 L371, 30.12.87). For its part, the Council has successfully amended the legal base of a proposal (in this case on the information market), changing it from article 100a to article 235, thus obviating the cooperation procedure's second reading. In this case, the Council formally re-consulted the EP to get a 'second opinion' which, however, lacked the force and significance of the cooperation procedure's second reading and deprived the EP of its attendant rights. Council–Commission collusion may also lead the Commission to support the Council over the EP. Indeed, it should not be assumed that the Commission (or Council) easily find consensus as to a proposal's proper legal base. If contested, it may be decided by a simple majority vote.

The complex inter-institutional interaction and consultation and re-consultation of the EP required by the cooperation procedure leaves scope for politicking. Accordingly, as a bargaining ploy, the EP has put forward amendments on which it was prepared to compromise simply to pressurize both the Commission and the Council and to give itself leeway in creating an image of being reasonable and open to persuasion. The Commission can also side-step contentious amendments by suggesting that they become the subject of a further proposal. It has a vested interest in avoiding stale-mate and no decision being taken at the end of the second reading; in minimizing conflict with the Council and maximizing compromise with the EP. The importance of EP–Commission interaction should not be under-estimated. Not only does the Commission play a vital honest-broker role in the cooperation procedure, but it is increasingly inclined to take seriously the EP's inputs in view of the high quality of its amendments and 'own initiative' reports.

The Council has been more blatant in its attempts to curtail EP and Commission influence. In a sense, the EP and Commission share an interest in seeing proposals being made subject to the cooperation procedure, notably in the controversial area of competition policy. The committology row showed how keen the Council was to claw back executive powers conferred on the Commission by the Rome Treaty by enhancing the role and powers of national civil servants responsible for reviewing Commission implementing and executive decisions. The EP referred the committology issue unsuccessfully to the ECJ on the grounds that the Council's preference for Regulatory Committee procedures represented not the streamlining of Commission executive and management functions (as the Commission argued (EPWD A2-78/78/86; Lodge, 1987:18ff)) but a deviation from article 10 (SEA) and from the spirit of the SEA's Final Act.

The EP opposed Regulatory Committees as they permit the Commission to act only with the support of a qualified majority of member states and exclude the EP. The Commission advocated three main types of committee:

(i) Advisory committees that may give an opinion, after which the Commission takes the decision;
(ii) Management committees in which, by qualified majority, member states' representatives can overrule the Commission view and refer an issue back to Council; and
(iii) Regulatory committees where issues go to the Council unless the Commission has the states' qualified majority support.

The Regulatory Committee procedure is supposed to encourage the Council to adopt alternative measures to those advanced by the Commission within a three-month deadline. But, in practice, there is no incentive for the Council to act in a constructive way since it can block a decision by simple majority even when it is unable to put forward an alternative.

In September 1988 the ECJ ruled that the EP did not have the right to bring annulment proceedings before it even though it did have the right to intervene in such cases; could bring proceedings for failure to act; and could itself be subject to action before the ECJ.

The EP has reacted by seeking amendments to proposals that provide for the Regulatory Committee procedure. The Council has usually rejected such amendments. Consequently, the onus is on the Commission to keep the EP fully informed about executive decisions. The two Presidents formally agreed to this in an exchange of letters in 1988. Now, all draft implementing measures (save routine, secret or urgent management documents) are forwarded to the EP at the same time as they are sent to the committology committees. The EP President then transmits them to the appropriate EP committees and liaises with the appropriate Commissioner.

Regular and easy inter-institutional communication has become vital also where EP–Council interaction is concerned. The Council is obliged to reconsult the EP when its common position deviates substantially from the proposal accepted by the EP. However, so far reconsultation is fraught, being inevitably controversial and time-consuming. Consequently, optimal demands are sacrificed for expedience. This has the merit of seeing action take place, but the longer-term implications may be less satisfactory. Since the Council has been notoriously slack in providing the EP with sufficiently detailed information about its common position the EP has had to develop other means for finding out the state of play in the Council (see above).

The Presidents-in-Office of the various Councils now appear before the EP's appropriate committees twice during their state's Presidency. Information gleaned during informal 'corridor' chats can be supplemented by the information on the state of play in the Council that the EP can obtain from the Commission. In addition, the specialized Councils have invited EP committee chairpersons to participate in a Council session, and meetings and correspondence between them has increased markedly. At the level of officials, such contacts are especially important not least because the EP wants to extend to the Council its new arrangement with the Commission for agreeing on an annual legislative programme (subject to three-monthly review). Seen in this light, the EP's current support for relocation to Brussels takes on added significance.

There can be little doubt that the cooperation procedure has led to the EP being a more proactive participant in the legislative process. It has also resulted in a changed role conception. It acts as guardian of treaty amendments brought in by the SEA and exploits their possibilities to the full whenever possible. For example, by judiciously exploiting second-reading and budgetary deadlines, it managed as early as October 1987 to persuade the Council to accept amendments to its Medical Research Programme that it had formerly rejected (EPWD C2-173/87; A2-175/87). On another occasion, however, inter-institutional dialogue coupled with heavy pressure group lobbying of the EP during the second reading of a proposal on exhaust emissions led the institutions to compromise even though theoretically Denmark could have blocked the adoption of the Council's common position (EPWD C2-142/87; A2-184/87; C2-141/87; A2-185/87).

If the EP is to safeguard its positions and ensure that the Commission and Council do heed its views, effective follow-up is essential. Greater transparency has been injected into the legislative process through this and agreement on a presidential trialogue; computer-led recording of progress on items under the cooperation procedure; information exchange that records which officials are responsible for what items of legislation; and vastly increased informal contacts.

Progress report on the cooperation procedure

The EP had before its third direct election itemized the policy agenda for the next Parliament, earmarking for particular attention: the Single European Market and fiscal harmonization; EPC and security; environmental protection; R & D; monetary integration (including the role of the ECU and a federal bank); solidarity and convergence between the centre and periphery regions; and the EC's budget and own resources. The EP had also swiftly learned how to adapt to the new demands of the cooperation procedure and has developed ways of helping MEPs fully to exploit the opportunities opened by the procedure for significantly improving the EP's ability to play a legislative role both internally and in respect of influencing EPC issues.

From the outset, the EP was convinced that the cooperation procedure was but a first step in a process of increasing its legislative inputs. Not surprisingly, the fruits of the cooperation procedure have been quantified, assessed and found to be wanting by the EP. While the Commission on first reading has taken up just over 78 per cent of EP amendments, the Council has accepted just under half. In second reading, the EP approved in the first year of the cooperation procedure just over 50 per cent of common positions and tried to amend the rest (sometimes reinserting amendments that had fallen at first reading, or amendments arising out of the Council's amendment of the Commission's first-reading drafts approved by the EP). The EP's second-reading amendments stand a far slimmer chance of survival. Indeed, on a few occasions the Commission rejected all the EP amendments; and the Council deleted over 50 per cent of those agreed by the Commission. The EP has clearly been successful in securing some amendment to legislative items. It has also identified ways of improving the chances of successful EP action to alter legislation. These do not rest simply on arguments in favour of extending the cooperation procedure into areas subject to the old 'standard' decisionmaking practices. Instead, they seek to consolidate existing gains and to exploit procedures that have not been fully explored so far. One of the second elected EP's legacies to the new EP is a series of proposals for exploiting and extending the scope of the conciliation procedure. As long ago as July 1983, all the EC institutions and EC members (save Denmark) agreed that this was desirable in principle, a view endorsed by the Ad Hoc Committee on Institutional Affairs in 1985. Even Mr Papantoniou, who had entered a reservation against joint EP–Council decisionmaking, applauded the improvement and extension of the conciliation procedure. Even though the Council can act by majority vote in this sense, little has happened.

The need for more effective inter- and intra-institutional policy management and coordination since the introduction of the cooperation procedure depends on communication. Previously, the conciliation procedure had virtually fallen into disuse. Excessively time-consuming and ill-managed, it took the Council, for example, four years to transmit a common position on a July 1982 Commission proposal for a modifying regulation on own resources on which the EP had emitted its opinion in December 1982. Moreover, only rarely did conciliation produce successful or partially successful outcomes from the EP's viewpoint.

However, the system of two readings under the cooperation procedure places a premium on EP–Commission cooperation and especially EP–Council compromise at all stages. While the first reading is crucial to the EP as it is, it is at this stage that it stands the best chance of securing amendment to draft proposals, conciliation with the Council at second reading could prove invaluable to both the EP and the Council.

If the EP rejects a proposal at second reading, the Council must be unanimous to overrule it. This heightens the EP's bargaining power and opportunity to build or to thwart the attainment of the necessary coalitions within the Council. Both parties' interests may be best served by compromise. To achieve such compromise, an appropriate mechanism must be developed. More importantly, it should be brought into play before the Council takes its common position. The conciliation procedure (primarily designed to resolve budgetary differences between the Council and EP) offers a ready-made mechanism which is being examined afresh.

Has the cooperation procedure lived up to expectations? Has it augmented the EP's role in policymaking? The answer to both questions must be a qualified 'yes'. Expectations of what the cooperation procedure would deliver for the EP were modest and ill-defined. Experience has shown that the procedure has helped to make the EP one of a number of important actors in policymaking – a 'co-player' – and so has augmented its role. It has not, however, put the EP on a co-equal footing with the Council and Commission. Proposals rejected by MEPs can become law, a fact which reinforces the idea of parliamentary democracy at EC level remaining weak even if stronger than before the SEA. MEPs have not been overly impressed with the suggestion that because over seventy Council decisions were taken by majority vote during the first year following the SEA's implementation, EC decisionmaking has become more effective and democratic. The Council can still seek and obtain unanimity.

Awareness of this has led MEPs to discuss the need for further refinements of the cooperation procedure, further amendments to the treaty and the revival of the draft Treaty establishing the European Union. MEPs' disquiet at the functioning to date of the cooperation procedure revolves around areas identified above: the legal base of legislation; the Commission's executive powers; and the first and second readings. The Legal base of proposals was bound to prove contentious. Indeed, MEPs suggest a degree of arbitrariness in the choice of legal base that mirrors the somewhat arbitrary division of policy areas subject to the cooperation procedure.

These problems illustrate how the EP's ability to influence policy outputs can be undermined. They also contribute to EP dissatisfaction over its role in policymaking and impatience over the limited scope of the SEA's amendments. These, it is felt, will prove insufficient to allow the EC effectively, efficiently and democratically to confront the demands of the 1990s towards 2000.

However, contemporary policymaking has to be seen as an octopus, for the tentacles of apparently discrete areas stretch out into other domaines and many of those rejected in December 1985 are being revived as essential for the EC's future prosperity and coherence. They concern, moreover, critical aspects of the SEM's 'external aspects', of the EC's desire to ensure that the SEM is not ridiculed as an 'infernal market'. Central are: a development policy (advanced before the SEA's conclusion by the Dutch and Danes); energy policy (an ignored Danish suggestion); cultural cooperation (rejected despite backing from the Commission, Italy and the Netherlands); and aspects of citizens' rights (to which Denmark drew particular attention). More sensitive still are: a common currency and monetary policy; and above all aspects of defence and security policy that presuppose a higher degree of foreign policy concord than is currently sought by the member states. The external dimensions of the SEM highlight incongruities between the member states' professed goals and current practices. It is these issues that need to be addressed more than the rather sterile debate about EC sovereignty and the EP's alleged role in eroding that of the member states. Clearly, the newly elected EP will have to confront important procedural and institutional questions immediately. There can be little doubt that the EP will try and use the 1992 review of aspects of the Single European Act (notably in respect of EPC) to introduce significant reforms to advance European Union and a transparent, democratic, effective, responsive and efficient legislative process.

Apart from their policy achievements, the most remarkable feature of both the elected European Parliaments has been their constitutional legacies to incoming MEPs. The eve of each new election has been sealed with a promise of progress towards the democratization of the EC's policy process coupled with a vision of European Union with clear principles and boundaries. The EP's legacy to the electorate in 1984 – the EUT – led to the SEA, 1992 and all that it signifies. The EP's legacy in 1989 commits its successor to take up the battle for an efficient, democratic legislative process responsive to citizens. In the 1980s, the EP has come to play the role of the EC's founding father. No other EC institution is bold enough or politically capable of sketching out the future constitution for a united Community. That the EP should have adopted such a bold stance owes much to its skilful exploitation of the cooperation procedure.

Inevitably, the growing role of the EP and the altered state of inter-institutional relations has repercussions for changing policy networks and for other actors in the policymaking process. More than ever, national parliaments need to know what is happening in the EP and to liaise with it effectively and reform their own internal practices accordingly. They need to recognize it as the guardian of parliamentary power in the EC even if many oppose the EP assuming a constituent role after the 1989 Euro-elections.

Note

1. Key reports during the 1980s were those on the completion of the customs union and internal market: EPWD numbers: 1-241/81; 1983/84 (Albert/Ball); A2-180/85; A2-169/86; and on 'non-Europe', The Catherwood report EPWD A2-39/88. Related resolutions can be found on OJ C260, 12.10.81 p.68; C287, 9.11.81 p.64; C127, 14.5.84 p.8; C117, 30.4.84 p.34; C315, 26.11.84 p.111; C175, 15.7.85 p.229; C36, 17.2.86 p.53; C227, 8.9.86 p.52; C297, 24.11.86 p.86; C7, 12.1.87 p.105, C187, 18.7.88; OJ Annex (June 1988) No 2-366, p.157; and COM(88)134 final.

References

There is a voluminous literature on the EP. This is just an overview.

Berghe, G. van den (1982), *Political Rights for European Citizens*, Aldershot, Gower.

Bieber, R. et al (1985), *An Ever Closer Union*, Brussels, Commission.

Butler, D. and Kitzinger, U. (1976), *The 1975 Referendum*. London, Macmillan.

Bourguignon-Wittke, R. et al (1985), 'Five Years of the Directly Elected European Parliament', *Journal of Common Market Studies* 23, 31-53.

Cardozo, R. and Corbett, R. (1986), 'The Crocodile Initiative', in J. Lodge (ed) (1986), *European Union: the European Community in search of a Future*, Macmillan, London.

Herman, V. and Hagger, M. (eds) (1980), *The Legislation of Direct Elections to the European Parliament*, Farnborough, Gower.

Herman, V. and Lodge, J. (1978), *The European Parliament and the European Community*, London, Macmillan.

Holt, S. (1988), 'The Budget as a Future Political Instrument of the European Parliament', in R. Hrbek (et al) (1984), *The European Parliament on the Eve of the Second Direct Elections: Balance Sheet and Prospects*, Bruges, De Tempel.

Jacqué, J.-P. (1983), '*Conquêtes et Revendications: l'évolution des pouvoirs législatifs et budgétaires du Parlement européen depuis 1979, Journal of European Integration* 6, 155-82.

Lodge, J. (1975), 'Britain and the EEC; Exit, Voice or Loyalty; *Cooperation and Conflict*, 10, 199-216.

— (1982), 'The European Parliament after Direct Elections: Talking Shop or Putative Legislature?' *Journal of European Integration* 5, 259-84.

— (1984),'European Union and the First Elected European Parliament: the Spinelli Initiative' *Journal of Common Market Studies* 22, 377-402.

— (ed) (1986), *Direct elections to the European Parliament 1984*, London, Macmillan.

— (ed) (1986a), *European Union: the European Community in Search of a Future*, London, Macmillan.

— (1987a), 'The European Parliament and Foreign Policy' in M.L. Sondhi (ed), *Foreign Policy and Legislatures*, Dehli, Abhinav.

Lodge, J. (1987b), 'The Single European Act and the new legislative cooperation procedure: a critical analysis', *Journal of European Integration* 11, 5-28.

Lodge, J. and Herman, V. (1982), *Direct Elections to the European Parliament: A Community Perspective*, London, Macmillan.

Loewenberg, G. (ed) (1971), *Modern Parliaments: Change or Decline?* New York, Aldine Atherton.

Louis, J.V. (ed) (1985), *L'Union Européenne*, Brussels, Université Libre de Bruxelles.

Nicoll, W. (1986a), La procédure de concertation entre le Parlement européen et le Conseil, *Revue du Marché commun*, no.293, 1986, 3-10.

— (1986b), 'Les procédures Luns–Westerterp pour l'information du Parlement européen', *Revue du Marché commun*, no.300, 475-76.

Palmer, M. (1983), 'The Development of the European Parliament's Institutional role within the European Community', 1973-83, *Journal of European Integration* **6**, 183-202.

Pinder, J. (1988), 'Role Concepts for the EP and their implications', TEPSA, Strasbourg.

Pridham, G. and P. (1981), *Transnational Party Cooperation and European Integration*, London, Allen and Unwin.

Reif, K -H. (ed) (1984), *Ten European Elections*, Aldershot, Gower.

Sasse, C. et al (1981), *The European Parliament: Towards a Uniform Procedure for Direct Elections*, Florence, EUI.

Sharp, M. and Shearman, C. (1987), *European Technological Collaboration*, London, RKP.

Wallace, H. (1973), National Governments and the European Communities, London, PEP.

— (1983), 'Negotiation, Conflict and Compromise: the elusive pursuit of common policies,' in Wallace, H., and Webb, C. (eds), *Policy-Making in the European Community*, Chichester, Wiley.

Weiler, J.H.H. (1983), 'The Genscher-Colombo Draft European Act: The Politics of Indecision' *Journal of European Integration* **6**, 129-154.

Part II Internal perspectives

4 Introduction: internal perspectives

Juliet Lodge

The 1990s are clearly going to be preoccupied with issues arising out of the attempt to realize the Single European Market (SEM). An artificial distinction can be made between what might loosely be defined as 'internal' and 'external' policies. However, it must be remembered that internal policies have external effects and the idea of an impenetrable barrier separating the two is misleading. By 'internal' policies, we mean that group of policies whose goals are directly related to the accomplishment of targets within the EC: they are inner-directed; they seek to modify in some way policy activities within the domestic settings of the EC and its member states. 'External policies' are outer-directed and aim at producing a degree of agreement and/or consensual policies among the Twelve towards non-EC, often known as 'third', states. An example of the latter would be the Lomé Conventions.

However, 'domestic' policies like the CAP, attempts to manage difficult sectoral areas (like steel and textiles) and to advance EC monetary integration, fiscal harmonization and capital and labour mobility as well as new efforts in the environmental and information technology (IT) trade spheres spill-out into the external arena. As a result, the EC's own arrangements for initiating, managing and executing policies in those sectors become stressed by the absence of appropriate mechanisms to manage effectively external effects of domestic policies that are often highly sensitive. Moreover, the goal of achieving a common market (as in the 1950s) and now a SEM inadvertently encourages policymakers at all levels from the EC itself through national government down to local government to focus on internal problems and on the difficulties associated with member states having to adjust to new policy environments and conditions. Since the effects of policies are largely unknown at the outset, and since subsequent wrangling is likely to result from unpalatable effects within certain sectors or member states, it is to be expected that policymakers will not necessarily anticipate possibly deleterious external effects. Moreover, in dealing with them (as in the case of Mediterranean enlargement), they have to adopt some means of prioritizing the claims of those who feel that their interests (usually trade interests) have been harmed as a result. The criteria they choose will almost always be contested.

It is obvious that neither a common market nor the SEM can be established without often unwelcome consequences for third states. The mere establishment of a Common External Tariff demands adjustments both by members of the bloc applying that tariff and by those who export to the bloc. Various forms of protectionism and market support also have trade diversifying effects. The year 1992 has become shorthand for the completion of the SEM. While its consolidation will extend beyond the 1990s, many third states and commercial interests within them are operating as if the SEM will assume concrete shape by 1992. This is especially true of the EC's major trading partners, including the rump EFTA (Hine, 1985: 114ff). Renewed speculation exists over EC entry bids by Norway and even Austria, Switzerland and Sweden. Turkey applied to join the EC in April 1987, Morocco may follow and by 2002 Cyprus is to complete a customs union. Third states are forced to adapt to the EC's policies and its anticipated effects. EC rim states seem to be following parallel actions, at a minimum, to minimize anticipated difficulties from the SEM's establishment.

While such effects are largely an unknown quantity, they are recognized. Predicting and managing them is, however, difficult. Equally, the internal consequences of a limited range of inner-directed policies are often overlooked, or insufficient resources are set aside to encourage appropriate supranational-led action. Economic and political considerations explain this. Certainly this has been the EC's experience. The accent on the removal of obstacles to trade within the EC led, for example, to the EC being castigated as a 'rich man's club'. The SEM has been similarly construed as a commercial ploy whose uncertain benefits would gravitate towards already rich centres – the Golden Triangle – wealthy elites and powerful companies already in a position to benefit from the hypothesized economies of scale consequent upon the SEM (Pelkmans and Winter's, 1988; Cecchini, 1988). Whereas the Rome Treaty establishing the EEC made some provisions to assist poorer sectors, it did not 'flag' them in the way in which Commission President Delors did.

The qualitative difference to European integration in the 1990s inheres not simply in the modifications to the Rome Treaty introduced through the Single European Act, but in the way in which they have been interpreted in the public domaine. The politico-economic context in which the SEA unfurled partly accounts for this. The era of Green parties on mainland Europe and generalized high unemployment with its attendant social problems meant that something more than mere lip-service had to be paid to sectors that clearly were high on the member states' domestic political agenda. Equally important, however, was M. Delors's intention to define the EC's *raison d'être*. Since its inception, this issue had been side-stepped (Lodge, 1989). The Monnet–Schuman visions and methods stressed the establishment of concrete achievements to create real solidarity and to realize the common good. However, the goal of European Union had been obfuscated by the process. Gradualism reigned supreme: indeed, had to assume centre stage at a time when national sovereignty was not only sorely tried but was still being slowly granted to the new West German state by its Western allies.

The phrase 'an ever closer union' disguised or hid the likely extensive implications of the creation of a common market for thirty years. National governments occasionally protested loudly at steps likely to augment the authority and competence of the EC's institutions. Such protestations seemed to reflect anxiety over an inability to make others in the EC follow a line prescribed by one state's national interest. A well thought-out understanding of what the various sectoral policy measures to advance integration implied in the longer term for both the member states' and the EC's capacity to deliver the goods proved elusive. No matter how serious and protracted disagreements among the member states, it was clear that the EC was not only an acceptable forum for the pursuit of goals but one which soon attracted more members. The effect on the EC of many states using it instrumentally to advance national interests was, paradoxically and contrary to the assumptions implicit in many integration theories, to reinforce and consolidate rather than weaken it. Many appreciated that the political implications of the processes of economic integration could not be forever ignored. Few appreciated that greater political integration would have consequences for macro and microeconomic sectoral integration.

It was comparatively easy in the early stages of European integration to deride and dismiss the future visions as 'federalist rantings'. By the 1980s, as Mrs Thatcher was to learn, this ceased to be the case. Many still abhor 'federalism' (often without understanding what it implies). But it is also clear that the EC's *raison d'être* needs some clarification. Public and elite expectations of what it can deliver exceed its capacity. The notion that the EC is a political animal is accepted. M. Delors tried to set out some parameters and to project a vision of a future EC. The precise details of the vision are less important than the fact that the vision makes clear that domestic and external policy sectors are irrevocably intertwined; that any benefits from economic integration must be shared in the name of social justice and its disadvantages offset. While the 'Social Europe' package was disappointing, the highlighting of different tranches of the SEM has imprinted a socialist element firmly on the EC.

A faint socialist watermark is clear in the Rome Treaty. Conscience calls for measures to deal with the negative effects of integration. Some incentives exist for labour mobility. By and large, however, the 'social' aspects of integration have played a secondary role. Attention has focused on removing barriers to trade and other forms of economic discrimination that might adversely affect intra-EC trade. The creation of the SEM and an industrial base for the EC remains frustrated by weaknesses in the EC's policy processes, the absence of consensus over macroeconomic goals and the continuing wrangling among the Twelve over the locus of authority.

Problems also inhere in the piecemeal approach to policymaking, the identification and implementation of sectoral policy goals that require a horizontal rather than a vertical approach to ensure rational and optimal outcomes. Moreover, the domestic organization and funding of agencies and departments charged with implementing and enforcing EC policy varies so greatly as to further frustrate rational and approximately common outcomes. Moreover, the EC lacks an overall economic plan (the SEM only partly disguises this). Instead of coherent over-arching economic policy, the EC has a series of economic instruments, often designed to prevent national actions that will distort competition (such as non-tariff and technical barriers to trade, state aids,[1] export premiums, preferential energy and freight rates for exports, for example) or that unfairly give or allow companies to abuse a dominant position (EEC, Art. 86). In certain areas, the level of aids (which may lead to states trying to outbid each other in a scramble to attract investment) has grown rapidly. Whereas in 1981, France, the UK and the FRG gave approximately the same amount of aid (around £2.8bn) and Italy double that, over the next five years UK aids fell sharply, French aids remained steady, German aids rose steadily but Italian aids rocketed to £16bn, that is nine times the UK level. Hence, there is concern to review the situation on export aids, general investment aids, industrial policy aids, aids through capital injection and the position of nationalized industries and state holding companies.

This section of the book will give an overview of some of the EC's important 'domestic' or 'internal' policy sectors that are critically linked into key EC policy sectors (discussed in more detail in separate chapters). It cannot deal with them all. However, it is important to realize that EC action extends well beyond the boundaries of the sectors examined.

The Economic context of policymaking

Title II of Part Three of the EEC Treaty 'Policy of the Community' is entitled 'Economic Policy' and divides into three chapters: conjunctural policy (Article 103) (short-term economic measures); balance of payments (Articles 104-9); commercial policy (Articles 110-16). Economic policy connotes something grand. In a broad sense it is used to describe the pursuit by governments of economic goals (for example zero-inflation, minimal unemployment) through the use of economic instruments (for example money supply, taxation, public expenditure). Governments may also resort to import quotas to protect their home market. In a customs union, the latter cannot be unilaterally applied (though derogations and transitional periods are, in the EC, permitted) without the ethos of the customs union being seriously undermined and partner states' interests being directly affected. The EEC treaties do not try to overcome, only to minimize, likely problems. Member states are required to 'regard their conjunctural policies as a matter of common concern' (Article 103(1)) and to 'coordinate their economic policies' (Article 105(1)). They are also required to pursue policies to promote stable balance of payments, stable prices, confidence in their currencies and a high level of employment (Article 104). An underlying (and unfounded) presupposition is that consensus exists over the way in which national economies should be run – whether there should be more or less state intervention, for example. Political factors inhibit such consensus.

Nevertheless, member states pursuing different economic goals or purporting to pursue convergent or identical goals while employing economic instruments in widely differing manners are bound to find that a degree of common action may prove beneficial given the potential for even greater growth in intra-EC trade. Obstacles that limit the potential for growth in the EC economy include: macro and microeconomic problems, such as those consequent upon monetary fluctuations which are only partly controlled by the European Monetary System (which the UK refuses fully to enter); divergent inflation and loan interest rates; and transport and energy costs, for example, as well as problems inhering in the application of the competition policy, the approximation of laws, merger policies, lack of a common fiscal system, differing VAT rates (Pearson and Smith, forthcoming), inadequate liberalisation of capital movements, insurance and services and so on. The SEM aims to eliminate such obstacles.

While the member states have taken numerous measures to promote the creation of the customs union, each has employed procedures in breach of the existing treaties to protect or give 'unfair' advantage to its nationals. Treaty infringements are brought before the EC's Court of Justice, and the guilty parties have to acquiesce and/or be convicted and fined. Attempts to harmonize standards upwards have been notoriously complicated (Cosgrove Twitchett, 1981) though CEN and CENELEC should prove helpful in certain sectors in future. Nevertheless, breaches continue since some economic advantage may be gained by a party that either postpones enacting a given EC regulation or directive or implements it partially. Regulations and notably directives are implemented at different rates in the member states and with different results.

Consequent effects on the drafting of future EC legislation are rarely acknowledged.

Even so, member states have realized that common action can prove beneficial. Whether it occurs within or outside the framework of the EC depends on the goal to be attained as well as political sensitivities and expedience. The particular sector that such action addresses is often evaluated in terms of its contribution to promoting supranational results: negative or positive integration is seen as the outcome. Negative integration refers to the removal of barriers to trade, of discrimination in economic practices, rules and policies. Positive integration refers to the transfer of public market rules and policies from member states to the EC's common institutions (Pelkmans and Winters 1988: 122). Progress towards EMS and an Economic and Monetary Union complete with a Central Bank and a common fully convertible currency is vital to the success of the customs union and now, of course, the SEM (see next chapter). However, many goals have been elusive or only partially attainable largely because of the compartmentalized, sectoral policymaking process. The EC's limited regional and meagre industrial policy initiatives have not been related to one another. There is a pattern of disjunction between related policy sectors across EC policy activities. The year 1992 has helped to encourage awareness of the need for integrated policy action to further goals that cut across neat sectoral divisions, but the appropriate adjustments are only beginning to be made. Before going on to examine some sectors in greater detail, it will be useful to try and briefly illustrate impediments to policy coherence by providing a glimpse at problems in a macro (industrial) and micro(transport) sector, policy areas whose importance will grow over the next few years and whose goals require integrated action across policy boundaries.

Industrial perspectives

The EC lacks an industrial policy but has economic instruments through which industrial aims may be pursued. These relate to the harmonization of laws, trade liberalization, an EC competition policy – sectoral actions and mechanisms that on an *ad hoc* basis try and cope with industrial sectors in crisis. The piecemeal approach has resulted in an imbalanced series of EC measures to attenuate the negative effects of industrial decline in the face of competition, and to regulate through a competition policy practices that impede the creation of the common market (EEC Articles 85-94; Parry and Dinnage, 1981). The EC's regional and social policies are both manifestations of this process and, until recently, have been imbued by the same *ad hoc*ery. Indeed, regional policy (often seen as an important instrument of industrial policy) was partly conceived as a compensatory mechanism for the British rather than as instrumental to an EC industrial strategy.

Member states have turned to the possibilities of EC action when they have realized the inadequacies of lone national action. However, by and large, neither governments nor the social partners have wanted a comprehensive EC industrial policy. Even British unions' conversion to union action at the EC level has been triggered more by frustration at the national level than by conviction. The more recent political awareness of the potential for EC industrial policy stems both from concern over the EC's relative decline in competitiveness in the international political economy and especially from the commitment to realize the Single European Market (and earlier the customs unions and common market – an area for which the EC has always had competence). However, EC activities have necessarily been divorced from a comprehensive EC-wide industrial strategy and have consequently seemed to relate simply to crisis management in sectors like steel, or to the technicalities of harmonization.

Harmonization has often been described as the key to the creation of a customs union and the modifications to the critical article of the Rome Treaty (Article 100) under the SEA are designed to expedite the realization of the internal (Single European) market. Progress has, however, been notably fraught. This is in part because of the tendency to confuse harmonization with unification. Moreover, the provisions of the Rome treaty that give effect to the principle of harmonization use terms like 'approximation', 'coordination' and 'harmonization' interchangeably (Dashwood 1981; 1983). In practice, the process is concerned with mutual adjustment of national regulations to an agreed EC standard, with the approximation of member states' laws to the extent required for the proper functioning of the common market.

Harmonization measures are often assessed in terms of their positive or negative effects on the progress of integration. 'Positive harmonization' refers to measures 'designed to attune the [member states'] legal systems to the [EC's] common policies' such as those mentioned by the Treaty (CAP, transport, common commercial policy and economic and social policy) and those introduced through Article 235 (EEC) such as energy, environmental and regional policies. (Dashwood, 1981: 15) Harmonization measures usually take the form of directives rather than regulations since they do not replace national laws but require adjustments to them. However, they may be drafted in such a way as to leave national authorities little scope for discretion in their implementation. On the other hand, directives can be so loose as to tempt states to omit adopting legislation that fully corresponds with the directives' intention and so to postpone enacting certain parts of it (on grounds of expense, for instance) until challenged by the Commission and ultimately the ECJ. The ways in which local, domestic agencies are organised and funded can also significantly hinder uniform implementation and enforcement of directives and EC goals. Combating fraud, for example, is far from simple (Siedentopf and Ziller, 1988). However, the flexibility inherent in directives is valued not least because it permits incremental progress. Significantly, the Commission chose the directive as the means to advance 1992 and by the end of 1988 had two-thirds of them in place.

The issue of harmonization looms large in considerations of EC industrial policy. An industrial policy, *per se*, does not exist. Sectoral action has been the norm. An EC-wide industrial strategy or consensus on the broad aims of a common or coordinated economic strategy does not exist. Conflicts between *dirigiste* and market economy member states partly account for this. Moreover, there is no consensus on whether an EC industrial policy should be comprehensive in scope or whether the haphazard selectivity to date is adequate. Different states now seem to want to mitigate the ill-effects of industrial decline and to support sunrise industries. The sectoral approach to integrating certain industries gives the impression of industrial actions being disjointed and haphazardly formulated. Until the 1970s results were rather intangible. The Council record for stalling decisions on Commission proposals was worst in the industrial and technology policy sectors. By 1979, a third of industrial policy proposals tabled before 1972 awaited a Council decision (Hodges, 1983: 266). Indeed, not until 1980 was there a Council meeting of Ministers responsible for industry and this was only an informal meeting from which the French and Germans were absent. The EC had failed to act usefully on the Colonna Report (Butt Philip, 1979; Woolcock, 1981). The Commission's 1977 programme aimed at defining a common strategy in advanced technology sectors and concentrated mainly on crisis areas (steel, ship-building and motor vehicles) but corresponding action on growth industries (IT and so on) was hampered by financial constraints and lack of political vision. Efforts to manage declining industrial sectors was not balanced by measures to foster internationally competitive new industries until the 1980s (see chapter 11).

Apart from textiles and more recently perhaps steel, it proved extremely difficult to enforce common strategies and rationalization. Rising unemployment in the wake of the oil and energy crises exacerbated this and undermined many of the premises about how resources could be redistributed and how industrial-belt prosperity would attract people from the land. The CAP had to cope with generalized recession and EC enlargement. The impact of measures (or lack of appropriate action) in given sectors on adjacent areas must not be overlooked. Regional policy was one response among many that was inadequately funded from the outset and inadequately integrated with other relevant sectoral policy measures (such as those under social policy provisions and the CAP). Not until the 1980s did experiments with integrated operations programmes and continuing budgetary strictures lead the EC to adopt measures to ensure that an integrated approach operated in regions that were to receive focused aid from several EC sources. By then, the idea that several EC states could proceed with projects (like the A300 Airbus) without all members being involved (and even with the participation of non-EC states) had become accepted. The demonstration effect was telling. States had to consider whether they might be denying themselves benefits that would not otherwise be attainable on a national basis by excluding themselves from collaborative EC and wider European ventures. Indeed, there seemed to be little alternative to such an approach given the absence of consensus among the Ten, then Twelve. Moreover, Europe *à la carte* seemed a useful strategy for achieving European Union. It was not, however, a helpful means of achieving economic and monetary union. Indeed, the absence of an EC industrial policy has been seen as a major impediment to EMU because it is believed to be crucial to ensuring effective coordination of economic policies among the member states. Against this, EC regional and social policies seem to amount to no more than token patching-up operations.

The relative ineffectiveness of the regional policy and the problems arising out of the absence of an overall industrial policy led several states not only to seek the strengthening of the EMS but to call for major steps forward in the creation of a genuinely coordinated economic space. The greater use of the ECU and the establishment of an EC Central Bank are instruments to that end. As with the creation of the EC itself, however, it was realized that major economic goals could not be promoted unless they were politically legitimized. Frustration increased support for pro-integrative statements that implied that those (like the UK) who opposed majority goals could relegate themselves to a second or third tier of the EC: the majority would no longer wait for the slowest ship in the convoy. Such potent threats forced the laggards into some hard thinking. Tindemans had raised the prospect of two-speed Europe in the 1970s. The 1980s were to test the members' will to see it eventuate. The prospect of 1992 was to push commercial interests into exploring the threats and opportunities the SEM was likely to present. In particular attention turned *inter alia* to company law, cross-frontier cooperation, patents, trademarks, public procurement issues, intellectual property rights, mergers and the EEIG. In the UK there was continued anguish over the UK becoming a full member of the EMS (with Mrs Thatcher objecting lest national macroeconomic aims be constrained and others insisting that governments could still deploy fiscal measures to manage counter-cyclical policy) (Pelkmans and Winters, 1988: 124; Butler, 1986). Moreover, the wider implications of an evolving EC industrial strategy began to exercise commercial and government interests as Delors made it clear that just as, in his view, the SEM was an irreversible process so too was the creation of a 'social space'. Yet while attention turned to eliminating the technical, fiscal and physical barriers to free movement of goods and persons, the years of neglect in the transport sector were put into sharp relief by the decisions both to realize the SEM and to build the Chunnel.

Industrial policy and transport

A common transport policy (CTP) would seem to be an essential feature of a customs union where the transport of goods and persons is an integral part of general economic activity. The ECSC's Treaty of Paris recognized the importance of transport (of coal, iron and steel). Translating this sectoral activity into the broader one demanded of the EEC (Article 3; 74;84 EEC) and now of the SEM proved far from easy partly because the free market thinking that underpinned it has been seriously challenged (Whitelegg, 1988: 10) and mainly because the provision of transport services within states is highly decentralized and fragmented. Technological advance, tourism, questions of land use, environmental considerations and greater labour mobility have implications for member states' transport policies, including their divergent practices regarding state intervention, regulation, competition, finance, infrastructure development and subsidization of public transport. States have traditionally used transport policy as 'an instrument of social and distributional policy' (Gwilliam, 1983). Economic distortions between different transport systems remain vast and the liberalization heralded by the SEM may generate economic growth having very uneven spatial and social impact and considerable disbenefits for some groups (Whitelegg, 1988: 4). Slow progress has been made on introducing a free competitive market in transport services to take advantage of the expected relaxation of border controls. The introduction of the Single Administrative Document (SAD) in 1987, designed to expedite and simplify matters, did not initially greatly reduce delays and attendant costs.

Awareness of the economic costs of different (often protectionist) national practices (most public in the case of airlines) grew throughout the 1970s. Though the EP challenged the Council successfully before the ECJ on its inaction on transport policy, little change occurred as a result. Sustained pressure on air transport only slowly had any effect. Road, rail and maritime and inland waterway transport remained problematic. By the 1980s, the estimated cost of the lack of integrated transport to freight hauliers was about two per cent of each consignment's value (Cecchini, 1988: 9). De-regulation was seen as but one means of cutting costs and developing a free market in transport itself.

While the costs of 'non-Europe' to road hauliers have been analysed, little attempt has been made to explore the logistical needs of an integrated transport system for the EC as a whole. As with other sectors, transport has been taken out of context and disjointed incremental policy outcomes have been the result even though from the time of the Commission's ambitious 1961 report on a common transport policy, there have been repeated attempts at designing an integrated EC-wide system. The 1972 Paris summit recognized the need for integrity between transport policy and other sectors (Gwilliam, 1983: 172), but there was little in resource terms to support necessary infrastructural development.

Reorganizing transport on a national and EC-wide basis would clearly affect numerous related sectors. Moreover, the big discrepancies in the degree of liberalization in transport between member states meant that any harmonization measures would demand extensive EC intervention both in road haulage and railways with their state backing and different perceptions of obligations to provide a public service. Politically, the issue was fraught. States employed restrictive practices that hindered the creation of a competitive free market in transport. Not surprisingly, therefore, EC action had to address such problems on a piecemeal basis before anything realistic in terms of an overall transport strategy could be devised. This helps to explain the preoccupation with fiscal harmonization (taxing fuel in tanks, for example), social harmonization measures (drivers' conditions, the tachograph, etc) and technical harmonization (axle weights, emission standards, etc) (Gwilliam, 1983; Butt–Phillip, 1988). The complexities and political niceties involved, however, were discouraging.

The Commission did not abandon visions of an integrated transport policy. Rather it addressed problems as they arose, identifying traffic bottlenecks and seeking *ad hoc* solutions to them. The Chunnel, the Messina Straits Bridge and Alpine crossings commended themselves but, as with other sectors, the EC's budget did not stretch to major infrastructure investment programmes. However, by the 1980s, as governments began exploring faster surface transport systems to capitalize on the Chunnel, the broad view held attractions. Dissatisfaction with the British end of the Chunnel (notably the absence of any fast public rail freight and passenger network both to London and to the regions) highlighted how the realization of the SEM may not reduce non-Europe's costs nearly as much as had been suggested. The Chunnel's impact on local communities, employment and the environment underlined the need for a re-think about the role of non-road transport systems. Moreover, the EC's Mediterranean enlargement meant that maritime shipping and civil aviation loomed far larger in the EC's transport policy than hitherto.

However, the overall impression of the CTP is that not only has it developed in an incremental way with negative effects across the EC but that the SEM will intensify them and the anticipated dislocation of economic activities. This is partly the product of the CTP having to operate through the disparate transport policies pursued at various levels in the member states. It is partly the result of the CTP still being conceptualized in the very limited terms of a cost minimization exercise. The CTP must be integrated into the wider preoccupations of Social Europe and a People's Europe. Transport systems and commuting affect citizens directly. As Whitelegg has trenchantly observed, the absence of a CTP that is sensitive and responsive to social, environmental and infrastructural factors is at best a lost opportunity for the improvement of living and working conditions in Europe. At worst the existing CTP is 'an ineffective policy pursued in an indifferent manner based on simplistic economic notions' (Whitelegg, 1988: 201).

Criticisms aside, there can be little doubt that the 1980s has witnessed a quiet revolution in the EC's and member states' approaches to common problems. EC institutions (for example, the EP through its bold initiatives on economic problems and the costs of 'non-Europe', and the Commission) led the way to the EC's politico-economic revival. This is the aspiration embedded in '1992' and the SEM. Indeed, by 1988 disillusionment with progress over the trickier 1992 directives led to doubt being voiced over whether or not the SEM could be realized before 1999 and whether or not 1992 was a legally enforceable deadline or simply a target. As Declaration 8a of the SEA shows, 1992 is but a target. The Declaration itself in a sense shows concern lest states that have not fully complied with the 1992 legislation by 1992 be impugned before the ECJ. They want to avoid such a situation. Nevertheless, 1992 has assumed important psycho-politico-economic dimensions in government, private and public-sector circles.

Note

1. The treaty identifies three types of 'legitimate' aids: 'social aids to individual consumers not linked with the origin of the product (for example, food vouchers to pensioners, or Christmas butter); emergency aids in the wake of disasters; and special FRG aids to help West Berlin and regions flanking the East bloc.

References

General

Cecchini, P. (1988), *The European Challenge 1992*, Aldershot, Wildwood.
El-Agraa, A. (ed.) (1983), *Britain within the European Community*, London, Macmillan.
Pelkmans ,J. and Winters, A., (1988), *Europe's Domestic Market*, London, Routledge, Kegan Paul.
Pelkmans, J. (1987), 'The Internal Market of the EC' in R. Beuter and P. Tsakaloyannis (eds), *Experiences in Regional Cooperation*, Maastricht, EIPA.

Industrial policy

Allen, D. (1983), 'Managing the Common Market: The Community's Competition Policy' in H. Wallace, and W. and C. Webb(eds), *Policymaking in the European Community*, Chichester, Wiley.
Butler, Sir M. (1986), *Europe: More than a Continent*, London, Heinemann.
Butt Philip, A. (1979), 'The Harmonisation of Industrial Policy and Practices' in Cosgrove Twitchett *op. cit.*

— (1983), 'Industrial and Competition Policies: A New Look', in A. El-Agraa (ed.), *op. cit.*

— (1988), 'The Application of the Transport Regulations by the Administrations of the Member States', in H. Siedentopf and J. Ziller (eds), *Making European Policies Work, vol.1*, London, Sage.

Colonna Report (1979), *Memorandum on Industrial Policy in the Community*, Luxembourg.

Commission of the European Communities (1961), *Memorandum on the General Lines of a Common Transport Policy*, Brussels.

— (1988), *Third Report from the Commission to the Council and the European Parliament on the implementation of the Commission's White Paper on completing the internal market.* COM (88) 134 fin., 21 March, Brussels.

Cosgrove Twitchett, C. (ed.) (1981), *Harmonisation in the EEC*, London, Macmillan.

Dashwood, A. (1981), 'The Harmonisation Process' in Cosgrove Twitchett, *op. cit.*

— (1983), 'Hastening Slowly: The Path towards Harmonisation' in H. and W. Wallace and C. Webb (eds), *Policymaking in the European Community*, Chichester, Wiley.

Gwilliam, K. (1983), 'The Future of the Common Transport Policy' in A. El-Agraa (ed.), op. cit.

Hine, R. (1985), *The Political Economy of European Trade*, Brighton, Wheatsheaf.

Hodges, M. (1983), 'Industrial Policy: Hard Times or Great Expectations?' in H. and W. Wallace and C. Webb (eds), *op. cit.*

Lodge, J. (1989), 'EC Decisionmaking towards the SEA' in D. Urwin and W. Paterson (eds), *Politics in Western Europe Today*, London, Longman.

Parry, A. and Dinnage, J. (1981), *Parry and Hardy: EEC Law*, London, Sweet and Maxwell.

Pearson, M. and Smith, S. (forthcoming), '1992: Issues in Indirect Taxation', *Fiscal Studies*.

Pelkmans, J. an Winters, A. (1988), Europes Domestic Market, London, Routledge, Kegan Paul.

Siedentopf, H. and Ziller, J. (eds) (1988), *Making European Policies Work, vol. 1*, London, Sage.

Whitelegg, J. (1988), *Transport Policy in the EEC*, London, Routledge.

Woolcock, S. (1981), 'Industrial Adjustment: The Community Dimension', in M. Hodges and W. Wallace (eds), *Economic Divergence in the European Community*, London, Allen and Unwin.

5 The Single Market: a step towards European Union

John Pinder

Why a single market?

The programme to complete the single market by 1992 has occupied centre stage in the European Community. Completion of the single market, or the internal market as it is often called, is an economic objective: to enable people and firms to buy or sell, lend or borrow, produce or consume throughout the whole EC as they have hitherto done within their own countries. Producers should be more efficient, consumers should get a better deal and the economy should be more dynamic in such a big market. But the why and the how of the single market programme will not be understood if the political motives that lay behind it are forgotten.

After World War Two there was a deep desire to replace Europe's system of rival nation–states by a new European polity, in which Europeans would become fellow citizens. When the Schuman Plan, which resulted in the European Coal and Steel Community, was launched in 1950, it was presented as a first step towards a European federation. When the ensuing attempt to establish a Political Community based on integrated defence forces was defeated in 1954 by a combination of nationalists and Stalinists in the French National Assembly, it became clear that a direct assault on national sovereignty was not likely to succeed. But the movement towards political union was not abandoned. It was instead channelled into the economic field.

While the political motive was fundamental, it would have run into the sands if it had generated a project that was not valid from the economic viewpoint. But Europe really did need the common market that was at the centre of the European Economic Community, established in 1958. An economic system was wanted that would be strong enough to be proof against any tendency to revive the rabid protectionism that had preceded the war; and Europeans were highly conscious in the 1950s of the dominance of the American economy, which was attributed, at least in part, to the vast size of the American market. Thus the backbone of the Rome Treaty that established the EEC was the creation of the customs union, through a phased programme to remove all tariffs and quotas from trade between the member countries over a twelve to fifteen year period, and at the same time to give them a common tariff on imports from outside the Community.

As the tariffs and quotas were removed from the internal trade, it grew twice as fast as world trade, quadrupling in the decade after the Economic Community was set up; and the EC economy grew twice as fast as that of the United States. While it cannot be scientifically established how much of the fast growth was due to the freeing of trade within the EC, there are good reasons to attribute some of it to what are called the dynamic effects of the opening up of markets. (Pelkmans, 1984, Pinder, 1988) These are the effects on the dynamism, or growth, of the economies because economies of scale and specialization are encouraged, technological progress is accelerated, business investment is boosted, and markets acquire a more competitive structure.

Despite this economic progress, which enabled Europeans to catch up with Americans in producing the goods such as cars and consumer durables which were typical of the second industrial revolution, Europeans remained nervous about American technological dominance (see Servan–Schreiber, 1967). By the 1980s, with the third industrial revolution, based on microelectronics and information technology, rapidly gathering pace, the Europeans had serious cause for alarm. American and Japanese firms were evidently superior in the new technologies, while in the more conventional production some of the newly industrializing countries were pressing the Europeans hard from behind. Various reports expounded the grounds for concern about the EC's competitiveness (Albert and Ball, 1983; Pelkmans, 1986: 41-50).

Through this concern about competitiveness, a consensus began to develop that a major cause of the lack of dynamism in Europe was once again the fragmentation of the European economy into national markets. The tariffs and quotas had, to be sure, been removed, but the national markets were now separated by non-tariff barriers. These barriers stemmed partly from the attempts to prop up old-established sectors that were hard hit by the stagflation of the 1970s; thus steel, ship and textile manufacturers in most countries were heavily subsidized to protect them against the competition of more efficient producers, whether from within the EC or outside it. Yet more significant in blocking technological progress was the tendency for products embodying the more advanced technologies to be subject to national specifications and public purchasing as well as subsidies, all of which could fragment the EC market for such products (Pelkmans, 1986: 44; Pelkmans and Winters, 1988: 109).

Thus the same economic motive that inspired the customs union, free of internal tariffs and quotas, led also to the idea of 'completing' the single market, by freeing it of internal non-tariff distortions: what could be seen as a customs union in modern dress. Lord Cockfield, as the Commissioner responsible for the internal market, presented a comprehensive programme for achieving this to the European Council in 1985 (Commission, 1985). The European Council approved it; and the member states embodied their commitment to it in the Single European Act (SEA).

The programme to complete the single market by 1992

The programme which removed tariffs from the trade between member states was stipulated quite simply in the EEC Treaty. These tariffs were to be reduced by an average of one-tenth on six occasions at stated intervals of a year or eighteen months, with the balance to be eliminated in the four subsequent years according to a timetable to be agreed before that final stage. It would be impossible to stipulate in a similarly simple fashion a programme to remove non-tariff barriers, which comprise an enormous mass of heterogeneous detail. To give one example: differing product specifications are, as we shall see, among the most significant barriers that fragment the market. Each one is defined by a law or a standards institute. In 1983 it was estimated that there might be 100,000 of them (Cecchini, 1988: 27).

The Commission imposed some order on this mass of detail by establishing a general objective, a date by which it should be attained, and a list of some three hundred measures that would have to be enacted by the EC with a timetable for their enactment. The objective was to remove all restrictions that impede goods, services, capital and people from moving freely throughout the EC, as they already do within each member country. The date was 31 December 1992. The measures cannot be so briefly summarized. But they can be analysed in groups such as those dealing with frontier controls, product specifications, service regulations, public procurement, state aids, competition policy, company law, capital controls and tax. This is the way in which they are analysed in the following text.

Frontier controls

In the winter of 1983-4, much of the trade between EC countries was brought to a halt by a lorry drivers' strike. The drivers were not striking against their employers, but against the frontier controls that kept them waiting for hours and even days in queues at frontiers, in all weathers. This is frustrating and sometimes painful for them, and expensive for their firms and for the European economy. The frontier controls impose other, less obtrusive but yet heavier costs, such as the clerical and managerial work of providing documentation. A study for the Commission has measured the costs of importing or exporting a consignment to or from a number of member countries. The average cost ranged from 'only' ECU26 for imports to Belguim, up to ECU250 for exports from Italy. (One ECU is, at the end of 1988, equal to about two thirds of a pound sterling.) The cost of exporting a consignment from the Netherlands and importing it into the UK was ECU125, while for exporting from Italy and importing into France it was ECU297 (Cecchini, 1988). While such costs may not bear so heavily on the large consignments which large firms will often buy or sell they can be prohibitive for smaller firms, which may simply be discouraged from venturing into such trade.

If public expenditure on controlling the frontiers is added to these (much larger) private costs, the total cost to the EC economy is estimated at ECU 8-9 billion (Cecchini, 1988: chapter 2 and p.84). The Commission has proposed that all frontier controls between member countries be abolished; and the SEA appears to commit the member states to this (Article 8A). But some member governments are resisting, on the grounds that it would become harder to control tax evasion and crime.

The extent to which stopping people at frontiers helps to control terrorism and the drug trade is certainly controversial. But there is no such doubt about the objective of ensuring free movement of EC citizens to take up jobs anywhere in the Community. This has in the past been impeded by differing requirements for professional qualifications; but in 1988 the EC enacted legislation which will contribute largely to the removal of this restriction on the freedom of at least its more highly qualified citizens.

Specifications and regulations

Specifications are established, either by law (technical regulations) or by standards institutes (standards), in order to guarantee to the consumer the safety and quality of a product. They can also ensure 'plug compatibility', which means literally that an electric plug bought from one manufacturer will fit into a socket bought from another: and this term is used, by analogy, for such vital matters as the inter-operability of systems for electronic data processing. (de Robien, 1986: 47). Specifications, differing from one country to another, fragment the EC market, making it impossible to sell a product made in one member country to a buyer in another, or at least imposing an additional cost to adapt the product to another specification. It has been estimated that it costs an additional ECU286 million to develop a volume car for sale in the various European markets with their differing specifications (Cecchini, 1988: 27); and since several such cars are produced for the European market, the total extra cost for each generation of cars runs into billions of ecus. Beyond that, there are the extra costs of producing the car for each market once it has been developed; and beyond that again, the manufacturer for such a market becomes less dynamic than one based on a homogeneous market such as Japan or the US, because of the factor known as the learning curve, whereby the cost of production is reduced as the volume which has been produced is increased. Differing specifications are one of the elements that slow the rate at which production builds up in Europe, impairing competitiveness not only by raising costs but also by holding up the attainment of maximum efficiency and the pace of further product development.

The impact of differing specifications is severe on many other industrial sectors including electrical engineering, mechanical engineering, pharmaceuticals, medical equipment and foodstuffs, where veterinary and food regulations are a particularly sensitive subject. Yet EC attempts to deal with the problem by harmonizing specifications had been painfully slow. From 1962 to 1984, the Council adopted directives to remove technical obstacles at a rate of only seven a year (Lauwaars, 1988: 154-5). In some sectors, the rate of development of new national specifications to cover new products was outstripping the rate of European harmonization of the old ones; and these were precisely the sectors in which Americans and Japanese were increasing their technological lead.

To confront this situation, the Cockfield White Paper proposed a 'new strategy' and a 'new approach'. The idea for the new strategy came from a judgement of the Court of Justice. German regulations prevented the import into the Federal Republic of a French drink called Cassis de Dijon on the grounds that its alcohol content was too high for wine but too low for spirits. The Court ruled that the French regulations under which Cassis de Dijon was produced ensured a safe and healthy drink and must be recognized as such by the German authorities (ECR 649 of 1979; see VerLoren van Themaat, 1988: 115, 118). This established the principle that is known as 'mutual recognition'. Products such as Cassis which conform with the specifications of one member state must not be excluded from another unless they can be shown to be damaging to health, safety, the environment or other aspects of the public interest. Thus the Court later found that the German authorities must allow the sale of beer brewed to the specifications of other member states; and the Germans had their revenge when the Italians were obliged to recognize the legitimacy of German pasta.

The Commission saw mutual recognition as an excellent way to bypass the slow, laborious process of seeking agreement on European specifications among the government representatives in the Council, or more precisely among the officials of member states in the myriad of committees that are supposed to prepare the ground for the ministers. The new strategy was to rely as far as possible on mutual recognition to overcome the barrier of differing standards and regulations. The strategy evoked a positive response from member governments that were pursuing a policy of deregulation. The German Economic Advisory Council articulated this view when it recommended that harmonization should be replaced by competition among rules, leaving the consumers to judge which rules they preferred (Joerges, 1988: 222-3). But where health and safety are concerned, the consumer cannot always know whether, say, a new medicine from one of the eleven other member countries can be expected to be safe; and the consumer's personal interest in using, for example, a fuel that damages the environment may differ from that of the public. In such cases, the deregulation implied by mutual recognition has to be replaced by re-regulation at the EC level.

Because the making of detailed EC regulations was such a laborious process, the Commission proposed its 'new approach' to technical regulation, whereby the law enacted by the Council would be short, limited to the objectives such as health and safety that the specifications were intended to attain: the detailed specifications would then be drawn up by approved standards institutes, without the political and procedural problems of securing agreement among the member governments. This method had been used already in 1973 for what became called the Low Voltage Directive (Lauwaars, 1988: 156). Although low-voltage equipment is far from being the hardest case – it is less perilous to poke your finger into low-voltage than into high-voltage equipment – this approach was seen as a speedier and less bureaucratic way of arriving at European specifications; and the enactment of regulations has indeed been speeded up since it was adopted.

In addition to the new strategy and the new approach, which were defined in the Cockfield White Paper, the new voting rules for the Council, laid down in the SEA, have also helped to speed the removal of technical barriers. Unanimous agreement among government representatives is the typical procedure for intergovernmental organizations, whereas majority voting is used in a federal system. The EC treaties provided for majority voting on some occasions and unanimity on others; but for the harmonization of laws, regulations or administrative actions unanimity was stipulated (Art.100, EEC). This procedure gives each member government the chance to block or delay in the hope of getting its way, as was borne out by the experience with harmonization of technical regulations. One of the SEA's important aspects was, therefore, its replacement of unanimity by the majority procedure in a number of cases, particularly relating to the completion of the single market and including harmonization under Article 100.

By these various means, the removal of technical barriers had been accelerated since the 1992 programme was adopted and the SEA passed. The removal of such barriers presents many genuine difficulties (see Joerges, 1988). But they are being overcome and the EC is making substantial progress with this aspect of completing the single market (SEM).

Just as specifications are stipulated for the sale of goods, so there are regulations to control the sale of services. It is hard for an individual to judge whether a bank will be able to repay a deposit in financially difficult times or an insurance company to honour a life insurance policy several decades hence. The likelihood of this depends on criteria of prudent financial management which are the subject of regulations. Thus like the market for goods, the market for services is a growing sector of the economy. In the London area, for example, financial services provide one-fifth of total employment. The cost and efficiency of such services has a big effect on other parts of the economy, moreover; thus the cost of borrowing affects business investment, and trade is impeded if the cost of changing currencies is high. Telecommunications and transport services are likewise vital to the health of the economy. It is not hard to see why a special section of the Cockfield White Paper was devoted to completing the SEM for services.

Public procurement and state aids

Goods and services purchased by the public sector are a substantial part of the EC's economy, about 15 per cent of gross domestic product. The portion that could be bought from other member countries is estimated at 7-10 per cent of GDP; but the amount that is in fact so bought is less than one-fiftieth of this, at only 0.14 per cent of GDP (Cecchini, 1988: 16). Studies have shown that governments, particularly of the larger member countries, often pay as much as a quarter more for a product than they would if they bought from another member country (Commission, 1987: 41). Europeans are, once again, doing themselves a damage through unnecessary fragmentation of their market.

Article 30 EEC stipulates that 'quantitative restrictions on imports and all measures having equivalent effect shall ... be prohibited between Member States'. The innocent reader might suppose that the refusal of a public authority to buy from another EC country would be a measure 'having equivalent effect' to a quota of zero. But the EC's juridical system, despite its impressive record in many respects, does not seem to have tackled this problem. Despite directives requiring publication of calls for tender in the EC's *Official Journal*, only a quarter of the value of contracts in the fields covered had been published in this way (Commission, 1985, para.82). This raises the whole question of the implementation of EC law, which varies widely in its effectiveness from one member country to another and has been hampered by shortages of staff in the Commission which should be bringing more cases to Court (see Weiler, 1988). Nor could the Commission and the courts work effectively without directives covering procedures such as the calls for tender; yet in such important fields as energy, transport, water and telecommunications, such directives still remained to be enacted when the single market programme was devised, over a quarter of a century after the establishment of the Economic Community.

With new vigour being put into completing the SEM, the process of implementing the law should become more effective, at least with respect to standard goods and services where discrimination through buying national is easier to detect. With complex products, however, where qualities that meet particular requirements can be more important than price, discrimination can be very hard to prove; and public authorities may have an enhanced motive for favouring local firms in order to promote their technological development. Here results may come more quickly from changes in industrial structure which make production more multinational, thus giving more member countries an interest in the success of a given supplier. The SEM programme has itself induced much restructuring along such lines; and it has been argued that EC policy could be orientated to promote it more strongly (Toulemon, 1988).

Governments also distort trade in the private sector by giving firms subsidies. These may increase trade by promoting exports which would not otherwise be competitive; but in the EC they have more usually been aimed to protect firms against more competitive imports, including those from other EC countries. The term 'state aids' is used in the EC also to include tax breaks, low-interest loans, cheap public services and other ways of granting firms financial advantages. The sum total of state aids was estimated in the early 1980s as amounting to 2-5 per cent of industrial costs in Germany, 5-10 per cent in France, Italy and the UK, and more than 15 per cent in Belgium (Pelkmans and Winters, 1988: 32-4). While by no means all of this is a support for inefficiency – for example incentives for research can stimulate technological development – much of it has been a barrier to competitive trade and a drag on the EC's dynamism.

Legislation stemming from the EEC Treaty provides an adequate basis for preventing the abuse of state aids; and the Commission had acted energetically to prevent it in such outstanding cases as steel, shipbuilding and textiles. But it is hard for the Commission to be sufficiently effective against the stubborn resistance of governments and their representatives in the Council; and the scope of state aids is so wide that eradication of their abuse is an enormous task. This is one that is not likely to be completed by 1992.

Another huge task on which the Commission has worked effectively is the competition policy, aiming to prevent distortions of competition perpetrated in the private sector. The Commission has, however, convincingly claimed that EC law should be extended to cover control over mergers that would create dominant positions in the EC which become more of a problem as the SEM comes nearer to completion; and the EC seems likely to agree to this.

There has been more difficulty in the field of company law. The project for a European company has been stalled by differences about the role of employees or company boards and advisory councils. This is seen as another impediment to the most efficient exploitation of the EC market; and the Cockfield White Paper listed some other ways in which the legal framework could be improved so as to facilitate cooperation among enterprises as well as to encourage innovation and investment through EC wide protection of intellectual and industrial property (Commission, 1985, paras 133-49).

Capital movement controls

Controls over the movement of capital across frontiers have been a major instrument of macroeconomic policy in many countries. Although some European countries, notably Germany and Britain, had dispensed with them, others such as France and Italy retained them until after the commitment to the free movement of capital by the end of 1992 was enshrined in the SEA.

Such controls impair the efficiency of capital markets as they do for goods and services; but the damage in the case of capital goes deeper because it can affect the whole range of business investment by preventing firms from seeking capital where it can be obtained on the terms that are most favourable for them. Investment and hence economic and technological development are thus impeded.

Capital controls have also stood in the way of other steps towards monetary union. Public authorities in Germany as well as Britain have made liberalization of capital movements a condition of such steps; and conversely, the integration of capital markets can be seen as making the integration of monetary policies, and the institutions and instruments associated with them, more necessary.

The EC's decision in 1988, to free all capital movements between member countries by the middle of 1990, with a delay until 1992 for some member states with special difficulties, was therefore one of the most significant to be taken under the single market programme. The condition set by France, that progress be made first with the harmonization of taxes that affect capital transactions, is a good example of the political, if not technical, linkages between different parts of the programme.

Tax

The Commission has argued that frontier controls cannot be abolished if indirect taxes in the different member countries remain too far apart. The White Paper focused on value-added tax (VAT) and on excise duties levied in particular on tobacco, alcoholic drinks and petrol (Commission, 1987, Part Three). In the light of American experience it concluded that such tax rates could differ from one state to another by not more than 6 per cent. Since most VAT rates in the EC are within a range of 14-20 per cent, often with a range of 4-9 per cent for goods regarded as more essential, such as foodstuffs, the Commission proposed that member states' rates be kept within those bands. The variations among excise rates are much wider and the Commission proposed to align them on an average rate. This would prevent distortions of trade due to differing patterns of tax rates and would minimize the incentive to evade tax by importing across open frontiers from countries with lower rates to those with higher rates.

These proposals met with objections from various angles. The French Prime Minister said that the French government could not afford the loss of revenue from reducing its higher rates of tax on items such as cars. The British government had made an election pledge not to allow any VAT on food and small children's clothes. The excise duty on cigarettes in France and Greece is one-half that in the Netherlands, one-quarter that in Britain and one-sixth of that in Denmark. The British and Danes, who have strong policies for restraining smoking on grounds of health, would hardly accept a cut in the excise so deep as to align on a rate that would be bearable for the French and Greek consumers. Some fear widespread tax evasion even with bands as narrow as 6 per cent. Others object that fiscal sovereignty should not be removed from the member states, or that competition among tax regimes, as among technical regulations, would be the best solution. In a more moderate version of the latter argument, the need to make a maximum as well as a minimum rate obligatory has been convincingly contested.

There are two possible outcomes. One is that harmonization is limited to what member governments find convenient, and enough frontier controls remain, at least for an indeterminate transitional period, to deal with attempts to evade tax by importing from lower-rate to higher-rate countries. The problems that would necessitate such controls are sufficiently limited to allow them to be fairly light. Thus general VAT rates are within the 14-20 per cent band in all member states except Denmark and Ireland, where they are higher, and Luxembourg, with a lower rate. The smuggling of zero-rated British food and children's clothing to the Continent would be inhibited by the transaction costs associated with cross-Channel importing, which could outweigh the difference between a rate of zero and one of the proposed minimum of 4 per cent. In order to reduce the costs and inconvenience of frontier controls, countries such as France and Italy may wish to reduce their higher-than-normal rates on certain products over time. The normal mechanism that discourages evasion of VAT, that each transaction is due to be reported twice, once by the seller and once by the buyer, applies also to cross-frontier transactions. The products subject to excise mostly come from large producers whose consignments can be readily controlled for tax purposes. The frontier controls could be reduced to a residual which might then wither away (see Easson, 1988; and Pelkmans and Winters, 1988: 93-8).

The other outcome is that the abolition of frontiers will be agreed, at least by most member states, because the changes in VAT rates required are limited enough to make this possible, particularly if there are exceptions to general rules of harmonization where transaction costs, or other means of control (such as bonding of goods subject to excise, or licensing of cars), can reduce the dangers of tax evasion or unfair competition to acceptable dimensions. (See also Biehl, 1988, where the merits of the tax union principle as against the destination principle of taxation currently used in the EC are discussed.)

Will the single market be completed by 1992? With what effects?

The Cockfield White Paper outlined a vast programme of legislation and implementation. Much of it should have been done years ago if the commitments of the EEC Treaty had been honoured. There were plenty of sceptics who doubted whether the EC could be made to mend its ways and who therefore thought that the 1992 deadline was a mirage.

By the end of 1988, however, the *Financial Times* published an article entitled 'Irreversible Steps to a New Community' which concluded that the 1992 programme was by then assured of substantial success. With the commitment by member goverments embodied in the SEA and the greater use of majority voting that followed from it, not far short of half the measures listed in the White Paper had been enacted. More important, perhaps, business people have begun to plan on the assumption that the single market is going to happen. The idea of the 1992 programme was strongly backed by many leading firms from the outset. When they and others have restructured themselves and made investments for the single market, they will exert powerful pressure to ensure that the EC does substantially complete it.

This does not mean that every aspect of the Cockfield programme will be completed. Tax harmonization will probably fall short of what he intended. The legislation to open up public purchasing may be enacted, but implementation may still fall far short of creating a single market in the public sector. The same goes for the control of the protection afforded by state aids. But as far as the dynamism of the economy is concerned, it is not perfection that is required, but a critical mass of legislation and implementation such as convinces business people that they must plan and act on the basis of the single market. Here, the removal of technical and regulatory barriers is very important. This has been going well; and the response from business is such as to give grounds for the optimistic title of the article in the *Financial Times*.

When the Commission was still far from confident about the success of the programme, it adopted the idea that a major study of the effects on the economy of completing the SEM would help business and the public to see what advantages would ensue for them, and thus swing opinion round to stronger support. To carry weight, the study had to be good enough to stand up to intelligent criticism; and the result is, indeed, an impressive piece of work, based on twenty-eight special studies of particular problems and sectors, including also a sample survey of 11,000 firms and a macroeconomic model to give a second opinion. The whole is brought together in a detailed two-volume summary report (Commission, 1988) and in a short book written in a more popular style (Cecchini, 1988). The report is commonly known as the Cecchini Report, after the special adviser to the Commission who directed the study.

The Cecchini Report estimated that completing the SEM would bring the EC a gain of around 5 per cent of its gross domestic product over the medium term. Only about one-twentieth of this – although even that amounts to the significant sum of ECU8-9 billion – comes from the removal of 'customs formalities and related delays'. The remainder is divided into three parts. The largest comes from the more direct effects on costs of removing 'barriers to production', that is protective public procurement, divergent standards, regulatory diversity and other restrictions on services and manufacturing. Next are the economies of scale, which would arise quite quickly as higher production brought fuller use of existing capacity, and, more importantly, as new investments are made to take fuller advantage of the potential economies. Then come the gains to efficiency as industrial structures and management methods respond to the more competitive climate (Cecchini, 1988: 83-5). While these estimates include some of the dynamic effects which appear to have been so important a result of the customs union, including economies of scale and the medium-term benefits of greater competition, they do not account for other dynamic effects which are less quantifiable or longer term. Most significant among these would be a faster rate of innovation and new forms of business strategy in response to the wider horizons; being longer term or less quantifiable does not mean being less important. Rapid innovation and intelligent long-term strategies may be the keys to Europeans' economic success in the next century. While parts of the Cecchini estimates are inevitably broad-brush, it is as likely that he has understated rather than overstated the gains that the SEM can bring, by excluding such effects from his forecasts.

The effects on production are not the only ones to be considered. Prices, employment, budgets and the external balance will also be affected, and the Cecchini estimates cover these too. He expects that, while GDP is boosted by some 5 per cent, the single market will cause prices to be around 6 per cent lower than they would otherwise be, employment 1.8 million higher and the budget and external trade balances improved by the equivalent of 2.2 per cent and 1 per cent of GDP respectively (Cecchini, 1988: 98). Given the starting point of high unemployment in the EC, the value of 1.8 million new jobs does not need to be stressed. Cecchini suggests that more expansionary economic policies in the EC could, by accepting a reduction of the downward pressure on prices, raise employment and production considerably more: with a price effect of minus 4.5 per cent instead of minus 6 per cent, he suggests that employment could rise by 5 million and production by 7 per cent (Cecchini, 1988: 101). Monetarists may contest the idea that there is such a trade-off between employment and inflation, except perhaps in the short term. But whatever one's view of this, the single market should bring a reduction of inflationary pressure in the economy as the more open competition begins to bite; and this should enable policies of any brand to be less of a constraint on the EC's economic and technological development. Under any scenario, moreover, EC consumers would gain, with lower prices and wider choice; and taxpayers will gain in so far as public purchasing becomes more economical and efficient.

Beyond the effects on such indicators of welfare as production, employment, prices and tax rates, there are broader implications for the political economy, the polity and the citizen. The citizen is more free if jobs can be obtained in the other EC countries and goods can be bought and sold across the frontiers between member states. A genuinely single common market requires more EC laws and more common economic policies; and this in turn, it will be argued, requires development of the EC institutions to correspond more closely to the norms of governmental efficiency and parliamentary democracy that are expected by the citizens of the member countries. It is on such large questions that the final part of this chapter concentrates.

Why the single market is a step towards European Union

There are two contrasting views of the EC's future. One is that its essential task is to establish the SEM and that any political implications should be confined to the minimum required for this. The other is that the Schuman Plan was rightly seen as the first step towards a European federation and that, even if the process of taking the remaining steps is lasting half a century or more, that is indeed the process in which the EC is engaged. There are of course many views that lie between these two. But the reader should be warned that this author takes the latter view, and sees the completion of the single market as a step towards a European Union, then a federation.

Since the terms 'European Union' and 'federation' are sometimes used loosely, the meanings they are given here will be explained. A 'federation', following the many existing examples of which the most venerable European one is the Swiss, has federal institutions with powers over trade, money, enough tax for its budget, armed forces and external relations. The federal institutions include a legislature comprising a house of the people and a house of the states, an executive which can be called a government, and a federal court. Whereas in international organizations the relationship of the international institutions with the citizens passes through the states, the federal institutions deal direct with the citizens. While in a unitary state the central government exercises all the powers under the constitution, even if it chooses to delegate some to provincial or local authorities, in a federation the member states hold their powers by right under the constitution, and powers are reserved to them except where it can be shown that the larger size and resources of the federation are required to perform the functions effectively.

The essential powers of the European Union, as defined by the EUT, are similar to those of a federation apart from the control over armed forces; and its institutions are similar to federal institutions. The single market is a step towards Union because it gives the EC, when SEA is added to the existing EC treaties, full powers over both internal and external trade. Although the EC already has monetary and budgetary powers, they fall short of those required for a Union; and the EC institutions would likewise have to be reformed in order to be able to exercise their powers effectively and democratically. External policy depends on security as well as economic instruments; but the Union would already have a substantial basis for its external policy if it could add a measure of cooperation in security matters to the full range of its economic powers.

The SEA provided not only for the completion of the SEM but also for the development of EC competences in the monetary, technological, environmental, social, regional and external policy fields, as well as for some reforms of the EC institutions. It was not, it will be argued, by chance that these measures accompanied the single market programme: if the SEM is to become and remain complete and to bring its full benefits to EC citizens, the EC will have to develop along such lines so as to become a European Union.

Monetary union, cohesion, the budget

As the member states integrate their capital markets, they lose autonomy over their monetary and macroeconomic policies. Monetary events in one member country transmit their effects directly into the economies of the other members, making an autonomous policy harder to substain. Hard, but perhaps not impossible, if the member governments retain control of their exchange rates and change them more frequently and sharply than those that participate fully in the European Monetary System have done in recent years. But more fluctuation of exchange rates would replace the old ways of fragmenting the market with a new one. It would dilute the certainty about the terms of access to the EC market that is a mainspring of the expected strengthening of competition, investment and technological development. This points towards the alternative solution: accept that the SEM reduces the separate autonomies of the several member states and gain a common autonomy by making macroeconomic policy together.

This is the connection between the single market and the monetary union that was recognized as an EC objective in the SEA's preamble; and this is why the European Council in June 1988, under German Presidency, set up a special committee, chaired by Commission President Jacques Delors, to propose steps towards monetary union. While various steps are possible, such as promoting the private and public use of the ECU, using the ECU for collective EC intervention in international currency markets, or collaboration in setting member states' monetary targets, the objective of monetary union must imply the establishment, sooner or later, of a European federal bank with the power to issue European money: in fact, the monetary institution and instrument of a European Union.

Monetary integration, like the creation of a single market, raises fears among the economically weaker groups, regions or member states that they will lose out to the stronger. So they tend to demand instruments of economic and social solidarity to accompany the market integration. Thus the Italians obtained the European Investment Bank and the Social Fund in the EEC Treaty and the British the Regional Development Fund soon after their accession. The Greeks for their part got the Integrated Mediterranean Programmes and the Spaniards led the demand for economic and social 'cohesion', which was accepted in principle in the SEA and in practice in the doubling of the 'structural funds' (regional, social, and agricultural guidance funds) by 1992, and was agreed in the budgetary reform decided by the European Council in June 1988.

With monetary union this function of social solidarity, which is a normal expression of citizenship in a federal system, would almost certainly have to be further developed; and this will raise the question of further budgetary reform (see Commission, 1977). The budget is likely to move closer to the size and shape of a Union budget, with more resources and a better articulated redistributive function.

Industrial, social, environmental policies

We have seen that the SEM itself, offering greater scope to the more dynamic firms, is expected to be one of the keys to Europe's future technological development. But the expenditure on research and development by almost all governments, right, left or centre in political orientation, shows that the market alone is not thought to be enough. The resources and risks associated with some of the most important potential developments are greater than a single firm will bear; and the public benefits of much R and D spread far beyond the body that undertakes them, not only for the more basic research but also in the spin-off from much technological development. (See Shonfield, 1981).

State aids to firms to encourage R and D, particularly in the form of favourable tax arrangements, are therefore viewed kindly by the Commission in its function as supervisor of the legitimacy of such aids in the member states. But the EC also has its common research programmes, financed in part from its own budget, in order to facilitate a collective effort by enterprises and governments from the member states, all of which in some ways are hampered because the national economies are so much smaller then those of Japan or the US. The Esprit programme, bringing together the main manufacturers in the EC's information technology sector for joint research and, as a consequence, other forms of cooperation, (de Robien, 1986) is the best example so far. The member governments also initiated the Eureka programme on a purely intergovernmental basis. The SEA gave these various programmes a foundation in the treaties, and at the same time indicated that there is a link between the single market and not only the macroeconomic policies to keep it developing on an even keel, but also the microeconomic policies designed to deal with particular industrial problems which will, increasingly, have a European dimension on the scale of the SEM itself. The same goes for the dimensions of environmental controls. Car exhausts are seen as killers of trees and dangerous for people's lungs. Standards for petrol and car exhaust equipment have to take account of that fact. Smoke from power stations and chemical emissions in the Rhine do not respect frontiers, so member states' standards for regulating them have to allow for other members' needs. The SEA commits the EC to high standards of health, safety, environmental and consumer protection when it is harmonizing laws and regulations (Art. 100A.3 SEA).

The EC is committed to go far in its common measures for environmental protection, partly because, as in the case of car exhausts, it has to have a common standard in order to complete the single market for road vehicles, and partly because the member states feel a degree of political solidarity that requires them to deal with such common problems together. But environmental threats do not respect the Community's external frontiers any more than the internal ones. Swiss as well as French chemicals pollute the Rhine that flows through the Netherlands. British power stations emit acid into the clouds that drop rain over Norway even more than over EC members. Radiation from Chernobyl hit Cumberland and Bavaria as well as the Soviet Union. The EC is as responsible as others for the damage to the ozone layer and will suffer with them as a result. In short, EC policies must take account of its neighbours and of the world as a whole as well as of itself. Having developed a collective capacity to act in this field, thanks in fair measure to the requirements of completing the single market, it needs to use its collective weight to help with environmental protection in the rest of Europe and the world: to act, indeed, as a good world citizen. The SEA also requires high standards of health and safety at work and the improvement of the working environment (Art. 100A.4, 118A SEA). The link between this and the SEM is similar to that of the cohesion policy, seen through the other end of the telescope. Whereas the cohesion policy reflects the concern of the industrially less-developed member countries that their industries may be flattened by the more-advanced, the worries about the working environment reflect the fears of workers in the more-advanced countries that their standards will be undermined by the competition from countries where working conditions are more primitive: fears of what has become known as 'social dumping'. It is significant that, although in the spring of 1988 58 per cent of manual workers in the EC as a whole expected that the SEM would bring them advantages in the job market, only 41 per cent of manual workers in FRG thought the same (*Eurobarometer*, 1988). Public opinion in West Germany could turn against the SEM if workers with such worries are not reassured that their working conditions will not deteriorate. Such are the hard, practical considerations that link these aspects of social policy with the single market, even before weight is given to the requirements of solidarity among EC citizens.

Positive integration and EC institutions

Many of these implications of the single market can be explained by the concept of positive integration (Pinder, 1968). Negative integration can be defined as the removal of barriers or other distortions in transactions among economic agents in the member states. This gives many economic and social problems a Community dimension, at the same time depriving the member states of some of the policy instruments with which they hitherto tried to deal with them. Hence the need for positive integration, bringing common institutions and instruments to make laws and policies to meet objectives beyond that of an undistorted single market.

There is not a simple dichotomy between positive and negative integration. When the EC determines a standard for car exhausts, it is both removing the distortion whereby the differing standards previously fragmented the market, and taking a view as to the sort of environment it wants to have and the amount it is prepared to pay for it: such objectives go way beyond the simple need for an undistorted market. When the EC establishes a monetary union, it is both removing the distortion of variable exchange rates and providing itself with the instruments for a common macroeconomic policy which also implies objectives beyond that of removing distortion. While the distinction between positive and negative integration should not be pressed too far, it is useful in helping to show why the SEM brings the need for other common objectives and policies in its train.

The SEM requires, at the very least, institutions that will apply the rule of law to the regulation of the market: the vast programme of EC legislation outlined by the White Paper and the activity of Commission and courts to ensure that it is implemented. The view presented here, however, is that this minimum is not enough: that the EC's powers in the field of trade need to be supplemented by the powers to create a monetary union and to have a budget of correspondingly greater importance, with adequate policies for technological development, social solidarity and cohesion and environmental protection; and that the existing EC institutions need to be reformed so as to be sufficiently efficient and democratic to carry these responsibilities. In short, if the SEM is to succeed it must be accompanied by other steps to create the European Union.

Towards a European Union in a uniting world?

When the founder members of the EC decided to establish the customs union, many people outside it, particularly in Britain, saw it as an inward-looking, protectionist bloc. Yet thanks partly to the initiative of the US under President Kennedy and partly to the Community's liberal response, the customs union presaged instead a series of international trade negotiations through which the tariffs of advanced industrial countries were cut by half. Now that the EC is creating a single market, outsiders have expressed a similar fear again, this time using the slogan of 'fortress Europe'.

Since non-tariff barriers are the typical contemporary instruments of protection, such critics claim that when the EC decides on common standards or technical regulations, or on common rules for public purchasing, these are likely to be protectionist. They point to the EC's record in agriculture and in imposing 'voluntary export restrictions' on Japan and NICs.

But it seems too pessimistic to assume that a Community which has embarked on a great programme of internal liberalization will apply the opposite philosophy in its relations with other countries. On the contrary, a Community that was stagnating because of internal protection would be more likely to protect against outside suppliers than one that is dynamic thanks to internal liberalization. The EC is a greater exporter than importer of manufactures and services and its interests would not be served by a move towards autarky in the international economy.

The idea that the EC could be a catalyst for growing interdependence and integration in the international economy is more interesting and no less realistic.

This is, after all, what followed on the creation of the customs union. The same could happen if the EC's new experience in removing non-tariff barriers were used as an example for wider international movement in that direction; and if the EC succeeds in creating a monetary union, this should be followed by a better balanced international monetary system, just as the EC's customs union was followed by a better balance in the trading system, hitherto dominated by the US.

If a healthy and open world economy is in the interests of the EC, a stable international political framework is yet more so. This is not only a condition for a stable and open international economy, but also for the security that is so vital for the people of the Community, concentrated as they are at one small end of Eurasia. The European Union would not be complete without cooperation in the security as well as the economic elements of external relations. The SEA moved in this direction by giving a treaty basis for cooperation among the member states in foreign policy and in the political and economic aspects of security (Art. 30.6a SEA).

The single market programme and the SEA have thus not only given the EC an impulse towards monetary union, social solidarity, foreign policy and security cooperation, budgetary and institutional reform, but also an impulse towards the European Union, which many see as the prime political project for the present stage of the EC's development (see Lodge, 1986; Pryce, 1987). The EC also has the chance, if it moves in this direction, to become a powerful agent for unifying the increasingly interdependent world. None of this is easy, let alone assured. Positive integration may prove to be beyond the present political capacity of Europe, let alone the world. Even negative integration may be too hard, although the EC has already made much progress with it. But this writer's view is that a European Union in a uniting world is desirable; it is possible; and the Community's single market can be seen as an important step towards it.

References

Albert, M. and Ball, R. J. (1983), *Towards European Recovery in the 1980s, Working Documents 1983-84*, Luxembourg, European Parliament.

Bieber, Roland, Dehousse, Renaud, Pinder, John, Weiler, Joseph H. H. (eds) (1988), *1992: One European Market?*, Baden-Baden, Nomos.

Biehl, Dieter (1988), 'On maximal versus optimal tax harmonization' in Bieber *et al*. ibid.

Buchan, David (1988), 'Irreversible steps to a new Community', *Financial Times*, 30 December.

Cecchini, Paolo with Michel Catinat and Alexis Jacquemin (1988), *The European Challenge: 1992: The Benefits of a Single Market*, Aldershot, Wildwood House.

Commission of the EC (1977), *Report of the Study Group on the Role of Public Finance in European Integration* (the MacDougall report), Brussels.

Commission of the EC (1985), *Completing the Internal Market: White Paper from the Commission to the European Council* (the Cockfield White Paper), Luxembourg.

Commission of the EC (1986), *Single European Act*, Luxembourg.

Commission of the EC (1987), *Efficiency, Stability and Equity* (the Padoa–Schioppa report), Brussels.

Commission of the EC (1988), *The economics of 1992: An Assessment of the Potential Economic Effects of Completing the Internal Market of the European Community, Vol. One: Basic Studies: Executive Summaries, Vol. Two: Studies on the economics of integration* (the Cecchini report), Luxembourg.

Easson, Alex J. (1988), 'The elimination of fiscal frontiers', in Bieber *et al.*, *op. cit.*
Eurobarometer (1988), No.29, June.
Joerges, Christian (1988), 'The new approach to technical harmonization and the interests of consumers: reflections on the requirements and difficulties of a Europeanization of product safety policy in Bieber *et al.*, *op. cit.*
Lauwaars, Richard H. (1988), 'The "Model Directive" on technical harmonization' in Bieber *et al.*, *op. cit.*
Lodge, Juliet (ed.) (1986), *European Union: the European Community in Search of a Future*, London, Macmillan.
Pelkmans, Jacques (1984), *Market Integration in the European Community*, The Hague, Martinus Nijhoff.
Pelkmans, Jacques (1986), *Completing the Internal Market for Industrial Products*, Luxembourg, Commission of the EC.
Pelkmans, Jacques and Winters, Alan (1988), *Europe's Domestic Market*, Chatham House Papers 43, London, Routledge.
Pinder, John (1968), 'Positive integration and negative integration: some problems of economic union in the EEC', *The World Today*, **24**, 88-110. Reprinted in G. R. Denton (ed.), (1969), *Economic Integration in Europe*, London, Weidenfeld and Nicolson. Michael Hodges (ed.) (1972), *European Integration*, Harmondsworth, Penguin.
Pinder, John (1988), 'Enhancing the Community's economic and political capacity: some consequences of completing the common market', in Bieber *et al.*, *op. cit.*
Pryce, Roy (ed.), (1987), *The Dynamics of European Union*, London, Croom Helm.
Robien, Emmanuel de (1986), 'The role of European industry in European standardization' in Rita Beuter and Jacques Pelkmans, *Cementing the Internal Market*, Maastricht, European Institute of Public Administration.
Servan-Schreiber, Jean-Jacques (1967), *Le défi américain*, Paris, Denoël.
Shonfield, Andrew (1981), 'Innovation: does government have a role?' in Charles Carter (ed.), *Industrial Policy and Innovation*, London, Heinemann Educational Books.
Toulemon, Robert (1988), 'Achievement of the single market in information technology' in Bieber *et al.*, *op. cit.*
Sunstein, Cass R. (1988), 'Protectionism, the American Supreme Court, and integrated markets' in Bieber *et al.*, *op. cit.*
VerLoren van Themaat, Pieter (1988), 'The contributions to the establishment of the internal market by the case-law of the Court of Justice of the European Communities' in Bieber *et al.*, *op. cit.*
Weiler, Joseph H. H. (1988), 'The White Paper and the application of Community law', in Bieber *et al.*, *op. cit.*

6 Free Movement of Goods, Workers, Services and Capital

Scott Davidson

Article 2 of the Rome Treaty lays down the objectives of the EEC. These are the promotion of a harmonious development of economic activities, a continuous and balanced expansion, an increase in stability, an accelerated raising of the standard of living and closer relations between the member states. Although these objectives are primarily economic, the phrase 'closer relations between the member states' hints at the political aspirations implicit in the Treaty (Spaak Report, 1956). To achieve these objectives, Article 3 provides the EC with two mechanisms: the establishment of a common market and the approximation of the economic policies of the member states. The first requires the abolition of all public barriers to the free movement of all factors of production and is sometimes referred to as 'negative integration'. The second mechanism, which requires a rather more creative dimension in coordinating the economies of the member states, is referred to as 'positive integration (Mathijsen, 1985: 108). Although the original Treaty did not contain a definition of what constituted a common market, this has been remedied by the Jursiprudence of the ECJ[1] and the SEA – an amendment to the Treaty. Article 8A of the amended Treaty provides that 'the internal market shall comprise an area without internal frontiers in which the free movement of goods, persons, services and capital is ensured in accordance with the provisions of this Treaty'. It is clear from the context of this provision that the concept of the internal market is synonymous with the common market.

Free movement of goods

Free movement of goods in the EC is ensured by the establishment of a customs union (Articles 9-29), the elimination of discriminatory internal taxation (Articles 15-99) and the elimination of quantitative restrictions and measures having equivalent effect (Articles 30-6).

The customs union

The significance of the customs union in the scheme of the Treaty is apparent by virtue of its location at the head of Part Two entitled 'Foundations of the Community'. Indeed, Article 9 provides that 'the Community *shall be based on a customs union*' (Emphasis added). The customs union is to cover all trade in goods and requires the prohibition between member states of customs duties on imports and exports and of all charges having an equivalent effect, and the adoption of a common customs tariff in relations with third countries. It is the latter which differentiates a customs union from a free trade area which has no common policy as regards goods originating outside the area. (GATT, Article 24; Wyatt and Dashwood, 1987: 13; Swann, 1978).

The term 'goods' is not defined in the Treaty, but the ECJ in the First Art Treasures case (Case 7/68) defined them as 'products which can be valued in money and which are capable as such, of forming the subject of commercial transactions'. Clearly raw materials, manufactured products and agricultural products are 'goods', but this term has also been held to apply to pornographic literature, gold coins which are not legal tender and even rubber dolls (Cases 34/79; 7/78; 121/85). It matters not where the goods originate since the provisions cover goods originating both within and outside the member states (Reg. 802/68; Forrester, 1980). In the case of the latter, however, the goods must be in free circulation, that is all customs formalities must have been complied with.

The customs union for the original Six was to have been completed within twelve years from the entry into force of the Treaty but was achieved within ten (that is by 1968). The extension of the customs union to the first, second and third accession states has been accompanied by transitional periods of lesser duration. It is envisaged that the completion of the customs union involving the Iberian states will be achieved by 1 January 1993.

The completion of the customs union was achieved by two means: a 'standstill' on all customs duties on imports and exports and the gradual elimination of customs duties and charges having equivalent effect. The standstill provision, Article 12, which prohibits the introduction of any new customs duties on goods was held to be directly effective by the ECJ in the landmark case of Van Gend en Loos (Case 26/62). Although the provision was contained in a treaty which normally only creates rights and duties for the states' parties, the ECJ decided that it also created rights and duties for individuals and that they might therefore rely upon it before their national courts. (Freestone and Davidson, 1988: 28; Hartley, 1988: 183). The device of direct effect therefore enabled individuals to exercise an effective policing role in detecting breaches of the Treaty. Note that the Treaty refers not simply to the elimination of customs duties, but also to 'charges having equivalent effect'. The reason for this is that if member states were able to introduce charges which were customs duties in substance though not in name, they would be able, either wittingly or unwittingly, to undermine the customs union. The most common form of charges having equivalent effect which have been levied by member states have been charges levied for a variety of services, for example veterinary and phytosanitary inspections, and quality control. In the Statistical Levy case (Case 24/68) the ECJ held that very small charges levied by the Italian government for the purposes of collecting trade information constituted charges having equivalent effect, and defined such charges as 'any pecuniary charge, however small and whatever its designation and mode of application, which is imposed unilaterally on domestic or foreign goods by reason of the fact that they cross a frontier, and which is not a customs duty in the strict sense'.

It is apparent from the ECJ's jurisprudence that it attaches supreme importance to the customs union and it has been rigorous in proscribing any member state activity which tends to jeopardize its attainment. It is abundantly clear from the case law that the ECJ will not be diverted by claims that a particular charge is non-protective in effect or that it was not intended to infringe the Treaty provisions (Case 283/69). The ECJ has, however, entertained the notion that certain charges may be justifiable if they are *bona fide* charges for services rendered. Here, such charges must confer a precise benefit upon an individual trader, they must represent the actual consideration for the service levied and they may only be levied in exceptional circumstances (Cases 46/76; 39/73; 63/74; 132/82).

The creation of the customs union was accompanied by the formation of the Common Customs Tariff (CCT) which, in effect, establishes a trade barrier between the EC and the rest of the world. The CCT was also introduced over a transitional period, and it establishes the duties to be paid entering the EC from third countries. Because of the introduction of the CCT, member states no longer have the competence either to determine customs duties nor to interpret their effect; this is entirely a matter of EC competence (Case 38/75). The duties collected under the CCT are an important part of the EC's 'own resources'.

Discriminatory internal taxation – Article 95

The free movement of goods throughout the EC may not only be hindered by customs duties and charges having equivalent effect, but also by the unequal application of internal tax systems. For example, a purchase tax applied at a higher rate to foreign goods increases their price *vis-à-vis* domestic goods and is likely to make them less competitive in the domestic market (Swann, 1978, 123-9; Swann, 1983, 58-65). Protectionism of this kind can reflect deeply entrenched traditional local markets (for example in alcoholic beverages) which member states may be unwilling to dismantle. Thus the provisions of the Treaty dealing with internal taxation of a discriminatory nature are the natural complement to those establishing the customs union.

Article 95 of the Treaty prohibits the imposition of any direct or indirect tax on products of another member state which is in excess of that which is levied upon similar domestic products. It also prohibits discriminatory taxation on the products of other member states where it is of such a nature as to afford indirect protection to other products. These are clearly two different but interrelated situations. The notion of similarity has been defined by the ECJ as existing when the goods in question fall within the same tariff classification or where consumers view the products as affording the same possibilities of utilization (Cases 27/67; 45/75; Wyatt and Dashwood, 1987: 112-15). The notion of indirect protection of other products is rather more difficult since a precise point of reference for determining the competitive relationship of the products may be difficult to identify. Nevertheless, from ECJ case law it appears that where the products in question do not exhibit the criteria of similarity in Article 95(i) but may still be regarded as being in competition, indirect protection will occur if there is evidence of a protective effect (Cases 169/78; 171/78). The ECJ has made it clear, however, that the economic relationship between such products must be enduring and not merely fortuitous (Case 27/67).

As long as member states conform to the requirements of Article 95 they are free to choose their own systems of internal taxation. Inevitably, however, differences in fiscal rates between member states produce lingering trade barriers because, for example, it is necessary for imported goods to be subject to various kinds of turnover equalization taxes and exported goods to have part of their VAT reimbursed. The delays associated with the administration of fiscal disparities and customs formalities have been estimated by the Commission at 112 billion ECUs and represent one of the major remaining barriers to trade in the EC (EC Commission, 1987).

The Cockfield Plan envisages the harmonization of all member states' turnover taxes by 1992 in line with the deadline set for the completion of the internal market. It remains to be seen whether this ambitious plan will be able to overcome the political hostility of some member states such as the United Kingdom.

Quantitative restrictions – Articles 30-6

Quantitative restrictions are among a state's traditional weapons for protecting its domestic market. They usually take the form of quotas the effect of which is to predetermine the number value or quantity of foreign goods entering the domestic market. The Treaty not only provides for the abolition of quantitative restrictions but also measures having equivalent effect. Whereas quantitative restrictions are reasonably easy to identify, measures having equivalent effect can be rather more difficult. Directive 70/50 contains a number of measures both discriminatory and non-discriminatory which are prohibited. These include laying down conditions as to pricing, subjecting imported products to conditions in respect of shape, size, weight, composition, presentation, identification or putting up and subjecting imported and domestic products to similar conditions, but which make the former more difficult to import. Directive 70/50 has, however, largely been superseded by the direct effect of Article 30 which has been held to embrace both discriminatory and non-discriminatory measures (Oliver, 1982).

In the Dassonville case (Case 8/74), which involved Belgian criminal law concerning the requirement of the certification of origin of spirits, the ECJ defined measures having equivalent effect as: 'All trading rules enacted by member states which are capable of hindering directly or indirectly, actually or potentially intra-Community trade'. It is clear from this wide formulation that intra-EC trade need not necessarily be affected; it is sufficient that potential hindrance exists. At one stage it was thought that discrimination was a necessary element for the existence of a measure having equivalent effect within the meaning of Article 30. However, the landmark case of Cassis de Dijon[2] made clear that discrimination was not required. This case resulted from a German law prohibiting the import of liquors having an alcohol content of less than 25 per cent. The plaintiff in this case wished to import Cassis, a French blackcurrant liqueur, which has an alcohol content of some 15-20 per cent. He was not permitted to do so. The ECJ recognized that in the absence of common rules regulating the organization of the market in alcohol, such competence still resided in individual member states, but it went on to say,

obstacles to [free movement of goods] within the Community resulting from disparities between the national laws must be accepted in so far as those provisions may be recognised as being necessary in order to satisfy mandatory requirements relating in particular to the effectiveness of fiscal supervision, the protection of public health, the fairness of commercial transactions and the defence of the consumer.

The net effect of the decision in Cassis de Dijon has been to make clear that minor differences in technical and similar standards within the member states may not be used to justify the hindrance of intra-EC trade, unless such requirements are objectively necessary (from the ECJ's viewpoint) to protect certain fundamental requirements relating to the welfare of individuals within the member state. In Cassis for example, the FRG argued that the need to state a minimum alcohol level in liquor was necessary in order to protect public health because low-strength liquors had a rather more insidious effect on consumers which might lead to alcoholism. The ECJ rejected this reasoning arguing somewhat pragmatically that spiritous liquors were, in most cases, drunk in diluted form anyway!

Following the Cassis judgment the Commission issued Communication 256/2 in which it stated its view that a product lawfully produced and marketed in one member state must, in principle, be admitted to another member state (Gormley, 1981). This position has been criticized in some quarters on the grounds that it reduces product standards to the lowest common denominator. Others, however, have welcomed the decision on the grounds that it now opens the markets of EC member states to the local specialities of other member states. Certainly, the Commission was obliged to rethink its position on harmonizing technical and product standards after Cassis. However, disparate technical standards throughout the EC member states constitute, together with differential fiscal standards, one of the most persistent barriers to the completion of the internal market. Nevertheless, the SEA has given new impetus to the legislative programme for harmonizing such standards in accordance with the programme enunciated in the Commission's White Paper of 1985. With the SEA's entry into force a new timetable has been introduced for the completion of the internal market by 1992 which involves an accelerated legislative programme. Within this programme the Commission is to report to the Council in 1990 and 1992 on the progress which has been made towards achieving the internal market (Article 8A). The introduction of these new dates for the completion of the internal market has not been universally welcomed (Pescatore, 1986).

Derogation from the free movement of goods – Article 36

Member states may derogate from the free movement of goods' provisions on the grounds of 'public morality, public policy or public security; the protection of health and life of humans, animals or plants; the protection of national treasures possessing artistic, historic or archaeological value; or the protection of industrial and commercial property'. Such derogation must not, however, constitute a 'means of arbitrary discrimination or disguised restriction on trade between member states'. Since Article 36 is an exception to the general rule of free movement, it has been interpreted strictly by the ECJ (Case 95/81). Although member states quite clearly retain the right to make an initial determination of what constitutes a threat to public policy, the ECJ has ruled that it is the final arbiter of what is objectively acceptable by way of derogation. Although there have been a number of justifiable derogations, in order to control the import of pornography for example, there have also been a number of unacceptable measures such as over-rigorous inspections or import bans which have proved to be no more than disguised protectionism (Case 40/82).

Particular tensions exist between the completion of the internal market and justifiable derogations to protect industrial and commercial property rights under Article 36. Industrial and commercial property rights are also known generically as intellectual property and include copyrights, patents and trademarks. Inevitably such rights confer territorial protection and therefore have a tendency to partition the internal market along national lines and thus restrict the free movement of goods. Furthermore, Article 222 of the Treaty declares 'this Treaty shall in no way prejudice the rules in member states governing the system of property ownership'. The ECJ has therefore gone to some length in an attempt to resolve the conflict between the two apparently irreconcilable objectives of property protection and the maintenance of the internal market. It has done so by drawing a distinction between the existence of nationally conferred intellectual property rights and their exercise. Whereas the grant of property rights remains unaffected by EC law, their exercise may be so affected if they interfere with the free movement of goods (Mann, 1975: 31-43; Jacobs, 1975: 643-58). Thus once the property rights are, in the terms of the ECJ 'exhausted', that is once they have fulfilled their basic objective of protecting the creativity of the inventor or proprietor and the goods are put into free circulation in the market, they are subject to EC rules on free movement.

The conflict between the protection of intellectual property rights and the internal market clearly calls for a European resolution of the problem. Patent rights are now dealt with by an overlapping system of conventions. The Convention for the European Patent for the Common Market 1975 (the Luxembourg Convention) (OJ L17/1 1976) creates for the EC a single patent within the wider framework of the Convention on the Grant of European Patents 1974 (the Munich Convention) (International Legal Materials) which creates a European patent for a wider number of states. The conventions have developed a unified system for granting, contesting and protecting patent rights within Europe, and these tasks are performed by the European Patent Office in Munich. The Common Market Patent is administered by a special section of the Patent Office in the Hague and is subject to the jurisdiction of the courts of the member states which can make reference to the ECJ for an interpretation of the Luxembourg Convention. National patent laws, however, still coexist with the European system so disputes concerning the protection afforded by patents granted under domestic law are still likely to arise.

Trademarks, that is rights in specific product names or distinctive features (for example the shape of bottles) are not yet subject to European control. In 1980, the Commission published two proposals for EC trademarks (OJ C 351/1, 1980; OJ C 351/5, 1980), but nothing has come of these yet (Gormley, 1981: 464).

The regulation of competition – Articles 85-90

The drafters of the Rome Treaty recognized that in order to maintain a single market it was not enough to dismantle public trade barriers since powerful private enterprises could also create restrictions on the free movement of goods. Hence Article 3(f) of the Treaty requires the implementation of a system 'ensuring that competition in the common market is not distorted'. The relevant substantive provisions here are Article 85 which prohibits a wide range of collusive anticompetitive activities between undertakings and Article 86 which forbids the abuse of a dominant position. It should be noted, however, that the competition rules are not concerned solely with the prohibition of certain anticompetitive practices, they are also concerned with the promotion of effective competition with all the benefits which are assumed to flow from this (Van Gerven, 1974). As the Commission stated in its *First Report on Competition Policy*:

Competition is the best stimulant of economic activity since it guarantees the widest possible freedom of action to all. An active competition policy pursued in accordance with the provisions of the Treaties establishing the Communities makes it easier for the supply and demand structures continually to adjust to technological development. Through the interplay of decentralised decision making machinery, competition enables enterprises continuously to improve their efficiency which is the sine qua non for a steady improvement in living standards and employment prospects within the Community. From this point of view, competition policy is an essential means for satisfying to a great extent the individual and collective needs of our society. [p.11]

As a statement of politico-economic ideology nothing could be clearer: competition in a free-market economy is simply the best way to achieve the objectives of the EC.

The Commission is charged with the task of enforcing the EC's competition policy (Kerse, 1981; Korah, 1986) and its role has been described as 'a federal agency operating directly within the territory of the member states and having exclusive competence' (Jacobs, 1980: 205). Council Regulation 17/62 gives the Commission extensive powers in the area of competition which it uses not simply in individual cases, but also to develop an effective system of competition as required by Article 3(f). The Commission is empowered to investigate cases on its own initiative or following a complaint by individuals or undertakings (Article 3, Regulation 17/62). Investigations are inquisitorial with the Commission engaging in a fact-finding mission to determine whether a breach of the competition provisions has occurred. It can visit an undertaking's premises and inspect documents (Article 14, Regulation 17/62). Should an undertaking be unwilling to comply with the Commission's requests the latter may impose fines ranging from 100-1,000 ECUs per day, as well as drawing the appropriate inferences from the non-compliance (Article 16, Regulation 17/62). If a violation of the EC's competition rules is discovered by the Commission it may impose fines upon an undertaking of up to one million ECUs or 10 per cent of a group's undertakings (Article 15, Regulation 17/62). Undertakings may, however, seek review of such a decision by recourse to the ECJ under Article 173. The Commission also has an implied power to grant interim relief under Article 3, Regulation 17/62 prior to making a final decision in a case (Case 792/79). Such measures, which are similar to domestic law injunctions or interdicts, may be taken where an undertaking is likely to suffer irreparable harm because of the anticompetitive activities of other undertakings. However, as the Commission has indicated, it is not the best body for securing interim protection because its procedures and ability to police infractions are inadequate. In the Commission's view the most effective forum for securing the protection of such rights is the courts of the member states where plaintives may rely upon the direct effect of Articles 85 and 86 (Davidson, 1983: 353).

The Commission has also claimed that it possesses the power to apply the EC's competition provisions extraterritorially much in the same way as the United States claims extraterritoriality for its antitrust rules. In several cases it has imposed fines on undertakings which, although not registered in the EC, have engaged in anticompetitive conduct the effects of which have been felt in the EC (Cases 48, 49, 51-57/69). It is arguable whether the ECJ has unequivocally accepted this 'effects' doctrine. Certain writers suggest that the doctrine is now firmly established whereas others consider that the ECJ has not gone this far and has preferred to find that anticompetitive behaviour in the common market has been produced by foreign undertakings acting through their wholly-owned subsidiaries (see Lasok, 1980: 183 and Jacobs, 1980).

It will be seen from this brief explanation of the Commission's powers and procedures that it undertakes a variety of functions: it is a policymaker, investigator, prosecutor and adjudicator. Whether it is able to fulfil all these roles effectively is arguable. Some commentators feel that the inquisitorial powers of the Commission need to be strengthened, while others question whether it can simultaneously develop a coherent competition policy as well as make decisions in individual cases.

As indicated above, Articles 85 and 86 prohibit certain types of anticompetitive behaviour. Article 85 prohibits collusive behaviour, whereas Article 86 deals with abusive monopolistic or oligopolistic behaviour. As the ECJ has indicated, these articles are not mutually exclusive; they operate on different levels, but have the same end – the maintenance of effective competition in the common market (Case 6/72).

Article 85(1) catches a variety of anticompetitive practices. It prohibits formal and informal agreements between undertakings, agreements between associations of undertakings and concerted practices which affect trade between member states. Agreements are reasonably easy to identify, but collusive activities falling short of agreements but which nevertheless have a deleterious effect on the internal market may be rather more difficult to discern. These latter are known as 'concerted practices' and have been defined by the ECJ as 'a form of coordination between undertakings which, without having reached the stage where an agreement properly so called has been concluded, knowingly substitutes practical cooperation between them for the risks of competition'. An example of a concerted practice is the Dyestuffs case where the ECJ found that the major producers of aniline dyes in the EEC by raising their prices by almost identical amounts on similar dates had, without an agreement having been concluded, acted in concert and hence in breach of Article 85(1).

Although agreements may technically infringe Article 85(1), the Treaty provides by Article 85(3) that agreements which fulfil certain criteria may be exempted from the rigours of its application. Article 85(3) requires that potentially infringing agreements must (1) contribute to improving the production or distribution of goods or (2) promote technical or economic progress while (3) allowing consumers a fair share of the resulting benefits. The agreements must not impose on the undertakings concerned restrictions which are not indispensable to the attainment of the aforementioned objectives or afford such undertakings the possibility of eliminating competition in respect of a substantial part of the products in question. Agreements may only be exempted if they are notified to the Commission, and notification provides immunity from fines (Article 4, Regulation 17/62). When the Commission found that it was receiving a vast number of notifications which it was unable to deal with within a reasonable time, it resorted to the use of administrative letters or 'comfort letters' by which it informed the notifying undertaking that it could see no reason to proceed to a decision and that it was therefore closing the file. Although this has undoubtedly expedited the Commission's decision-making, comfort letters do appear to lack the legal security which attaches to a decision (Korah, 1986: 37-39). The Commission has also adopted a number of bloc exemptions whereby an agreement falling within the terms of the bloc exemption is automatically exempted without the need to notify the Commission. This practice has served further to reduce the administrative burden.

Article 86 makes abuse of a dominant position illegal. It is not the existence of a dominant position but its abuse which is forbidden. Dominance is an indication that an undertaking has been a successful competitor and it is arguable that success should only be penalized when it becomes prejudicial to the maintenance of effective competition and the single market. As Judge Learned Hand said in the context of American antitrust law: 'The successful competitor having been urged to compete must not be turned upon when he wins'. In EC law, undertakings are said to be in a dominant position 'when they have the power to behave independently, which puts them in a position to act without taking into account their competitors, purchasers or suppliers' (Case 6/72).

Once a dominant position is achieved, abusive behaviour can be varied; a non-exhaustive list of examples of abuse is contained in Article 86. These include monopoly pricing (General Motors) (Case 26/75); differential pricing and excessive profit taking (United Brands) (Case 27/76); refusal to supply (Commercial Solvents) (Cases 6 & 7/73) and, in one bold decision, corporate mergers (Continental Can) (Case 6/72).

Although there has been some criticism of the way in which the EC's competition policy has been implemented (Korah, 1986: 145; Hornsby, 1987), it nevertheless remains one of the most important foundations of the internal market.

Free movement of workers

The provisions governing the free movement of persons are to be found in Part II Title III of the Treaty and as such fall under the heading of 'Foundations of the Community'. Like free movement of goods, the free movement of persons is one of the means set out in Article 3 by which the EC's objectives are to be attained. A strictly literal interpretation of these provisions might lead one to believe that the underlying rationale for the free movement of person was predominantly economic. However, the ECJ in interpreting the relevant provisions has consistently endowed them with rather more human concerns.

Although the economic considerations may originally have inspired the provisions on the free movement of workers, it is clear that these provisions now find a justification in the objective expressed in the preamble [of the Rome Treaty], of creating even closer relations between the people of the member states. [Parry and Dinnage, 1980, p.244].

Furthermore, paragraph 4 of Council Regulation 1612/68 (OJ 1968, L257/2) on free movement of workers within the EC states that such movement 'constitutes a fundamental right of workers and their families', thus making it abundantly clear that the EC is directly concerned with the human dimensions of this particular factor of production.

The legal basis for the free movement of workers is to be found in Article 48 of the Treaty which secures the right of workers to move freely throughout the member states to accept offers of employment actually made, to reside in the member state where he is employed and to remain in that territory after his employment has ceased. These rights do not, however, apply to employment in the public service (Article 48(4)), and a member state may also at its discretion limit their exercise on grounds of public policy, public security or public health(Article 48(3)). Article 48 also requires 'the abolition of discrimination based on the grounds of nationality as regards employment, remuneration and other conditions of work and employment'. The precise ambit of Article 48 was discussed in the Code Maritime case (Case 167/73) where the ECJ held it to be directly effective in the sense discussed above.

The framework established by Article 48 has been implemented by a number of EC legislative measures which deal in detail with the rights of a worker and his family to enter, reside in and to continue to reside in the state of the worker's employment after it has ceased. The legislation also deals with equality of treatment in employment and the tax and other social advantages which flow from the employment relationship, together with the circumstances in which a migrant worker may be refused entry or continued residence in another member state.

Of these provisions Directive 68/360 (OJ 1968, L257/15) deals with the abolition of restrictions on the free movement and residence of workers and their families within the member states. Member states are to grant their nationals the right to leave their territory in order to take up activities as employed persons (Article 2(1)) and other member states must allow such persons entry to their territory upon production of a valid identity card or passport and letter of engagement from an employer (Article 3(1)). Several issues arise from an examination of Directive 68/360. First, who is a 'worker' for the purposes of the Treaty and Directive? There is no definition of the term to be found in either of these instruments. Second, is a seeker after work a 'worker'? The relevant instruments are silent here also. Third, which members of a worker's family will be entitled to accompany him to his place of work?

Turning to the first question, the ECJ has made it clear that the term 'worker' in the Treaty and its implementing instruments may be defined solely by reference to EC law (Cases 75/63; 53/81; 139/85; 66/85). Although the Court has not given a full definition of the term, it has, in Levin (Case 53/81), described certain of its characteristics. First, it is clear that there must be a relationship of employment. Second, it matters not whether that employment is full time or part time, as long as it is real and effective and not simply marginal or ancillary. Hence, as in the English case of R. v. Secchi (1975, 1 CMLR 383), a squatter who did occasional work washing-up in restaurants would not qualify as a worker. Third, a worker's status is not affected by a level of remuneration lower than that demanded by a member state's statutory minimum, presumably as long as they do not become a drain on the state. And, finally, a worker's intention in taking up employment in a particular member state is irrelevant for the determination of his or her status.

As regards the second question, there is no explicit provision in EC law giving an individual the right to move throughout the EC to look for work. There are, however, a number of indirect indicators which signify that individuals may do so. First, when the Council drafted Directive 68/360 it was agreed that individuals should be able to look for employment for a period of three months. As Hartley argues, reliance on this is hardly satisfactory since 'the minutes of the Council are not published and this statement is only known through indirect means' (Hartley, 1978: 191-207). Nevertheless, Article 69 of Regulation 1408/71 (OJ 1971, L149/2) buttresses this position by providing that seekers after work in another member state are entitled to draw social security for a period of three months. There are also a number of dicta by the ECJ that the right to take up employment also embraces the right to look for work (Cases 53/81; 48/75). Moreover, the member states themselves have introduced measures permitting entry for limited periods in order to seek employment.

As regards the member of a worker's family who are entitled to accompany him or her to their place of employment, Article 10(1) of Regulation 1612/68 provides that the following persons are entitled to install themselves with a worker:

(a) a spouse and descendants who are under the age of twenty-one or who are dependants;
(b) dependent relatives in the ascending line of the worker and spouse.

It should be noted that 'spouse' here refers to a marital relationship and does not include cohabitation or arrangements falling short of marriage (Case 59/85).

In addition to the above requirements, member states are to facilitate the admission of any other member of a worker's family who does not fall within the categories described but who is nevertheless dependent upon the worker and who lives under his roof in the state whence they came (Article 10(2)). Members of a worker's family will, however, only be allowed to install themselves if the worker is able to provide them with housing which is considered normal for national workers in the region where he is employed (Article 10(3)).

Once a worker can produce an identity card or passport and a document of confirmation of engagement from an employer he is entitled to be issued with a residence permit as proof of his right of residence (Article 4 (2) Directive 68/360). It should be noted that the residence permit is only probative of the right to residence which is itself derived from the Treaty (Case 48/75). The worker's family is also entitled to be issued with residence permits if they produce a valid identity card or passport together with a document proving their relationship to or dependence upon the worker(Article 4(3)). Unless the worker is to be employed for a period of less than twelve months (in which case a temporary residence permit will be issued) he and his family are entitled to be issued with a permit which must be valid for a period of five years (Article 6(1)). Such a permit is automatically renewable for a further period of five years upon its expiration and it may not be withdrawn solely on the grounds that a worker has become involuntarily unemployed or incapable of work through illness or accident (Article 7(1)).

The principle of equality

As indicated above, Article 48(2) requires the abolition of any discrimination based on nationality as regards employment, remuneration and other conditions of work and employment. This particular aspect of the Treaty is implemented by Regulation 1612/68, Article 1 of which gives any national of a member state the right to take up and pursue employment in the territory of any other member state. The Regulation also prohibits particular discriminatory practices including, *inter alia*, special recruitment procedures for foreign nationals, the restriction of advertisements of vacancies in the press or subjecting vacancies to conditions other than those normally applied to employers carrying on their activities in a particular member state, and impeding recruitment of individual workers where they do not reside in the territory of the state concerned. When taken in conjuntion with Article 7 of the Treaty these provisions are a substantial weapon in the hands of individuals who consider that they have been discriminated against on the grounds of nationality.

Article 48(2) and Regulation 1612/68 not only deal with equality regarding eligibility for employment, but also with equality of treatment when employment has been secured. Article 7 of the Regulation provides that the national of one member state who is employed in the territory of another member state is not to be treated differently from national workers by virtue of his or her nationality. This precludes both direct and indirect discrimination.

In Ugliola, (Case 15/69), for example, an Italian employed in the FRG was required to return to Italy to undertake mandatory military service. On returning to work he found that his period of military service had not been taken into account when calculating his seniority. German law required national service in the Bundeswehr to be taken into account for such purposes. Ugliola argued that he had been discriminated against by virtue of his nationality. Despite the FRG's attempt to argue that both nationals and non-nationals were treated equally on the entirely theoretical basis that a German serving in the Italian army would not have his service taken into account, the German law was found to be inapplicable being in conflict with EC law. Nevertheless where it is possible to show that difference in treatment between nationals and non-nationals results from the application of objective criteria there will be no infringement of the Treaty or its implementing legislation (Case 152/73).

Regulation 1612/68 also provides that workers are to derive specific benefits as regards access to training in vocational schools and retraining centres; the right to belong to and vote in trades unions; the enjoyment of social and tax advantages; and the same rights and benefits as national workers in matters of housing. Workers' families are also to enjoy certain rights under Regulation 1612/68. These include the admission of the children of a worker to a member state's general educational, apprenticeship and vocational training courses under the same conditions as nationals (Article 12). Thus the ECJ held in Casagrande (Case 9/74) that the son of a deceased Italian worker was entitled to a grant to allow him to pursue higher education in Germany. The ECJ has developed its jurisprudence in this area by giving an extremely expansive interpretation to the Treaty and its implementing provisions. For example in Fiorini (Case 32/75), French law allowed certain families to receive identity cards allowing railway travel at reduced prices. The question arose whether Fiorini, the widow of an Italian worker who had worked in France, was entitled to such a card. The ECJ held that such a card amounted to a 'tax or social advantage' within the meaning of Regulation 1612/68 which extended not simply to workers (despite the plain meaning of the Regulation) but also to their families. The ECJ reached this view on a broad construction of Regulation 1612/68, relying on the preamble which stated that free movement was not simply a right of workers but also of their families.

Exceptions to free movement

Article 48(3) provides that a member state may exclude persons falling within the scope of Article 48 from its territory on the grounds of public policy, public security or public health. Such prohibition on entry must apply to the whole of the state in question and not only to parts of it, unless similar restrictions can be placed upon a member state's own nationals (Case 36/75). Article 48(3) is implemented in detail by Directive 64/221 (OJ Sp.Ed. 1963-4, p.117; Wooldridge, 1977), and both have been declared directly effective by the ECJ (Case 41/74).

Although member states are allowed discretion in applying the public policy proviso, the ECJ has made it clear that this discretion is circumscribed by EC law. The operation of the proviso may only be based exclusively on an individual's 'personal conduct' (Article 3(1)) and previous criminal convictions are not in themselves sufficient to allow its operation (Article 3(2)) (Case 6/74). But if an individual's past conduct demonstrates that he has a propensity to behave in a particular way and that criminal convictions are evidence of personal conduct posing a present threat to public policy, he may be excluded or deported from the territory (Case 30/77; Barar, 1981). The individual's conduct must, however, constitute a genuine and serious threat to a public policy and affect one of the fundamental interests of society (Case 36/75). Diseases which might threaten public policy are included in two non-exhaustive annexes attached to the Directive and include, *inter alia*, tuberculosis, syphilis, drug addiction and profound mental disturbance.

The failure of an individual to comply with the requirements of obtaining a residence permit does not entitle a member state to deport a foreign national since, as indicated above, the right of entry and residence is derived from the Treaty itself and does not depend upon the issue of a permit (Cases 48/75; 157/79). Member states may, however, impose penalties on non-nationals for failing to comply with reasonable immigration requirements, but penalties for violations of such requirements must not be excessive and must be proportionate to the offence (Case 118/75).

Freedom to provide services

Free movement in the Treaty is guaranteed not only to those who are employees of others, but also to the providers of services, that is someone who is established (that is having their principal place of business) in one member state and providing services in another member state. It is also interesting to note that freedom to provide services is also taken to imply the freedom of recipients of services to move to other member states to receive those services (Art. 1(1) (b) Directive 73/148, OJ 1973, L172/14; Case 26/83).

Article 59 provides for the abolition of restrictions on the freedom to provide services. This became directly effective after the end of the transitional period (Case 33/74). Services are defined in Article 60 as being such 'when they are normally provided for remuneration' and are stated to include activities of an industrial, commercial, professional or craftsmanlike nature. The right to provide services must be guaranteed by member states under the same conditions imposed by them upon their own nationals, thus discrimination on the grounds of nationality is forbidden. This provision also applies *pari pasu* to recipients of services. Nevertheless, member states may impose certain restrictions upon non-nationals seeking to provide services within their territory where this is necessary for the prevention of evasion of rules relating to professional conduct, professional rules, ethics or other forms of professional supervision (Cases 39/75; 279/80). There must, however, be no other less restrictive way of ensuring compliance with such professional requirements.

Exceptions to the freedom to provide services

As well as restrictions on the provision of services on the grounds of public health, public policy and public security, restrictions may also be based upon circumstances where the provider of services may be required to exercise powers of public authority, even if only occasionally (Article 55, EEC).

Free movement of capital

Unlike free movement of goods, there is, as yet, no common market in capital. There are, at the present stage of development of the EC, good reasons for this. Transfers of capital remain a highly sensitive political issue because of the adverse effects which a free flow of capital may have on a state's economy. In a perfect market capital will be invested wherever the best returns are to be had and it will be unnecessary for states to guard against the adverse effects of capital export by way of exchange control regulations. In the EC's current state of development, however, member states cannot be so sanguine about the long-term effects of free capital flow between them (Swann, 1978; Ress, 1983: 318-21). Thus Article 67 requires that member states progressively abolish all restrictions on the free movement of capital belonging to their residents. The provision further requires that discrimination based on nationality or place of residence of investors is to be progressively abolished. It is clear, however, that the abolition of restrictions is only required to the extent necessary to ensure the proper functioning of the common market. In interpreting this provision the ECJ has made it quite clear that the extent of the abolition of restrictions is relative and must depend upon a balancing of the advantages and risks which a liberalization of capital transfers may involve at any particular stage in the development of the internal market. It is apparent therefore that Article 67 lacks the mandatory quality necessary for it to be directly effective (Case 203/80).

The primary responsibility for developing the liberalization of capital flows rests upon the Council pursuing a legislative programme in accordance with Article 69. Here the Council is to act on a Commission proposal, and the Commission itself is to consult with the Monetary Committee. A number of directives have been adopted, the most recent in 1986 (OJ 1986, L 332) amending the Council's first Directive of 1960. The latter directive placed a requirement upon member states to relax certain restrictions on the transfer of a capital for the purposes of direct and indirect investment and the purchase of land. The amended directive extends this relaxation to long-term credits, securities not dealt on stock exchanges and the admission of stocks and shares of companies to the stock exchanges of other member states.

Exceptions to the free movement of capital

Because of the political sensitivity attached to capital movements, a member state may take protective measures to prevent disturbances in its capital market either with the authorization of the Commission or, where there is a situation of great urgency or the necessity to preserve secrecy, it may act unilaterally. Member states also retain certain powers in the economic field by virtue of other treaty provisions, for example conjunctural policy or regulation of short-term economic cycles (Article 103); protection of balance of payments (Articles 104, 108, 109) and exchange rates (Article 107).

Conclusion

There can be li tle doubt that significant advances have been made in integrating the economies ι f the member states since the foundation of the EC in 1958 and through its subsequent enlargements. Yet dissatisfaction has been expressed in many quarters that the speed of integration has not proceeded rapidly enough (Freestone and Davidson, 1988; Lodge, 1986). It is undoubtedly true that progress might have been achieved more rapidly but for the intransigence of the member states expressed through the medium of the Council and its insistence on unanimous voting. At present it is far from clear whether the modifications introduced into the Treaty by the SEA will lead to accelerated integration. Certainly the introduction of a new timetable aiming for completion of the internal market in 1992 has given an added political impetus to the integration process, but beyond these political developments (which could have been achieved without the Treaty in any event) it is difficult to see, as Pescatore argues, what significance a new, non-binding transitional date has. The mechanisms for achieving a completed common market were already in place in the unamended Treaty; all that was required was the political will to use them effectively. In all this, however, the ECJ should not be forgotten. It is arguable that the Court's pro-integration approach manifested through its teleological interpretation of the Treaty and implementing instruments has done as much, if not more, than the other institutions to further economic integration. Of course, this form of judicial activism has not remained free from criticism (Rasmussen, 1986; Capalletti, 1987), and there may well be substance in the accusation that the ECJ has exceeded its adjudicatory role. But looking down from the high point of Cassis de Dijon, who can say that the Court has not served its Community well?

Notes

1. See for example Case 207/83 *Commission v UK* (1985) 2 C.M.L.R. 259 in which the ECJ said, 'the Treaty, by establishing a common market and progressively approximating the policies of the Member States, seeks to unite national markets into a single market having the characteristics of a domestic market'.
2. Case 120/78 *Rewe-Zentralfinanz v. Bundesmonopol-verwaltung für Branntwein* (1979) ECR 649; (1979) 3 CMLR 337. See also D. Wyatt (1981), 'Article 30 and non-discriminatory trade restrictions', *European Law Review*, 6, pp.185-93; and Oliver, and R. Barents (1981), 'New Developments in Measures having Equivalent Effect', *Common Market Law Review*, 18, pp.271-303.

References

Barav, A. (1981), 'Court Recommendations to Deport and the Free Movement of Workers in EEC law', *European Law Review*, 6, 139-61.

Capalletti, M. (1987), 'Is the European Court of Justice Running Wild?', *European Law Review*, 12, 3-17.

Davidson, S. (1983), 'Actions for Damages in the English Courts for Breach of Article 86', *European Law Review*, 8, 353-57.

Easson, A. (1980), 'The Spirits, Wine and Beer Judgments: A Legal Mickey Finn?', *European Law Review*, 5, 318-30.

EC Commission (1987), *Europe Without Frontiers: Completing the Internal Market*, Office for Official Publications of the EC, Luxembourg.

European Court of Justice:

Case 26/62 *Van Gend en Loos v Nederlandse Adminstratie der Belastingen* (1963) ECR 1; (1963) CMLR 105.

Case 75/63 *Hoekstra (née Unger)* (1964) ECR 533; (1964) CMLR 319.

Case 27/67 *Fink Frucht* (1968) ECR 223.

Case 7/68 *Commission v Italy* (1968) ECR 423; (1962) CMLR 1.

Case 24/68 *Commission v Italy* (1969) ECR 199; (1971) CMLR 611.

Case 15/69 *Ugliola* (1969) ECR 363; (1970) CMLR 194

Cases 48, 49, 51-57/69 *ICI and Others v Commission* (1972) ECR 619; (1972) CMLR 557.

Case 283/69 *Sociaal Fonds voor de Diamandarbeiders v Brackfeld & Chougal Diamond Company* (1969) ECR 211; (1969) CMLR 335.

Case 6/72 *Continental Can v Commission* (1973) ECR 215; (1972) CMLR 690.

Cases 6 and 7/73 *Commercial Solvents v Commission* (1973) ECR 357; (1973) CMLR 361; (1974) ECR 223; (1974) I CMLR 690.

Case 39/73 *Rewe-Zentralfinanz v Landwirtschafts-Kammer* (1973) ECR 1039.

Case 152/73 *Sotgiu v Deutsche Bunderspost* (1974) ECR.

Case 167/73 *Commission v France* (1974) ECR 359: (1974) 2 CMLR 2/6.

Case 8/74 *Procureur du Roi v Dassonville* (1974) ECR 837; (1974) 2 CMLR 436.

Case 9/74 *Casagrande* (1974) ECR 773; (1974) 2 CMLR 423.

Case 33/74 *Van Binsbergen v Bedrijfs Vereniging Metaalnijverheid* (1974) ECR 1299.

Case 41/74 *Van Duyn v Home Office* (1974) ECR 1337; (1975) 1 CMLR 1.

Case 63/74 *Cadskey v Istituto Nazionale per il Commercio Estero* (1975) ECR 281.

Case 67/74 *Bonsignore v Oberstadt-direktor Koln* (1975) ECR 297; (1975) 1 CMLR 472.

Case 26/75 *General Motors v Commission* (1975) ECRT 1367; (1976) 1 CMLR 95.

Case 32/75 *Fiorini v SNCF* (1975) ECR 1085; (1976) 1 CMLR 573.

Case 36/75 *Rutili v Minister for the Interior* (1975) ECR 1219; (1976) 1 CMLR 140.

Case 38/75 *Nederlandse Spoorwegen v Inspecteur der Invoerrechten Accijnzen* (1975) ECR 1439.

Case 39/75 *Coenen v Sociaal-Economische Raad* (1975) ECR 1547.

Case 45/75 *Rewe-Zentrale v Hauptzollamt Landau Pfalz* (1976) ECR 181.
Case 48/75 *Procureur du Roi v Royer* (1976) ECR 497; (1976) 2 CMLR 619.
Case 118/75 *Publico Ministero v Watson & Bellman* (1976) ECR 1185; (1976) 2 CMLR 552.
Case 27/76 *United Brands v Commission* (1978) ECR 207; (1978) 1 CMLR 429.
Case 46/76 *Bauhuis v Netherlands* (1977) ECR 14.
Case 30/77 *R v Bouchereau* (1977) ECR 1999: (1977) 2 CMLR 800.
Case 7/78 *R v Thompson* (1978) ECR 2247; (1979) 1 CMLR 47.
Case 168-171/78 *Commission v France, Italy, UK & Denmark*.
Case 169/78 *Commission v Italy* (1980) ECR 385.
Case 34/79 *R v Henn & Darby* (1979) ECR 3795; (1980) 1 CMLR 246.
Case 157/79 *R v Pieck* (1980) ECR 2171; (1980) 2 CMLR 220.
Case 792/79 *Camera-Care v Commission* (1980) ECR 119; (1980) CMLR 334.
Case 203/80 *Casati* (1981) ECR 2595.
Case 279/80 *Criminal Proceedings against Alfred John Webb* (1981) ECR 3305.
Case 53/81 *Levin v Staatsecretaris van Justitie* (1982) ECR 1035; (1982) 2 CMLR 454.
Case 95/81 *Commission v Italy* (1982) ECR 2187.
Case 40/82 *Commission v UK* (1984) ECR 283.
Case 132/82 *Commission v Belguim* (1983) ECR 1649.
Case 26/83 *Luisi and Carbone* (1984) ECR 377.
Case 59/85 *Netherlands v Reed* (not yet reported).
Case 66/85 *Laurie-Blum v Land Baden-Wurttemberg* (not yet reported).
Case 121/85 *Conegate v HMS Customs & Excise* (1986) 1 CMLR 739.
Case 139/85 *Kempf v Staatsecretaris van Justitie* (not yet reported).
Forrester, I. S. (1980), EEC customs law: rules of origin and preferential duty', *European Law Review*, 5, 167-87 and 257-86.
Freestone, D. and Davidson S. (1988), *The Institutional Framework of the European Communities*, London and New York, Routledge.
Gormley, L. (1981a), 'Cassis de Dijon and the communication from the Commission', *European Law Review*, 6, 454-9.
— (1981b), 'The Commission's proposals on trademarks – part II', *European Law Review*, 6, 464.
Hartley, T. C. (1978), 'The internal personal scope of the EEC immigration provisions', *European Law Review*, 3, 191-207.
— (1988), *The Foundations of European Community Law*, Oxford, Clarendon Press.
Hornsby, S. B. (1987), 'Competition in the 80's: more policy less competition?', *European Law Review*, 12, 79-101.
International Legal Materials, 1974, 13, 270.
Jacobs, F. (1975), 'Industrial property rights and the EEC treaty – a reply', *International and Comparative Law Quarterly*, 24, 643-58.
— (1980), 'Jurisdiction and enforcement in EEC competition cases', in F. M. Rowe, *et al.* (eds), *Enterprise Law of the 80's*, Washington, DC, American Bar Association Press.
Kerse, C. S. (1981), *EEC Antitrust Procedure*, London, European Law Centre.
Korah, V. (1986), *EEC Competition Law and Practice*, Oxford, ESC Publishing.
Lasok, D. (1980), *The Law of the Economy in the European Communities*, London, Butterworths.
Lodge, J. (1986), *European Union: The European Community in Search of a Future*, Macmillan, London.
Mann, F. A. (1975), 'Industrial Property Rights and the EEC Treaty', *International and Comparative Law Quarterly*, 24, 31-43.
Mathijsen, P.S.R.F. (1985), *A Guide to European Community Law*, 4th edition, London, Sweet and Maxwell.
Oliver, P. (1982), *Free Movement of Goods*, London, European Law Centre.
Parry, A. and Dinnage, J. (1980), *Parry and Hardy: EEC law*, London, Sweet and Maxwell.
Pescatore, P. (1986), 'The Single European Act', *Europe*, no. 1397.

Rasmussen, H. (1986), *On Law and Policy in the European Court of Justice*, Dordrecht, Nijhoff.

Ress, F. (1983), 'Free movement of persons, services and capital', in EC Commission, *Thirty years of Community Law*, Luxembourg, Office for Official Publications of the EC.

Spaak Report, (1956), *Rapport des Chefs de delegations aux ministres des affaires étrangères*, Brussels, Secretariat of the Intergovernmental Conference, Brussels.

Swann, D. (1978), *The Economics of the Common Market*, 4th edition, Harmondsworth, Penguin.

— (1983), *Competition and Industrial Policy in the European Community*, London and New York, Methuen.

Van Gerven, W. (1974), 'Twelve years EEC competition law (1962-73) revisited', *Common Market Law Review*, 11, 38-61.

Wooldridge, F. (1977), 'Free movement of EEC nationals: the limitations based on public policy and public security', *European Law Review*, 2, 190-207.

Wyatt, D. and Dashwood, A. (1987), *The Substantive Law of the EEC*, 2nd edition, London, Sweet and Maxwell.

7 The Budget of the European Community

Michael Shackleton[1]

The budget of any organization offers important insights into the workings of that organization; the EC's budget is no exception. By examining where the EC's money comes from, how it is spent and the process by which its allocation is determined, this chapter will therefore identify those characteristics which distinguish the EC from traditional international organizations and discuss the relationship between EC institutions and the twelve member states. This relationship is not a static one but based on a delicate balance, which is maintained and revised through a constant process of negotiation. The budget offers a fruitful way of examining that balance in that it is of sufficient dimension to acquire political salience and to prompt argument about the procedure for and the content of the distribution of resources.[2]

Revenue

The financing of all international organizations has traditionally been guaranteed by national contributions calculated on the relative wealth of the states concerned. Until 1970 this was also the case in the EC: the budget was divided into several parts and the EC of Six agreed on keys for national contributions which took account of both national wealth and the relative benefit derived by each state from the part of the budget concerned. In 1970 a very major change took place. It was agreed to replace national contributions and progressively to give the EC its 'own resources', divided into three categories: first, customs duties collected at the frontiers of the Community; second, agricultural levies applied on the import of agricultural products from outside the EC (these two together are commonly called 'traditional own resources'); and third, a proportion of national receipts from value – added tax (VAT), not to exceed 1 per cent of the VAT base or the total value of all transactions in the Community subject to VAT calculated on a harmonized basis.[3]

The importance of this change cannot be over-emphasized. It meant that the EC was no longer dependent upon the member states agreeing to provide national contributions, but that it could call upon these resources and consider them as collective Community property. The situation in other international organizations is very different. United Nations' members, for example, often either refuse to make their full contribution or claim that they are unable to pay it at the time when payment is due. By contrast, members of the EC are not entitled to withold payments under the system of 'own resources'. When Britain in 1983 delayed crediting her own resources for the month of April to the

Commission's account, the issue was taken before the European Court of Justice (ECJ) and the Court ruled in December 1986 (Case 93/85) that Britain was not entitled to act in this way and indeed was obliged to pay interest in respect of the delay. However, member states are reluctant to accord 'own resources' the same status as resources held by individuals or companies. The Community's monies are held by national governments in national accounts, but are not granted interest. So far the member states have not been willing to accept Commission proposals to revise the rules to permit these monies to earn interest.

One of the important features of the arrangements established in 1970 was that the rules applied in the same way to all member states regardless of their size or wealth. No account was taken of the fact that traditional own resources are collected in disproportionately large part by small countries like the Netherlands and Belguim who have major ports receiving goods in international trade. Equally, there was no attempt to take account of the capacity of member states to pay. As a general rule VAT constitutes a larger percentage of gross national product (GNP) in poorer states where consumption is more significant than production in the national economy, than it does in richer states where the reverse tends to be true. Hence the VAT burden tends to weigh more heavily on poorer states.

This principle of 'horizontal equity' whereby each member state paid according to the same rules survived until the Fontainebleau summit in June 1984. To understand why it survived as long as it did, as well as why the member states eventually agreed to allow it to be breached, it is necessary to compare the comparative gains and losses from the budget of the individual countries.[4] Table 7.1 shows the percentage contributions for 1985 of the then ten member states to the 'own resources' of the Community as compared with the payments from the budget made in those same states.

The pattern in Table 7.1, stable over many years, points to two major 'net contributors' to the EC budget, the FRG and UK. The former was generally prepared to accept the situation in the light of its high level of prosperity; the latter had always been determined to correct the imbalance.[5] In the early 1980s

Table 7.1　Winners and losers from the EC Budget 1985

Country	% contributions to EC 'own resources'	% of payments to Member States
Belgium	5.0	4.3
Denmark	2.4	3.7
France	20.4	21.9
FRG	28.2	17.0
Greece	1.5	6.9
Ireland	1.1	6.3
Italy	13.9	18.1
Luxembourg	0.2	0.03
Netherlands	7.2	9.0
UK	19.5	12.6
Allocation not available		0.2

Source: Annual Report of the Court of Auditors concerning the 1985 financial year (Official Journal C321 of 15 December 1986)

the EC agreed to meet the difficulty by making extra payments to Britain each year out of the budget. This proved unsatisfactory to Britain, notably because it sought a permanent mechanism which was not subject to the uncertainties of the annual budget procedure.

A long period of bitter negotiations followed and culminated in the Fontainebleau decision to deal with the British problem on the revenue rather than the expenditure side of the budget. It was agreed that instead of all members paying the same VAT rate, Britain's rate should be decreased by an amount corresponding to two-thirds of the difference between its percentage share of EC VAT resources and its percentage share of total allocated expenditure. In 1986, for example, the UK VAT rate fell from 1.25 per cent to 0.68 per cent, a drop equivalent to 1900m ECU or 40 per cent of the total volume of 'own resources' made available by Britain to the EC in that year.

This was a very significant concession as the reduction in Britain's revenue contribution had to be made up by the other member states. An important reason for its being granted was that the EC was no longer able to meet its expenditure needs within the VAT ceiling agreed in 1970. Up until the early 1980s, that 1 per cent level had proved quite sufficient to meet the EC's needs. In 1982, however, the VAT call-up rate jumped from 0.78 per cent to 0.92 per cent, and the following year the ceiling was effectively reached. At this point Britain was in a very strong position to force a change in the nature of the resource system because any increase beyond 1 per cent required unanimity in the Council as well as ratification by all member state parliaments; the other member states proved willing to accept the change as part of a deal assuring more revenue for the EC budget.

The increase in 'own resources' agreed at Fontainebleau was for the VAT rate to be raised from 1 per cent to 1.4 per cent in 1986, when Spain and Portugal were expected to become members, with the possibility of a further increase to 1.6 per cent at the beginning of 1988. It turned out to be based on a hopelessly unrealistic assessment of the development of EC expenditure. After intergovernmental agreements were used in 1984 and 1985 to finance the deficits that were incurred, the new 1.4 per cent limit was immediately exhausted in 1986, the first year of its operation. In 1987 effective expenditure went far beyond the 1.6 per cent level which back in 1984 had only been envisaged as a possibility for the following year. As a result, the only way to keep the budget in balance (an obligation imposed by the EEC Treaties) was to delay expenditure by a variety of ingenious but artificial devices.

This situation was the subject of heated debate in the EC. In February 1987, the Commission prepared a report (COM(87)101) which urged that in future the overall volume of resources available be calculated in terms of overall Community GNP. This offered the possibility of the budget being directly linked to the overall fortunes of the European economy, as it had not been previously. Hitherto the volume of 'own resources' was governed by the total available from customs duties, agricultural levies and the 1.4 per cent VAT rate. However, with customs duties in decline as rates of duty tended downwards and agricultural levies dropping with the increase in the EC's self-sufficiency in agricultural products, traditional 'own resources' offered a contracting revenue base. At the same time, VAT revenue was seen to be growing less quickly than total Community economic activity, as consumption went down as a percentage of GDP.

The Commission proposed a limit of 1.4 per cent of Community GNP for the period up to 1992. After three successive summit meetings (Brussels, June 1987; Copenhagen, December 1987 and Brussels, February 1988), it was decided to follow the Commission's basic idea but the overall volume of revenue was restricted to 1.2 per cent of Community GNP rather than 1.4 per cent. This assured an important degree of financial security to the EC. It meant that in 1992 the budget could reach 52.8 bn ECU[6] (at 1988 prices) or an increase of 20 per cent in real terms.

At the same time, it was necessary to determine the shape of the revenue system that would operate within the overall limit. The heads of state and government decided that the three existing types of 'own resource' should be supplemented by a fourth resource based on the relative GNP figures of the member states. In other words, once the expenditure for a given year has been determined, the total amount generated by customs duties, agricultural levies and the 1.4 per cent VAT rate is deducted and the balance paid by each member state in direct proportion to the level of its GNP. This change was designed to address the issue of capacity to pay, particularly in the light of the accession of Spain and Portugal. However, it had never before constituted an element in the 'own resource' system and it opened a whole new area of difficulty.

First, it introduced a resource which looked very much like a national contribution, thereby diluting the 'own resource' character of the system. This was all the more apparent given the fact that it was sure to become an increasingly significant component of the budget in percentage terms. Already for 1989 the Commission in its preliminary draft budget envisaged that it would be providing over 8 bn ECU or 18 per cent of the total.

Second, it threatened to alter the balance between member states in terms of their revenue contribution to the budget. Italy, in particular, was concerned that its contribution to 'own resources' would increase substantially. Indeed it had made strenuous efforts to ensure that the original Commission proposal for the 'fourth resource' be modified. The Commission had suggested that the prevailing VAT rate be reduced from 1.4 per cent to 1 per cent and that the fourth resource be calculated on the basis of the difference between the VAT component of GNP and the total amount of GNP. On this basis it calculated that Italy would have had to contribute something like 188m ECU extra to the financing of the 1987 budget, whereas Britain would have contributed some 306m ECU less (COM(87)101). The outcome of the negotiations was that the VAT rate was kept at 1.4 per cent and that the fourth resource was calculated on the basis of total GNP and not the difference between the VAT component and the total.

This example illustrates clearly the tension between the pressure for and resistance to change in the Community revenue system. No change is neutral in its effects but equally the status quo is constantly being challenged. The Brussels summit of February 1988 constitutes an important stage in the development of the system but it is certain not to constitute the last word. Amongst the member states, the application of the fourth resource is likely to arouse further debate, particularly as it will require agreement on the calculation used in measuring GNP. Moreover, the willingness at Brussels to extend the Fontainebleau arrangements relating to the revenue-side compensation to Britain is far from certain to continue indefinitely precisely because of the introduction of the fourth resource, with its favourable impact on Britain.

From within EC institutions there is sure to be pressure for further revenue to be found in the form of a Community tax of some kind. It is worth pointing out that the European Coal and Steel Community (ECSC) which has a separate budget from the rest of the EC, already has the right to impose a levy on coal and steel producers within the EC to finance a part of its activities. As a result, such producers have a major interest in influencing the Community process, whereby the levy rate is decided. An equivalent tax on, for example, energy imports would certainly cause individuals to be more aware of the importance of EC decisions. However, any such change would necessarily have a major impact on the balance of relations between the member states and the EC institutions. Taxation remains supremely a national prerogative in the perception of member states and it may be some considerable time before there can be any notion of such a tax being decided upon at EC level.

However, the debate about new forms of revenue will not take place in a vacuum. It will be strongly influenced by the decision taken as to the development of EC policies and the expenditure arising from them. The more limited the ambitions for the EC's future, the smaller the pressure for different sources of revenue; the wider those ambitions, the more likely it is that the existing revenue arrangements will have to be revised.

Expenditure

Where then does the revenue discussed in the previous section go to? If you open a copy of the EC budget, which is published as one volume of the *Official Journal of the European Communities*, you will find that expenditure is divided up into five sections with one section for each EC institution (see Table 7.2). One fact stands out clearly from table 7.2: the Commission budget dominates that of the budget as a whole, representing some 98 per cent of the total. The reason for this is twofold: first, the other sections only contain administrative appropriations, designed to enable the institutions to function; second, although the Commision budget does have one part which is devoted to administrative appropriations, amounting to around 1.2 bn ECU, it is overshadowed by the part devoted to operating appropriations. Unlike traditional international organizations, the EC devotes by far the largest proportion of its revenue to the policies which the Commission implements, with running costs constituting a relatively minor element. Again, the situation in the UN provides a useful contrast. Its budget for 1986-87 (excluding the specialized agencies with

Table 7.2 The Community Budget in 1988

		mECU
Section I	– European Parliament	400
Section II	– Council	
	(with Economic and Social Committee)	214
Section III	– Commission	43,083
Section IV	– Court of Justice	53
Section V	– Court of Auditors	28
	TOTAL	43,778

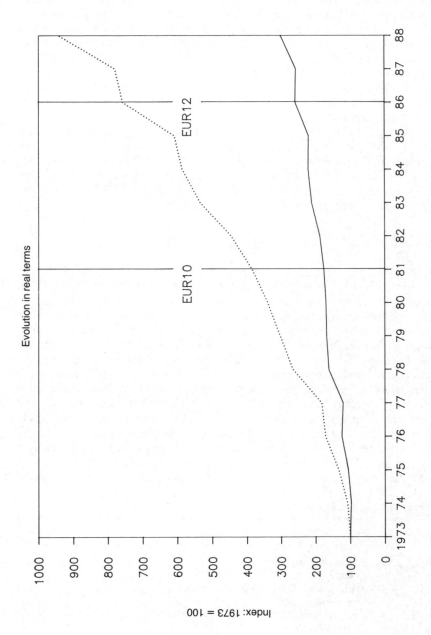

Figure 7.1 EC budget, 1973-88 *Source:* The Statistical Office of the European Parliament

Key: ...... Current prices ——— Deflated prices

separate budgets) was set at $1.6 bn (less than the EC's total administrative expenditure (UN Res. 40/253A)). Moreover, of that total, more than two-thirds is devoted to central activities in New York including staff salaries, the upkeep of buildings etc. The amount available for activities funded directly by the institution is correspondingly small.

The volume of operating appropriations may sound substantial but it is important to keep it in perspective. It remains at little more than 1 per cent of EC Gross Domestic Product (GDP) and some 3 per cent of the total spending by governments of the twelve member states. Moreover, the rate of increase has been relatively slow in real terms. Over the fifteen years since 1973, the budget increased more than ninefold at current prices, rising from 4.6 bn ECU to 43.8 bn ECU, but at constant prices its size only expanded by a factor of three (see Figure 7.1).

The development of the budget also has to be seen as a reflection of the relations between the EC institutions and the member states. The latter have been, reluctantly or otherwise, prepared to accept the gentle but regular upward pressure on EC expenditure. One of the significant features of the 1988 Brussels European Council was that for the first time, a summit communiqué contained a table indicating how the overall size of the budget, divided into major expenditure categories, was intended to increase between 1988 and 1992. Table 7.3 shows a commitment and guarantee that will be an important reference point over the next five years. All will be working on the assumption that the figures laid down will be respected. For the Commission it will mean being able to organize expenditure in the secure knowledge that the revenue necessary will be included in the budget; in the member states the national exchequers will be able to calculate reasonably accurately the level of their financial commitment to the EC as well as their receipts from the EC over the next five years. The importance of this level of financial security needs to be assessed in the context of the difficulties encountered by ordinary international organizations who do not have an own resources system and who, despite having much smaller budgets, are regularly finding themselves short of finance because member states are unable or unwilling to pay their subscription. In 1988, for example,

Table 7.3 Budget estimates for 1992 (commitments) in billion ECU (1988 prices)

	1988	*1992*
EAGGF guarantee section	27.5	29.6
Financing of de-stocking measures	1.2	1.4
Set-aside – aids to income	0	0.6
Structual funds	7.7	12.9
EPIDP (European Programme for Industrial Development in Portugal)	0.1	0.1
Total of structrural actions	7.8	13
Policies with multiannual allocations		
(Research – Integrated Mediterranean Programmes)	1.4	2.4
Other policies	1.7	2.8
Reimbursements and administration	3.5	2
Monetary reserve	1	1
TOTAL	44.1	52.8

the UN was owed some $700 million including $466 million from the US (Agence Europe, 30/31 May 1988: 17).

The increase in revenue is also important in the light of the severe financial stringency which all individual member states of the EC are exercising domestically. Most are attempting energetically to reduce the size of public spending and yet at EC level all have been prepared to witness the budget's size linked, for the first time, to a measure of overall EC wealth (GNP) and at a percentage which allows for substantial real growth. Certainly it is a tribute to the momentum of the EC's development that such growth was eventually agreed to unanimously. How is this overall volume of expenditure broken down? Table 7.4 shows for 1988 the distribution between the various Titles of Part B of the Commission budget, i.e. that devoted to policy expenditure. The most obvious feature of Table 7.4 is the very major imbalance in the pattern of expenditure. The Common Agricultural Policy (CAP) and particularly the two titles which provide the financial basis for the system of guaranteed prices dominate the EC budget as indeed they have throughout the EC's history. Between 1973 and 1988, EAGGF Guarantee made up less than 60 per cent of the total budget on only one occasion (1981) and twice, 1973 and 1977, it constituted more than 75 per cent. This domination is even more marked if one considers not just the appropriations entered in the budget but also those which are actually spent. In 1986, for example, over 99 per cent of EAGGF Guarantee expenditure entered in the budget was spent. In contrast, all other sectors of the budget failed to achieve implementation rates of over 94 per cent. Indeed, some fell to much lower levels: expenditure under Title 9 concerned with development aid was only implemented to 61 per cent of the total available by the end of the year (OJC 336 15 December 1987 p.165).

Table 7.4   The 1988 Commission budget by policy area

		m ECU	*per cent*
TITLES 1 & 2	European Agricultural Guidance and Guarantee Fund (EAGGF) – guarantee section	27,500	65.8
TITLE 3	EAGGF – guidance section and specific agricultural measures	1,219	2.9
TITLE 4	Common policy on fisheries and the sea	282	0.7
TITLE 5	Regional development and transport	3,211	7.7
TITLE 6	Social sector	2,841	6.8
TITLE 7	Energy, industry and technology; research; nuclear safeguards; information market and innovation sectors	1,121	2.7
TITLE 8	Repayments with aids to member states, loan guarantees and miscellaneous	3,688	8.8
TITLE 9	Cooperation with developing and non-member countries	893	2.1
TITLE 10	Other expenditure	1,049	2.5
	Total	41,804	100

The reason for the predominance of CAP expenditure arises from the particular character of the legislation governing the Guarantee sector. That legislation lays down and reviews each year the minimum prices that will be guaranteed to producers whatever the market price. It also ensures that for all sales on to the world market the difference between Community and the generally lower world prices will be financed out of the budget. As world prices are set in US dollars and in the recent past, the dollar has significantly weakened against the ECU, the cost of the CAP has been subject to upward pressure which the budgetary process has been unable to resist. In 1984, for example, it was agreed that agricultural spending should not increase faster than the rate of growth of the volume of 'own resources'. However, by 1987 it proved impossible to contain expenditure within this limit. It was calculated that the appropriations entered in the budget (22.9 bn ECU) would have to be exceeded by more than 4 billion ECU or around 20 per cent if the obligations of the EC were to be met. The member states were unable to agree on a supplementary budget. Instead the problem was 'solved' by a decision to prefinance agricultural guarantee spending with the EC effectively reimbursing that spending rather than providing the money in advance as had previously been the case. As a result, two months' worth of expenditure were 'saved' in 1987 and rolled forward into 1988, and hence indefinitely into the future.

The 1988 Brussels summit sought to address this issue. It proposed first of all that the annual growth rate of EAGGF Guarantee should not exceed 74 per cent of the annual increase of Community GNP. Since it was recognized that such a limitation by itself might be more effective than the guideline established in 1984, it was also decided to introduce a system of budgetary 'stabilizers' whereby expenditure on agriculture would be carefully monitored and if it appeared that it would exceed the volume of appropriations envisaged, then the Council would be invited to introduce the legislation necessary to bring expenditure into line with that entered in the budget. At the time of writing it is not possible to assess the success of a system which has yet to be applied. Certainly it represents an important attempt to alter the relationship between the law of the EC as established by legislation and that established by the budget in favour of the latter. But, even if it is successful, it will not lead to the dramatic drop in the percentage of the budget that CAP spending takes up which many – including the Commission (COM(87) 101) – had hoped to see. It will remain at around two-thirds of the total, thus showing the weight of the *acquis communautaire* in this domain.

In almost all other areas of policy, the relationship between the budget and legislation has operated rather differently. Rather than there being an automatic budgetary effect flowing from an established legislative framework, the EC institutions and in particular, the Commission, have found themselves confronted with the need to obtain agreement on a legislative framework and then to ensure that there are sufficient applications of adequate quality upon which the funds can be spent. The simple entry of appropriations in the budget has not proved a guarantee either that the necessary legislation will be passed or that projects and programmes to match the budget allocation will be presented.

In the transport area, for example, it has so far proved impossible to get agreement on an EC policy of any significant dimensions, despite a 1985 ruling that the Council was in contravention of its obligations under the Rome Treaty by failing to agree to such a policy. The EC, for its part as one branch of the budgetary authority (see below), has sought to provide impetus for such a policy by entering substantial appropriations in the budget. In the Joint Declaration signed by Council, EP and Commission in June 1982, the Council agreed that it would use its 'best endeavours' to ensure that legislation would be introduced by the end of May where it is needed as a basis for spending monies entered in the budget of any given year (OJC 194, 28 July, 1982). These best endeavours have proved to no avail but interestingly a substantial proportion of the appropriations entered for transport has been regularly spent: in 1985, 1986 and 1987 the Council agreed to finance a variety of *ad hoc* projects, thereby providing EC finance for a set of basically national projects.

Research policy offers a rather different perspective on the difficulties of modifying the balance of EC expenditure. In September 1987 the Council did adopt a framework programme for EC activity in the field of research and development for the period 1987-91. However, it took negotiations lasting over a year for the agreement to be reached, and when it was the Council agreed to a level of expenditure of 5,369m ECU, a sum substantially below that which the Commission had proposed (7,735m ECU). It is not necessary to enter the debate about funding in order to recognize that the resistance of member states to a substantial expansion of non-agricultural policies constitutes a major barrier to changing the shape of the EC budget.

Even when policies are agreed, it is by no means guaranteed that the funds allocated in the budget will be used: the recent history of the European Social Fund (ESF) illustrates the point. To make the argument clear it is necessary to digress a little by clarifying the distinction that exists in the budget between commitment and payment appropriations. The latter represent the expenditure that EC institutions are entitled to incur in a given financial year; the former constitute commitments that can be entered into in one year but where payment is made partly in that same year and partly in subsequent years. The budget thereby allows for a higher level of commitments than payments in that a substantial proportion of the commitments will only be paid out *after* the financial year in question. In agriculture the level of payments and commitments is the same since all monies are committed and paid out within one financial year, most other EC policies are multiannual in character. An initial payment is made at the outset of a project with a commitment to pay the balance on its completion. Only when the project is confirmed as having been completed (in a subsequent year) is the final payment made.

This system operates in the ESF but less than smoothly. In 1986 the Commission drew attention to an increasing volume of commitments which remained to be paid: at the beginning of that year over 20 per cent of all the commitments entered into since 1978 were still outstanding. When the member states were invited to look into the matter, it did prove possible to clear a large part of the backlog by the end of 1987. However, only just over half of this backlog was cleared through payments, the remainder, some 1.3 bn ECU, was cancelled. The comment of the Commissioner responsible, Manuel Marin underlined the frustrating nature of these cancellations:

The member states did not fully use all their possibilities concerning the use of the appropriations that had been allocated to them. This has meant that, faced with very important problems on the labour market and with very limited resources, other deserving actions could not benefit from the ESF's support. [Agence Europe, 16 Dec 1987]

The Commission used up the limited appropriations in the ESF for projects which were unsuccessful and without the member states apparently being unduly unconcerned. Again, this underlines the dependence of the EC upon member states to enable the budget to operate effectively and the difficulty of developing policies designed to change its shape.

These examples also illustrate a wider problem in that the EC budget constitutes a package of separate policies rather than a coherent whole with a clear underlying philosophy. The EC budget has developed in a rather haphazard way in response above all to national pressures. After Britain's entry the Regional Fund (ERDF) was created expressly to counterbalance the acknowledged imbalance arising from the existence of the CAP which gave Britain limited benefits. With Greek entry in 1981, it was agreed to establish Integrated Mediterranean Programmes (IMPs) which were designed to counteract the tendency of EC policy – agricultural and other – to benefit the wealthier regions of the north. And with the accession of Spain and Portugal in 1986, the increase in the number of less-prosperous states brought pressure to bear for the strengthening of regional, social and agricultural guidance activities (the so-called structural funds) which culminated in the agreement reached at the Brussels European Council meeting of February 1988 to double the size of the structural funds between 1987 and 1993.

This last example also brings out the conflict of principles that operates at the level of individual policies. At one level what happened at the 1988 Brussels summit was remarkable. In the negotiations leading up to the meeting, none of the wealthier member states gave the slightest indication that they would be willing to accept the proposed doubling of the structural funds. At the meeting itself, however, the poorer states were successful in gaining such a commitment for the period up to 1993 rather than up to 1992. The idea of the budget as a redistributive mechanism retains important political weight. Even a doubling of the funds may, however, have a relatively limited impact on reducing divergent levels of wealth in the Community. The total size of the budget in 1992 will still be less than half of what the MacDougall Report in 1977 considered to be necessary for the budget to begin to have a significant impact in redistributive terms (MacDougall Report). Nevertheless, the Brussels' decisions expressed the recognition of the wealthier states that the economic fortunes of the poorer members can be ignored by the EC only at its peril and demand a certain level of financial solidarity. Hence the idea of the budget as a redistributive mechanism retains important political weight.

However, it is one thing to create an EC policy, it is another to run that policy according to EC criteria. Take regional policy, for example: until 1985 the Regional Development Fund (ERDF) was subject to strict national quotas which guaranteed a certain level of funding to each member state. Since 1985, the policy has been amended by the creation of 'indicative ranges' which set upper and lower limits to what each member state can receive. Nevertheless, there remain important restrictions on the degree of discretion that the member states are prepared to concede to the Commission. Any attempt to measure the extent of regional problems in an objective way so as to determine priorities for expenditure inevitably raises important questions of equity which are difficult to resolve at the EC level. Should expenditure be concentrated only in the poorest regions or should all member states be assured some stake in the maintenance of the ERDF? Should account be taken of the relative wealth of a particular region in relation to other regions in the same state or should the comparison be cross-national? And how should the problem of industrial decline be compared with the problems of backward regions in the poorer member states?

These are not questions that can easily be solved, especially where they may lead to the Commission taking decisions beyond the reach of national governments. EC procedures remain sufficiently underdeveloped (or perhaps are sufficiently developed) for member states not to be willing to have complete trust in the outcome of decisions over which they have limited control. In this sense the shape of the budget also reflects the level of legitimacy that member states accord the EC process. As we shall see in the next section, the circumspect character of member states' attitudes is replicated in the process by which the budget is agreed, despite the very special role that the other institutions and in particular, the European Parliament play in that process.

The process of budgetary policy making

Just as the revenue and expenditure of the EC budget distinguish the EC from traditional international organizations, so the budgetary process is unique in character. It provides, through the Treaties, for the Commission and the EP to play an important role in the preparation of the budget and does not reserve decisions exclusively to the member states' Council representatives. It is also the subject of a constant process of review as the boundaries between EC and national competences are argued over and redrawn. The formal structure laid down by the Treaty only provides a partial picture of the way in which the process operates. None the less, it is important to understand the way in which the procedure is supposed to work, as it provides the framework within which budgetary negotiation actually takes place.

Article 203 of the EEC Treaty, as revised in 1975, lays down a clear timetable for the budgetary procedure and specifies precisely the role of the different EC institutions in that procedure. The process starts with the Commission preparing a preliminary draft budget which contains the estimates of expenditure for the following financial year, both of the Commission and of the other institutions (the EP, the Council including in an annex the ESC, the ECJ, and the Court of Auditors). This preliminary draft budget has to be placed before the Council 'not later than 1 September'. It is then the task of the Council to establish the first reading of the draft budget and to place it before the EP.[7] The EP then has forty-five days in which to adopt amendments or proposed modifications (this distinction will be explained below) before returning its first reading version of the draft budget to the Council. The same twofold procedure is then repeated: the Council has fifteen days after receipt of the EP's draft to prepare its second reading and thereafter the EP has a further fifteen days to react to the Council's new draft. When the procedure is completed, the EP President declares that the budget has been finally adopted and through his signature endows the budget with binding force *vis-à-vis* the institutions and the member states. Article 203 also allows for the EP to reject the budget in its entirety and to request that a new draft be presented to it: this has happened on two occasions, in 1979 and 1984, in relation to the budgets for the following years.

The process by which the preliminary draft budget is converted into the adopted budget is thus determined by two institutions, the Council and the EP, who are often referred to as the twin arms of the budgetary authority. However, it remains important to establish the degree of correspondence between the timetable and what actually happens, as well as the balance of influence within the joint budgetary authority.

First, although the Treaty presupposes that the timetable will be adhered to, there can be no certainty that it will be. It was a source of major consternation within the EC when in autumn 1987 for the first time since 1975 the Council proved unable to adopt a draft budget by the 5 October deadline. It eventually presented its first reading to the EP in March 1988 with the EP's second reading delayed until May. The EP, for its part, decided to take the Council to the ECJ for contravening its obligations under the Treaty, but the threat of such action was not sufficient to oblige the Council to respect the formal framework.

Second, the timetable laid down does not exhaust all the possibilities. At the end of 1986, for example, after the EP's second reading, the President was unable to sign the budget because the amendments adopted constituted an increase in expenditure which could only be made with the Council's assent, which was lacking. It was therefore necessary to have what amounted to a third reading in February 1987 before the President was able to sign the budget into law.

Third, the completion of the timetable does not necessarily end the debate on the budget. At the end of 1985, the EP President signed a budget which he considered legal but which the Council contested. It took the EP to Court and in July 1986, in case ECJ 34/86, the Council obtained the annulment of the budget. The budgetary procedure had to be reopened before the 1986 budget could be adopted in a final form acceptable to both branches of the budgetary authority.

All these examples demonstrate the conflict of interest between Council and the EP that is but thinly disguised in the words of the Treaty. Both sides use the framework available to exercise the maximum influence in the pursuit of the outcome that each considers desirable. Traditionally, this has meant the EP trying to expand the area of EC activity outside the agricultural domain with the Council more concerned to limit the extent of its power-sharing with the EP (Nicoll, 1986). Though both institutions enjoy the status of a part of the budgetary authority, it is not true that each enjoys the same level of influence within the process. This becomes immediately obvious when one considers more precisely the changes that each institution is entitled to make to the draft budget.

It was indicated above that the EP at its first reading can adopt either amendments or proposed modifications. This distinction reflects the existence of two kinds of EC expenditure, one which is designated compulsory, the other non-compulsory. These terms themselves are not to be found in the Treaty which talks rather of 'expenditure necessarily resulting from this Treaty or from acts adopted in accordance therewith' (compulsory expenditure), with non-compulsory expenditure corresponding to expenditure 'other than that necessarily resulting from this Treaty'. The precise boundary between these two categories has been the subject of continuous debate, although the broad shape of the two domains was settled by the Joint Declaration signed by Council, Commission and the EP in June 1982. As a result, one can identify as compulsory expenditure (CE) all the expenditure entered into under Titles 1 and 2 for EAGGF Guarantee, expenditure arising out of EC international agreements, and expenditure linked to reimbursements to member states (Title 8). Non-compulsory expenditure (NCE) is concentrated in the other titles of the budget in particular fisheries (Title 4), regional and social policies (Titles 5 and 6), research and development (Title 7) and cooperation with developing countries (Title 9). As the figures above (see Table 7.3) indicate, the balance between these two categories of expenditure is heavily weighted in favour of compulsory expenditure: it stands at approximately 75 per cent of the total and indeed has remained at about this level throughout this decade.

It is in this context that the EP's powers at first reading to adopt amendments to non-compulsory expenditure and proposed modifications to compulsory expenditure should be seen. Amendments require the support of a majority of MEPs (at present 260), whereas modifications only require a simple majority. However, the subsequent status of the two kinds of change is very different. The Council's decision on the proposed modifications at its second reading is final and the EP is not entitled to revive its proposals at second reading. In other words, for 75 per cent of the budget it is the Council which has the last word (although it requires a qualified majority to over-rule modifications that cut expenditure). As far as amendments are concerned, the EP is not bound by the decisions of the Council at second reading. Although it cannot introduce new amendments (other than compromises), it can re-establish its first reading amendments at second reading, provided they obtain not only the support of the majority of MEPs, as at first reading, but also three-fifths of the votes cast.

This right is, however, not unlimited in character: the EP is not free to increase non-compulsory expenditure (NCE) in the budget by whatever amount it considers appropriate. The limit upon the increase is determined by what is called the 'maximum rate'. This rate is a statistical measure of the growth in GNP, government spending and inflation in the member states which the Commission calculates and communicates to the budgetary authority before the outset of the budgetary procedure. For 1988, for example, the figure was set in March 1987 at 7.4 per cent thus providing a guideline as to the permitted expansion of non-compulsory expenditure in 1988 as compared with the volume of that same expenditure in 1987. The EP has the right (under Article 203, paragraph 9) to increase NCE from one year to the next by *half* the maximum rate and this amount is referred to as its 'margin for manoeuvre'. What usually happens is that the Council at its first reading increases NCE by half the maximum rate. The reason for this is that if the Council enters less than half, the EP can claim all the remaining percentage up to the maximum rate; if, on the other hand, the Council enters more than half, the EP is still entitled to an amount equal to half. At its first reading the Parliament has tended to enter much more than its margin for manoeuvre allows for. However, at second reading, it is obliged to limit itself to an increase commensurate with the maximum rate provisions, i.e. half the maximum rate beyond the Council's first reading, including those EP amendments which the Council accepted at its second reading.

This limitation is not one that the EP has been prepared to accept without major debate. The Treaty itself provides for the possibility of increase in the maximum rate being agreed by the budgetary authority if EC activities so require. However, during the 1980s there has been a major reluctance on the part of the Council to support such increases. In 1986, as we have seen, the Council took the EP to Court because the EP President signed a budget with a level of NCE which involved an increase in the maximum rate which the Council explicitly stated it was unwilling to accept. The reason for the EP's action in apparently violating the Treaty in this overt way illustrates the nature of the antagonism between the two arms of the budgetary authority and is therefore worthy of brief discussion.

The EP argued that 1986 was a special year which required an extra financial effort for two reasons: first, Spain and Portugal were due to join the EC and one could therefore not simply apply the maximum rate to 1985 expenditure and expect to have adequate coverage for an EC of twelve rather than ten; second, the EP accepted the Commission's argument that 1986 was going to witness an unusually high level of payments in the structural funds to cover commitments entered into in previous years (the problem was referred to as the 'weight of the past'). It was claimed that the budget had to be expanded if EC obligations to third parties were to be met. The Council recognized that both of these problems existed but refused to countenance the levels of increase the EP wanted. In the event, the Court ruled in favour of the Council, declaring that any increase in the maximum rate had to be agreed to explicitly by both arms of the budgetary authority. However, the EP could claim an important degree of satisfaction in that the budget for 1986 which was finally adopted did include levels of appropriations for the structural funds which were close to those voted by it some six months earlier. As a result, of course, the NCE base to which the maximum rate for the following year (1987) would be applied was substantially expanded.

The struggle over the maximum rate of increase has to be seen in a broader context. It is not simply a question of increases for their own sake but rather of increases linked to the issue of the overall shape of the budget. To this end the EP has sought to exercise its power of amendment in a varied way. It has, for example, consistently favoured using a large part of its margin of manoeuvre to support development aid, altering the allocation of expenditure within the non-compulsory sector. It has also taken advantage of the possibility of creating new budgetary lines as a way of providing an impetus for policy innovation. And it has used the budgetary reserve in Chapter 100 to freeze appropriations until it is satisfied with the Commision's plans for their use.

However, the amounts available for NCE and the rules governing that amount are very different from the equivalent amounts and rules applicable to compulsory expenditure. As we have already seen, there is a substantial imbalance in the budget between agricultural guarantee expenditure and the remainder, and this divide corresponds very closely to that existing between compulsory and non-compulsory expenditure. The volume of CAP expenditure is significant above all because of the rules governing its expansion: up to now it has proved impossible to contain that expansion through the budget.

The inability of the Council to maintain budgetary discipline is significant from two points of view. First, it underlines that the Council itself is not a single, monolithic block: it is made up of a whole series of different Councils responsible for the different areas of EC activity. Thus, when the budget is discussed, it is the national ministers responsible for budgets (in the UK case, not the Chancellor of the Exchequer as one might expect but the Minister of State to the Treasury) who take decisions. However, those decisions may more or less openly contradict the decision taken by the Council composed of agriculture ministers, whose concerns are rather different and who are subject to pressures from a well-organized lobby. As a result of this perhaps inevitable conflict it was agreed at the Brussels summit that if the deliberations of the

Agricultural Council appeared likely to lead to the agricultural guideline being exceeded then the final decision would be referred to a special joint meeting of the Council attended by the ministers of finance and the ministers of agriculture, who together would have the sole power to adopt a decision.

Second, the lack of budgetary discipline in agricultural spending has had an important effect on the EP's behaviour. It has constantly stressed the fact that the rules governing the two categories of expenditure have been interpreted very differently by the Council. Whereas since 1984, the Council has successfully refused to countenance any significant increase in the maximum rate, the agricultural guideline has proved much more malleable. As a result it is easier to understand why the EP has adopted such a combative role in seeking to protect and expand the non-compulsory part of the budget. How has the EP been able to influence the procedure? Part of its strategy has consisted in seeking to take advantage of the division within the Council. Thus at the end of 1986 when amendments were adopted going beyond a maximum rate acceptable to the Council, the intention was as much to increase pressure on the Agriculture Council to adopt reforms in the course of its marathon seven-day meeting as it was to increase the size of the budget.

Nor should it be forgotten that on particular issues, the EP has allies among the national delegations in the Council. This is particularly important in view of the rule that at its second reading, the Council requires a qualified majority to reject EP amendments. Each country has a certain number of votes, together totalling seventy-six. When a decision has to be taken, fifty-four votes are required for a qualified majority and twenty-three from at least four states for a blocking minority.[8] With Iberian enlargement in 1986 a broad alliance of countries has been established (Spain, Portugal, Italy, Greece and Ireland) with many common interests, including one shared with the EP, namely, a substantial increase in structural fund expenditure. As a result, in 1986 a blocking minority was able to prevent the rejection of many EP amendments. The difficulty, however, was that a qualified majority was also required to raise the maximum rate and the same states that voted against EP amendments were also able to prevent any such increase. In this instance the EP did not alter the final shape of the budget but it did have an important influence on the nature of the bargaining in the Council.

It is easy under such circumstances to claim that the EP's role is relatively marginal, but this would be to misunderstand the nature of the close relationship that the shuttle process between the two institutions generates. Considerable effort is expended by the Council in persuading the EP to come towards its point of view. Formal conciliation meetings take place before the Council's first and second readings at which an EP delegation is received and invited to present its view. The Council President, who chairs the meeting, responds and invites national delegations to do likewise. Sometimes this invitation is not taken up, as the members of the Council may not wish to air their differences openly, but on occasions a debate verging on negotiations can take place. At the same time, there are numerous informal meetings between ministers and MEPs at which both sides are able to speak freely about the possibilities of narrowing differences of opinion. And it is not true to say that the Council is unwilling ever to make concessions. In May 1988, for example, the German President of the Budgets Council came to Strasbourg and surprised MEPs (and some Council members) by saying that he was willing on behalf of the Council to accept all the EP's second reading amendments and thus to agree to an increase in the maximum rate for commitments. There was no need for him to act in this way but it constituted a limited but clear gesture of goodwill in the process of constant negotiation that goes on between the two bodies.

This negotiation has also to be seen in the context of the EC's general development: the budget decisions taken at the Brussels summit were part of a wider debate. In its report on the financing of the Community (COM(87) 101) the Commission made a specific link between its aim of financial security from 1988 to 1992 and the SEA's aims, in particular the determination to establish a single market by 31 December 1992. Indeed, it is in this way that the SEA's impact on the budget should be seen. The SEA introduced a number of important changes in the legislative area (notably by increasing the scope for majority decisions and strengthening the EP's role in the adoption of legislation), it did *not* touch the formal institutional balance in the budgetary field: there were no amendments to Article 203 of the Treaty, for example. However, the SEA did have important consequences for the budgetary process. Commission document (COM(87) 101) was specifically couched in terms of offering the financial means for achieving what had been laid down in the SEA, without the EC being subject to the severe budgetary crises arising out of shortage of revenue which had affected it on an almost continuous basis from 1984 onwards. Thus, for example, the report gave a financial expression to the promotion of 'economic and social cohesion' which had been enshrined as an objective in the Single Act with the Commission urging that the structural funds be doubled by 1992.

The EP strongly supported the Commission position and in this respect the decisions taken at the 1988 Brussels summit were very satisfactory. NCE increases were assured and went far beyond what the maximum rate would have allowed. Already for 1989 this rate was down to 5.8 per cent from 7.4 per cent in 1988 and 8.1 per cent in 1987. Thereafter it was expected to drop to below 4 per cent in value terms (just over 1 per cent in real terms) by the beginning of the 1990s. The Brussels summit opened the way to a five-year period in which the Council would no longer insist on the maintenance of the normal maximum rate, hence removing one important source of conflict between the two arms of the budgetary authority.

However, at another level, the Brussels' decisions were deeply disturbing as they undermined the EP's traditional role. Member states proposed to set annual limits on revenue for the period up to 1992 with the result that the actual size of the budget was likely to be effectively determined in advance of the budgetary procedure rather than being fixed at the end through the signature of the EP President. Moreover, within the budget a distinction was made between non-compulsory expenditure linked to the structural funds and other multiannual allocations such as research and development on the one hand and other non-compulsory expenditure on the other. Whereas the latter was to be subject to the maximum rate, the former would be allowed to expand in accordance with the commitments made at Brussels.

Remarkably, Council and the EP resolved, at least temporarily, these difficulties by signing in June 1988 an inter-institutional agreement which laid down a planned expenditure growth up to 1992 by broad policy area. It also set out rules governing any revision of this financial perspective which provided important guarantees for both sides. The EP was assured of a significant increase in the total amount of NCE that could not be endangered by an expansion of CAP spending. Indeed, it won the right to give its approval by qualified majority to any such increase in CE. The Council, for its part, was able to ensure that the extent of the EC's financial obligations for the next five years be formally agreed by the EP. The two are now locked into an arrangement whose character can only really be appreciated when it is put into practice.

First experiences of the new agreement have proved rather different than many expected at the time of its negotiation. In the second half of 1988 CAP expenditure fell dramatically. A reviving dollar and the American drought combined to cut the gap between world and EC food prices and to help cut the level of stocks held in storage. As a result, the Commission proposed that the size of the 1989 budget be cut by just under 1.4bn ECU and the budget finally adopted in December 1988 (44.8 bn ECU in payments) fell more than 2bn ECU short of the figure both the EP and Council had fixed as a limit for total spending in 1989 in the financial perspective.

In one sense, this was a satisfactory outcome for the EP. It gained an improvement in the balance between compulsory and non-compulsory expenditure in favour of the latter, with anticipated CAP spending falling below 60 per cent of the total budget for only the second time in the EC's history. However, the gain was more apparent than real. The EP was unable to prevent these savings from flowing directly back into national treasuries. Nor were any of the savings earmarked for the development of other EC policies. In part, this was due to the desire to have the budget adopted before the beginning of 1989, something that had not happened for five years; in part, too, the inter-institutional agreement had succeeded in creating a more cooperative climate of relations between the Council and the EP which few wished to endanger in the first year of its application. It would, however, be rash to predict that this 'honeymoon' will survive the continuing attempts of both sides to interpret the agreement to their advantage, particularly after the third direct elections in 1989.

Conclusion

This chapter has stressed three main points. First, the EC is very different from traditional international organizations: the system of own resources and the procedure by which expenditure is determined is unique in the degree of autonomy that it permits to supranational institutions. Such autonomy is limited, but nevertheless real.

Second, there is a substantial momentum in the budgetary process. The idea that the EC is constantly paralysed by crisis in the budget area as elsewhere overlooks the fact that important changes have taken place over a relatively short period of time and that those changes are witness to growth rather than decline. The revenue system has developed in important ways since the EC's inception. The 'own resource' system, introduced in 1970, has been modified and prompted major dispute in the EC, whether over the issue of Britain's revenue reduction – agreed at Fontainebleau – or because of the introduction of a fourth resource designed to take account of 'capacity to pay'. Similarly, expenditure has grown, slowly but surely, with no member state prepared to block any further increase. Rather the argument has been over where monies should be spent with constant efforts to control agricultural expenditure combining with a desire, particularly strong among poorer member states as well as in the EP, to increase spending on structural policies. And the process by which decisions are taken over expenditure and revenue has witnessed great variety in EP–Council relations which belies the bald language of the Treaty.

Finally, the debate about the budget must be seen as a debate about the EC's development. Those who wish to see the EC equipped with a larger more coherent budget, operating on EC criteria largely decided by the Commission and shaped by the decisions of the directly elected EP, are at the same time expressing their faith in a closer level of integration; those, on the other hand, who see the EC as little more than a common trading area will necessarily view any expansion of the budget and EC competence within it with much greater suspicion. One can say with some degree of confidence that the 1988 Brussels summit was a substantial blow to those of the latter persuasion. Whether its outcome will advance the cause of the integrationists remains to be seen.

Notes

1. The views expressed in this paper are entirely the author's own.
2. The themes of this chapter have been substantially influenced by Wallace, H. (1980), *Budgetary Politics: The Finances of the European Community*, London, George Allen & Unwin.
3. The 1 per cent VAT rate was not, as is often supposed, 1 per cent of national VAT revenue and was therefore not directly dependent on the volume of that revenue.
4. In recent years the Commission has declined to provide information of this kind on the grounds that the gains and losses of member states need to be assessed on a broader basis than that provided by the budget.
5. There is a considerable literature on this subject. One can note in particular, Denton, G. (1984), 'Restructuring the EEC Budget: Implications of the Fontainebleau Summit', JCMS, 23, pp. 117-40.
6. On 30 November 1987 one ECU was worth £0.688665. Hence the value in pounds sterling is roughly two-thirds of £35 bn.
7. The EEC Treaty still uses the term 'assembly', but the term 'parliament' was formally recognized by the member states themselves in the Single European Act adopted in 1986.
8. Germany, France, Italy and the UK have ten votes; Spain has eight, Belgium, Greece, the Netherlands and Portugal each have five, Denmark and Ireland each have three and Luxembourg has two.

References

Barnes, I. and Preston, J. (1988), *The European Community*, Harlow, Longman, p.23.
Commission of the European Communities (1977), *The Role of Public Finance in the European Communities*, (The MacDougall Report), Volumes I and II, Brussels.
— (1987), *Report by the Commission to the Council and Parliament on the Financing of the Community Budget*, COM (87) 101, Brussels.
Nicoll, W. (1986), 'From Rejection to Repudiation: EC Budgetary Affairs in 1985', *Journal of Common Market Studies* 25, 31-50
UN Resolution 40/253A of 1985 quoted in *Yearbook of International Organisations 1987/8*, edited by Union of International Associations, Munich, K.G. Saur (reference AA 3375).

8 The Common Agricultural Policy

John S. Marsh

At the end of the Second World War, Europe's industry was in ruins and Europe's people short of food. Agriculture, too, had been disrupted by the war and in the process of recovery was given a key role. Increased output was the goal and agricultural policy the means by which governments sought to attain it. Agriculture at that stage still accounted for a large share of total employment. It was Europe's biggest industry and the basis of social and community life for the rural regions which still made up most of Europe's land area. Its dominant economic and social role ensured its political importance. Regarded by many as a stabilizing influence reflecting the personal responsibility and entre-preneurship required of the small farm, the rural community was to some minds at least associated with a concept of national character. For political parties the support of the farm vote was seen as crucial to survival.

By the time the Rome Treaty was signed, the facts had changed. Food was no longer scarce. Industry had recovered and in West Germany an 'economic miracle' was under way. Despite this, entrenched attitudes ensured that in any attempt to weld together the economies of member countries, agriculture could not be treated like other industries. For most industries it was envisaged that competition within a framework of free internal trade and common external tariffs could determine what was produced and where production occurred. For agriculture, Article 38 of the Treaty, required that the industry should be brought into the Common Market by a 'Common Agricultural Policy' (the CAP). Article 39(1) sets out its principal objectives:

(a) to increase agricultural productivity by promoting technical progress and by ensuring the rational development of agricultural production and the optimum utilization of the factors of production, in particular labour;
(b) thus to ensure a fair standard of living for the agricultural community, in particular by increasing the individual earnings of the persons engaged in agriculture;
(c) to stabilize markets;
(d) to assure the availability of supplies;
(e) to ensure that supplies reach consumers at reasonable prices.

In effect this was 'Community creation' by administration rather than by the pressure of market forces. An analysis of the reasons for this choice and the decisions about policy to which it led forms an essential starting point for an understanding of the CAP, its problems and the options now open to the policymaker.

Why have a common policy for agriculture?

Policies exist to correct perceived failures in the spontaneous operations of societies to achieve the goals they value. Agricultural policies had focused on four such areas of concern: the risk of food shortages; the volatility of agricultural markets; the poverty of many farmers and farm workers; and the possible role of agriculture in relation to general economic objectives like employment, the balance of trade and economic growth.

In the 1950s the Six member countries who were to form the Community were still net importers of foods, requiring imports of 15 per cent of total cereal consumption and 36 per cent of maize.[1] Rationing was a recent memory and any government allowing a severe shortage to recur would face the wrath of the consumers at large. Food security is an ill-defined concept. In situations of famine it means a lack of adequate nutrients to sustain health. For affluent, well-fed groups it may represent little more than assurance of continuing supplies of each of the foodstuffs they choose to consume. Security can be achieved either by producing and holding a store of food or by acquiring sufficient wealth to be able to buy it from other countries when supplies are scarce and prices are high. The politics of food security are more straightforward. The farm lobby suggests that the only way to be sure of a supply is to produce it at home. They also emphasize the 'essential' nature of each type of food – an argument which side steps the adaptability of the human constitution to a variety of diets. Politicians, while recognizing that adequate supplies of exotics can be bought abroad, tend to accept the notion that indigenous foods ought to be encouraged at home. Such thinking formed much of the agricultural policy which pre-dated the CAP and has been embodied within it.

Agricultural markets are regarded as inherently volatile. The economic reasons for this stem from the low-price elasticity of demand for most farm products. Small increases in the quantity reaching a market result in more than proportionate falls in price. As a result the revenue of farmers from a 'good' crop may be less than from a poor harvest. At the same time, the quantity reaching the market is in the short term very insensitive to price movements. Although some products can be stored, this is a costly activity and therefore the market price may rise and fall steeply in response to the vagaries of a weather dependent production system.

The inherent instability of agricultural markets is accentuated on the world market by the activities of governments. Those who seek to avoid internal price falls by subsidizing exports, depress world markets which are unable to absorb additional quantities at existing prices. This may justify the actions of governments who seek to defend their producers by placing limits on imports, the results of which will further force down world prices. Similarly, if domestic supplies fall and governments subsidize imports to shield their consumers, prices in world trade will be forced up – a tendency reinforced by governments which impose barriers to exports to hold internal prices down. All these activities feature in the policies of major trading nations. As a result European governments have sought to insulate both their producers and consumers from this volatile world market.

Once the period of food shortage had passed, in the 1950s, the predominant goal ceased to be certainty of supply and became the protection of farm incomes. The income elasticity of farm products is often small and for most production is less than unity. Implicitly this means that as the economy grows the revenues of agriculture will grow, but less rapidly than those of other sectors. Simultaneously the products which farmers buy as inputs from the rest of the economy will have to be paid for at a price which reflects the value in other industries of the resources which produce them. Such a situation provides the basis of a cost/price squeeze which might depress incomes within the sector. Relief could be achieved, in terms of the per-capita income of those who remain, by a migration of agricultural labour to other sectors. Such out migration has unattractive social consequences. In remoter areas populations' age, public services for transport, health and education become relatively expensive and the opportunities for all the trades and industries which service the rural community, shops etc, become fewer. In areas close to towns the population may actually increase as urban workers seek rural residences. For the traditional village this change, too, may be hard to accept. Not least house prices may rise to a level at which local young people are unable to find a place to live near their home and so join the drift to the cities. The attempt to sustain farm incomes thus reflects concerns both about the personal welfare of farmers and farm workers and the social structure of the countryside. Farm lobbyists stress both elements. Article 39 (1)(b) [EEC] reflects a similar perception.

The macro-economics arguments for agricultural support reflect the varying pre-occupations of governments. In the UK, for example, an argument often used to encourage the expansion of home agriculture was that it would improve the balance of payments. In France a similar type of argument attempted to justify the expansion of subsidized agricultural exports. In depressed regions, maintaining agricultural activity has been seen as crucial to avoiding unemployment. Thus policies have attempted to aid especially hill and mountain areas. In some parts of Europe expanding agricultural production has been seen as part, if not the engine of, economic growth. Thus policies have tried to encourage expansion even where local markets have been saturated. Macro-economic arguments frequently owe more to common sense than analysis. They have, however, played a part in conditioning the public and political mind in favour of farm support. The CAP developed in an environment within which these arguments were generally accepted. They meant that the agricultural industry could not be integrated by the dismantling of protection. Instead the process has to be achieved through substituting a common protection system, which enabled goods to be free to move within the EC. This common policy had to replace the differing levels of support among member countries.

The Instruments of the CAP

Price support

A policy which allows goods to move freely implicitly affects their prices. Among the Six price manipulation was a key element in each state's home agricultural policy. The new Community followed suit. The key instrument used to support prices was the variable import levy. (See glossary at the end of this chapter for details of all technical terms.) Ministers specify a price level they wish to see within the Community, variously known as a target or guide price. World offer prices are then monitored and if they fall below the acceptable level (threshold price) an import levy, equivalent to the difference, is placed on all imports of the product. The operational details vary from product to product[2] but the principle is clear. Competition by imports, priced below an acceptable level, is ruled out. For major products this method of price support is reinforced by intervention purchase. This instrument is triggered when internal prices fall below a level indicated by the Council of Ministers. Member states' intervention agencies then purchase supplies of the product, provided it is of suitable quality and offered in appropriate quantities. In effect a floor is put in the market. Prices are free to move only between the 'intervention' and 'target' or 'guide' prices. Table 8.1 shows these prices for a number of key products.

Table 8.1   Expenditure on Export Refunds

	1974	1975	1976	1977	1978	1979	1980
Total Products	590.6	968.9	1,474.3	2,287.2	3,538.6	4,732.2	5,452.4
Monetary Compensatory Amounts in Extra Community Trade			191.7	209.8	211.0	249.6	242.6
				206.9[1]			
Total	590.6	968.9	1,666.2	2,703.9	3,749.6	4,981.8	5,695.0
USD/ECU Conversion Rate (End of Year)	0.795	0.858	0.885	0.816	0.726	0.695	0.718

	1981	1982	1983	1984	1985	1986	1987
Total Products	4,938.5	4,764.2	5,220.5	6,203.6	658.7	7,239.2	9,066.0
Monetary Compensatory Amounts in Extra Community Trade	270.0	289.1	339.2	415.8	128.4	170.10	117.0
Total	5,208.5	5,053.3	5,559.7	6,619.1	6,716.1	7,409.2	9,183.0
USD/ECU Conversion rate (End of Year)	0.896	1.021	1.123	1.267	1.310	1.016	0.867

[1] Effect of double rate
Source: Agricultural Situation in the Community 1981-1987
   Eurostat Review 1971-1980, 1976-1985
   Eurostat Eurostatistics 1978-1987

The third key instrument of the CAP is export restitution. The EC pays exporters a subsidy equivalent to the difference between the price at which they buy within the EC and the price they realize in third country markets. The amounts of these refunds and the quantities to which they apply are determined periodically by the Commission. For cereals there is a second system where exporters are invited to tender for export licences.

Co-responsibility levies

Import levies, intervention purchase and export restitutions formed the major tools of the CAP as it evolved in the 1960s. Today, however, these are reinforced by a number of others. As the problem of financing the CAP grew, the EC devised a system of co-responsibility levies. These are payments made by farmers in respect of the volume of product they sell. For example, a wheat producer might sell his product at £100 per tonne, but could then be required to pay a 3 per cent co-responsibility levy necessitating £3 per tonne to be sent to the EC. The logic here was to reduce prices to farmers, raise revenue for the EC and leave consumer prices unchanged. Two examples clarify these aims.

Initial co-responsibility levies were applied to the milk lake. The levy was invented both to discourage producers and aid disposal. The levy charged was small, some 1.5 per cent. Milk surpluses continued to grow until in 1984, faced by a bill for dairy support of 5,441.7, ECU – the EC decided to replace it by a quota system. For milk, there are two forms of levy payment on wholesale deliveries. Formula A, or the 'producer-based' quota, invokes a penalty on over-supply by an individual producer at a rate equal to 75 per cent of the target price. Formula B, or the 'dairy-based' quota, invokes a penalty on over-supply by an individual producer at the dairy level of a rate equal to 100 per cent of the target price. These penal levies are only charged if the country as a whole exceeds the allowable quota. In practice they have become virtually national quotas, and obviously conflict with the concept of free trade within the Common Market. Quotas on sugar were introduced much earlier. The system used defined three tranches of output. Each member state was allowed 'A' and 'B' quotas which it allocated to its sugar factories. At the initial 'A' quota level the EC guaranteed a high level of support. Support under the 'B' quota was much lower. Any excess over 'A' and 'B', is termed 'C', and cannot be sold on the internal market. It must either be stored or exported without the aid of export restitutions.

By 1988, faced with acute financial constraints, the EC began adopting a system of budgetary stabilizers which involves the Council determining in principle a ceiling level of production (Maximum Guaranteed Quantity) it is prepared to support. A co-responsibility levy is chargeable at the beginning of each marketing year, and will be reimbursed if the maximum guaranteed quantity is not exceeded. If it is, the intervention price may be reduced at a future date. Small producers will be exempted from the co-responsibility levy in some cases.

Monetary compensatory amounts

Prices within the EC are fixed in terms of the European Currency Unit, the ECU. Payments to farmers or exporters have to be made in national currencies. Thus a key element in determining what a farmer actually receives is the exchange rate between his currency and the ECU. Problems arise when exchange rate movements become frequent. In principle if a currency appreciates, prices fixed in ECUs should fall. Similarly if a currency depreciates farmers should receive higher prices. Both changes have been resisted by governments. A fall in prices to farmers in West Germany, (as the D-Mark rose against other currencies) was firmly resisted by the farm lobby. A rise in prices where currencies declined in value, for example in the UK or France, was opposed by governments anxious to avoid any stimulus to inflation. Countries whose currency had moved in relation to other members were reluctant to restore parity by altering the green conversion rate. Compensating action was required at the frontier to prevent advantages being gained by importers or exporters based on speculative movements of products bought and sold at prevailing exchange rates in member countries. To this end, the monetary compensatory amount (MCA) was introduced. It is a tax on agricultural imports from the rest of the EC to a country whose currency has appreciated together with an equivalent subsidy from that country for exports to the other members. The level of the tax/subsidy is set to offset the change in currency priorities so that trade can continue as before. For countries whose currencies depreciate an analogous system of taxes on exports and subsidies on imports exists.

Such an approach fragments the EC market. It distorts the co-ordination of competition between member states. It allowed agricultural prices, measured in terms of the volume of 'other' goods a given quantity of farm product would purchase, to vary more in the mid-1970s than in the mid-1960s. The Commission has made sustained attempts to reduce and remove MCAs, but they have persisted and grown in complexity as different rates have been applied to different products and attempts multiply to remove loopholes and anomalies. For the policymaker, however, adjustments in MCAs have become another instrument of policy affecting both the prosperity of farmers and the EC's aggregate level of output.

The policy instruments outlined here were the result of protracted argument and debate within the EC. That any agreement was reached is itself a major achievement. Without it the EC as a whole could not have come into existence. However, from a relatively early date it was clear that the CAP was seriously flawed. Since 1968 the Commission itself has put forward no fewer than twelve papers specifically discussing the adaption of the CAP. (A list of these papers can be found in the Reference section.)

Why the CAP now needs reform

Two distinct reasons have led policymakers to recognize the need for change in the CAP: first, changes in the EC economy; and second, failures to achieve the CAP's stated goals because of the nature of the policy itself. In each case, the attempt to manipulate an unreformed CAP to cope with these deficiencies has increased costs. For practical purposes, the main perceived reason for changing the CAP has now become its unacceptable cost.

The EC economy has changed as a result of enlargement, of new technology and of economic growth: the impact of each of those on the CAP must be considered. Enlargement occurred in two phases. In 1973 the UK, Ireland and Denmark joined; in the 1980s, Greece, Spain and Portugal.

Enlargement

The first enlargement brought in two countries (Denmark and Ireland) who depended to an important degree on agricultural exports, but the third, the UK, was a major food importer. Two important consequences arose. From a global point of view there was a significant diversion of trade from low-cost third-country suppliers to EC farmers. Within the EC, the UK found itself a perpetual net contributor to the cost of the CAP, payments which arose either in the form of higher prices paid for EC produced supplies or as import levies paid on imports from third countries. Farmers in the EC countries concerned found the price levels within the EC substantially higher than they had previously experienced. As a result they were encouraged to expand. The implications of applying the CAP to these countries heightened tension between the EC and other agricultural exporters; underlined a tendency for the UK to be isolated on the CAP within the EC; and increased the cost of farm support as EC supplies outstripped EC demand.

The second phase of enlargement introduced new problems. The new states were poor by north European standards. They had large farming populations: Spain increased the EC's agricultural labour force by 24 per cent and Portugal by 12 per cent (Commission of the EC, Agricultural Situation in the Community Report 1986: 278-9). Their products were characteristic of the Mediterranean region. CAP support was more generous for typical northern products – cereals, milk and beef – than for fruit and vegetables and wine, which formed a larger share of southern agriculture. The new members looked to the CAP to aid their farm sectors. This demanded not only more spending, difficult in the context of the existing budget cost of the CAP, but a rebalancing of benefits to the south's advantage. The second enlargement intensified some existing problems, not least those associated with the diversion of trade from traditional importers to EC sources. The United States, in particular, protested and sought adjustments in the CAP to allow it to continue its cereal sales to Spain.

New technology

Within the economic climate created by the CAP, farmers were encouraged to apply new technology. The price support system meant that as production grew there would not be a sudden collapse in prices. In effect part of the risk of innovation was transferred from the farmer to the state. There were many opportunities to introduce improvements. New and more productive seeds and breeding animals were developed. The agro-chemical industry provided plant nutrients in the form of fertilizer and crop protection through herbicides, pesticides and fungicides. New machines improved cultivation while innovation in irrigation, drainage and buildings improved the environment in which crops grew and animals were reared.

Two aspects of this new technology undermined the CAP. First, output grew more rapidly than demand. For example, since 1973 total cereal production has grown by 48 per cent but internal consumption by 17 per cent (Commission of the EC, Agricultural Situation in the Community, T/176 Report, 1987). For an increasing range of products the EC became a net exporter so the costs of support to the budget grew. Second, the new methods were generally capital intensive. They replaced labour and to a lesser extent land by bought-in inputs. Economically this meant that an efficient agricultural system could provide a particular level of income for each level of output for only a decreasing number of people; if the same number of people remained, the industry would become increasingly inefficient and its costs to the rest of the economy would grow.

In its early years the EC enjoyed a sustained period of rapid economic growth.

While this implied greater competition for resources used in agriculture, it also provided alternative employment opportunites for many rural people. The agricultural labour force fell rapidly: between 1964 and 1974 some four million people left farming – 35 per cent of the total agricultural labour force in 1964 (Commission of the EC, Agricultural Situation in the Community Report 1975: 355). As a result the global income of agriculture had to be shared between fewer people and living standards rose for those who still farmed. Precise measurement of this change is difficult. Many farm businesses are part-time. Household income, as distinct from income from farming may be relatively high compared with that in other sectors.[3] Farmers who own their farms, possess a significant capital asset. In these terms, if not in relation to annual income, they are relatively rich compared with most citizens. The position is also complicated by the wide dispersion of incomes within agriculture. Successful large farmers generally enjoy high incomes and many have the trappings of affluence. In contrast, the much more numerous small farm businesses managed with 'average competence' have only modest incomes. Those farm families which have depended solely on the income of a small farm for their living have found it difficult to keep pace with the living standards of fully employed workers in other sectors. Average income data, or data aggregated for the industry as a whole, do not provide a reliable insight into the fortunes of farm families.

Economic change

Following the oil crisis, economic growth slackened. Much new technology in industry was labour saving. In several external markets the products of newly industrialized countries provided enhanced competition. Within the EC unemployment rose and job opportunities for those leaving farming shrank. The rate of migration of manpower from agriculture fell. Between 1964 and 1968 (EUR6, that is six members) 1,853,000 people left agricultural employment. For 1974 to 1978 this figure was 568,000 (EUR9). Although farm incomes, in the EC as a whole, were maintained, falling by only 0.3 per cent in real terms from 1975 to 1979, the cost of farm support grew. EAGGF Guarantee section spending rose 4,8212.5 mil ECU in 1975 to 10,434.5 mil ECU in 1979. The relative stagnation of the EC economy did not mean that for all its people incomes ceased to grow. In the 'sunrise' industries personal wealth increased and this helped to fuel a demand for a more rural lifestyle based not on agriculture but on the activities of relatively new industries. In rural areas within easy reach of conurbations, new growth took place as former town dwellers came to live in villages and country towns. The impact on the traditional rural community was mixed. At one level it provided a new demand for services and a source of income. In the housing market in particular it pushed house prices beyond the reach of young agricultural families; in effect the value of income was depressed as the prices of assets essential to their survival in the countryside rose. For the CAP this process intensified the problem of maintaining farm incomes at a politically acceptable level.

The growing need to export EC farm products, in order to maintain CAP determined internal prices, placed a rising burden on the EC budget, which the decline in the relative value of the US dollar to the ECU greatly increased from 1985. World prices for most farm exports are denominated in US dollars. Thus if the dollar falls a given quantity of agricultural exports earns fewer ECUs. However, the CAP requires EC exporters to buy at the ECU price within the EC. As a result, the gap between EC and world prices grows, requiring the EAGGF Guarantee Section, responsible for subsidizing the exporter, to provide greater funding (refer to Table 8.2). The implication is that the budget will need extra resources to remove surplus production from the market.

The growing impact on the CAP of events over which the agricultural policymaker has no control has been intensified by limitations inherent in the CAP. The instrument upon which it depends, price manipulation, is incapable by itself of delivering all the goals which the CAP seeks to attain. A key target has been the maintenance of farm income. Price rises, however, tend to become capitalized into land values and to lead to growing purchases from other sectors. The benefit to farmers' incomes thus tends to erode over time. For new farmers, or those who seek to expand, the impact is more an increase in costs than an improvement in income. Further price rises, designed to restore incomes, are likely to prove equally futile while at the same time stimulating production. For the CAP, once the domestic market is supplied, this means that prices and incomes can only be sustained by budget expenditure, intervention or export restitution. As it stands therefore, the CAP is incapable of delivering both a satisfactory level of income and an appropriate volume of output. One or other or both must be sacrificed.

A second systemic problem relates to the distribution of income. Price support is related to the volume of produce sold. It benefits most large farmers, who, if they are reasonably competent, should not be poor. The farmer with little to sell, either because his farm is small or because he is situated in difficult farming country, benefits proportionately less. However, price support is supposed to have a social welfare function and sustain rural communities most of whose farms are small. While it is clear why the CAP has consumed 70-80 per cent of the EC's budget since 1973, the cost is seen as unacceptable given the EC's limited resources and growing demands on them. The CAP's reform is vital. In 1986, it was agreed to increase the EC's own resources by raising the VAT to which it was entitled to 1.4 per cent from 1 per cent. This increase was subject to the condition that agricultural spending should not rise at rates greater than the growth in the EC's resources. It was to be reviewed in 1988 with a view to increasing the VAT entitlement from 1.4 per cent to 1.6 per cent. Although the official level of VAT entitlement has been held at 1.4 per cent the inter-governmental advances required to cover legal expenditure obligations have pushed this figure over the 1.6 per cent level so far rejected by the twelve member countries. The actual VAT rates required to finance the EC budget are shown in Table 8.2. This picture of the CAP's cost is incomplete. Apart from contributing as taxpayers to the EC budget, citizens pay directly for the CAP through higher food prices. Thus the total transfers involved for the farm sector greatly exceed the apparent budget cost. The CAP also has an economic cost because it ensures that resources remain in agriculture, even when the value of their output is less than their cost. It makes the EC economy poorer. One aspect of this is a lower real income per capita; another is a loss of competitiveness by other industries on the world market. Such reduced competitiveness in turn implies fewer jobs in the EC. Measurement of these 'real' costs of the CAP is difficult. Several attempts have been made (Buckwell, 1982, Koester, 1984 and the Bureau of Agricultural Economics, 1985 are all interesting sources for

Table 8.2   VAT required for financing the community budget (% VAT rate)

	1983	1984	1985	1986	1987
Actual Budget VAT rate, including inter-governmental advances	1.00	1.14	1.23	1.40	1.39
Non-budgeted expediture					
– current deficit	—	—	—	0.10	0.23
– non-depreciation of agricultural stocks	0.13	0.08	0.08	0.10	0.03
– 'cost of the past'	0.09	0.06	0.09	—	—
VAT rate required for proper financing	1.22	1.28	1.40	1.60	1.65
Accumulated liabilities billions ECU	3.0	6.0	8.6	12.2	17.0

Source: COM(87)101 and Corringendum

reference) and while they differ on details the overall picture is clear: the CAP, as it stands, represents a heavy economic burden for the EC.

Proposals for Reform

Proposals to reform the CAP are almost as old as the policy itself.[4] Apart from official Comm ission papers there have been numerous suggestions from interested part es and outside observers. To describe these in detail would occupy too much space. At the end of this chapter, following the notes, there is a listing of references, organized by topic. It is, however, helpful to distinguish between what may be regarded as symptomatic and systemic proposals. The goal of symptomatic proposals is to remedy a specific perceived weakness of the policy – its cost, its balance or its income distribution. Systemic proposals seek a change in the nature of the CAP itself. In practice, specific 'reforms' may have both types of effect. The final section of this chapter will argue that while symptomatic reforms are likely to take place, the CAP can only reach stability if systemic changes are accepted.

A prime official reason for advocating change has been the CAP's unacceptable cost to the budget. Commission documents began acknowledging cost problems in 1975 (see COM(75)100, COM(79)710, COM(85)333 and COM(87)430). Three main targets of reform have been proposed: cutting rewards to farmers; limiting the EC's liability; and restricting the amount farmers sell. Several different possibilities exist under each heading.

Under the heading of a 'prudent price' policy, the Commission attempted the obvious route to reduce both supplies and liabilities by allowing real prices to fall. In fact the EC10 prices have fallen. The rate of decline has, however, been insufficient to contain the growth in output. The Council of Ministers has repeatedly shrunk from implementing the size of price cut the Commission believed the situation warranted. Political imperatives thus ruled out the sufficient application of the most obvious instrument of production control, lower prices. Apart from direct price reductions the Commission also proposed co-responsibility levies for a number of products which were in surplus. In effect farmers paid a tax on sales to the EC; their earnings were reduced;

consumers paid unchanged prices and the Commission received a modest addition to its budget revenues. The extent to which co-responsibility levies were applied was limited by the same political forces which inhibited price cuts. In practice, although farmers suffered a real reduction in returns, the incentive to produce was not sufficiently lowered to bring output under control.

The EC's liability to intervene can be restricted in a number of ways. Imposing more rigorous quality standards can eliminate part of the total output from support. Delaying or shortening the period during which intervention occurs can reduce the quantity likely to be offered. The export restitution system may be subject to competitive tender, to minimize the subsidy needed. Export restitutions may be suspended if world markets are especially weak. Since initial purchases at intervention are financed by national governments, payment of the accounting loss between intervention price and market price may be delayed for a substantial period after the product is sold from intervention. The delay in national repayment can save the EC considerable funds. More recently the EC sought to limit its liability through a system of 'Guarantee Thresholds' (in the 1988 negotiations the term Maximum Guaranteed Quantities was favoured). These refer to ceiling quantities which the EC is willing to support. The original intention was to cut prices the year following a breach of the ceiling. In fact this practice was not followed in June 1985, when the West German government refused to accept the price cut implied for cereals. In 1988 a more radical system of budgetary stabilizers was agreed. For example, in the case of oilseeds if production exceeded the ceiling, prices were to be cut in the same year. It remains to be seen how this will operate and whether it will be politically acceptable. The intention is clear – to limit the budget liability of the EC.

The third approach to reducing the budget cost of the CAP is to restrict the volume entitled to support. The most celebrated example of this is the milk quota system, hurriedly introduced in 1984 when dairy support accounted for 30 per cent of all guarantee expenditure (Commission of the EC Agricultural Situation in the Community Report 1985: 274). Despite co-responsibility levies imposed in 1977, this continued to grow. Quotas which limit the amount each dairy or each farmer can sell are not compatible with a competitive market but the urgency of the problem was such that the EC agreed to adopt an allegedly temporary system pegging output to only 1 per cent above the 1981 level.

Quotas remained as a major instrument of the CAP in the 1988 proposals. The quantity needing support has also been cut less directly by impeding competition from non-CAP products. The EC put quotas on isoglucose sales to shield its sugar regime which was in chronic surplus. It has also sought, unsuccessfully, to tax vegetable oils and fats (which are largely imported) to increase the domestic market for butter. A different approach to limiting quantity has been advocated by those who seek to impede the application of new technology: the EC has already imposed limits on the use of hormones in beef production. Many advocate limiting the use of nitrogen. Proponents of such proposals often relate them to other goals – protecting the health of the EC or its environment. Often scientifically flimsy the attraction of such ideas is their constraint on production.

Although budget problems have dominated much of the debate, the difficulties of ensuring an adequate level and distribution of farm incomes have never ceased to confront the policymaker. In the 1970s, the Commission briefly flirted with the so-called 'objective' method of price fixing. Calculations were made of changes to revenue and cuts and price proposals were introduced to restore incomes to an acceptable level. Such an approach faced practical and conceptual problems. At a practical level it was very difficult to measure changes satisfactorily. Some groups of EC farmers had done well, others had suffered losses of real income due to inflation. Conceptually an attempt to regulate income via price adjustment sacrifices control of the level of production. The rapid growth in surplus soon destroyed the credibility of the 'objective method'.

An inability to safeguard the aggregate level of income places especial stress on those whose incomes are lowest. The CAP has approached such problems by attempting to discriminate in favour of some groups of farmers. Aids, especially structural support increases, to farmers in designated 'less-favoured areas' have been more generous than for other farmers. The assumption that all farmers in such regions are poor is false. However, there undoubtedly exist in many remote, hill and mountain areas many of the poorest EC farmers. A more direct approach to discrimination in favour of small farm businesses runs into a different obstacle. Farm business sizes vary greatly between member states. In the UK most farm output comes from large farms. In most other EC countries there are few such farms. Discrimination in favour of the small would mean discrimination against the UK, Luxembourg and, to a lesser extent, some regions of France (see Figure 8.1). It is politically unacceptable on any significant scale.

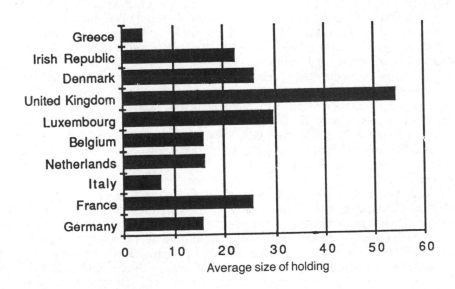

Figure 8.1   Average size of EEC farm holding over one hectare
Source: Loader, R.J. (1987, p.38)

The most straightforward approach to the income problem is direct income aids. These would be paid to people according to some principle unrelated to production. They could be based on past output levels, but are more usually proposed in relation to current social need. There are some severe problems. First, it is important that such aids should be production neutral. In a situation in which prices were allowed to fall this would be of little economic importance, except to the remaining commercial farmers. Under the CAP, however, prices continue to be administered at above-market clearing rates so any extra incentive to production adds to the problems of surplus. Second, income aids would have to be related to the Twelve's national social security policies as political problems would arise in differential treatment to the same sector by different states. The Twelve countries' social security policies vary greatly, reflecting in part the differing per capita incomes of their citizens. A level of income aid adequate in Portugal would leave German farmers very poor in relation to other Germans. Differential payments, with more going to the richer states, would be difficult for the Council of Ministers to accept. Third, direct income aids demand substantial budget expenditure. How much is needed depends upon the degree of support and numbers covered. The only way in which the CAP could find such funds would be by a drastic reduction in prices and price support. Such a move has so far proved politically unacceptable. Fourth, the most obvious way of accommodating different income levels and the shortage of EC funds would be for member governments to finance their own income aids. For many Europeans, including Commission officials, this smacks of the re-nationalization of the CAP.

The CAP's disintegration is the third issue reformers have addressed. Discussion has focused on the MCA system and the differing price levels to which this has led. Attempts were made to limit MCA's by defining a range of exchange rate movements for which no adjustment in MCA's would be allowed. At price reviews existing MCA's were to be negotiated away: small ones completely, large ones step by step. In 1984, the Council agreed to denominate common prices in terms of a special 'green ECU'. This meant that positive MCA's were removed by raising the common price, while negative MCA's disappeared by increasing prices in member states. The effect was to raise average prices paid to most EC farmers. The elimination of MCA's remains on the agenda for 1992. It is, however, hard to see how this can be achieved in the absence of a co-ordinated adjustment of national currencies. In turn this presupposes much greater co-ordination of economic management among the Twelve.

Pre-occupation with the symptoms of disorder in the CAP is wholly understandable among those responsible for administering this complex policy. However, from time to time both the authorities and outside critics have argued for a more radical 'systemic' approach. The economic rationale of such an approach is straightforward. Resources should be deployed in such a way that no movement would add more to the value of output than would be lost in current use plus the cost of the resource movement itself. To the EC the only true measure of what a product is worth is what it would cost to replace. No distinction can be made between internal supplies and those from imports. In both cases allowance has to be made for any uncertainty attaching to supplies and for positive and negative externalities associated with production. A thorough-going 'systemic' reform thus demands that the agricultural sector be fully integrated into other sectors and the world trading system. Official proposals do not go so far but they do bear some of the stamps of this approach.

As early as 1968 Mansholt could argue for the movement, in the Six, of five million hectares and five million people to non-farming activities (COM (68)1000). Current structural proposals for farm diversification and for set-a-side (the withdrawal of agricultural land from active cultivation to be laid to fallow, forestry or for use as grazing) have been influenced by the recognition that the CAP suffers not just from too much output but more fundamentally from too many resources committed to farming. Three areas of debate merit special mention.

First, the EC's traditional approach has focused on aids to retraining, retirement and the modernization of remaining farms. This approach was overtaken in the 1970s by rising unemployment. It remains, however, a positive attempt to achieve resource mobility in a more gentle way than simply bankrupting farm businesses. Elsewhere in the economy during the 1980s more faith has been placed in market forces and this may be applied to farming.

Second, for agriculture the externalities of its productive activities are of great importance. Some negative externalities are easy to identify: mud on roads; unpleasant smells; water pollution by fertilizers or pesticides or fields blackened by straw burning. Positive externalities, although less easy to spot, are equally real: for example, the appearance of much of the landscape; the maintenance of access to the countryside and the sustenance of many village communities. In determining the value of agricultural activities in Europe such externalities seem likely to play a growing role. Controls over pollution and aids for farming in environmentally sensitive areas already exist. The world market price of food cannot provide the only guide to the value of Europe's agriculture.

Third, the pressure of international opinion on the CAP is likely to grow. In part this is because as the world's largest food importer and second largest food exporter, the EC plays a leading role in the world market. Moreover, the CAP has sought to solve many internal problems by treating the world market as residual. It has dumped its exports, frustrated lower-priced imports and even, in 1974 when world prices of sugar rose, subsidized imports. Other countries do not believe that a fair trading system can co-exist with the CAP in its present form. The urgency of the issues has increased as a result of the decision in 1984 to embark upon a further round of trade negotiations in GATT. In common with other GATT signatories, the EC agreed that agriculture should be included and accepted that this would involve consideration of agricultural policy as well as trade itself. Moves in this direction all imply a systematic approach to CAP reform. New economic arrangements will be needed if EC agriculture is to respond to the future needs of the Twelve.

The prospect for reform

Great ocean liners require much water in which to change their direction. It is idle to expect that a policy so far-reaching, involving so many complex and competing interests as the CAP can be rapidly transformed. However, it is now accepted that it cannot continue in its original character. Politicians and officials are likely to minimize the need for change and to make great claims for the shifts which have already occurred. They seek to avoid the risk of lost votes or of avoidably alarming the farming sector. Not only farmers but many businesses which supply farm inputs and purchase farm products would feel threatened.

The result is that the debate on reform will continue to focus on the 'symptoms' and once budgetary solvency has been achieved there will be those who prematurely congratulate themselves on a successful 'reform'. The failure to face up to the CAP's systemic deficiencies means that fresh symptoms will occur and some existing ones get worse. Farm income problems are likely to grow. In remote, mountainous or inhospitable places populations will continue to fall. Continued support for farming will still make Europe less competitive as an economy in a world in which economic competition from the newly industrialized countries is growing. The single market will offer new opportunities for integration, but a CAP intent on safeguarding farm interests will tend to prevent this major sector from fully participating in the market. The steps taken in the 1980s to limit the CAP's budget cost are likely to prove successful. Already milk surpluses appear to be under control and cereals may be expected to respond to the more stringent application of guarantee thresholds and budget stabilizers. However, it seems very probable that in the 1990s 'Reform of the CAP' will still be on the European agenda.

Notes

1. Taken from Bureau of Agricultural Economics (1985).
Sources: a) Commission of the European Communities (1980) A Systematic Approach to Agricultural Forecasts for the European Community of Nine. b) Rokjo, Regier, O'Brien, Coffing and Bailey (1978). c) Gemmill, G. (1976). d) For coarse grains.
2. For a detailed account of import levy adjustments, see Harris, *et al.* (1983), pp.35-54.
3. The numbers of farmers supplementing their income from other sources in growing to such an extent that this aspect of income should no longer be ignored. The Ministry of Agriculture, Farms and Fisheries (1988, p.90) shows that only 15 per cent of farmers in the UK rely solely on their farm as their source of income. This trend was established in the early seventies. In Germany, in 1971, it was found that although the average farmer with a less than 5-hectare holding was only receiving an income of 2,700 DM from his farm, he was earning 11,900 DM via off-farm income. The figures for a 5-10 hectare holding are 6,500 DM farm income and 11,300 DM off-farm income. (OECD, 1977, 17).
4. *Agra Europe*, a weekly publication printed in London reports most major suggestions for CAP reform.

CAP reforms – a list of references by topic

Co-responsibility levy

French Farmers' Union, *Agra Europe*, No. 896, 26 September 1986, p.6.
Kiechle, I., *Agra Europe*, 20 December 1985, no.1164 p.1

Quotas

Curry, D., Report of the European Parliament's Agriculture Committee, discussed in *Agra Europe*, 11 November 1983, no.1056 p.1.
Harvey, D. (1984).
Woltjer, E, (1985). in Castle, *et al.*

Guarantee thresholds

COM(81) 608.
Pisani, E., 6 May 1983 a publication of the Development Commission on plans for the reform of the CAP reported in *Agra Europe*, no.1029, p.1.

Quantums

Pisani, E. (1985).

Market Forces

Marsh, J. (1981).
House of Lords (1983).
Confederation of the Food and Drink Industries of the EEC.
(CIAA) – reported in *Agra Europe*, 21.10.83, no.1053, p.1.
Castle, B., see Woltjer, E. (1985).
BEUC, statement reported in *Agra Europe*, 26.6.87, no.1241, p.3.
Priebe, H., see Marsh, J. (1981).
Ritson, C., speaking at conference. 'The CAP under Pressure' at the National Agricultural Centre, reported in *Agra Europe*, 13.3.81, no.919, p.2.
Pederson, J., in a memorandum to EEC Agriculture Commissioner, reported in *Agra Europe*, 26.4.85, no.1130, p.1.
Kearney, B., Irish Agricultural Institute, reported in *Agra Europe*, 26.8.83, no.1045, p.1.
Curry, D. European Parliament Agriculture Committee (1983).

Abolish MCAs

Curry, D., European Parliament Agriculture Committee (1983)

Nationalization of surplus disposal

Schmidt, H., in Statement to the Bundestag reported in *Agra Europe*, 28.11.80, no.950, pp.4-5.

Five-yearly price reviews

Tracy, M., at conference 'The Future of Agriculture in Europe' reported in *Agra Europe*, 7.11.86, no.1209, pp.2.

Low-input farming

Tracy M., (1984).
German Institute for Economic Research (DIW) reported in *Agra Europe* 23.8.85, no.147, p.2.

Diversification

European Parliament Agriculture Committee, opinions on Green Paper, reported in *Agra Europe*, 29.11.85, no.1161, p.4.

Set-a-side

Kiechle, I., speaking at International Green Week, reported by *Agra Europe*, 24.1.86, no.1168, p.4.
Jopling, M., discussion paper of Ministry of Agriculture, presented to EEC Prime Ministers, reported by *Agra Europe*, 26.9.86, no.1203, pp.1-4.
MacGregor, I., at the Oxford Farming Conference 1987, reported in *Agra Europe*, 9.1.87, no.1217, p.1.

Structures

Provan, J., reported in *Agra Europe*, 26.11.82, no.1007, pp.1, 2.
EP Regional Policy reported in *Agra Europe*, 11.4.86, no.1179, p.3.
Mackie, M., at the Oxford Farming Conference 1987, reported in *Agra Europe*, 9.1.87, no.1217, p.1.

References

Buckwell, A. (1982), *The Costs of the Common Agricultural Policy*, London, Croom-Helm.
Bureau of Agricultural Economics, (1985), *Agricultural Policies in the European Community; Their Origins, Nature and Effects on Production and Trade Policy*, Monograph No.2, (Canberra).
— Commission of the European Communities (1980), *A Systematic Approach to Agricultural Forecasts for the European Community of Nine*, Information on Agriculture No.77 (Brussels 1985).
Commission of the European Communities:
(COM) means Commission document published by the Commission in Brussels.
 Biotechnology in the Community, Stimulating Agro-Industrial Development, COM(86) 221/2.
 Commission of the European Communities Memorandum on the Reform of Agriculture in the European Community (The Mansholt Plan), COM(68) 1000.
 Improvement of the Common Agricultural Policy, COM(73) 1850.
 Stocktaking of the Common Agricultural Policy, COM(75) 100.
 Changes in the Common Agricultural Policy to Help Balance the Markets and Streamline Expenditure, COM(79) 710.
 Commission Report on the Mandate of 30th May, 1980, COM(81) 300.
 Guidelines for European Agriculture, COM(81) 608.
 Further Guidelines for the Development of the Common Agriculture Policy, COM(83) 380.
 Common Agricultural Policy – Proposals of the Commission, COM(83) 500.
 Perspectives for the Common Agricultural Policy, COM(85) 333.
 A Future for Community Agriculture, COM(85) 750.
 Commission Communication on Budgetary Discipline, COM(87) 430.
 Commission Communication Concerning a Review of Action taken to Control Agricultural Markets and Outlook for the CAP, COM(87) 410.
 Commission Communications Concerning the Implementation of Agricultural Stabilisers, COM(87) 452.
Gemmill, G., (1976), *The World of Sugar Economy: An econometric analysis of production and policies*, Agricultural Economics Report, No. 313, Michigan (Michigan State University).
Harris, S., Swinbank, A. and Wilkinson, A. (1983), *The Food and Farm Policies of the European Community*, Chichester, Wiley & Sons.
Harvey, D. (1984), *Price and Market Policies in European Agriculture*, in Thomson, K. J. and Warren, R. M. (eds) Department of Agricultural Economics, Department of Marketing, University of Newcastle upon Tyne.
House of Lords (1983), *Supply Controls*, Eighth Report of the House of Lords, European Communities Committee, London, HMSO.
Koester, U., Bale, M. (1984), *The Common Agricultural Policy of the European Community: A blessing or a curse for Developing Countries*, World Bank Staff Working Papers, No. 630, Washington, DC.
Loader, R. J. (1987), *The Structure and State of British Agriculture*, FMU Study No.13, University of Reading.
Marsh, J. (1981), *Alternative Proposals for the Common Agricultural Policy*, Irish Section, European League for Economic Co-operation (Dublin, Ireland).
Ministry of Agriculture Farms and Fisheries (1988), *Farm Incomes in the United Kingdom 1988*, London, HMSO.
OECD (1977), *Part-time farming Germany, Japan, Norway, United States*, (Paris).
Rojko, I., Regier, C., O'Brien, M., Coffing, P. and Bailey (1978), *Alternative Futures for World Food in 1985*, Volume 1, World GOL Model Analytical Report, US Department of Agriculture, Foreign Agricultural Economic Report No.146, Washington DC.

Statistical Office of the European Communities (1982), *Eurostat Review 1971-1980*, Luxembourg.
— (1987), *Eurostat Review* 1976-1985, Luxembourg.
Tracy, M. (1984), 'Issues of Agricultural Policy in a Historical Perspective,' Visiting Professor at Wye College, Presidential Address to the Agricultural Economics Society in Cambridge, April.
Treaty of Rome, (1957), 25 March.
Woltjer, E. (1985), in Castle, B., Woltjer, E., Pisani, E. (eds) *Reform of Common Agricultural Policy*, Luxembourg Socialist Group of the European Parliament
World Bank (1986), *World Development Report*, Washington D C, Oxford University Press.

Glossary

Co-responsibility levy is a tax imposed on the farmer for certain commodities. This provides a source of revenue to the EC while not implying a change in prices. The levy can either be a fixed rate (%) of the price received by the farmer or it may be variable according to the volume of commodity involved. Some levies may only be applied once a stated production limit has been exceeded (see *Quotas*).

Countervailing levy arises from the different import mechanism used for fruit, vegetables, wines, maize and new potatoes. The levy is calculated per shipment and is payable by the foreign supplier. It is calculated as the difference between the *reference price* (q.v.) and the foreign supplier's offer price. There is therefore no advantage to a foreign supplier in asking for a price lower than the reference price because the relative countervailing levy will absorb any difference.

ECU (European Currency Unit) is based on a basket of currencies weighted from member states with the weighting arising from the individual state's share of the Community GDP and associated factors. The calculation of ECU value is made daily. The ECU developed from the European Unit of Account (EUA).

Export Restitution is the subsidy paid to EC exporters by the EAGGF Guarantee section in order to bridge the gap between internal prices and world prices. Without this subsidy EC offer prices would be uncompetitive at world levels.

GATT (General Agreement on Tariffs and Trade) was originally brought into force in 1948. GATT lays down agreed rules for multi-national trade. It covers ninety-two countries (thirty-one others comply with the agreement on a *de facto* basis). The Commission represents the EC's interests in negotiations.

Green conversion rate is the rate which is used to convert CAP support prices from units of account to national currencies.

Intervention price is the guaranteed price at which the national intervention agencies are obliged to purchase all eligible (by volume and quality) EC produce offered them. For many products there is a Maximum Guaranteed Quantity (q.v.) in terms of volume beyond which intervention may be suspended. The intervention price thereby represents a 'floor' price in the wholesale market. The price the farmer can expect to receive has to allow for the deduction of marketing costs.

Lomé Convention was established in 1975 when an agreement was signed between the nine EEC states and forty-six ACP countries with an aim to establishing favourable trade relations. These terms are renegotiated at conventions held at approximately five-year intervals.

Maximum Guaranteed Quantity is the ceiling quantity which the EC is willing to support. Above this level the Council is empowered to make any necessary price adjustments. Intervention buying may also be suspended.

Monetary Compensatory Amounts (MCA's) are required to re-establish the common support prices arising where the value of a member state's currency has moved relative to the green conversion rate. It represents the gap between the price actually paid/received by the importer/exporter at the prevailing CAP support prices of that state and the common intervention price to be expected if prices for agricultural goods had been fixed at the market exchange rate.

Positive MCA's arise where the currency of a member state has revalued and thereby CAP support prices expressed in the national currency are above the 'common level'. There will be a tax on imports and a subsidy on exports.

Negative MCA's arise where the currency of a member state has devalued leaving CAP support prices expressed in national currency below the 'common level'. The result will be a subsidy on imports and a tax on exports.

Quotas specify a maximum desired output or the maximum amount of some resource (for example area of land) allocated for production by each farm or by a member country. They have the aim of limiting the quantity of production eligible for EC support. Usually a penalty will be incurred on producers who exceed the quota. This may take the form of a levy. Milk and sugar are two commodities to which quotas have been applied.

Reference price is calculated from average prices on representative markets over a period of years and is used to represent a minimum import price. Its use is limited to certain products: for example fruit, vegetables and wine (see countervailing levy). The term is confusing because it has alternative meanings when used in the context of the internal market. The above definition applies only to the reference price as used in the import mechanism.

Set-a-side refers to the withdrawal of agricultural land from active cultivation to be laid fallow or for use as grazing forestry. Recent proposals offer payments to farmers who reduce their crop area in this manner.

Support prices are those prices decided by the Council at the annual price review. They indicate the price levels to be expected within the Community. As such these prices differ from those which would exist in a free market situation.

Target price represents the desired level of price that producers should receive on sales of a particular commodity. The target price is the starting point for the derivation of other EC support prices (for example threshold and intervention prices).

Threshold price is the minimum entry price for imports from third countries, defined to ensure the prevailing Community price is not undercut. (See variable import levy, q.v.)

Variable import levy is a tool which ensures that imports are not offered below the threshold price. The levy is calculated as the difference between the lowest recorded world market price quotation and the threshold price, and is payable by importers. The same levy is payable on all imports of a particular commodity regardless of offer price so that price advantages are still held by the lowest offer prices.

9 Community Regional Policy

Harvey Armstrong

Introduction

Member states are anxious to strengthen the unity of their economies and to ensure their harmonious development by reducing the differences existing between the various regions and by mitigating the backwardness of the less favoured regions. [Preamble, Treaty of Rome, 1958]

In order to promote its overall harmonious development, the Community shall develop and pursue its actions leading to the strengthening of its economic and social cohesion. In particular, the Community shall aim at reducing disparities between the various regions and the backwardness of the least favoured regions. [Article 130A, Single European Act, 1986]

Despite thirty years of unqualified commitment to the cause of regional policy within the EC, regional disparities survive and pose a stumbling block to the full integration of the economies of the member states. It must be noted, however, that for much of the EC's history regional policy (as distinct from the individual regional policies of the member states) has been very weak. The EC's own onslaught on regional problems really only dates from the establishment of the European Regional Development Fund (ERDF) in 1975. The period since 1975 has witnessed a flowering of EC regional policy initiatives. The ERDF underwent major reform in 1979, and again in 1984. These reforms have been accompanied by a succession of other regional policy initiatives.

This chapter assesses the EC's regional policy, the ERDF, the extent of regional disparities within the EC and reviews briefly arguments used to justify an EC regional policy. It assesses the various initiatives designed to improve the coordination of the regional policy effort and briefly reviews the role of the European Investment Bank (EIB), the European Social Fund (ESF), the European Coal and Steel Community (ECSC) and the European Agricultural Guidance and Guarantee Fund (EAGGF) in helping to reduce regional disparities. An agenda for reforms to EC regional policy in the 1990s is presented.

Regional problems in the EC

The EC is one of the world's great economic powers, has 7 per cent of the world's population – a market of 320 million people. Such a vast economic entity is inevitably a diverse one. Not surprisingly, great differences exist from region to region in prosperity and job opportunities.

There is no single universally accepted method of measuring the economic well-being of a region. A variety of measures (or indicators) of a region's economic welfare exists. Measures of per capita income (or output) are very popular and suffer fewer of the drawbacks of traditional indicators such as rates of unemployment. It is possible for example, to measure the Gross Domestic Product (GDP) of a region in much the same way as is done for national economies. Figure 9.1 shows GDP per capita in the EC regions in 1985. This map highlights a number of key features of the regional problem in the EC. Apart from one or two exceptional areas (for example the Aberdeen region of Scotland which has benefited from North Sea oil exploitation), the EC's depressed regions are on the periphery and the highest per capita income levels are mainly in the centre. The 'centre-periphery' nature of regional disparities within the EC is a long-standing one (COM(73)550; Armstrong, 1978). Fundamental economic processes systematically favour the centre. Severe regional problems exist in the depressed Mediterranean periphery. Many of these southern disadvantaged regions suffer particularly deep-seated problems and have levels of deprivation rarely seen in the more northerly member states. The 'depressed south' is now the most important regional problem confronting the EC, and its greatest challenge.

Another very popular indicator of economic disadvantage is regional unemployment rates that are very difficult to compare. Each country has its own definition of unemployment and different criteria for claiming unemployment benefit. Unemployment rates confirm the broad 'centre-periphery' pattern of regional disparities. They do, however, pick out pockets of economic disadvantage in more central areas which GDP per capita figures do not. There is high unemployment in parts of Belgium, and in northern France in areas formerly dependent on coal mining and heavy industry. By contrast, large areas of Greece and Portugal which are low-income regions appear to have *low* unemployment rates. This apparent paradox is easily explained. In Greece and Portugal, unlike the Belgium and French coalfield areas, the problem is not one of industrial decline but rather of rural underdevelopment, with large numbers of people continuing to work in an impoverished agricultural industry. In rural agricultural areas the problem is largely one of low incomes and under-employment. People are rarely completely unemployed. As a result, unemployment rates understate the true scale of the problem.

The apparent anomalies revealed from the study of the unemployment rates hint at the extraordinary diversity of types of regional problem faced by the EC. Indeed, the EC Commission identifies several main types of disadvantaged region in the EC:

(i) *Underdeveloped regions* These regions have simply never enjoyed the benefits of industrial and economic progress and are particularly prevalent in the EC's Mediterranean areas. The preponderance of agriculture, often of a very inefficient kind, the exceptionally low incomes, and the lack of basic infrastructure, such as good roads and telecommunications, makes these regions especially difficult cases.

(ii) *Declining industrial regions* These regions have often been prosperous in the past but have now declined because of the loss of competitiveness of industries on which they were once dependent. Most of the depressed north and west of the UK is dominated by regions of this kind.

(iii) *Peripheral regions* The development of a single EC market for goods and services poses particularly severe problems for geographically isolated areas (for example island communities such as Sicily or Ireland) and for the mainland's periphery. Such regions face long-term problems related to lack of easy access to the markets of the EC.

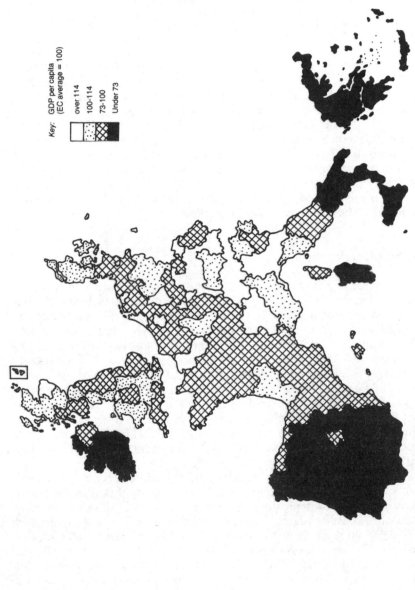

Figure 9.1 Regional gross domestic product per capita in the EC, 1985

Source: Commission of the European Communities, *The Regions of the Enlarged Community: Third Periodic Report on the Social and Economic Situation and Development of the Regions of the Community,* Brussels, 1987.

Key: GDP per capita
(EC average = 100)

over 114
100–114
73–100
Under 73

(iv) *Border regions* The creation of a common market poses particular problems for regions along the frontiers of member states. Areas close to national frontiers often develop distinctive types of industry which exploit legal barriers to trade between countries or which take advantage of the need to off-load and on-load freight (for example at Channel crossings). A distinction is often drawn between *internal* border regions (that is borders between pairs of member states) which face adjustment problems as frontier regulations are swept away; and *external* border regions whose traditional trade patterns with non-EC neighbours may be disrupted by the Common External Tariff and other external trade barriers.

(v) *Urban problem areas* The big cities of the EC face congestion, pollution, crime and social deprivation notably in the inner city areas of large metropolitan agglomerations.

There can be no doubt that the extent of the regional problems facing the EC is cause for great concern. Regional disparities are enormous by any standard. GDP per capita disparities in the EC are some two times and unemployment disparities three times as high as in the US. Moreover, things have worsened considerably in recent years. The entry of Greece, Spain and Portugal significantly widened the existing disparities. The rapid growth and gradually narrowing regional differences so characteristic of the EC of the 1960s and early 1970s has been replaced by much slower rates of growth and higher unemployment in the late 1970s and early 1980s. The harsher economic conditions of the 1970s and 1980s have resulted in a reversal of convergence trends in the EC. The challenge facing EC regional policy is immense.

The case for EC regional policy

The need for government to act to try to reduce regional disparities has long been recognized in Europe. All the EC's principal member states have their own well-established regional policies. In the UK, for example, regional policy has existed continuously since 1928 (Armstrong, 1988; Armstrong and Taylor, 1988). By contrast, the existence of a separate, EC regional policy is a very recent phenomenon. The ERDF was only established in 1975. The arguments for and against a distinctively EC-level regional policy are complex and controversial. At one extreme are those who would like to see members states' regional policies ended and replaced by a single comprehensive EC regional policy. At the other extreme are those who feel that the member states are the ones most qualified to administer regional policies and that EC involvement is at best unnecessary bureaucracy, and at worst interference with the effective operation of member states' own regional policies.

Four main arguments support a separate EC regional policy. First, the EC can improve the efficiency of regional policy by ensuring that regional policy spending is *concentrated* where it is most needed – that is in the most severely disadvantaged regions. At present, some member states are virtually depressed regions in their own right (Portugal, Greece, Republic of Ireland). Others, like Spain and the UK have many depressed areas within their borders whereas countries such as Germany, France and the Netherlands have few major problem areas. With the problem regions so heavily concentrated in certain member states, it is impossible for member states left to their own devices to target the most financial help on the most severely disadvantaged areas. Poorer member states simply cannot afford to pay the bill. There is a clear role for the

EC here: a fund like the ERDF can be used to channel resources into the most severely depressed areas.

The second argument for a separate EC regional policy concerns *coordination*. Twelve states each trying to solve their own regional problems produce chaos. Many regional agencies and governments actively promote industrial development and so too do many local authorities. With so many different participants great inefficiency can occur. Many member states, for example, have used their regional financial incentives to 'bid' aggressively for investment projects seeking a location within the EC. Many Japanese and US companies are wooed by the member states. Such 'competitive bidding' is very costly and inefficient. The EC has launched a whole series of regional policy initiatives to try to improve coordination. Coordination is also necessary amongst the different policies of each government. It is known, for example, that the CAP has tended in the past to favour farmers in the EC's more prosperous northern agricultural areas rather than in the chronically depressed Mediterranean. There is clearly a case for the EC to ensure that the regional effects of *all* of its own policies are carefully monitored and where possible redesigned to bring more help to the depressed areas.

The third broad argument concerns 'common interest'. Each EC member has a vested interest in what goes on in fellow member states. Depressed regions benefit no one. All benefit from all the labour in the EC being fully occupied and producing goods and services. High unemployment in certain areas is also very inequitable. There is considerable evidence that Europeans do feel that such inequities should be eliminated. An EC regional policy would therefore benefit all.

The fourth and final argument in support of an EC regional policy is a dynamic one. Regional disparities may be a severe barrier to further integration. The EC advances by way of the mutual consent of its members. Where large areas remain underdeveloped it is difficult to obtain the consent to move further along the road to economic and monetary union. The EC can only advance if everyone feels they are benefiting. In such circumstances a strong EC regional policy is essential.

Taken together, the various arguments in favour of a separate EC regional policy represent a powerful case. It should be noted, however, that there is no suggestion that the members' own regional policies should be abolished. The local knowledge and long experience of member states and local authorities are of great value. The EC must therefore seek to work with national and local governments to solve regional problems.

The ERDF

The ERDF was established in 1975. Prior to this EC regional policy was rudimentary: limited help was given by way of funds and programmes whose main functions were not regional policy. The ECSC and EAGGF gave some financial assistance to depressed areas simply because of the kinds of industries in which they were involved. The EIB provided loans to depressed areas. There was, however, little in the way of a systematic EC regional policy. Depressed regions were forced to rely almost entirely upon their own national governments for help. These disparate member state regional policies were themselves subject to a number of fairly ineffective EC competition policy regulations designed to try to prevent member state regional inducements being misused in ways which would undermine free trade and free competition. The ERDF's creation was a major turning point. The UK played an important role in the setting up of the new ERDF. The long experience of the UK in regional policy provision was of great value in the design of the ERDF. Since 1975 EC regional policy has steadily grown in stature. The EC has proved an innovator in its regional policy. Many new initiatives have been introduced in the years since 1975. Today's EC regional policy can be divided into three main constituent parts. First, there is the ERDF itself: the principal financial instrument of EC regional policy. Second, there are numerous EC initiatives to improve EC *coordination* of member states' regional policies, with those of regional and local authorities. Finally, a number of other EC funds and institutions operate with a deliberate regional bias.

The ERDF prior to 1984

Since 1975 the ERDF has undergone two major reforms – in 1979 and 1984 (Commission, 1981a, OJL 169 28/6/84). The history of the ERDF is largely one of a struggle to throw off the many restrictions imposed by the Council of Ministers in the original 1975 Fund Regulation. Most of the restrictions on the ERDF's field of action remained immediately prior to the major 1984 reforms. Table 9.1 compares the ERDF prior to the 1984 reforms with that set up afterwards. Before the 1984 reforms, the ERDF was divided into two parts: a quota and a non-quota section. The quota section took 95 per cent of ERDF allocations; the non-quota section was restricted to a maximum of 5 per cent of ERDF allocations.

Quota section assistance was hedged around with restrictions which limited severely the EC's discretion to decide exactly how its own fund's money should be spent. Only grants and interest rebates could be given. This represented a very limited range of types of assistance. On the other hand, quite a wide range of industrial investment projects (including craft and service industries such as tourism) and infrastructure projects were eligible for assistance. Quota section assistance was, however, restricted to those assisted areas designated by the member states for their own regional policies. The EC itself could not, therefore, decide where ERDF money was to be spent. The result was an extraordinary 'patchwork' of areas eligible for ERDF quota section assistance. Each member state had, of course, its own ideas on which areas were in need of help.

To make matters worse, the EC did not (and still does not) have the manpower to administer locally ERDF quota section applications. Applications were channelled through members' ministries such as the UK Department of Industry. This gave them a strangle-hold on the flow of applications and hence a considerable degree of control over who got ERDF assistance. A further limit on the EC's freedom of action before 1984 was the quota system itself. The predominant quota section was so-named because each member state was *guaranteed* a fixed annual share (or quota) of ERDF allocations. In 1984, these quotas were: UK, 23.8 per cent; Belgium, 1.11 per cent; Denmark, 1.06 per cent; France, 13.64 per cent; Republic of Ireland, 5.94 per cent; Italy, 35.49 per

Table 9.1 1984 reforms to the ERDF

	Before 1984	After 1984
Expenditure	Determined annually as part of the EC budget decision.	No change.
Project-by-project assistance	*'Quota' section* Assistance given on a project-by-project basis as a means of supporting the regional policies of the individual member states; this quota-section assistance formed a fixed 95% of all ERDF allocations: it derived its name from the fact that each member state was guaranteed a predetermined share (or 'quota') of this type of assistance. UK quota for 1984 was 23.8%.	*Project assistance* The previous distinction between 'quota' and 'nonquota' section is abolished; in place of a predetermined quota the United Kingdom was guaranteed a share of ERDF allocations between 1984 and 1987 of between 21.42% and 28.56% (the so-called 'indicative range'); the project-by-project assistance so characteristic of the quota section is retained as a separate category of ERDF aid–project assistance.
	(a) Type of assistance offered Principally investment grants given as a percentage of eligible capital expenditure; also interest rebates on other EC loans.	*(a) Type of assistance offered* Principally investment grants; also interest rebates – especially on loans made to small- and medium-sized enterprises.
	(b) Eligible activities Eligible projects must exceed 50,000 European units of account (Eua); must also be benefitting from member state aid; and, in the case of assistance to industrial projects must create or maintain jobs. Projects must be justifiable as part of the member state's regional development programme.	*(b) Eligible activities* As before.
	(c) Eligible areas The assisted areas as designated by member states for their own regional policies.	*(c) Eligible areas* As before; exceptionally, a small part of the ERDF resources may be allocated to infrastructure projects outside of the member states' Assisted Areas where the project is 'an essential complement to the infrastructure of an assisted area' (CEC, 1984).
	(d) Eligible industries Industrial, handicraft, and service industries (that is those services concerned with tourism or which have a choice of location); infrastructure *projects* also eligible.	*(d) Eligible industries* As before.

(e) *Rates of grants*
Industry, craft, services 20% of the investment cost (up to a maximum of 50% of aid given by member states to the same project); cost-per-job ceilings of 100,000 Eua per job created or 50,000 Eua per job maintained; aid may exceed 20% for handicraft and service projects (up to 50% of member state aid and with a 100,000 Eua cost-per-job ceiling); infrastructure-10%-30% of the expenditure incurred by member states (up to 40% in the case of projects of particular importance for the regions).

Programme assistance

'Nonquota' section
5% of ERDF allocations; assistance offered not to individual projects but through programme contacts; these are multiannual programmes of assistance, agreed jointly by the EC and member states involved, to tackle specific Community regional problems (for example to counter adverse effects of other EC policies); three programmes initially agreed for the United Kingdom-Ulster-Eire border regions, shipbuilding areas, and textile areas.
Each programme encompasses many projects and coordinates EC, national, regional, and local aid; not limited to member states' Assisted Areas and a flexible range of types of assistance permitted (not limited to investment grants and interest rebates).

(e) *Rates of grant*
Industry, craft, services 50% of aid granted by member states to the project; infrastructure-30-50% of the expenditure being met by the member states' public authorities (55% for projects of particular importance).

Quota and nonquota sections abolished; the programme contract approach is, however, retained and greatly expanded; programmes are expected to increase to 20% of all ERDF operations within three years (at expense of project assistance).

Two distinct types of programmes:
(1) *Community programmes:* agreed with the member state but initiated by the EC and intended to 'directly serve Community objectives' to be given priority over other types of programme; normally will encompass more than one member state; aimed at new activities and not simply the reorganization of declining industries such as steel or textiles; above all, aid is given much more flexibly under programmes than project-by-project assistance.
Programme aid need not be confined to member states' Assisted Areas, can be up to 55% of member state contributions, and can be given in a whole variety of ways (that is, not confined to investment grants and interest rebates).

(2) *National programme of Community interest:* initiated by the member state to which they are confined, but jointly agreed with the EC; up to 50% of member state aid (55% in exceptional cases).

Before 1984	After 1984

Other provision

Before 1984:

(a) *Indigenous development*
Nonquota section used to pioneer more flexible types of assistance for small firms (see 'after 1984' reforms).

(b) *Integrated development operations*
ERDF resources devoted to pioneering integrated operations in Belfast and Naples; these are closely coordinated schemes (EC, national, regional, and local agencies involved) to tackle the problems of specific small areas; coordinated and flexible assistance.

(c) *Studies*
The ERDF also funds studies on regional policies and problems.

After 1984:

(a) *Indigenous development*
Special provision is made for measures designed to exploit the indigenous development of regions especially for small firms which involve assistance of up to 55% of aid given by the member state, and a variety of types of assistance (for example, assistance in obtaining consultancy advice, aid for local research organisations, aid for tourist promotion etc).

(b) *Integrated development operations*
To be continued and expanded.

(c) *Studies*
As before.

Coordination initiatives

Before 1984:
A variety of initiatives exist to try to coordinate EC, member state, and, to a lesser extent, regional and local involvement in regional policy, these include the regional development programmes of member states; the periodic report on regional problems in the EC; the Commission's regular guidelines and priorities for regional policy; the regional impact assessment procedure; annual reports from member states to the EC and the use of programme contracts and integrated operations.

After 1984:
All previous initiatives retained and strengthened, especially substantial strengthening of programme contracts and integrated operations.

Source: Armstrong, 1986.

cent; Luxembourg, 0.07 per cent; Netherlands, 1.24 per cent; Germany, 4.65 per cent; and Greece, 13.0 per cent. Finally, the quota section before 1984 was subject to a Fund Regulation which contained numerous restrictions on the precise terms and conditions under which an ERDF grant could be given (for example rates of assistance, 'ceilings' on funds offered, types of eligible project etc). Moreover, assistance could only be given on a project-by-project basis, greatly hampering EC attempts to put together carefully planned and closely coordinated programmes of regional assistance.

The small non-quota section of the pre-1984 ERDF was much less hampered by regulations and restrictions and proved to be an important break-through when it was introduced in 1979. The EC had much greater freedom of action with non-quota section assistance. For example, non-quota assistance could, if necessary, be spent partly or wholly outside member state assisted areas. Moreover, fewer restrictions were placed on the types of help which could be given and on the terms of the assistance. The EC, slowly at first after 1979 and then with gathering momentum, began to put the non-quota section finance to use in a radical new manner. The concept of a *programme contract* was developed with finance from the small non-quota section. A programme contract is a coordinated 'package' of initiatives, jointly agreed between the EC and member states, and specifically designed to alleviate a clearly identified regional problem. The programmes are designed to run for several years (and, indeed, have been frequently re-financed with new tranches of assistance). They draw together many different projects and initiatives.

The early programmes set up between 1979 and 1984 tended to concentrate on areas heavily affected by the run-down and restructuring of particular industries, especially those industries where the EC was encouraging a radical restructuring. By 1984 the UK was (together with other member states) benefiting from five programmes (or 'specific Community measures' as they had by then come to be known):

1. Steel areas programme;
2. Shipbuilding areas programme;
3. Border areas programme (along the Northern Ireland border);
4. Textile areas programme;
5. Fisheries programme.

All but one (the Border areas programme) were designed to encourage new types of industry in areas affected by the run-down of a local staple industry. These 'specific Community measures' continue to be financed. By 1991 it is estimated that the UK will have received about £180 million from these five programmes (ERDF: Twelfth Annual Report). The early 1979-84 experimental programmes proved a successful 'model' for the many new types of programmes now being introduced in the EC. In addition to programme financing, by 1984 initiatives had been introduced which greatly improved the EC's role in the coordination of regional policy. A comprehensive system for monitoring and analysing states' regional policies had been introduced in 1979. Member states were required to plan their regional policy efforts and to coordinate with other member states (see below).

The 1984 reforms of the ERDF

The 1984 reforms of EC regional policy proved to be the most important since the ERDF was set up in 1975. Full details of the 1984 reforms are set out in Table 9.1. Two 1984 reforms have significantly strengthened the degree to which the EC itself actually takes decisions concerning the ERDF and have weakened the power of the member states.

The quota/non-quota distinction was abolished in 1984. Quota section assistance continues in the form of Project Assistance and non-quota assistance as Programme Assistance. Radical changes have been made in the operation of these two sections. Project Assistance (that is project-by-project help in the form of grants and interest rebates) while the dominant part of the ERDF is being systematically cut. Project Assistance was cut from 95 per cent to 80 per cent within three years of the 1984 reforms and is being further reduced. Programme assistance (programme contracts of the type pioneered between 1979 and 1984) is being rapidly expanded. Since programme contract assistance is more flexible and more at the discretion of the EC, the expansion of Programme Assistance greatly strengthens EC control of the ERDF.

The 1984 reforms weakened member state influence over ERDF decisions in other ways. Before 1984, Project Assistance was allocated to member states on the basis of pre-determined shares or 'quotas'. This is now no longer the case. Rigid quotas have been replaced by a system of 'indicative ranges' for Project Assistance. For example, before 1984 the UK was guaranteed 23.8 per cent of quota section assistance. Immediately after the 1984 reforms this was changed to an 'indicative range' of between 21.42 per cent and 28.56 per cent. The introduction of 'indicative ranges' gives the EC a greater say in where ERDF money is spent. The UK is guaranteed a minimum amount (21.42 per cent between 1984 and 1987), but if it wants more must persuade the EC to agree to assist more of the project applications sent to Brussels. The 'indicative ranges' have, of course, been altered with the entry of Spain and Portugal. On entry, Spain was given an 'indicative range' of 17.97-23.93 per cent while Portugal's was 10.66-14.20 per cent. Naturally, the United Kingdom's 'indicative range' has had to be cut – to between 14.50 per cent and 19.31 per cent.

In addition to relaxing quotas, the 1984 reforms relaxed some of the many detailed restrictions on the way in which Project Assistance can be given. Of even greater importance are the changes to the non-quota section (i.e. 'Programme Assistance'). Programme Assistance has been substantially reformed. An attempt was made to move programme contracts away from being sector-specific (i.e. steel, shipbuilding, textiles and fisheries areas programmes) and into more varied types of programme contracts. The 1984 reforms defined two distinct types of programme:

(a) *Community Programmes* are jointly agreed by the EC and member states but initiated by the EC. These EC-wide programmes are meant to 'directly serve Community objectives' (OJ LI69 28/6/84).
(b) *National Programmes of Community Interest (NPCI)* are initiated within a member state and EC approval is sought. Normally they are specific to a single member state.

The ability to initiate Community Programmes, and the need to be actively involved in National Programmes, has increased EC influence in the ERDF. Moreover, priority is given to Community Programmes over National

Programmes. It was envisaged that Community Programmes would gradually grow until they dominated the Programme Assistance section of the ERDF.

The impetus given to regional policy based on coordinated programmes of help by the 1984 reforms was strengthened by two further changes introduced by the 1984 Fund Regulation. First, the go-ahead was given for a rapid expansion of *Integrated Development Operations* (IDOs). Between 1979 and 1984 the EC had experimented with two IDOs, one in Belfast, the other in Naples. IDOs are designed to redevelop and revitalize severely deprived inner-city areas. As well as ERDF, the IDOs draw upon other EC finance, and assistance from national and local governments in the cities concerned. Second, the 1984 reforms gave the go-ahead for more transfrontier programmes designed to tackle regional problems which straddle national frontiers.

Finally, the 1984 reforms signalled a major change in the direction of EC regional policy. For a number of years it had become increasingly obvious that the traditional approach of encouraging large manufacturing plants to move from prosperous to depressed areas was not working: regions need to be helped to grow 'from within'. Stimulating indigenous development means helping small firms and service industries as well as manufacturing. Small firms have special needs. Simple cash grants for investment in plant and machinery are not enough. Small firms need advice. They need to hire consultants. They need help with research and development, and they need to share common services such as accountants and lawyers. The 1984 reforms included special types of assistance to help to stimulate indigenous development of depressed regions. Such measures attract higher rates of ERDF assistance.

The ERDF: the way forward

The ERDF can claim a considerable degree of success. Despite compromises between the EC and member states which have been an inevitable feature of successive Fund Regulations, much good work has been done. The ERDF has ensured that the greatest volume of assistance has gone to the most depressed regions. Southern Italy, the Republic of Ireland, Northern Ireland and the north of Britain have been the principal beneficiaries. Greece has also had considerable assistance. Spain and Portugal have, as yet, received only small sums from the ERDF despite their serious regional problems but will get much more help in future. ERDF expenditures in the UK have grown steadily to over £2.7 billion since 1975, both in nominal and real terms. This is in marked contrast to the real values of expenditures by the Department of Industry on UK government regional policy initiatives. The ability of the ERDF to continue to increase its expenditures in real terms over a prolonged period when the UK government has been cutting back on its own regional policy budget is very impressive.

Despite its many successes a number of serious criticisms can be levelled against the ERDF that point the way forward for future reform.

Table 9.2 Allocations from the ERDF to UK regions, 1979-87

£ million
Project assistance

Region	Industry	Infrastructure	Studies	National Programmes of Community Interest	Total
North	84.68	309.96	0.53	14.82	410.00
Yorkshire/Humberside	23.28	204.92	0.42	0.00	228.62
East Midlands	7.58	32.19	0.55	0.00	40.32
South-west	8.35	121.04	0.24	0.00	129.64
West Midlands	6.10	156.52	0.10	14.82	177.54
North-west	53.13	251.79	0.46	61.47	366.85
Wales	77.79	329.65	0.85	9.83	418.12
Scotland	151.33	447.92	0.95	54.37	654.58
Northern Ireland	94.54	190.47	0.80	0.87	286.67
Multi-regional	60.00	14.25	1.06	2.65	77.96
Total United Kingdom	566.78	2,058.71	5.96	158.83	2,790.28

Notes: 1. 'Multi-regional' assistance is assistance which encompasses more than one region simultaneously.
2. Figures are not shown for Community Programmes. Being definitive, such programmes encompass the whole EC and the UK share of such aid is not known in advance of the money being spent.

Source: Commission of the European Communities, *Press Release* ISEC/3/88, 27 January, 1988

The size of the ERDF budget. Despite what appears superficially to be large sums of money, the ERDF is wholly inadequate for the task it confronts. In 1987 the ERDF was allocated 3.3 billion ECUs (1 ECU = £0.697 in September 1988), some 8 per cent of the EC budget. This is an improvement on the 1970s but the budget now has to serve twelve states. ERDF spending continues to be dwarfed by the Twelve's regional policy spending. Yet even the combined activities of both the EC and the states have failed to prevent a serious widening of regional disparities in the EC.

In February 1988 the Council of Ministers announced that the 'structural funds' (the ERDF, the European Social Fund and the Guidance Section of the European Agricultural Guidance and Guarantee Fund) would be doubled in size between 1987 and 1993 (OJC245, 12/9/87). This a is a radical decision. It gives little in the way of grounds for optimism, however. Enlargement has greatly increased the number of regions in need of urgent help. Much of the new money is earmarked for regions which are particularly severely depressed (that is with a GDP per capita of less than 75 per cent of the EC average), most of which are in the south of the EC. In the UK, for example, only Northern Ireland falls into this category. Of course, the UK may benefit more even though it obtains a small share of future allocations, since the Fund itself is to be doubled. The full effects of enlargement on the United Kingdom allocation have yet to be felt. In addition, the SEA envisages 1992 as marking much greater internal integration of the EC economies. Further economic integration will inevitably widen regional disparities. The accessible central regions will become even more attractive locations for industry. Improved integration will increase the size of the task which confronts the ERDF. This, in turn, places greater burdens on the enlarged ERDF.

The CAP is the root cause of the inadequate size of the ERDF. It absorbs over 60 per cent of the EC budget – and cost over-runs are endemic. A properly funded ERDF must await effective measures to control CAP spending.

Additionally as a concept. The problem of the ERDF's small size is compounded by the tendency of some member states to substitute ERDF spending for spending under their own regional policies. The EC, not unnaturally, is keen to see its spending being used in an 'additional' manner, and not for member states simply to view it as a convenient means of financing their own budgets. Vigorous EC attempts to persuade states to use ERDF aid in a truly 'additional' manner have, unfortunately, in many cases been met simply by deception. It is impossible to estimate how much ERDF money represents a genuine increase in regional policy spending. Considerable substitution has clearly occurred and directly undermines the ERDF's effectiveness.

The predominance of assistance to infrastructure projects. Between 1975 and 1987 (tenth allocation) some 84.3 per cent of all Project Assistance went on infrastructure projects (and Project Assistance comprised 96.3 per cent of all assistance, with programmes accounting for only 3.7 per cent). The predominance of infrastructure assistance, and the paucity of help for industrial projects is a source of serious concern. (Even in the UK, a country with a long history of giving grants to industrial projects, infrastructure projects took 73 per cent of all ERDF Project Assistance between 1975 and 1987.) The reasons for the high proportion of ERDF help going to infrastructure projects lie partly in the fact that infrastructure grants are easier to apply for and obtain, and partly because of the severe recession of the early 1980s which choked off industrial investment (and therefore the flow of applications to the ERDF). A better balance of infrastructure and industrial assistance is clearly needed.

The slow development of Programme Assistance. The painfully slow development of programmes is beginning to speed up dramatically. Not until October 1986 were the first two Community Programmes approved, and the money is only now beginning to flow freely. The first two Community Programmes were the STAR programme, designed to improve access to modern telecommunications for depressed regions; and the VALOREN programme, designed to tap local energy supplies and improve the efficiency of energy use in the depressed regions. Progress on other Community Programmes has, however, been slow.

National Programmes of Community Interest (NPCI) were also rather slow off the mark. A wave of NPCIs is now being introduced in all member states. The early UK NPCIs (such as the Tees Corridor and the Mersey Basin programmes) are now being joined by many more, for example NFCs in Birmingham and West Lothian were approved in 1988. Interest in devising new programmes in the UK is now intense. The EC approved fourteen NPCIs in 1986 and twenty-seven in 1987. Genuine Community Programmes (as distinct from NPCIs) are still thin on the ground. Particular attention needs to be directed at proposals for stimulating the indigenous potential of depressed regions where small firms are the main target. In 1987 there were still only eighteen such 'indigenous development' measures approved by the ERDF.

The balance of power between the EC and member states. The 1984 reforms have strengthened the EC's hand in the ERDF at member states' expense. This is a good development. In the past member states tended to dominate ERDF decisions through their control of applications for Project Assistance and by way of the tight constraints built into the Fund Regulation. A worrying feature of the existing ERDF is that no attempt has ever been made to spell out precisely what the balance of powers between the EC and member states should be. The ERDF has simply moved from one compromise to another. The programme approach to regional policy means that the EC and member states must work together (Croxford, 1987). Both have a role to play in regional policy. What is missing at present is a clear statement of 'who should do what' (Armstrong, 1985, 1986). Too much state control of the ERDF is a bad thing; no member state regional policies whatsoever would be even worse. The balance must be carefully calculated and rigorously adhered to.

The paucity of formal evaluation of ERDF activities. Evaluating the effectiveness of ERDF assistance has proved extremely difficult not least because to evaluate its effects one must calculate what would have happened had there been no help. This is a difficult concept to quantify. To make matters worse, ERDF help is always given in conjunction with help from other sources (for example from the member state). Disentangling the effects of ERDF help from that of other organizations is an extraordinarily difficult task. Great efforts are now being made to devise methods to evaluate formally ERDF assistance. They must be given priority. No policy can ever be made effective unless it is properly monitored and evaluated.

Coordination of regional policy

The EC is uniquely placed to help to improve the coordination of regional policy in the EC. A number of different types of coordination are now being developed.

Coordination between EC and member states' regional policies

The most important task facing EC regional policy in the 1990s is the need to improve the cordination of member states' regional policies one with another and jointly with the EC itself. To this end the EC has introduced three main initiatives.

Competition policy regulations. The EC uses its competition policy regulations to try to control and coordinate member state regional policies. A system of ceilings has been established which places limits on the total amount of financial help which can be offered to a project by governments (Deacon, 1982). These ceilings are highest in depressed regions and lowest in prosperous regions. In addition, competition policy regulations are used to try to prevent member states from using 'opaque' financial incentives (that is incentives whose true value is hard to ascertain), and to limit the use of continuing subsidies (for example labour subsidies paid week-in, week-out). EC competition policy regulations have not been very successful as a coordinating mechanism. They face enforcement problems. More importantly, they are restrictions and as such tend to impede states' room for manoeuvre.

Monitoring and analysis. In 1979 a comprehensive system for monitoring and analysing member states' and EC regional problems and policies was introduced. Member states are required to produce regular annual reports and information statements on regional policy activities. In addition, each member state must produce and regularly update a Regional Development Programme setting out regional policy plans. The EC produces major biennial periodic reports on regional problems in the EC that form the basis of sets of Commission regional policy guidelines and priorities to guide the EC and member states in their regional policy decisions. The EC's Regional Policy Committee also analyses regional issues and advises the Commission.

Community and national programmes of the ERDF. These, as we have seen, bring the EC and member states together in jointly mounted attacks on specific regional problems. Integrated Development Operations perform a similar function in the urban areas.

All three initiatives are welcome. There is scope for tightening the competition policy regulations further, particularly by bringing into the regulations more member state industry policy subsidies (that is, subsidies offered everywhere in a member state and therefore, by definition, not part of regional policy). Great caution must, however, be exercised. The regulations must not be allowed to develop in ways which hamper states' regional policies for it is the member states and not the EC which continue to provide most help for the depressed regions.

The comprehensive monitoring and analysis system is also very welcome. One can question, however, how effective the Commission's guidelines have been in influencing the ERDF's activities and those of the member states. Many member state Regional Development Programmes also seem to carry too little weight in the decision-making process. It is the ERDF's own programme contracts which, paradoxically, offer the greatest immediate opportunities for improved EC–member state coordination. Programmes are, by definition, joint ventures between the EC and member states. They literally force the two sides to work together. This is fine at the level of an individual programme – in the fine details of its implementation and in decisions on who is helped and how the help is given. But who is to coordinate the programmes? Only time will tell whether the EC can ensure that programmes are accepted or rejected in a logical and consistent manner and in a way which ensures that those that are accepted genuinely complement the regional policy activities of the member states. Moreover, there is little sign as yet of member states such as the UK taking similar steps to coordinate national regional policy activities with the ERDF. UK regional assistance continues to be given on a project-by-project basis and with precious little reference to EC activities in Britain.

Coordination between the ERDF and other EC policies

The EC has made a serious attempt to improve coordination between the ERDF and other EC policies. All major EC policies have their own distinctive geographical pattern of effects. This has long been known. Indeed, some EC funds and institutions have played a major role in helping the depressed regions. Since 1952 the ECSC has been helping the coal and steel industry and the mostly very depressed areas dependent on it. As well as financial help the ECSC subsidizes the retraining and resettlement of redundant coal and steel workers, and gives 'conversion' loans to new companies (in any industry) setting up in coal and steel areas. In 1987, 238 million ECUs of 'conversion' loans were made in the EC, of which 9.2 million were in the UK.

The European Investment Bank gives loans and loan guarantees (often on very favourable terms) in many depressed areas of the EC. The EIB operates with a strong and deliberate regional bias. In 1987 no less than 58 per cent of the 7,450.4 million ECUs loaned by the EIB in the EC were for regional development purposes. The European Social Fund (ESF) also operates with a deliberate regional bias, helping to finance training, retraining, resettlement and other schemes to help many different groups of people. In 1987 44 per cent of the 3.15 billion ECUs allocated from the ESF was spent in the most depressed regions. The UK took 19 per cent of ESF allocations in 1987. The EAGGF's Guidance Section also helps depressed regions. Farmers receive financial assistance in many ways: for farm investment projects, land consolidation, early retirement, environmentally sound production methods etc., amounting to 917 million ECUs in 1987. It should be noted, however, that the EAGGF Guidance Section is dwarfed by the farm price support system which swallowed a massive 22,988.5 million ECUs in 1987. Unfortunately, the price guarantee section of EAGGF tends to help farmers in the richer north of the EC much more than poorer farmers in the south and in hill farm areas (for example, Scotland).

The four funds and institutions discussed above (ECSC, EIB, ESF and EAGGF Guidance Section) have been the subject of a series of reforms designed to improve their contribution to the depressed regions even further. A recent Commission proposal (OJC 245, 12/9/87) to reform the structural funds (ESF, ERDF, and EAGGF Guidance Section) has now been accepted. As well as doubling in size by 1993, they are to be more closely coordinated and their regional bias is to be sharpened with more money being directed at the worst affected regions.

The success achieved in coordinating the ERDF with the ESF, EAGGF Guidance Section, the EIB and the ECSC should not obscure the real failures of the EC coordination effort. Foremost among these is the CAP: EC price support policy is distinctly anti-regional. It tends to help the farmers in the richest areas. The EC has, as yet, been unable to rectify this anomaly. The huge size of the amount spent makes this a truly alarming failure of coordination. The EC has a well-established system of *Regional Impact Assessment* (RIA) designed to discover the geographical pattern of effects of major EC policies (Regional Policy Series, 28-29), but as the CAP shows, it is one thing to identify a need for coordination with the ERDF; it is something else to achieve it.

Conclusion

Much has been achieved by EC regional policy in the years since the ERDF was established in 1975. Much remains to be done in the 1990s. The next decade will witness new and severe demands on EC regional policy. Turkey has applied for EC membership and Morocco waits in the wings. The entry of these two extremely disadvantaged Mediterranean countries would exacerbate the ERDF's problems. There is a demanding EC regional policy agenda for the 1990s. Six steps in particular are urgently needed:

(a) The ERDF must be greatly increased. Doubling the fund by 1993 will not be sufficient to allow the ERDF to begin reducing regional disparities. Without more the disparities will widen.
(b) The extra finance should be at the expense of the agricultural price guarantee policy, itself profoundly anti-regional.
(c) The EC urgently requires greater powers to try to force member states to use ERDF money in a truly 'additional' manner.
(d) There is a need to reduce the amount of money the ERDF gives to infrastructure projects and, instead, direct more to industrial projects and to small firms.
(e) The EC has been only partially successful in coordinating the ERDF and member states' regional policies. Simply relying on the new generation of programme assistance schemes will not be sufficient in itself to achieve the required extra coordination.
(f) Improved evaluation of the effectiveness of ERDF operations is needed.

Finally, for too long EC regional policy has been viewed as something separate from EC industrial policy as a whole. With the EC now finally beginning to assemble an active industry policy it is essential that regional policy be seen as an integral part of industry policy. Ideally, the two would be part of a single policy. The essence of regional problems is industrial change. In responding to the challenge of industrial change at EC level the Community must simultaneously mount attacks on the geographical problem areas which emerge as industrial change occurs.

References

Armstrong, H.W. (1978), 'community regional policy: a survey and critique', *Regional Studies*, **12**(5), 511-28.
— (1985), 'The reform of the European Community regional policy', *Journal of Common Market Studies*, **XXIII**, (4), 319-43.
— (1986), 'The division of regional industrial policy powers in Britain: some implications of the 1984 policy reforms', *Environment and Planning: C Government and Policy*, **4**, 325-42.
— (1988), 'Regional problems and policies', in B.F. Duckham *et al.* (eds), *The British Economy Since 1945*, Oxford University Press.
— and Taylor, J. (1985), *Regional Economics and Policy*, Philip Allan Ltd.
— and Taylor, J. (1988), *Regional Policy: The Way Forward* (Revised Version), London, The Employment Institute.
Commission of the European Communities (1973a), 'Proposals for a Community regional policy', *Official Journal*, OJ C86 of 16/10/1973 and OJ C106 of 6/12/1973.
— (1973b) *Report on Regional Problems in the Enlarged Community*, COM (73)550 final, Brussels.

— (1975), 'Regulations establishing a Community regional policy', *Official Journal*, OJ L73 of 21/3/1975.

— (1981a), 'Principal regulations and decisions of the Council of the European Communities on regional policy', *Office for Official Publications of the European Communities*, Luxembourg.

— (1981b), *Study of the Regional Impact of the Common Agricultural Policy*, Regional Policy Series 21, Brussels.

— (1983), *Study of the Regional Impact of the Community's External Trade Policy*, Regional Policy Series 22, Brussels.

— (1984), 'Council regulation (EEC) No. 1787/84 of 19 June 1984 on the European Regional Development Fund', *Official Journal*, OJ L169 of 28/6/1984.

— (1985), *The Effects of New Information Technology on the Less Favoured Regions of the Community*, Regional Policy Series 23, Brussels.

— (1987a), *The Regions of the Enlarged Community*, Third Periodic Report on the Social and Economic Situation and Development of the Regions of the Community: summary and conclusions, Luxembourg.

— (1987b), 'Proposal for a Council Regulation on the tasks of the structural funds and their effectiveness and on coordination of their activities between themselves and with the operations of the European Investment Bank and the other financial instruments', *Official Journal*, OJ C245 of 12/9/1987.

— (1988), *European Regional Development Fund: Twelfth Annual Report (1986)*, Luxembourg.

Croxford, G.J., Wise, M. and Chalkley, B.S. (1987), 'The reform of the European Regional Development Fund: a preliminary assessment', *Journal of Common Market Studies*, **XXV** (1), 25-38.

Deacon, D. (1982), 'Competition policy in the Common Market: its links with regional policy', *Regional Studies*, **16**(1) 53-63.

Hansen, N.M. (1977), 'Border regions: a critique of spatial theory and a European case study', *Annals of Regional Science*, **XI**, (1), 1-14.

Keeble, D., Owens, P.L. and Thompson, C. (1982), 'Regional accessibility and economic potential in the European Community', *Regional Studies*, **16**(6), 419-31.

McCrone, G. (1971), 'Regional policy in the European Community', in G.R. Denton (ed.), *Economic Integration in Europe*, London, Weidenfeld and Nicolson.

10 The Mediterranean Challenge: cohesion and external preferences

Kevin Featherstone

Introduction

The EC has been obliged to develop a Mediterranean policy serving two distinct and, at times, rival groups of countries. The first, an internal one, is composed of those member states on its southern flank; the second is an external collection of those member states within the basin with whom the EC has sustained close trading relations. This chapter examines both these dimensions, and assesses the kind of tensions which have developed between them. The policy adopted towards one group has important ramifications for the other; to consider one in isolation could thus be highly misleading.

The questions raised by this dual approach are of major and wider significance. EC policy towards both groups of Mediterranean nations highlights some of the pressures and constraints acting upon an endeavour of international regional integration. Such a project raises tensions in policy alternatives externally between protectionism and openness, and internally between uniformity of treatment and preferential resource allocation. Both sets of alternatives are interrelated: for example the ease of access for imports from outside has differential consequences for member states and this affects demands for special treatment internally. The reality of choosing between these polar opposites involves further complexity: the search for an optimal compromise between the two sets of alternatives, the capacity for long-term planning rather than *ad hoc* decision-making and the experience of policy initiation as opposed to reaction. Moreover, the eventual policy outputs have broader external and internal implications. Galtung (1973:68) judged the EC's early trading relations with less-developed economies in terms of exploitation, fragmentation (among the third countries), and penetration (dependency). Pomfret (1986:104) concluded that the EC's preferential trading agreements with outside Mediterranean countries showed that 'economically weak countries ... have most to gain in the long run from a liberal and multilateral trading system'. Internally, the regional inequalities between member states have led to various opinions on how to cope with them: integration according to two speeds (involving a faster pace for those countries which could manage it); variable geometry (a differentiation between the core policies of the *acquis communautaire* and selective collaboration for other projects); or a concerted attempt to maximize 'cohesion' (a reduction of those very inequalities) (Wallace, 1985). The creation of an international bloc thus raises questions as to its external relations and the pace of the integration process.

How and why did the EC develop its ties with the Mediterranean basin? How did the EC respond to the accession of the new southern European states? What

186

was the initial impact on those new states? What were the external consequences of enlargement (for the other Mediterranean economies)? Looking to the future, how will the completion of the EC's internal market be affected by Mediterranean enlargement? These very broad and major questions can only be dealt with briefly. Relevant issues rather than comprehensive answers will be raised.

The opening to the Mediterranean

The very existence of the EC, and its customs union, meant it was inevitable that neighbouring states would seek easier access to what was an important and expanding internal market. This was nowhere more crucial than for the non-member countries in the Mediterranean basin: many of these relatively weaker economies were dependent on the EC for their limited range of exports and many also suffered a large trading deficit with the bloc. Moreover, there were still colonial and former colonial ties with the basin that the EC had to take account of: Algeria was still part of France (until 1962) and Morocco and Tunisia were independent members of the franc zone. For its part, the EC had political and strategic interests at stake in the basin: seeking stability on its doorstep and a favoured role for itself. The Six also wished to protect their considerable Mediterranean export markets, and commercial policy was the prime instrument available to serve both economic and political objectives.

At first the EC granted privileged trading access on an *ad hoc* bilateral basis. This response was the result of the EC's complex and differential ties with basin countries, the varying initiatives that the Mediterranean countries took towards them and the sensitivities the rest of the world felt about such trade discrimination in the context of the Kennedy Round of the GATT negotiations in the 1960s. Moreover, the new EC was concerned with internal priorities, notably the establishment of the customs union and the adoption of the CAP. Both had direct implications for the EC's external trading relations, and the

Table 10.1   The development of trading agreements between the EC and the Mediterranean Countries

Association under Article 238		Co-operation agreements		Preferential trade agreements		Non-preferential trade agreements	
Greece	1961	Israel	1975	Spain	1970	Israel	1964
Turkey	1963	*Maghreb:*	1976	Israel	1970	Lebanon	1965
Morocco	1969	(Algeria, Morocco,		Egypt	1972	Yugoslavia	1970
Tunisia	1969	Tunisia)		Lebanon	1972	Yugoslavia	1973
Malta	1970	*Mashreq:*	1977	Portugal	1972		
Cyprus	1972	(Egypt, Lebanon,					
		Jordan, Syria)					
		Yugoslavia	1980				

Note: Years given refer to date of signature of agreements, not their implementation. Subsequent protocols have not been included.

Sources: General Reports on the Activities of the EEC/EC (various years), Brussels.

ramifications for the Mediterranean basin were likely to be significant. Thus the initial EC stance towards the non-member Mediterranean countries was hesitant, but also reactive.

The development of the EC's ties with Mediterranean countries is shown in Table 10.1. The Rome Treaty included provision for the members' existing colonies and dependencies; thereafter, various types of trading concessions were granted to other Mediterranean countries, creating a patchwork of relations. Greece (1961) and Turkey (1963) obtained association agreements under Article 238 of the Rome Treaty; both left open the possibility of a transition to full membership, but in the case of Greece the reference was much stronger.[1] A major revision of relations with other countries occurred as a result of the 1972 Paris Summit declaring it attached 'essential importance ... to the fulfilment of its commitments to the countries of the Mediterranean Basin with which agreements have been or will be concluded, agreements which should be the subject of an overall and balanced approach'. This so-called 'global' approach led to the Maghreb and Mashrek agreements which provided for customs-free access for industrial goods, a variety of concessions for agricultural produce and financial aid via the EIB. The agricultural concessions were limited, however. The tariffs did not disappear completely, and the system and levels of minimum prices under the CAP served as effective restraints. With this sequence of agreements in the 1970s, the EC was left with trading agreements with all Mediterranean basin countries except Albania and Libya. The trading bloc had thus established a comprehensive network of relationships, with itself as the dominant partner.

The EC's first agreement (under Article 238), signed with Greece in July 1961, was also its most ambitious. Unlike subsequent agreements, the Athens Treaty sought to provide 'support' in order to 'in future facilitate the accession of' the new partner 'into the EC'. The economic provisions thus took on the character of a pre-accession accord. A customs union was to be established in stages: by 1974 Greece would accept a common external tariff and trade between it and the EC would be tariff-free; however, Greece would have until 1984 to eliminate such barriers on industrial goods coming from the EC (Swann, 1984:309). The Athens Treaty covered a range of policies affecting the free movement of labour and of services and competition rules, but special reference was also made to agricultural produce. Article 35 endeavoured 'to ensure equality of treatment between [agricultural] products of member states and like products of Greece'. However, subsequent negotiations over the harmonization of farm prices, in the context of the EC's new CAP, proved inconclusive when the Six rejected the Greek demand for agricultural aid from the FEOGA scheme, despite the references to 'equality of treatment' in the Athens Treaty (Verney, 1987:258). Athens was also disappointed that a financial protocol which had envisaged $125m of capital loans to Greece from the European Investment Bank over a five-year period had only been partially realized. By the end of 1966 only $63m had apparently been lent (Swann, 1984:309).

Greece's relations with the Six were interrupted by the Colonels' coup in April 1967. The EC limited the Association Agreement to its 'current administration' on 26 November 1967. The Agreement was effectively frozen: tariff reductions continued on schedule, but discussions on agricultural harmonization were stopped, as the $56m of potential capital loans (Verney, 1987:258). Trading access thus continued; 'Greek industrial exports have enjoyed free access since 1968, earlier than originally envisaged, while by 1974 two-thirds of EC exports entered Greece duty-free' (Tsoukalis, 1981: 31). Nevertheless, the EC had differentiated its stance towards the Colonels from that of the USA while Washington was implicated both in the events leading up to the coup and to its demise as a result of the Cyprus fiasco in 1974.

The fall of the Colonels' regime was followed by widespread anti-Americanism, and increasingly Greek elites saw 'Europeanism' as a suitable supplement or, indeed, alternative to Washington's embrace. Moreover, the EC had been enlarged in 1973 and was now behaving as a more cohesive bloc, with talk of 'European Union'. Supporters of accession did not wish Greece to be disadvantaged by being on the outside. There were also powerful economic reasons for entry: the full benefits of the CAP were being denied to Greek farmers, though domestic industry was already suffering from EC exports, and Greece's preferential position with the EC in 1961 had been undermined by the latter having signed a series of trading agreements with Greece's Mediterranean competitors (Verney, 1987:258).

The Greek Prime Minister after 1974, Constantine Karamanlis – the returning 'hero' – lodged an application for full EC membership on 12 June 1975. The entry bid was supported by the right and centre of Greek politics, but not by the left, and public opinion seemed uncertain. Karamanlis also faced problems with Brussels. The Commission feared the EC becoming embroiled in Greco–Turkish disputes and, after entry applications were received from Spain and Portugal, contemplated dealing with all three together. Karamanlis responded wit' vigour. In March 1976 the Council of Ministers unanimously accepted the G eek application, putting aside the Turkish problem, and later Karamanlis successfully pressed his claims for Greece to be treated as a special case as a result of the 1961 Agreement (Tsoukalis, 1981: 138-9).

The negotiations with Greece proved protracted: they began in July 1976 and finished with the signing of the Accession Treaty in May 1979. The first team of negotiators accused the Karamanlis government of seeking entry at any economic cost, while others in Athens accused the EC of stalling. In 1978 the real negotiations began. The Commission accepted that Greece should be granted a five-year transition, as had its three predecessors in 1973, but that for free movement of labour, peaches and tomatoes a seven-year period would apply. It was also agreed that Greece should not become a net contributor to the EC budget during the transition (Tsoukalis, 1981:142). Greece became a full member in January 1980, just ahead of the subsequent parliamentary elections.

When the Greek Socialists (PASOK) swept to power in October 1981, the party was expected to re-examine relations with the EC. PASOK originally opposed entry, on the grounds that it would further undermine Greece's struggle to lessen its external dependency; the EC would 'consolidate the peripheral role of the country as a satellite of the capitalist system', in the words of its 1977 manifesto. In 1981 PASOK called for a referendum to allow a choice between full membership and 'a special agreement' with the EC (Featherstone, 1988: 179-80). However, it was recognized that, as President, Karamanlis would refuse any government request for a plebiscite. The Papandreou government thus submitted a memorandum to the EC Commission in March 1982 asking for 'special arrangements' to help Greece's economic development. It sought increased agricultural and regional aid, as well as temporary derogations from EC policies. Such 'special arrangements', the government indicated, 'would constitute the minimum possible' basis on which membership would not be 'in conflict with basic Greek national interests'.

The following year, the Commission allowed Greece a special derogation on certain imports, and in March 1983 it published a comprehensive reply to the Greek Memorandum. The Commission accepted PASOK's five-year economic plan, which included a number of protection clauses to help small businesses which ran counter to EC competition policy. The Commission also proposed that a number of special projects should be established to give greater assistance to Greece and, more generally, it saw the majority of problems being reconciled within the context of a developing EC policy for the Mediterranean. Athens responded favourably, and the government announced its intention of staying in the EC. Later, in October 1985, the Papandreou government secured a 1,750m ECU loan via the Commission (under the facilities of Article 108 of the Rome Treaty) – a loan which avoided an embarrassing recourse to the IMF. PASOK had thus come to accept EC membership as a means of helping Greece's economic development.

Portugal and Spain's relations with the EC developed after those of Greece. Portugal, under Salazar's dictatorship, joined EFTA in 1960, given its need for continued access to the UK market and its concern that membership of the EC, even if it were to be allowed, would threaten its cherished hold over its African colonies. Portugal asked for the opening of entry negotiations with the EC, following Britain's first application in 1961, and in 1962 the Franco regime in Spain also sought full integration into the EC (Featherstone, 1988:287). After the rejection of Britain's application, the Six were slow to respond to Portugal and Spain. In June 1970, Spain signed a trade agreement with the EC, and in July 1972 a similar agreement was reached between Portugal and the EC, as part of the latter's negotiations with the remaining EFTA countries. It was clear, however, that while Portugal and Spain were subject to dictatorial rule they would remain excluded from full EC participation.

The fall of the Caetano regime in Portugal, following an almost bloodless army coup in April 1974, and the death of Franco in November 1975 provided the opportunity for both countries to launch their entry bids. In contrast to Greece, the Portuguese and Spanish socialist parties share the major responsibility for their countries' accession to the EC. In Portugal, it was the first socialist government under Dr Mário Soares which submitted the entry application in March 1977, and it was Soares' third administration (June 1983–October 1985) which conducted the final phase of the negotiations. The Spanish application was lodged by the centre–right Government of Adolfo Suárez in July 1977, but later negotiations were conducted by Felipe González's socialist administration, following the PSOE's election triumph in October 1982. In both countries EC entry had been supported by a broadly based consensus, with the exception that while the Spanish Communists (PCE) supported membership, their Portuguese counterparts (PCP) objected on the grounds of it being an exclusively Western European entanglement and an overtly capitalist one at that.

Portugal and Spain's entry negotiations proved very difficult, raising problems in agriculture and fisheries for the existing EC members. Both Spain and Portugal have large and relatively inefficient agricultural sectors, and while Spain would be the EC's fourth poorest member (as measured by GNP per capita), Portugal would be by far the poorest.[2] Particular difficulties were posed for Italy and France, as a result of Iberian production of similar agricultural commodities. Enlargement became a major issue in the March 1978 French elections: both the Gaullists (RPR), led by Jacques Chirac, and the Communists (PCF), led by Georges Marchais, came out strongly against the accession of any of the three Mediterranean applicants. By contrast, 'enlargement never became a political issue in Italy because all parties were agreed on its desirability' (Tsoukalis, 1981:151). The Commission published its opinion on Portugal's application in May 1978, and on Spain's in November 1978. The response to Portugal's submission was less guarded than that to Spain's as the latter's economy was likely to have a greater impact on the rest of the EC (Tsoukalis, 1981:142). Negotiations with Portugal began in October 1978, and with Spain in February 1979.

Another sensitive area was that of social policy and migrant labour. Fears were raised as to the damaging effects on employment and on social security systems if large numbers of workers moved north from the Mediterranean to find jobs. As a safeguard, it was agreed that free movement of labour for Spain and Portugal would be introduced over a seven year period; that is, after the envisaged completion of the EC's internal market, when a range of barriers will be removed for all countries. Moreover, the high peaks of migration in the 1960s and 1970s had already been undermined in the 1980s by the recession. Allocations from the EC Social Fund were revised after enlargement: the highest recipients in 1985 – Italy, Britain, France and Ireland – by 1987 had seen their share fall by an average of 5.5 per cent, with Spain receiving the third highest grant, Portugal the fifth, and Greece the seventh. The budget for the Social Fund, as well as for the other structural funds, had been significantly increased, however.

After Greek entry, negotiations with the two Iberian governments became entangled in the new PASOK government's demands over the EC's proposed 'Integrated Mediterranean Programmes' (IMPs). Indeed, Papandreou threatened to veto Spanish and Portuguese accession (at the December 1984 Dublin Summit) unless adequate funds were found for Greece under the IMPs. Agreement on this latter issue was finally reached at the March 1985 Brussels Summit (European Council), by which time all other outstanding questions had been resolved on the Spanish and Portuguese applications. This allowed the accession treaties to be signed in Lisbon and Madrid on 12 June 1985, with entry agreed as of January 1986. At the March Brussels Summit, four governments (those of the Bénelux countries and West Germany) declared in the minutes of the meeting that the decisions reached constituted the EC's final response to the Greek Memorandum of 1983. The first phase of the EC's response to its second enlargement was thus complete. The three countries had acceded to full membership and the EC had agreed on the IMPs as a means of helping those regions affected by enlargement.

The EC's response to Mediterranean enlargement

The EC's response to its Mediterranean enlargement resulted in several policy initiatives designed to tackle the new economic problems it faced. These initiatives were taken during a period when the EC was setting itself more ambitious and wider objectives – the completion of the internal market by 1992

– and thus developments in each area came to be seen as interrelated. In short, Mediterranean enlargement has not so far retarded the intensification of the integration process, rather it has been absorbed into a broader stimulus towards its realization.

The most notable initiatives involved payments to existing members likely to suffer economically as a result of enlargement, and financial aid to the entrants designed to strengthen their economies and bring them closer to EC norms. The transfers of resources were thus a recognition of the principle that regional inequalities ought to be controlled within the integration process.

As noted, the creation of the IMPs was a direct response to the threat faced by EC regions by the accession of Spain and Portugal. The European Council had agreed on them in principle at its March 1984 Brussels meeting, and it decided upon the level of funding at its 1985 session. IMPs were to last from 1986, the year of Iberian accession, to 1993, by which time the transitional arrangements for Spanish and Portuguese accession would be almost complete. Areas eligible for IMP funding were defined as being the whole of Greece, the greater part of Italy (not the north), and southern France, with the exclusion of certain urban centres, in the latter two cases. The population of these areas was fifty million, and in 1984 they received almost a third of all EC grants and loans (more than 3,600m ECU or £2,125m), itself a recognition of their special needs. In March 1985 it was agreed that 6,600m ECU (£3,894m) would be allocated to the IMPs over the seven-year period: 2,500m ECU from the existing structural funds; an additional budget contribution of 1,600m ECU; and loans of 2,500m ECU via the European Investment Bank (EIB) and the New Community Instrument (NCI). Within this Greece was to get 2,000m ECU (£1,300m) from the structural funds and the additional budget contribution, and payments to France and Italy were primarily to come under EIB and NCI appropriations. By the end of 1987, all the Greek and French IMPs, under the first allocation, had been launched and the Italian IMPs were to be implemented in 1988.

The level of such expenditures remained low, however, in comparison to the total EC budget. In 1987, 20.5 per cent of the budget was allocated to all the structural funds (for example agricultural investment, regional policy, social policy) while the IMPs represented just over 0.5 per cent of the overall budget. Finance available for the IMPs over seven years represented less than 18 per cent of the budget available for a single year (1987).

Special provision within the EC budget was made for Portugal. A December 1980 agreement provided for pre-accession aid – notably grants for projects in agriculture, fisheries and technical assistance, which in 1985 totalled 96m ECU – and loans via the EIB. After her accession, a regional aid scheme was developed for Portugal entitled PEDIP (Programa Especifico de Desen-volvimento da Indústria Portuguesa). The programme was endorsed by the extraordinary meeting of the February 1988 Brussels European Council, and was designed to further the modernization of Portuguese industry between 1988 and 1992. The finance – involving a special allocation under the enlarged structural funds – was to total 1,000m ECU (approximately £0.66m) over the five-year period. No such scheme was created for Spain. It had also received aid via the EIB in the pre-accession period, but thereafter its needs were dealt with under the general programmes of the structural funds as well as the EIB. The level of aid to Spain was significant (see Table 10.2).

Wider financial strains were quickly to become apparent, however. EC

Table 10.2 Financial relations between the EC and the new member states

	Greece (million ECU) 1981	Greece (million ECU) 1986	Portugal (million ECU) 1986	Portugal (million ECU) 1987	Spain (million ECU) 1986	Spain (million ECU) 1987[3]
Total payments to EC	254.5	632.4	110.9[1]	202.6[1]	2,320.6	986
Receipts from:						
EAGGF: Guarantee	146.2	1,386.9	30.4	145.3[2]	271.4	627
EAGGF: Guidance	—	86.2	—	30.8	—	17
ERDF (Regional)	122.0	309.1	188.8	230.9	314.3	346
ESF (Social)	6.6	107.1	109.2	174.8	174.9	270
Others[3]	119.9	15.8	169.4	30.8	1,654.9	2
Total receipts	394.7	1,905.1	497.8	612.6	2,415.5	1,262
Balance	140.2	1,372.7	386.9	410.0	94.9[5]	276

Notes:
1. Figures supplied by Portuguese government. Total payments in 1986 were 278.6m ECU and in 1987 were 344.8m ECU, but reimbursements reduced these amounts to those given above. Exchange rates used are the average for both years: 1986, 1 ECU = esc. 147.5; 1987, 1 ECU = esc. 162.427.
2. Figures supplied by Portuguese government.
3. Figures supplied by Spanish government, converted at exchange rate of 1 ECU = pta 139, valid as of December 1987.
4. Includes 'specific measures' of aid to each country immediately after accession, of some magnitude.
5. Figures from the EC Court of Auditors given here show a positive balance, while Spanish government figures show a small deficit.

Source: All figures came from *Eurostat Review* (EC) unless otherwise indicated.

expenditure had outgrown available revenue: demands for an increase in the structural funds, notably from the southern members and Ireland, were countered by calls for greater budgetary discipline and UK and FRG resistance to increasing the EC's own resources. The two European Council (Summit) meetings in 1987 both ended without agreement on a package of measures to overcome a situation which was becoming increasingly critical (see Chapter 7). Eventually, an extraordinary European Council meeting agreed to a compromise deal, which explicitly stated that the size of 'the Structural Funds will be doubled in 1993 by comparison with 1987'. By 1992, the structural funds would involve 13,000m ECU.

The impetus for such increased expenditure came in the context of the drive towards liberalizing the internal market and the concern of the southern members in particular that such policies should not serve to exacerbate economic and social inequalities within the EC. Indeed, the SEA's Article 130A provided that the EC 'develop and pursue its actions leading to the strengthening of its economic and social cohesion ... [and] aim at reducing disparities between the various regions and the backwardness of the least-favoured regions'. Moreover, another revision (Article 130B) declared that, 'The implementation of the common policies and of the internal market shall take into account the objectives set out in Article 130A'.

The policy agenda for the objectives of economic and social cohesion represented a second stage in the EC's response to the challenge of Mediterranean enlargement. Distinct from the accession of new member states and the IMPs, the concern for cohesion stemmed from fears as to how peripheral economies might fare in the context of more intense competition in the new internal market after 1992. De-regulation was thus to be tempered by market intervention at EC level, to engineer desired economic and social objectives.

The initial impact of membership on the Mediterranean states

Acceding to a major grouping such as the EC produces a widespread impact on the internal development of the new member state. The concern here will be with the economic advantages and disadvantages, as measured in terms of payments and receipts from the EC budget and imports and exports to other EC countries. However, other impacts can be noted in the political and social domains; albeit in a less discernible fashion. Elites who have become exposed to wider European interactions can experience significant changes, in both a cognitive and affective manner. In Spain and Portugal, such European-wide ties often met with a popular and emotional response, as they signalled the end of the relative exclusion experienced during the years of dictatorship. For Greece, participation was initially more controversial, and these divisions were only overcome as PASOK became reconciled to membership.

Participation in the EC obliged the new members to contribute to, and receive payments from, the budget. All three benefited as net recipients of funds from the EC (see Table 10.2). The level of payments to Greece increased significantly between 1981 and 1986, the first year of Iberian membership. Greece, and later Spain, came to benefit most from CAP suppport mechanisms (EAGGF Guarantees), followed by money from the regional and social funds. For Portugal, structural support from the regional and social budgets outstripped that from the CAP. Such inflows of funds were essential to each of the new member states, if their economies were to be able to face up to increased external competition.

Easier trading relations with the EC did indeed involve problems for the new members. The Spanish economy, in particular, had been buttressed by import tariffs prior to accession, and it had enjoyed a large trading surplus with the rest of the EC. After accession, all three countries had a trading deficit with the EC, though in the case of Portugal this only occurred in the second year of membership (see Table 10.3). The imbalance for all three rose to significant levels: the flood of imports outstripped the capacity of their domestic economies to export. Accession also affected trade patterns: before entry, Portugal's largest export market was the UK; since then exports to France and the FRG have outstripped those to Britain. Moreover, trade between Spain, Portugal and Greece grew significantly after 1985.

The problem of balancing the benefits from inward investment aid with the dangers of increased imports had been foreseen well before enlargement took place. However its resolution, in the context of competing interests, seems likely to remain as a major challenge to the EC as a whole as progress towards de-regulation and the completion of the internal market continues.

Table 10.3 Trading flows of new member states
(m ECU)

		Between rest of EC and:		
		Greece	Portugal	Spain
1981	Imports	4,011	—	—
	Exports	1,671	—	—
1985	Imports	6,424	4,586	13,745
	Exports	3,225	4,647	16,371
1986	Imports	6,033	4,134	17,046
	Exports	3,253	4,221	16,423
1987	Imports	—	7,121[1]	23,626[2]
	Exports	—	4,434[1]	19,210[2]

Notes:
1. Figures transposed from Portuguese escudos at exchange rate of 1 ECU = 168.280, as of December 1987.
2. Figures transposed from Spanish pesetas at exchange rate of 1 ECU = 139.338 as of December 1987.

Sources: Eurostat Review (EC); *Balance del segundo año de la adhesión de España a la CEE* (1987); *Portugal Nas Comunidades Europeias* (1987); and *Basic Statistics of the Community* (1982), EC.

The external consequences of enlargement

Access to the EC market is of crucial importance to Mediterranean states outside the bloc; for most of them, the EC is their largest trading partner. Conversely, as their main supplier the EC has to be sensitive to their vulnerability. The second enlargement of the EC represented a major threat to the trading position of the Mediterranean countries on the outside: before accession, Spain alone exported more non-fuel products to the EC than all the other Mediterranean countries put together; it was also the largest outside supplier of Mediterranean agricultural products, (Pomfret, 1986:99). Inside the EC, easier access for Spanish products posed dangers for the Mediterranean countries on the outside.

Moreover, the second enlargement occurred at a time of heightened economic difficulty for the Mediterranean countries. They had suffered not only as a result of the recession in the EC reducing the scope for their exports, the EC had also imposed restrictions on imports of goods in its so-called 'sensitive' industries, such as textiles and clothing, which were important to some of them. To the Mediterranean countries such moves contradicted the promises of free entry for manufactures foreseen in the EC's global approach heralded at the start of the 1970s.

The Commission was aware of the conflicts of interest. A discussion paper produced for it and published in 1985 (EC and Mediterranean: 3-4, 1985) commented: 'In short, there will be a variety of interests, most of them southern, though not all by any means, which will want the Community closed as much as possible against outside exporters of typical Mediterranean products ... On the contrary, the northern regions of the Community ... will have primary interests in a dynamic Mediterranean as an outlet for their agricultural and industrial goods as well as services.' This clash of interests clearly affected the internal policy of the EC towards its southern members and regions, and it seems likely to remain a factor in the negotiation of trading relations with excluded Mediterranean states.

The economic cost to the Mediterranean countries of the EC's second enlargement can be expected to vary according to the country and the trading product involved. Pomfret (1986:98) noted that it 'should not have a great effect on manufactured goods'; as any sensitivities were likely to involve more than the new entrants. It is in agricultural trade that the strongest clash of interest exists: 'the countries most affected ... will be those whose exports most clearly resemble those of Greece, Portugal or Spain' (Pomfret, 1986:99). Of these, Spain represents the greatest threat and Portugal the least, as the latter's agricultural exports are relatively untypical. The consequences were most serious for the associate members Cyprus and Turkey, the Maghreb countries, especially Morocco, and Israel (Pomfret, 1986:99). In a very basic sense, the clash remains an unequal one. There is an enormous gap in economic weight between the EC and its Mediterranean partners. Pomfret has made the point succinctly: 'Economically one-sided preferential agreements, like those in the Community's Mediterranean policy, are inevitably subject to the priorities of the dominant partner' (1986:100).

Before Spanish and Portuguese accession, the Commission had brought forward proposals in March 1984 to 'maintain and strengthen' preferential trade agreements between the EC and the Mediterranean countries (EC General Report, 1984:682). In 1985 the Council of Ministers agreed (30 March) to do 'all in its power ... to ensure that traditional trade patterns were maintained', and it subsequently established the directives on which the Commission was to negotiate revisions of the appropriate trading agreements' (EC General Report, 1985:831). In 1986 the Spanish government delayed the negotiations by insisting on special protective measures for Spanish fruit and vegetables, but agreements were finally concluded with Tunisia, Egypt, Lebanon, Israel and Turkey. Further revisions to the various co-operation and association agreements were signed in 1987 with Algeria, Tunisia, Egypt, Jordan, Lebanon, Cyprus and Turkey. Only the revision of Malta's association agreement and Morocco's cooperation accord remained outstanding.[3] Earlier, the association agreement with Turkey had been affected by the imposition of military rule in Ankara: it had continued to operate, but new financial resources had remained frozen until 1986. In April 1987, Turkey made a formal application for full EC membership, but, because of its economic position, Greek objections and the EC's concern with the internal market, Turkish entry does not seem likely until well after 1992.

The co-operation agreements with the Mediterranean countries involve financial aid from the EC budget and EIB loans. The current 1987-91 agreement with the Maghreb and Mashreq countries plus Israel provides for 1.6bn ECU of aid (see Table 10.4), two-thirds of which is available in loans. This is substantially less than that allocated to Greece, for example, under an earlier IMP agreement.

A full analysis of how the Mediterranean countries have fared in the 1980s is beyond the scope of this chapter, but it can be noted that (i) new agreements

Table 10.4 Financial aid to Mediterranean countries
(in million ECU)

Recipients	First Protocol	Second Protocol	Third Protocol
Maghreb countries	339	489	786
Mashreq countries	300	486	769
Israel	30	40	63
Total	669	1,015	1,618

have been signed with almost all the relevant countries; (ii) as before, the EC has dealt with each country separately; and (iii) the level of aid to them has not risen significantly. The relationship thus remains much as before, with adjustments having been made to the trading agreements to take account of the interests of the new member states.

'Cohesion' and the internal market

The emphasis placed on the 'cohesion' of the EC was a direct result of the SEA agreement on the internal market reached at the December 1985 Luxembourg Summit. Commission President Delors commented at the time that the SEA was

a splendid opportunity for the Community to emerge from what it is at present – a free trade area, plus budgetary transfers ... cohesion is a new idea, the idea that convergence of economic and social policies – and not merely budgetary transfers – will in ten years' time enable every Member State, including the poorest, to say that all in all Community life has been of benefit. [Bull. EC **11**, 1985:17]

For the southern members, an increased budget supporting expanded EC programmes was very much to their basic economic self-interest. It was also seen as facilitating a 'pay-off' in two senses: as one of the major benefits of accession for the new members and, more generally, as a necessary bulwark for all the peripheral economies facing the dangers of more intense competition as a result of the completion of the EC's internal market. An increased budget was not agreed, however, until February 1988; thereafter, programmes could be expanded and the new concerns taken seriously.

The southern EC governments attached great importance to the need for 'cohesion'. The four-year programme of the Spanish socialists (PSOE) adopted in 1986 seeks 'the construction of a United Europe'. However, the strongest emphasis is in the economic domain: the objective should be 'to organise the internal market on the criteria of economic cohesion, to seek a re-equilibrium of the EC by means of reform of the measures that [aim to] promote the development of the southern regions and peripheries'. Their Portuguese counterparts and, indeed, the Lisbon centre–right coalition government of Cavaco-Silva, also pressed similar claims. Both the Portuguese and Greek governments appended separate declarations to the SEA arguing that progress towards the internal market should 'not damage sensitive and vital sectors' of their economies. Greek Premier Papandreou identified the EC's structural programmes and the acceptance of cohesion – for which he himself, not unreasonably, took credit – as the justification for his government's change of heart over participation in the EC. 'From the moment it became evident', he said, 'that Greece's insistence on the necessity for solidarity towards the countries of the European south had been accepted by the wealthier northern partners, we judged the country's interests to be better served inside, rather than outside, the EC' (*Financial Times*, 1.7.88).

Moreover, at a critical stage in the development of the EC's internal market policies, southern European governments were provided with the opportunity to emphasize the importance of cohesion. From July 1988 to the end of 1989 the presidency of the Council of Ministers and the European Council was held successively by the Greek, Spanish and French governments; each, moreover, headed by socialists. Early in 1988, Papendreou indicated that his emphasis would be on the social dimension of the internal market, and in May 1988 President Mitterrand stated that France's chief priority 'will be the creation of a unified social space, an initiative undertaken by Greece'. Delors, in a speech to the ETUC (12 May 1988), also argued that a unified social space was fundamental to the establishment of an internal market. The PASOK government was thus set to take up concerns expressed more broadly across the EC, 'from unions in high-wage, high-labour standard countries like West Germany and Denmark, who are afraid that jobs in a free-trading Europe might otherwise flow to those countries with lower standards' (*Financial Times*, 1 July 1988). Papandreou was clear about the need for a new emphasis:

Some governments in the EC believe it is enough to remove obstacles to trade and encourage competition to obtain growth and stability. The key to our presidency is the social dimension – standard of living, health, unemployment benefits and salaries. The worker will be at the centre of our presidency. [*The Independent*, 1 July 1988]

Social equality, greater protection for workers in industry and unemployment were themes likely to be stressed by the southern governments; a heightened role for the EC in these spheres might help their domestic economies to approximate more closely the higher standards in wealthier European economies.

At the same time, increased attention was being given to monetary integration and financial stability (the Integrated Financial Space). At its Hanover meeting in June 1988, the European Council set up a committee of experts to propose 'concrete stages leading towards [economic and monetary] union', and it was due to discuss their report in Madrid in June 1989. On the controversial question of a European Central Bank, the Greek government supported the Commission's proposals, while their Portuguese and Spanish counterparts reserved their position (Programme for the Greek Presidency). Unlike the UK, sensitivities over supranationality did not figure so prominently in Lisbon or Madrid. Like the British currency, those of Greece, Spain and Portugal were not part of the central stabilization mechanism of the EMS, though the pressure has been on each of them to enter before 1992. A more active role for the EC in promoting financial and currency stability could help support the weaker southern currencies.

Conclusions

The EC's second enlargement highlighted the clash of interests between the new entrants and those countries left outside; a clash refereed by the older and larger member states. Once inside, the new entrants were able to seek a revision of policies and of resource allocation to lessen the inequalities between the centre and the periphery of the integration process. Mediterranean countries outside the bloc were left to secure the most favourable trading preferences available in the light of the changed situation in the basin.

The response of the other EC states indicated the extent of the change. The first new entrant, Greece, was rewarded with aid under the IMPs, designed to settle complaints over its original membership terms and to protect it from the effects of the Iberian enlargement. Portugal received special consideration under PEDIP to tackle its economic under-development and to avoid any later attempts at 're-negotiation' along the Greek pattern. More generally, southern states were successful in pressing for a doubling of the EC's structural funds by the end of 1992. In economic and social matters the EC had been changed by the creation and extension of particular aid schemes; an increase in the flow of funds across national boundaries. But the period of enlargement had a crucial impact on the emerging debate over the EC's long-term objectives; in particular it affected the ideological and political input into the debate over the completion of the internal market. A 'unified social space', backed by an increase in structural funds, looks set to establish a strong interventionist role for EC institutions in the new barrier-free economy. National de-regulation will not prevent EC regulation and intervention.

Less quantifiable changes came from the inclusion of domestic elites and organizations in Community-wide politics, and the inculcation of West European norms and practices. At the political level, the southern European input also had an impact on the foreign policy deliberations of the EC (EPC). The most obvious cases initially involved Greece: its neutralist stance over East–West relations (dissenting from declarations agreed by others), its support for the Palestinian and Arab cause and its stance against Turkish aggression in Cyprus and the Aegean (also involving a threatened veto over Turkish entry into the EC). The Iberian governments seemed to wish consciously to avoid such radical dissent, but their potential for special inputs on Latin American and African issues was also significant.

Wider questions remain to be judged in the light of future developments. The creation of a trading bloc inevitably raises issues as to access for imports from outside, involving general tariff policy and a system of preferences. Critics attack the EC for being an exclusivist and protectionist club of the wealthy, and to some extent it must be found guilty as charged by virtue of its very existence. In a deeper sense, however, it must be judged according to particular sets of external linkages, differentiating its relations with less-developed countries from those with other industrialized economies. The latter can also be criticized for their own protectionism. As the EC faces the end of the twentieth century, how it manages its own internal market and CAP will have direct implications for its generosity towards weaker nations on the outside.

The EC developed its Mediterranean ties in an essentially *ad hoc* and reactive manner. Its second enlargement involved a new form of differentiation between countries in the basin. The Greek Memorandum of 1982 was, perhaps, a salutary lesson as to the need for policy coherence and planning. Many feared that the second enlargement would weaken and retard the integration process; in the event, such concerns seem to have been exaggerated. Mediterranean demands have largely been absorbed into wider, long-term objectives. Moreover, the second enlargement served to clarify some basic policy choices – such as the need for increased interventionism in the new internal market – and has thus given new emphasis to politics and ideology in debates about the future of the EC.

Notes

1. See Burrows (2:1985). He notes that:

Turkey's relations with the EC are at present governed by the Association Agreement of 1964, extended by the Supplementary Protocol of 1970. These agreements provide for a gradual reduction of barriers to trade; financial assistance; and an approach to free movement of workers, which should have been completed by 1986. Overall they provide that Turkey should be in a position to accept customs union by 1995, thus permitting consideration of full membership, but with no guarantee that this would be accorded.

In April 1987, as noted elsewhere in the text, the Turkish Government announced its intention of applying for full EC membership.
2. The *World Development Report 1984* for the World Bank lists the GNP per capita in 1982 for Portugal as $2,450; for Greece $4,290; Ireland $5,150; Italy $6,840; and the UK $9,660.
3. The Commission's proposals on Morocco were, in mid-1988, still to be agreed. The Greek Presidency in 1988 stated that it expected the Malta Government to apply for full membership.

References

Balance del Segunda año de la adhesión de España a la CEE (1987), Secretaria de Estado Para Las Comunidades Europeas, Madrid, Oficina de Informacion Diplomatica.
Burrows, B. (1987), 'Turkey and the European Community', *Federal Trust Working Paper*, 3, London.
Commission of the EC, (1984) 'Integrated Regional Development Programmes', DG for Agriculture, 89/1984.
—, (1988), 'Recommendation for a Council Decision concerning the conclusion of a Protocol to the Co-operation Agreement between the EEC and the Kingdom of Morocco consequent on the accession of the Kingdom of Spain and the Portuguese Republic to the Community', COM (88) 168 final, 23 March 1988.
—, (1988), 'Amended Proposal for a Council Regulation (EEC) on the tasks of the structural funds and their effectiveness ...', COM 88, 144; 23 March 1988.
Communiqués of European Council meetings: March 1985–June 1988.
Council Regulation (EEC) No 2088/85 of 23 July 1985, concerning the integrated Mediterranean programmes.
Delors, J. (1988), 'Discours dévant la Congres de la Confédération Européene des Syndicats', Stockholm, 12 May 1988.
Featherstone, K. (1988), *Socialist Parties and European Integration: A Comparative History*, Manchester, MUP.
Galtung, J. (1973), *The European Community: A Superpower in the Making*, London, Allen and Unwin.

General Report on the Activities of the European Communities, Commission of the EC, Brussels: various years.

Ginsberg, R. (1983), 'The European Community and the Mediterranean', in J. Lodge, *Institutions and Policies of the European Community*, London, Frances Pinter.

Greek Foreign Ministry (1988), 'Programme for the Greek Presidency of the European Community; July–December 1988', Athens (in Greek).

Harrop, J. (forthcoming), *The Political Economy of Integration in the European Community*, London, Edward Elgar.

Leigh, M. (1978), 'Nine EEC Attitudes to Enlargement' and van Praag, N. (1978), 'European Political Co-operation and the Southern Periphery', *Sussex European Papers*, No 2.

Pomfret, R. (1986), *Mediterranean Policy of the European Community: A Study in Discrimination in Trade*, London, Macmillan/Trade Policy Research Centre.

Portugal Nas Comunidades Europeias (1986), Ministéro dos Negócios Estrangeiros, Primeiro Ano, Lisbon.

— (1987), Ministéro dos Negócios Estrangeiros, Primeiro Ano, Lisbon.

Philip, A. Butt (1988), *Implementing the European Internal Market: Problems and Prospects*, London, RIIA.

Pollack, B. (1987), *The Paradox of Spanish Foreign Policy: Spain's International Relations from Franco to Democracy*, London, Frances Pinter.

Sampedro, J.L. and Payno, J.A. (eds) (1983), *The Enlargement of the European Community: Case Studies of Greece, Portugal and Spain*, London, Macmillan.

Swann, D. (1984), *The Economics of the Common Market*, Harmondsworth, Penguin.

Telex Mediterranean, Brussels, various editions.

To Vima, Athens, various editions.

Tsoukalis, L. (1981), *The European Community and its Mediterranean Enlargement*, London, Allen and Unwin.

Verney, S. (1987), 'Greece and the European-Community', in K. Featherstone and D.K.K. Katsoudas, *Political Change in Greece: Before and After the Colonels*, London, Croom Helm.

Wallace, H. (1985), *Europe: The Challenge of Diversity*, London, RIIA/RKP.

11 The Community and New Technologies

Margaret Sharp

Introduction

The term 'the new technologies' is loosely applied to a number of fast growing sectors of the economy whose current success emanates, at least in part, from underlying changes in technology. Perhaps most obviously it applies to what is now termed the information technology sector – electronics, telecommunications, computers, robotics and the associated hardware and software to create the networks and systems which link them all together. The biotechnologies provide another grouping in which developments in science are beginning to have major impact – so far mainly upon the pharmaceutical and health care sectors, but with potentially major impact upon agriculture, food production and processing and the chemical industry. New materials technologies are themselves largely emerging from the chemicals sector but may have major impact upon metallurgy and the engineering industries, while an industry such as aerospace, as a major user of new technologies, helps to push the science and technology forward to meet new challenges and answer new problems.

New technologies have gained a new importance in the 1980s as the general slowing down of world growth rates has thrown a new prominence on fast growing sectors of the economy. The underlying movement is seen by some (for example Freeman *et al*, 1982) to be part of the long-term dynamics of the world economy in which economies oscillate between periods of rapid technological change and the slower processes of assimilation and maturation; and by others (Lawrence and Schultze, 1987) to be part of a man-made cycle of macroeconomic mismanagement. Be that as it may, policies which help promote this process of change have been in vogue both at the national and international level. Each European country has its own panoply of programmes to promote new technologies, ranging from general measures to expand and promote the science base underpinning these fast growing areas of technology to specific incentives to encourage firms to apply and use the new tools and techniques being developed.

These efforts have been mirrored at the Community level by a series of EC initiatives which, as time has gone by, have become more focused and more effective. There is a sense in which cooperation in science and technology can be described as 'the lowest common factor' of cooperation. At times when there has been little else to cooperate over, common programmes promoting scientific exchange or pooling funds on expensive research programmes have been dredged up to show a modicum of good will. Such 'lowest common factor' policies have tended, however, to be shallow: once crossed by national interests they were often, as we shall see, discarded in favour of the national programmes. This is no longer the case: the need for collaboration is now backed by economic necessity. The interesting feature of the 1980s has been the demise of the national champion and the rise of European-based multinationals with a capability to compete at a global level. This chapter argues that the European Community programmes, particularly ESPRIT, have played a seminal part in this shifting of perspectives from the national to the global level.

Early Community initiatives in the promotion of new technologies

The concept of a European Technological Community has never been far below the surface for those seeking to create a united Europe. Indeed, it formed an explicit part of the programme of Jean Monnet's Action Commitee for a United States of Europe,[1] and was subsequently translated into an action plan in Christopher Layton's book, *Europe's Advanced Technology: A Programme for Integration* (Layton, 1969). It has recently resurfaced in Narjes's call in 1985 for the creation of a Technological Community to be centred upon the Community R & D programme and its various new technology initiatives (see below).

There has always, however, been a schizoid element in the advocacy of a European Technological Community, and tension between the free-market ideologues whose emphasis has been upon diminishing the internal barriers and inherent fragmentation of the European market, and the European chauvinists who have constantly warned against Europe's increasing dependence on American (and latterly Japanese) technology and whose vision centres upon a far more positive and interventionist approach (Servan-Schreiber (1967). (See Williams (1973) for a discussion of these trends).

One of the reasons for this schizoid element was that the Treaty of Rome did not endow the Commission with explicit powers to promote research, development or, for that matter, industry. It provided for a range of policy powers which could be used to determine the regulatory framework and help shape the market environment: competition policy, freedom of movement for capital and labour, the right of establishment, the regulation and harmonization of state aids. But no general policy framework was established for either industrial or technological policy. This left the Commission to operate only through unanimous decisions of the Council of Ministers and hostage, therefore, to any national interests considered to be of over-riding importance. Belatedly the Single European Act has simultaneously extended both the Commission's competence to act in this sphere of policy and, of course, introduced majority voting. Together these have now greatly strengthened the Commission's role.

The need to operate via consensus among the Council of Ministers helps to explain the stop-go nature of some of the early experiments. DG III, responsible for industrial affairs, was not established until 1967, and then took some time to decide what its proper role should be. Initially it decided on an active stance, encouraging trans-national mergers and the development of large European companies (EC Commission 1970), but became caught between West German advocacy of free-market principles and the more interventionist philosophy of the French. Attempts in the early 1970s to create an Industrial Policy Committee under the joint auspices of the Council of Ministers and the Commission failed, leaving Community industrial policy in limbo until the turn of the decade.

In the mid-1970s all European countries were overtaken by excess capacity in their older industries – textiles, shipbuilding, steel, motor cars, even chemicals. Uncertain how far it represented merely a cyclical downturn after the oil crisis or a more far-reaching adjustment to the fundamental structure of the economy, nearly every government responded with subsidies and protection. The situation threatened to get out of hand with beggar-my-neighbour action which led to strong EC intervention in 1977-8 to limit state aids to shipbuilding, steel and textiles. Crisis cartels were established for steel and, briefly, man-made fibres, until DGIV ruled the latter out of order. An attempt to recreate a chemical cartel was also stamped on quickly. Overall, however, it meant that both national and EC authorities were pre-occupied by the problems of the old industries until the early 1980s.

Science and technology policy, fared little better. The first meeting of the Council of Science Ministers was held in 1967, and in a flurry of activity they commissioned studies of the potential for Community action in six broad areas of technological development – transport, oceanography, metallurgy, environmental issues, data processing and telecommunications – but detailed discussion of proposals was held up by Britain's application for membership. Eventually the initiative led to the establishment in November 1971 of COST (European Cooperation in the field of Scientific and Technical Research), a grouping centred on the Community but comprising, in fact, all nineteen OECD Western European members including Switzerland, Sweden and Austria (Williams, 1973). COST has become a useful, if low-key, framework for the preparation and implementation of pan-European projects of applied scientific research, but because of its extensive membership it has tended to shift outside the EC framework with separately negotiated agreements of cooperation for each project. Besides the original six areas identified for development in 1967, it has added four more: meteorology, agriculture, food technology and medical research. In the latter half of the 1980s, the COST framework has been overshadowed by the EUREKA initiative, embracing as it does a similar group of European countries but enjoying high-profile encouragement from national governments anxious to play down Commission initiatives (Sharp and Shearman, 1987: 28 and 59-60).

In the computing sector where Servan-Schreiber (1967) specifically warned of the growing power of IBM, European initiatives were particularly slow to get off the ground. Several attempts were made during the 1960s to develop cross-national groupings, but most turned out to be inconclusive. In 1962, for example, Siemens, Olivetti, Elliott Automation (later the core of ICL) and Bull began talks to create a cross-Europe grouping, but these came to nothing. Later, in 1969, the Eurodata consortium – ICL, CII, Philips, AEG-Telefunken, Saab and Olivetti – was established to tender for the ESRO (European Space Research Organization) computer requirement, but this collapsed under pressure from the German government, largely because Siemens had been left out. The subsequent attempt in 1973 to bring Siemens, CII and Bull together under the Unidata umbrella collapsed because the French government negotiated a separate deal with the American company Honeywell behind the backs of the German government! While hopes for the success of Unidata were still riding high, the Commission had pushed through in 1974 a Council Resolution backing a medium-term programme on the application, development and production of data processing systems. The hope had been that this would mark the beginning of a major EC programme in computers and electronics. With the failure of Unidata this initiative fizzled out, leaving nothing but a series of small and isolated Commission initiatives and illustrating well the problems of trying to create a coherent programme when the susceptibilities of national champions were at stake (Sharp and Shearman, 1987: 46-7).

In the 1960s nuclear power was, of course, seen to be one of the most important areas of new technology, and the Commission's powers in this sector derived directly from the Euratom Treaty of 1958. Euratom's broad objectives were to encourage the creation and growth of the civil nuclear power industry in Europe through a programme of joint research and development. Four joint research centres were set up – at Karlsruhe, West Germany; Ispra, Italy; Geel, Belgium and Petten, the Netherlands. Areas of research included fast breeder reactors, high-temperature gas reactors, nuclear ship propulsion and nuclear applications to agriculture and medicine. Of these, the quest for a European reactor was potentially the most important but in practice the most neglected, with governments unable to agree a mutually acceptable financial framework within which to pursue the research, or even the research agenda to be pursued. In this respect developments were the casualty both of mistaken assumptions about the future role of nuclear power, which many in the 1960s saw as central to the future economic prosperity of the industrialized world, and the nationalistic ambitions of the individual power plant manufacturers, who lobbied their respective governments accordingly. But the achievements of Euratom were not negligible. In spite of its failures in what should have been its main function, Euratom has assumed (and continues to do so) important regulatory functions in relations to civil nuclear energy and safeguards in the handling of radioactive materials; and its fast breeder reactor programme has survived, despite vicissitudes, into the 1980s, with the French model, Superphenix 1, the product of a fruitful and continuing collaboration between the French and Italian partners (Sharp and Shearman, 1987: 29-33).

Of all the new technologies of the 1960s and 1970s, the one success story of European collaboration – aerospace – owed nothing to the EC and much to the determination of governments and their respective national champions to see collaboration through to success. Admittedly, both for aviation and space, economics rapidly ruled out an individual firm from acting alone unless heavily supported by government subsidy (which of course happened in the military sectors, but not in civil aviation), and even, in time, inhibited individual governments from acting alone. The lessons culled from, first Concorde, and then Airbus, are of the long, slow haul to collaboration; of the importance of the learning process in collaboration itself; and of the advantage in allowing industry, not governments, to dictate the scope for collaboration, allowing it to be market, not government, driven (Hayward, 1986).

The space story is also interesting, and illustrates another aspect of success – the need to pursue a coherent strategy with patience and determination over a long period of time – for with new technologies gestation periods can be very long. The precedents for European collaboration on space were not good. In the 1960s the European Launcher Development Organization (ELDO) and the European Space Research Organization (ESRO) both had their teething troubles and financial problems, but the merged European Space Agency (ESA) which developed in the 1970s drew in all European countries with a keen interest in the sector. As a narrow but functionally orientated collaborative framework, it has helped to produce a coherence of objective and purpose in the closely knit space community of policy makers, scientists, engineers and industrialists, and has ensured that, by the mid-1980s, Western Europe has the range of space capabilities sufficient to give it a degree of autonomy. Like Airbus Industrie, ESA is not without its problems, well illustrated by Britain's vacillations over membership. So far much of its success has derived from the pro-active leadership of the French; but with the shift from experimental to commercial, other partners may wish to have more of a say and consensus leadership may prove less coherent. There are also incipient problems over its military role. To date it has firmly eschewed any military connection (and has among its members a number of European neutrals), the ethos of its founding charter pledging it to a civilian and 'peaceful' role in space (RIIA, 1987).

What lessons are to be learned from the experiences of the 1960s and 1970s? For the EC perhaps above all the limitations of EC action. Arguments among governments, differences in national policies and the difficulties in establishing effective management formulae were all major constraints on effective EC action. But experience among national governments in promoting new technologies had not been happy either and there has been understandable cynicism about any bureaucracy's ability to 'pick the winner' and fears that expensive mistakes at a national level would be translated into even more expensive mistakes at the supranational level where accountability was weakened. The lessons were not all negative. There had been some successes, and these suggested certain characteristics to be espoused. First was the need for flexibility – to recognize that not all programmes had to conform to a uniform EC pattern with participation from all EC countries, but needed to be tailored to circumstances, with scope for reappraisal and review. The 'variable geometry' that was to become an increasingly important theme of the 1980s was already apparent. Second was the need for functional specificity. Programmes with limited but clear objectives were more likely to meet with success than grandiose programmes which promised the earth but could deliver nothing. Equally, it was crucial that the partners perceived sufficient benefit in the longer term to sustain their commitment through the short run and provide the incentive to reconcile major differences in outlook and interest. In this respect the Franco–German axis was crucial. Programmes which won support from these two partners were more likely to be successful. Third was the need to align the government and industrial roles into one that was mutually reinforcing. There was little point in governments promoting programmes which were of no interest to the industrial community. In this respect programmes needed to be drawn up in line with the 'grain of the market', not against it.

ESPRIT – a watershed in the development of EC programmes

In retrospect it is easy to see how these lessons were heeded in the developments of the 1980s and how they led to a whole new style of EC programme. At the time, it was a matter of groping forward in the dark, hoping that the new ideas and new institutions would achieve the desired change in attitudes. And as so often in history, it was a matter of the right person delivering the right message at the right time. The person was Vicomte Davignon who, in 1977, had taken over the Commission's industrial portfolio (DG III) determined to transform its image from one of supporting lame ducks (or condoning such support from national governments) to one of actively helping to create a new industrial structure for Europe. The problems which beset him in shipbuilding, steel and textiles were to prove less tractable than he hoped, but a number of factors played into his hands in relation to the promotion of new technologies. His interest in industrial R & D became evident at the same time as DG XII's forward-looking 'Europe + 30' exercise reached fruition and the FAST (Forecasting and Assessment in Science and Technology) studies on the information society, biotechnology, and work and employment brought to light Europe's weakness in translating basic research into industrial activities.

By the early 1980s many industrialists began to express concern at Europe's relative decline in the Information Technology IT sector. Within the industry as a whole, the EC supplied a mere 40 per cent of its own market and only 10 per cent of the world market. Whereas in 1975 the EC balance of payments in IT goods and services had been positive, by 1982 a large deficit had arisen. Japan meanwhile seemed intent on becoming the (IT) industry's second world leader. In the mid-1970s it had put in hand its VLSI (Very Large Scale Integration) Programme which had brought together its major electronics manufacturers and targetted major Japanese entry into the volume commodity chip manufacture with the 64K-RAM chip. Japan's fifth generation computer programme, involving some $200-500m of government financial investment, was launched in October 1981. The United States, too, was far from complacent. Department of Defense collaborative programmes included work on VHSI (Very High Speed Integration), the STARS programme in software engineering the Strategic Computing programme to develop supercomputers performing high-speed calculations.

Individually, of course, various European governments were supporting their own IT industries. The French had run a series of *Plans Calculs* and *Plans Compositants* aimed at upgrading the computer and components sector; the British had had a series of support schemes for microelectronics aimed at raising both productive capabilities and industrial awareness and the Germans had had a succession of programmes aimed at upgrading performance and usage of computers and components. The contrast between the relative failure of the separate European initiatives and the success of MITI's coordinated and collaborative VLSI programme was stark, and the lesson did not go unheeded. Under Davignon's guidance the Commission began to develop a more strategic approach to the IT sector. The broad outline of a programme for microelectronic technology was produced in 1979-80 and agreed by the Council in November 1981. The Commission then took the unorthodox step of inviting representatives from the major companies to establish a working group to draw up the detailed programme which was to develop into ESPRIT, the European Strategic Programme for Research in Information Technology.

Davignon played a vital role in developing the ESPRIT programme. In his evidence to the 1985 House of Lords' Select Committee on the European Communities, he outlined the three factors which had motivated his attempts (House of Lord, 1985: 169). In the first place, he had been struck by the 'very distinctive difference in performance' between the industries of USA, Japan and the EC. Second, he had felt that the time had come for Community competence to be upgraded to reflect more accurately the state-of-the-art; and, third, he had been aware of the fact that no real incentive existed for cross-border collaboration. Any EC-level solution therefore needed a new approach to policy development. Until then the Commission had tended to work with research directors or their equivalents, and initiatives had come unstuck because they had been unable to carry them higher up the hierarchy. Davignon determined to liaise with only the very highest levels of company management, to define priorities with them and thus secure their commitment to the subsequent programme.

Over 1979-80 Davignon therefore invited the heads of Europe's leading electronics and IT companies to a series of round table discussions. The 'Big Twelve', as they came to be known, comprised ICL, GEC and Plessey from Britain; AEG, Nixdorf and Siemens from Germany; Thomson, Bull and CGE from France; Olivetti and STET from Italy; and Philips from the Netherlands. Davignon received a more favourable response than the Commission had received from their lower-level counterparts in earlier years. A technical committee was established which set up a number of panels and workshops, and discussions continued for two years. Initially the thought was that they would establish a series of Airbus-style joint companies to manufacture products within Europe. Such production activities, however, proved difficult to organize, whereas the concept of carrying out a major collaborative research programme seemed a more appropriate activity for organization on a Community basis (House of Lords, 1985). Discussion therefore began to focus on the pre-competitive end of collaborative research, a stance which from the Commission's viewpoint neatly avoided the issue of competition policy. Under Articles 85 and 86, collaboration for the purposes of pre-competitive research is granted a block exemption; collaboration at the development stage (competitive research) is not allowed.

The emergence of a round table consensus on the five areas of research where a European programme was deemed essential quite clearly reflected the high level of industrial commitment to the idea of collaboration. Discussions had been lengthy and detailed at a time when the possibility of any form of Community programme or funding was uncertain. But industry's willingness to commit itself was also the result of the intensified competition in IT globally. In particular, two events were seminal in changing attitudes – the prospective deregulation of AT&T, which would allow AT&T, long constrained by the US anti-trust authorities to operate *only* in the US, to move into European operations; and the settlement of the longstanding dispute between the US anti-trust authorities and IBM which gave IBM *carte blanche* to move into the telecommunications sector. Behind the scenes there was also the influence of the Gyllenhammer Group. This is an informal grouping of European manufacturers, ranging from Philips to Volvo and Pilkingtons, who keep a watching brief on infrastructure issues affecting Europe in general. Their acknowledgement of the inefficacy of promoting solely national policies played a part in the establishment of ESPRIT, as did the careful preparatory work of DG XII officials, while the newly formed alliance between the Commission and industry brought pressure to bear on national governments to recognize the logic of the Community position.

The first outline proposal for ESPRIT was produced in September 1980. The idea was to develop a European strategic programme based on the collaboration between the major European companies and their smaller counterparts, and universities and research institutes. By May 1982 these had been worked into a full proposal and the Commission's paper 'Towards a European Strategic programme for Research and Development in Information Technology'[2] was put to the Council, and subsequently to the Versailles European Summit in June 1982. The response was favourable and by December 1982 the Commission had the go-ahead for the first pilot phase costing 11.5 mECUS (£8.5m).

The pilot phase was a deliberate part of the Davignon strategy. Given the doubts he encountered from the participants in his round table, in particular over the capacity of the Commission to mount an effective programme which would not become bogged down in bureaucratic delays, his strategy was one of the 'toe in the water' – see how the pilot phase goes before making a further commitment. A special task-force, many recruited from industry, was set up to handle applications and to cut through the Brussels red tape. The call for proposals went out in February 1983, and contracts began to be signed in May that year. By September thirty-eight projects had been launched which were later to be incorporated into the main part of the programme. Over 80 per cent of the first round of contracts went to the twelve 'round table' companies (comprising, it has to be said, 70 per cent of the industry). The majority of projects involved participants from two to three member states. Of the total number of organizations associated with the pilot phase, twenty-seven were located in Britain, twenty-one in Germany, ten in the Netherlands, eight in Belgium, four in France and two in Italy. Examples of the projects were: the Thomson-CGE partnership with Plessey and GEC with the Universities of Newcastle, Southampton and Montpellier in the development of an advanced interconnect for VLSI; the collaboration between Siemens, System Designers Ltd, CIT Alcatel and Philips on software production and maintenance management systems; and that between Olivetti and Nixdorf in broad-based office communications systems.[3]

Encouraged by the success of the pilot phase, the Commission rapidly pushed ahead with its full plans. Those comprised a ten-year programme (1984-93) with an overall budget of 1.5 billion ecus (approx. £1 billion). The first five-year phase was to concentrate on the pre-competitive stage of developing the technology in three areas (microelectronics, advanced information processing and software technology) and two fields of application (office systems and computer-integrated manufacturing). These plans were put to the Council in November 1983, but held up until February 1984 by UK and German reservations over budgetary costs.

The first call for proposals under the full programme went out in March 1984 and met with a huge response. The 201 projects eventually selected for the programme's first phase involved 240 firms (57 per cent of these from firms with less than 500 employees) and 210 research institutions. Three-quarters of the research projects involved collaboration between firms and academic research units. By January 1987, a total of 1.36 bn. ECUS (approximately £900m) had been committed, almost the whole of what had originally been seen as a ten-year programme.

A crucial feature of ESPRIT has been the openness and commitment it has required of the firms linked into it. Project proposals have to be submitted in reply to open invitations. Each project must involve at least two independent industrial partners from separate member states. Costs are generally co-financed by the EC and industry on a 50/50 basis. Research results are shared between all the participants in any given project who are free to apply them commercially, and preferential access is then granted to other ESPRIT participants outside that project. These guarantees are the cornerstones of the whole ESPRIT process.

The Council decision adopting the full ESPRIT programme required its progress to be reviewed as soon as 60 per cent of the first phase budget had been committed. This point was reached by the end of 1984 and a three-person review board was set up under Dr Pannenborg, ex-head of Philips, which reported in October 1985. By and large ESPRIT was given a clean bill of health. The review panel concluded that the programme had been successfully established and was well on its way to meeting its original objectives. Certain changes in the selection procedure and evaluation of proposals were suggested, together with improvements in project management and additional channels of communication. For future development the panel suggested a continued emphasis on the pre-competitive aspect of research, a consolidation and restructuring of research areas and, finally, the addition of focused demonstration projects with a large user involvement (European Commission, 1985).

These suggestions have been incorporated in the second phase of the programme originally scheduled to start in 1987, but delayed by the problems over the agreement of the Framework Budget of which ESPRIT was a major part (see below). Phase II is roughly twice the size of ESPRIT I with a budget of 2 billion ECUS (£1.4bn). The review board's suggestions for stream-lining the programme into three main areas of research – microelectronics, IT processing systems and application technologies – were accepted, as were the greater focus on what is called 'demand driven' aspects of the programme, for example the greater emphasis on the Application Specific Integrated Circuit (ASIC) technology. The review board's call for demonstration projects is incorporated into what are called 'Technology Integration Projects' (TIPs), the aim of which is to pull the various strands of work together to show their usefulness to one another. For example, work on desk-top work-stations is being linked to the more theoretical work on parallel architectures, and if successful, this combination will considerably enhance the processing and presentation capabilities of the work-stations (European Commission, 1986). Although nominally pre-competitive research, a good part of ESPRIT II is in fact competitive research as those involved in the earlier research projects seek to stretch and develop some of the ideas exploited in that phase. The increasing popularity of ESPRIT is evident from the fact that the call to tender for the first phase of ESPRIT II was ten times oversubscribed, (*Financial Times* 12 April 1988).

Other EC Initiatives of the 1980s

A series of other EC programmes promoting new technologies have been launched in the wake of ESPRIT. Although differing substantially in subject matter and detail, they retain the ESPRIT characteristics of being functionally specific with clearly identified objectives, an open tendering system and quick decision-making processes (once the Framework Programme had been approved – the long wait over ESPRIT II was the hold-up in 1986-7 over agreement on the Framework Budget).

After ESPRIT, the most significant EC programme is the RACE (Research in Advanced Communications in Europe) programme. Unlike ESPRIT, which essentially looks to cooperation among firms and research institutions across the whole community, RACE has to operate through the national PTTs, and through them with national governments. The ESPRIT model has therefore not been appropriate and the Commission has instead had to approach the main 'actors' (that is the PTTs) more indirectly via member governments (though having paved the way with ESPRIT help). RACE reflects a new consensus that the currently evolving narrowband Integrated Services Digital Network (ISDN) should gradually be replaced by an Integrated Broadband Communications Network (IBCN),[4] and the programme is designed to establish the technological base essential to the introduction of a Community-wide IBCN infrastructure and services. The programme's definition phase (1985-6) aimed at agreeing an IBCN reference model, identifying the relevant R & D design work, developing a consensus among PTTs on the functional and technoeconomic characteristics of the network itself, and evaluating the technical environment and the applications and/or services made possible by the new network (COM (85) 145 final).

February 1986 saw the formal go-ahead for the first 'definition' phase of RACE. The programme, costing 40m ECUS (£30m), involved thirty-two projects and 109 organizations ranging from equipment manufacturers through broadcasters and telecom administrators to university researchers. The R & D falls into four main areas – integrated circuits, optoelectronics, broadband switching and communications software – but the broad objectives of the programme embrace both design work on the system equipment and standards specification for what is called the Integrated Advanced Network. The second phase of RACE, approved as part of the Framework Budget for the five years 1987-92 with a budget of 500m ECUS (£395m), likewise backs both equipment R & D and work on the formulation of common proposals for specifications and standards, (*Financial Times* 11 May 1988).

Liberalization of EC telecom markets somewhat undermines the concept of IBCN which looks to benefits derived from full interactive network provision, the idea being to provide the whole range of voice, video and data communications through a single cabled network. This may explain why, with the exception of the UK, the European PTT authorities have opted to keep the network provision as a public monopoly service rather than introducing competition into network provision (as the UK government has through Mercury). Technology is, however, also rapidly eroding the monopoly, with satellite and cellular radio both competing as transmission facilities. To date, business demand has shown a preference for the cabled network facilities which suffer much less from interference (especially important for data transmission). It is interesting, for example, that in the de-regulated environment of the US, business (and the telecom authorities) are currently both pushing the development of ISDN networks as precursors of IBCN networks, (*Financial Times*, 19 December 1987). The full cost of installing an IBCN network across the whole of the EC is likely to be in the region of 350 billion ECUS (£245 billion) but spread over at least ten years. Given that ordinary domestic consumers seen unlikely to want the full range of services potentially on offer, there is some dispute as to how extensive the network should be. Here the ambitions of the individual telecom authority will determine the outcome. The FRG is committed to providing a broadband fibre optic cabled network to as many subscribers as possible, but France, under the Chirac government

(1986-8), dropped its ambitious plan for interactive video in every home and now has more modest plans involving cabling only the main cities. In the UK, competition between BT and Mercury for the lucrative big business accounts has led to prime attention being given to business networks (Financial Times, 11 May 1988).

It was against this background that the Commission launched its Green Paper on telecommunications in June 1987 (COM(87)290).[5] Building on experience in the first phase of RACE (and complementary to the proposals put forward for the second phase) the Green Paper called for a radical restructuring of the European marketplace in telecommunications, proposing considerably more competition in the equipment and service sectors while safeguarding the right to monopoly of network provision. In line with the complete liberalization of the internal market by 1992, the Commission called for a series of actions ranging from the establishment of a European Telecommunications Standards Institute (ETSI), which would be responsible for formulating all European standards, to the harmonization of tariffs across Europe. The most disputed proposals have been those calling for the liberalization of satellite services (for this erodes the PTTs' primary monopoly), and those advocating the harmonization of tariffs, which, though the logical development from the unifying of the internal market, is nevertheless unthinkable for most PTTs at present. Overall, there has been a surprising degree of consensus that liberalization of the equipment and peripherals markets has to come. We have yet to see whether the PTTs and the respective national governments will practise what they preach!

The significance of the Green Paper on telecommunications, however, lies in the evidence it provides that the Commission, not national governments, is now in the driving seat on telecommunications. While the European market remains fragmented by differing standards and regulations, Europe's commerce and industry remain at a disadvantage *vis-à-vis* their US and Japanese counterparts. The Commission recognizes this; hence its push to simplify and standardize telecommunications services throughout the EC. How far it succeeds will be an indication of how far governments and business in the EC really are committed to following through the logic (and advantages) of the internal market.

Apart from work on IT and telecommunications, a number of other EC programmes deserve mention. One of the Commission's more recent initiatives has been the BRITE (Basic Research in Industrial Technologies for Europe) programme. Unlike ESPRIT and RACE this programme is not aimed at pushing forward new frontiers in mainstream areas of new technology, but at stimulating the use of new technologies in older industries. Nine major technological themes have been identified. These are the problems of reliability, wear and deterioration of materials and systems; laser technology and power metallurgy; joining techniques; new testing methods; computer-aided design and manufacturing; polymers, composites and other new materials; membrane science and technology; catalysis and particle technology; and new technologies applied to articles made from flexible materials.

BRITE follows the ESPRIT model in terms of its organization and the emphasis on pre-competitive research. The rules and procedures for project selection, partner criteria and property rights are also similar. So too are the funding arrangements. The first phase (1985-8) has a project budget of 125m ECUS (£87m), and the programme to date involves over 400 organizations across the EC. One quarter of these are small or medium-sized businesses (SMEs),

21 per cent are research institutes and 19 per cent universities (*Financial Times*, 25 September 1987).

The EC has also begun to develop a number of programmes which, like BRITE, cut across sector boundaries. Two examples are COMETT (Community in Education and Training for Technology), designed to foster cooperation between universities and industry for training in new technologies, and SPRINT (Strategic Programme for Innovation and Technology Transfer) aimed at helping firms, particularly SMEs, identify and access specialist services across a range of skills and competence, the idea being that the organization of contacts between people of different backgrounds and skills is a vital plank in the present day innovation process. Compared to ESPRIT or RACE both programmes are modest in their funding, but are seen by many as important complements to the innovation process.

Finally it is worth mentioning another group of programmes which are helping to promote a very different group of new technologies – biotechnology programmes. Again, in money terms these have been overshadowed by ESPRIT. The Framework Programme for the years 1987-92 sets the biotechnology budget at 150m ECUS (£105m or approx £20m per annum) compared with ESPRIT's budget of 200m ECUS (£1.4m). Nevertheless current expenditures represent a doubling of previous expenditures.

Back in the 1970s, biotechnology was, in fact, one of the first areas seen by the newly constituted DG XII (Research and Technology) as ripe for collaboration. Proposals aimed at advancing strengths in genetic engineering and enzymology were first put forward in 1974, but it was not until 1981 that the Commission was given the go-ahead to introduce its Biomolecular Engineering Programme (BEP). This ran for four years (1982-5) with total expenditures of only 15 million ECUS (£12m), and it concentrated on supporting programmes that promoted post-doctoral training and exchange, and projects that linked academic research and industry. Its main thrust was towards the agri-food sector, not pharmaceuticals (Narjes, 1986).

BEP was succeeded in 1986 by the more ambitious Biotechnology Action Programme (BAP), which has a budget of 50 million ECUS (£36m) for five years (1986-90). Emphasis still rests on enzyme, genetic and protein engineering, but the programme now has two main thrusts: first, as before, to promote basic research and training; and, second, to promote what are termed 'contextual' developments, specifically 'biotic' collections (that is cell and gene banks) and 'bio-informatics' (data banks of gene sequences, etc.). BAP has been considerably oversubscribed with only about 15 per cent of applications being funded. Most of these involve university and research institutes' collaborations across Europe, but 40 per cent of those funded also involve some industrial participation (Cantley, 1987). When compared with the ESPRIT requirement of at least two industrial partners, this 40 per cent figure gives some indication of how biotechnology is still at a much earlier stage of development. Plans are currently being discussed for a successor to BAP to be called BRIDGE (Biotechnology Report for Innovation, Development and Growth in Europe) to run for the period 1990-4 in which an enhanced industrial role is seen, while a major initiative ECLAIR (European Collaborative Linkage of Agriculture and Industry through Research) aims to harness biotechnology for the conversion of agricultural output into useful industrial products and, vice versa, for the development of industrial products such as biodegradable plant protection products which use biotechnology for the benefit of agriculture. ECLAIR's expenditures are projected at 80m ECUS (£56m) over the five-year period 1988-93, and form a separate part of the Framework Programme from the biotechnology budget (European Commission, 1987).

On the biotechnology front, there is also the Concertation Unit for Biotechnology in Europe (CUBE), a development from the FAST programme, which had identified the Bio-Society as a vital area of future development and had recognized the need for some coordination at a European level. CUBE's main functions are to help the EC (both Commission and member governments) 'get its act together'. In this capacity it is linked both to the BAP and, via its Biotechnology steering group, to a range of activities across the Commission such as raw material supply, agriculture, intellectual property rights, regulatory development and patents. Though seemingly a minor activity, as with telecoms, the development of the regulatory environment will in the long run be a crucial factor in helping promote the competitiveness of European business in this sector (European Commission, 1988).

The Framework Budget

The saga of the Framework Budget illustrates well the tensions between the member states over, on the one hand, how much to spend in total on this element of the EC budget, and, on the other, how best to bring pressure to bear for fiscal rigour within the EC. A good starting point is the EC Budget, set for the fiscal year 1987-8 at 36.6 billion ECUS (£27bn), but overrunning this total by some 5 billion ECUS, making a total of somewhat over 40 billion ECUS (£29.2bn). Three-quarters of that sum, approximately 30 billion ECUS (£22bn) is devoted to supporting agriculture through the CAP, the remainder going to finance the competing demands of the social and regional funds, administration, Third World aid and, of course, science and technology. Of this, the science and technology budget has been rather less than 0.8 billion ECUS (£500m a year); even the new Framework Budget has only brought it up to just over 1.1 billion ECUS (£800m) a year. In other words even at the higher rate of spending only two and a half per cent of the EC budget is going on science and technology.

As indicated, ESPRIT introduced a different type of policy into the science and technology portfolio. Gone were the heavy-handed attempts at coordinating a Community mega-project as had been seen in the various Euratom projects. Instead, with ESPRIT the Commission was orchestrating a series of linked and complementary projects, whose common ground was that they all fell within identified IT priority areas: they all involved cross-border collaborations between firms and research institutions, with at least two firms among the partners, and the project proposal had come from below – from the partners – rather than being imposed from above. It was a formula which had immediately proved popular. As a result, as we have seen, the Commission immediately began introducing other programmes along similar lines.

Flushed with the success of ESPRIT and the support for such programmes expressed at the Fontainebleau Summit in the summer of 1984, DG III (Industry), DG XII (R & D) and DG XIII (IT) began planning a major expansion. Commissioner Narjes (Industry), in the early spring of 1985 called for the establishment of a European Technological Community (ETC), a plea that in part provoked the EUREKA initiative as a response from member states, primarily Britain and France, jealous of sovereignty and suspicious of EC initiatives in this area. Narjes followed up his called for an ETC by suggesting that the budgets of all the Community's R & D projects be aggregated together into one 'framework' (the French use the word 'envelope') budget, and in 1986 put forward ambitious plans to triple the budget from its 1983-6 level of 3 billion ECUS over four years (£2.1 bn or approximately £0.5 bn a year), 50 per cent of which went on energy, to a 10 billion ECUS budget (£7 bn) over the five years 1987-92, with information technology, not energy, taking the lion's share (*Financial Times* 7 March 1985).

This 10 billion ECUS bid was quickly scaled down to 7.7 billion ECUS (£5.3m) since it was clear it had little support from member states. (On an annual basis, however, even the 10 billion ECUS programme was still only 5 per cent of the EC's total budget.) This figure was acceptable to the smaller countries (who have relatively smaller national research efforts) but opposed strongly by the British and German governments, both of whom regarded the proposals as representing fiscal profligacy (in that they more than doubled existing spending levels) and hoped that pressure on this budget would help bring other budget expenditures into line (to a degree they were prepared to trade an easier line on this budget with a tougher line on agriculture). From mid-1986 onwards, therefore, the Framework Budget proposals were caught up with the overall EC budget problems and Britain's wish, in particular, to see fiscal discipline injected into EC proposals, especially on the agricultural budget. As the row dragged on into 1987, a number of programmes which had been scheduled to come on-stream in early 1987 had to be postponed and the budget was successively trimmed to 6.8 billion (£4.7bn), then 5.7 billion ECUS (£4 bn), with the British demanding a cut of 3.6 billion (£2.5 bn). At such a level it would have been very little above its 1983-6 level which would have made it difficult to mount any of the more ambitious programmes planned by the Commission (*Financial Times* 9 April 1987).

To the dismay of all but the British government, the disagreements continued through the spring of 1987 and were not finally settled until after the British general election in June that year. In the end the British settled for a budget of 5.6 billion ECUS (£3.9 bn), a figure which had been mooted back in December 1986. It is no wonder that the British stance was unpopular – nine valuable months could have been saved if they had settled then. The whole issue is a prime example of the continuing Gaullism of some member states – especially Britain – and their unwillingness to put Community before national interest. It is ironic in the light of their stance that the general election also brought a reassessment of domestic R & D policy by the UK government and the recognition that Britain was getting good value for money from ESPRIT. Indeed, by early 1988, that same UK government was cutting back its national IT programme and urging firms to participate in EC schemes!

How effective have EC programmes been in promoting the new technologies?

In the previous section the central issue was the size of the Community R & D budget. The key question, however, should not be how much is spent, but whether the money is being spent effectively. One of the main arguments used by the UK government in their opposition to the Framework Programme was that a good part of the budget was not being used to promote worthwhile research. In particular they were critical of the sums being devoted to energy research (1.7 billion ECUS (£1.2m) over the five years) where the EC now funded the previous Euratom programmes on fast breeder reactors and fusion and supported the four research centres at Ispra, Karlsruhe, Petten and Geel. There were also criticisms of some of the other programmes for funding dubious 'collaborations' which had come together purely for the purposes of collecting EC subsidies.

Without undertaking detailed evaluations of each programme it is difficult to answer these criticisms. Britain was not alone in questioning the value of the energy research programmes and it is notable that even since the agreement on the Framework Budget, there have been substantial cutbacks on the joint research centres.[6] General opinion seems increasingly to doubt whether fast breeder reactors will ever prove an economic proposition while the viability of fusion power recedes continuously ever further into the future.

The other issue – whether EC programmes were funding too many 'dubious' collaborations – raises the issue of additionality. The concept of additionality is that programmes which offer a financial incentive to participation should aim to fund projects which are 'additional' – that is which would not have been undertaken if the incentive payments were not available. Ideally, of course, every project undertaken should be additional, but it is widely recognized that this is a counsel of perfection. Commission officials vet projects to screen out blatant cases of opportunism, but it is impossible to impose any rigorous set of criteria since, if asked, firms and/or research institutions will always claim they would not have gone ahead without EC funding. There are also other objectives – for example the development of EC-wide regulations; the promotion of cross-border collaborations – which these programmes promote. And although the notion of *juste retour* (that countries should benefit according to contribution) does not apply in any precise form, EC officials also recognize that it is necessary to get a good spread of projects across the different member states and that for the high-tech projects it is not always easy to find partners in countries such as Greece or Portugal; but it is also important to develop the capabilities of these countries. Putting all these things together, therefore, officials have to accept that on any programme of the nature of ESPRIT, BRITE or BAP, there will be some 'deadweight' (projects which are dubiously funded). The hope is, however, that taking one thing with another the gains will exceed the losses. To keep check on this they maintain a regular programme of monitoring and evaluation.

It is in the broader context that the ESPRIT programme has really made its mark. There is not space here to detail the changes that have been taking place in the European electronics industry (Sharp, forthcoming). Suffice it to say that the latter half of the 1980s has witnessed a major realignment of strategies and capabilities around three main 'poles' of competence: Siemens, with its broad thrust of interests across the electronics sector from semiconductors through to telecommunications; Philips, the Netherlands-based multinational, which has switched from being a geographically decentralized enterprise to a highly centralized operation which integrates up-stream capabilities (for example semiconductors, where it is linked with Siemens in the Mega-project) with its major operations in consumer electronics; and Thomson, the French firm which used to be the national champion *par excellence,* and now, via a route of acquisition and disposal, has Europe-wide (indeed world-wide) interests in semi-conductors, consumer electronics and defence electronics. Likewise, in telecommunications, again three main 'poles' of competence are emerging in Europe – Siemens, Ericsson (the Swedish firm) and the French firm, CGE, which has not only taken over all Thomson's telecommunications interests but, via its purchase of IT's European interests, has become the second largest producer of telecommunications equipment in the world. In this sector what we have seen in the last few years is the transformation of some of the former national champions into global firms competing and operating in global markets.

This is a remarkable transformation and it is worth asking what role has ESPRIT played in all this? Outwardly surprisingly little. Its 1.5 billion ECU (£1bn) budget spread over the five years 1984-9 was small beer compared with the investments being poured into the IT sectors by firms such as Siemens and Philips. Moreover, concentrating as it does on pre-competitive research, the emphasis is not so much on products that can be brought to market as on developing the tools and techniques to enable those products to be made. Prime among successes is the use of the Inmos transputer in the Parsys super computers, developed jointly with the French; and the work on developing software standards for manufacturing and office automation systems has been invaluable in helping to open up these markets to European manufacturers.

Psychologically, however, ESPRIT has played a vital role in three important respects. First, ESPRIT has provided an important channel for cooperation. The need for cooperation should be set in the context of the early 1980s; the fragmented European industry gradually waking up to the realization that it had allowed the US and then the Japanese multinationals to acquire a seemingly dominant technological lead; the increasingly high cost of R & D and initial set-up costs in most high-tech sectors, combined with the uncertainties of the shortening product cycle; and the threat posed by the impending entry into the European arena by AT&T once deregulation opened the door to such entry. The tide of Japanese inward investment into consumer electronics illustrated how limited was the value of protection when capital was freely mobile. There was no alternative but to meet the threat head-on, which in turn meant rapidly acquiring technological capabilities not possessed in-house. Links with US and Japanese firms made sense technologically, but not strategically, since the objective was to decrease rather than to increase technological dependency. The figures speak for themselves. In 1983 the EC Commission recorded thirty-two US-EC link-ups in firms in the IT sector to six internal Community link-ups. By 1986, they were almost in balance; forty-nine US-EC link-ups to forty-six internal Community link-ups. Some would, of course, have taken place without the existence of ESPRIT, but there is little doubt in the minds of many participants that the existence of ESPRIT (and other programmes such as BRITE and EUREKA) have encouraged the European route.

Second, ESPRIT has provided a mechanism for creating among top level decision-takers in this industry convergent expectations about the future, and about the sort of measures needed to meet the competitive threat from the US and Japanese multinationals. The power of such convergence should not be underestimated for it becomes self-fulfilling – if all decision-takers make investment decisions in the light of common expectations, production will expand as expected! The Japanese VLSI and fifth generation programmes are based upon this principle; the young Turks from MITI effectively act as a mechanism which ensures that all firms act on a common set of expectations which then have a tendency to become self-fulfilling. In the case of ESPRIT, Davignon's round table fulfilled this same function. For the first time, Europe's fragmented electronics industry confronted the threat of competition together. They discovered that there was among them 'convergent expectation' that competition would get tougher, that tariff or export constraint protective barriers were ineffective given the free mobility of capital and that national champions protected by public purchasing ran the risk of being out of touch with market developments. Thus these major European companies came to recognize that to compete successfully even within Europe they needed to set their sights on global markets and global competitiveness. In this context, the national champion becomes irrelevant.

Third, ESPRIT has created an important constituency pressing for the completion of the internal market and the abolition of all remaining internal barriers to trade such as divergent standards and regulations. Once the major electronics firms had discarded their 'national champion' role, it was logical that they should begin to look to Europe as their 'home base' and to see in the divergent European standards, for example, on data transmission, major hindrances to their effective operation in those markets. This has been reinforced by the very successful programmes within ESPRIT aimed at establishing Europe-wide standards for IT products. For example, it has created a set of software called Communications Network for Manufacturing Applications (CNMA) which allows different types of robots to work together within an automated factory, which in turn prevents the phenomenon that is seen so often with IT products, of tying customers into one particular range of equipment. A similar software has been developed for office systems (Office Document Architecture) which enables documents to be passed from one computer to another without loss of formatting etc. Recognizing the advantages of these common standards has created companies such as Siemens, Bull and ICL into a constituency which recognizes and promotes the virtues of the single European market.

Finally, ESPRIT has for many firms provided an important learning process in collaboration. The history of successful collaborations, such as Airbus Industrie, illustrates only to well the fact that collaboration is a slow process of building up mutual trust and respect among partners. Collaborations cannot be created and expected to be successful overnight. For many European firms there has been no experience of collaboration with other European firms, for European operations were frequently directed from a home base, whereas US and Japanese operations were conducted through local licensees who often became natural partners in any collaboration. For many such firms ESPRIT has been the first experience of collaboration with other European firms. The fact that over 1,000 applied in spring 1988 to participate in the second phase of the programme starting in January 1989 is testimony to the positive response the experience has provoked.

Looking back over the history of the EC's efforts to promote new technologies, the 1980s has seen a sea change both in policies and in perceptions of success. The EC's rather heavy-handed efforts at 'top down' coordination, typified by the ambitious, mega-projects of Euratom, have been replaced by a much lighter 'orchestration', where the EC seeks to encourage and channel innovation in certain directions, but where the drive for innovation is market-led by the participants. The change coincided with a period of disillusion among European governments with the achievements, or more precisely non-achievements, of industrial policy and a desire to find policies which work with, rather than against, the grain of the market. And there were lessons also to be learned from the experience of the 1960s and seventies – from the failures of projects such as Unidata compared to the success of the (privately organized) Airbus Industrie. The timing, too, was propitious. The Euro-pessimism which pervaded European thinking in the early 1980s provided fertile ground upon which to seed thoughts of collaboration across European frontiers. Perhaps, above all, the experience has confirmed the prejudices of those who argue, as Jean Monnet did at the outset of the Community, that political will follows the establishment of mutual economic interest. Confronted by the double challenge to competitiveness from the US and Japan, the large and powerful companies who had been the 'national champions' of the 1970s, recognized the logic of the market-place in espousing collaboration, but in so doing immediately created a strong constituency calling for closer and more complete integration of the European market-place. 1992 is as much a product of the EC's technology policies of the 1980s, as it is of the grand strategies of any European politician.

Notes

1. The Action Committee for the United States of Europe was founded in October 1955, on the initiative of Jean Monnet, by the Socialist, Christian Democrat and Liberal parties, and non-communist trade unions of six EC countries: Belgium, France, West Germany, Italy, Luxembourg and the Netherlands.
2. For a useful summary of Esprit Phase 1 documentation, see the European Commission's publication 'Official Documents on the Esprit Programme', COM (84) 608 (Brussels, Commission of the European Communities, 1984). For details on Phase 2, see COM (86) 269 final.
3. A full list of Esprit projects can be obtained from the Commission of the European Communities Directorate General for Information Technologies and Telecommunications, (DG XIII).
4. ISDN allows voice, data, text and video to be carried. IBCN represents a higher capacity network which will evolve from and ultimately subsume the present services and network structures of, for example, ISDN, cable TV and mobile communications.
5. For details see 'Towards a Dynamic European Community: Green Paper on the development of the common market for telecommunications services and equipment', COM (87) 290, Commission of the European Communities, Brussels, November 1987.
6. *Financial Times*, 12 April 1988. 'Ministers give go-ahead to High Tech projects' reports doubts on both the JET and other research centre projects. See also *Financial Times* for 29 September 1986, 'Brussels plan to cut cash for joint research centres'.

References

Cantley, Mark (1987), 'Biotechnology Developments in Europe and the Evolution of EEC Policies', paper presented to USDA Biotechnology Challenge Forum, Washington DC, Feb 1987. Mimeo Obtainable from CUBE, DGXII, Rue de la Loi B-1049, Brussels.

European Commission (1970), *La Politique Industrielle de la Communauté* (The Colonna Report) COM (70) 100-final, Brussels, Commission of the European Communities.

European Commission (1984), *Official Documents of the ESPRIT Programme* COM (84) 608, Brussels, Commission of the European Communities.

European Commission (1985a), *Communication from the Commission to the Council and Parliament concerning a review to assess the initial results of the Programme ESPRIT*, COM (85) 616 Final, Brussels, Commission of the European Communities.

European Commission (1985b), *Proposal for a Council Decision on Preparatory Action for a Community R & D Programme in the field of Telecommunications Technologies*, R & D in Advanced Communications technologies for Europe, COM (85) 113 final.

European Commission (1986) *ESPRIT, the First Phase: Progress and Results*, COM (86) 687, Brussels, Commission of the European Communities.

European Commission (1987), *Proposal for a Council Decision to adopt a first multi-annual Programme (1988-93) for Biotechnology-based agro-industrial research and technological development*, COM (87) final Brussels, December.

European Commission (1988), *CUBE Report 1984-1988, Retrospect and Prospect*, Draft Mimeo XII/F-1 CUBE DGXII, Brussels.

European File, 1986, *The Sprint Programme*, Luxembourg.

Freeman, C., Clark J. and Soete, L. (1982), *Unemployment and Technical Innovation: A Study of Long Waves and Economic Development*, London, Frances Pinter.

Hayward, Keith (1986), *International Collaboration in Civil Aerospace*, London, Frances Pinter.

HMSO Cmnd. 278 White Paper, 'DTI – the department for enterprise', HMSO, London, 1988.

House of Lords Select Committee on the European Communities (1985), *ESPRIT (European Research and Development in Information Technologies)*, Session 1984-85, 8th Report, London, HMSO.

Lawrence, R.Z., and Schultze, C.L. (eds) (1987), *Barriers to European Growth: A Transatlantic View*, Washington DC, Brookings Institution.

Layton, Christopher (1969), *European Advanced Technology: A Programme for Integration*, Allen & Unwin, London.

Narjes, Karl-Heinz (1986), 'The European Commission's strategy for Biotechnology', in D. Davies (ed.), *Industrial Biotechnology*, London, Frances Pinter.

Royal Institute of International Affairs (RIIA) (1987), *Europe's Future in Space: A Joint Policy Report*, Chatham House Special Paper, London, Routledge and Kegan Paul for the Royal Institute for International Affairs.

Servan-Schreiber, Jean Jacques (1967), *Le Défi Américain*, Paris, De Noel.

Sharp, Margaret L. (forthcoming), 'Corporate strategies and collaboration: the case of ESPRIT and European electronics, in M. Dodgson (ed), *Technology Strategies and the Firm: Management & Public Policy*, London, Macmillan.

Sharp, Margaret and Shearman, C. (1987), *European Technological Collaboration*, Chatham House Paper No. 36. Routledge and Kegan Paul for Royal Institute for International Affairs.

Williams, Roger (1973), *European Technology: the Politics of Collaboration*, London, Croom Helm.

Part III External perspectives

12 European Political Cooperation: towards the 1990s

Juliet Lodge

Introduction

There can be little doubt that the 1990s will see the EC playing a wider and more politicized role in the international arena. This is not to say that it will pursue a unified, common foreign policy *per se*. Rather, the artificial distinction maintained so far by the EC between its 'external relations' and 'political cooperation' will be fudged as it becomes increasingly difficult to compartmentalize neatly aspects of the EC's international dealings that clearly fall under the Commission's external relations' competence and those that affect member states' security and defence postures. The globalization and politicization of international trade makes the demarcation between the two questionable. The overall effect is to complicate the way in which the EC's institutions and the member states manage not only their inter-relationship in international affairs, but how they manage and coordinate 'external relations' and 'political cooperation' at the supranational and domestic levels. Ignoring for a moment the fact that neither exists in an international vacuum, at the most basic level of policymaking within the member states the need for inter-departmental consultation, cooperation and coordination will grow. The push for 1992 may Europeanize domestic ministries in unanticipated ways; it will require domestic issues to be seen against a broader international context. The question of who has responsibility for and is accountable for policy outputs has yet to be determined. Moreover, this is a singularly sensitive issue. This is because the breaching of the 'external relations/political cooperation' divide implies major qualification, if not abandonment, of EC doctrines carefully constructed since the EC's inception.

The federal spectre

The evolution of European Political Cooperation (EPC) has to be seen in historical perspective. It is instructive that a process that began by encouraging greater *rapprochement* among the member states' foreign policies should shy away from terms implying federalism. Thus cooperation implies inter-governmental action and the maintenance of national sovereignty. Even the SEA employs the term. All references in Title III of the SEA are to the High Contracting Parties and not, as elsewhere, to the member states. They remain ambivalent towards the extent and effect upon them of the EC's extensive and expanding involvement in the international arena. All seek to use the EC instrumentally in pursuing national foreign policy goals. For all the EC is a primary frame of reference. Many, however, remain uncertain as to the balance between the costs to their national sovereignty and the benefits they derive from pursuing a common or harmonized EC stance in international affairs.

This ambivalence can also be explained in terms of the EC's history – the failure of the clearly federal European Defence Community in 1954 and the European Political Community. Common action in the high political security sphere implies a quantum leap in integration for which few states are psychologically prepared or politically ready. Moreover, many would interpret such endeavour as confirming the EC's evolution into a unitary federal state – even a super-state – in which the central government assumes almost exclusive control of foreign relations even where the component member states retain an international capacity.

It has commonly been argued that the spectre of an external threat may impel sovereign states to seek alliances of a federal nature. As public international law sees the world as composed of unitary actors, states in federations effectively are seen to cede what they were once pleased to interpret as the *domaine reservé* of their own executives to the federal centre. Even where constitutional provisions afford the constituent parts a role in international issues (such as the conclusion and ratification of a treaty for example), this is of a different order than that possessed by independent states. The role is not about the advancement and protection of a national interest but the legitimization of a federal, internal process of policymaking that has produced a foreign policy outcome affecting the interests of its constituent parts. In practice, while their positions may be safeguarded by constitutional provisions, the appearance of sovereignty having been pooled or ceded to the centre creates the impression that the centre has an independent external identity and legal personality – both of which may be necessary for maximizing the overall interests of the constituent units and the influence of the federation itself – but which are easily conflated with the idea of statehood. This is one of the main reasons why the notion of the EC having common foreign policy goals and the attendant instruments and policymaking and policy implementation capacities provokes such anxiety among the states.

Moreover, the EC's extensive involvement in the international arena and the push towards 1992 have highlighted the extent to which international considerations impinge on domestic ministries' jurisdictions that are already assailed by the EC. The problem for the member states is that even in areas where the EC does not have explicit external competences, experience has shown that the successful pursuit of internal policies demands an expansion of the EC's external jurisdiction and a concomitant lessening of member states' autonomy (Weiler, 1988: 236; and see below). Moreover, states can be tempted to try and deal themselves with questions in EPC subject to EC competence to avoid the tighter discipline and obligations incurred in the EC.

Furthermore, the old dichotomy between trade and defence has been fudged as the EC's prosperity has been recognized as being dependent on international peace. The term 'security' is now recognized as having economic dimensions for the EC with the result that the member states cannot credibly reserve exclusively to themselves the pursuit of high politics and diplomacy. This reality may have been privately recognized years ago. Article 224 (EEC) obliges member states to consult each other with a view to together taking steps to minimize disturbance to the functioning of the common market by measures that a member state may need to take in the event of;

- serious internal disturbances affecting the maintenance of law and order;
- war or serious international tension constituting a threat of war; or
- in order to carry out obligations it has accepted for the purpose of maintaining peace and international security.

While a degree of cooperation in defence matters may be inferred from this, the issue remains extremely sensitive (not least because of the close interrelationship between sovereignty and defence of the realm). The question of security cooperation within EPC has now been formally codified in the SEA. Moreover, within eighteen months of its coming into force, the Spanish Council Presidency publicly indicated the possibility of the EC being imbued with authority for an EC defence policy. How then have the EC's external relations and EPC evolved?

External relations

In the 1950s, the recent history of the EC's founding members was such that none could be convinced that any attempt to create a common foreign policy would not result in one state at worst dominating and at best determining the foreign policies of the others. The French Fouchet proposals in 1960 did nothing to allay such fears. From the EC's inception, defence and security issues were excluded from its authority. Such matters were dealt with within NATO and the WEU. The twofold implications of this were that member states would retain exclusive competence for their foreign policies while consequent upon the creation of the customs union the EC would have competence for 'external relations'. The latter were construed in strictly economic and commercial terms with little regard to their inseparability from the wider political context of international relations. This division between 'high' and 'low' politics was advantageous in that it enabled the EC to deal internationally as a 'civilian power' devoid of overt-political imperialistic intent. Its disadvantages lay with the plethora of differing commercial and trade agreements that its members concluded with non-EC states as part of their broader foreign policy strategies.

Wide divergence among these proved problematic: the states created an external impression of disunity that non-EC states could exploit. The results could prove politically embarrassing and economically costly. There was a compelling need for creating a semblance of group coherence and consensus out of the diverse individual strategies which inevitably undermined the sense of commonality that was supposed to inform the EC's 'external relations' through the common commercial policy (CCP).

The CCP was a recognition of the external effects of the EC's establishment. The avowedly 'economic' intent of the European Economic Community led to the disingenuous attempt to separate the political and the economic. Art.113 of the Rome Treaty restricted the EC's treaty making power to international trade:

the [CCP] shall be based on uniform principles, particularly in regard to changes in tariff rates, the conclusion of tariff and trade agreements, the achievement of uniformity in measures of liberalisation, export policy and measures to protect trade....

The Commission was empowered to negotiate and the Council to conclude such agreements on the EC's behalf. The original supranational intent was undermined from the outset by the member states' insistence on both the setting up of a special Council committee to help the Commission in negotiations, so reducing the latter 'to a mere plenipotentiary status' (Weiler, 1988: 240), and the conclusion of agreements by the EC and the member states together. Special provisions were to apply in the event of economic difficulties arising for one or more member states. Such problems were bound to occur given the demands of the completion of the common market and the trade diversifying effects arising from it for EC members and their trading partners. On occasion, these led (as in the case of the UK accession) to special protocols being concluded to protect outside traders' interests (Lodge, 1982).

The EC was also empowered under Art.238 to conclude association agreements with a third state, a union of states or an international organization involving reciprocal rights and obligations, common action and special procedures (for example as with Greece and Turkey, and the Yaoundé, Arusha Agreements and the Lomé Conventions). Obviously such agreements had to take national interests into account. In so doing, the idea that the EC's external relations could simply be conducted by the use of economic instruments was challenged and found wanting. It quickly became apparent that even if different economic instruments were appropriate for different stages of economic integration – usually ranged in ascending order from free trade area through customs union, common market, economic union and monetary union to an ultimate political union – the political and legal effects of these instruments and the external effects of internal policies could not be nearly so neatly compartmentalized.

While it may be argued that the way in which the EC was constrained by its members in the conduct of, its external relations limited the opportunity for external relations to become subject to federalizing influences and made for intergovernmentalism, the demands of the CCP, and more especially those arising out of a series of 'internal' policies and those necessary to the functioning of the common market, made greater centralization inescapable. This is not the place to explore in detail the nature and experience of the EC's economic instruments but it is helpful to allude to some important features. (For a detailed analysis see the lucid account by Molle and van Mourik.) Normally portrayed as economic instruments, all have political effects that have been neglected or taken out of context.

The CCP as an external manifestation of the customs union designed to abolish internal tariffs relies on a common external tariff (CET), non-tariff barriers (NTBs) (for example quotas and export controls) and the promotion of EC exports on world markets. The customs union was achieved with the CET in 1968 (Molle and van Mourik, 1987). The CET has been differently applied and subject to cuts and protracted wrangling in GATT (in which the EC participates). NTBs embrace tax laws, import quotas, border controls, technical regulations, public procurement, aid policies and an array of other devices (such as voluntary export constraints and orderly marketing arrangements) designed to protect markets. Finally, the CCP's scope is so wide that all manner of other issues fall into the supposedly 'low political' competence of the EC, including instruments of export competition (export credits (soft loans), subsidies (notably in agriculture)) which quickly bring industrial and competition policies into the reckoning of those concerned with external relations. Moreover, as the Cecchini report and its predecessors reveal, the creation of the Single European

Market will affect not just the liberalization of trade and service but also industrial and competition policy, capital movements, monetary policy, investment, energy, transport and labour (founded on Article 7 of the Rome Treaty). As the row over 'Social Europe' shows, this in turn has myriad implications for a range of welfare issues formerly deemed the exclusive domaine of national government.

The external effects of these instruments and burgeoning policy areas have political effects on the member states and compromise the desirability of their pursuing unilaterally independent foreign policies. The EC's external relations' economic instruments underline this as does their legal basis. The EC by various mechanisms encroaches on virtually all areas of foreign policy once the exclusive domain of the member states.

The EC is a major international actor with extensive involvement in international trade, international organizations (UN, OECD) and multilateral arrangements. Articles 210 and 211 of the Rome Treaty give the EC 'legal personality' under international law. Its rights and obligations, its legal capacity depend on its functions and the purposes for which it was set up. The ECJ has accordingly ruled (Costa v. Enel) that it has limited competences in the sphere of international relations. The member states, by contrast, are believed to have unlimited competences. Furthermore, as Schwarze argues, the EC's powers rest on the principle of *competence d'attribution*: 'the Community only holds those powers ... confirmed upon it by the Treaty' (Schwarze, 1987: 71). As shown, Article 113 and all that flows from it gives the EC potentially vast scope since it also has an implied power whenever it has the necessary internal powers and those needed for the performance of its duties (this concept is known as the principle of 'parallel powers'). The EC is enabled to use its internal competence to deprive member states of external power because 'according to the Court, once an internal power has been used, the respective external power exclusively stays with the Community, at least as long as the internal order requires a unitary use of external powers towards third states' (Schwarze, 1987, citing Case 1/76: 74). No wonder the member states insisted on the conclusion of 'mixed agreements', dividing powers between the EC and themselves and, in effect, asserting their sovereign status. These considerations should also help to clarify why EPC was gradually set up in parallel to rather than as an integral part of the supranational Community.

European Political Cooperation

EPC's origins coincide with developments in the 1970s that could be interpreted as signs of the attractiveness and deepening of European integration. Four states had applied to join the EC, the EC's democratization through the holding of direct elections was being discussed and the issues of economic and monetary union were on the agenda. Various reasons for the sudden stimulus to integration can be inferred at the end of a decade dominated by Gaullism, institutional paralysis and the drift towards intergovernmentalism. Important motivational factors were then, as they were to prove again in the early 1980s, the Six's desires to consolidate their achievements and to determine the future agenda in advance of the accession of new members, and to enhance the EC's ability to respond to international developments.

The decision to create a Framework for Political Cooperation emanated from the 1969 Hague summit meeting of the Heads of Government or State. They argued that a means had to be found to enable 'a united Europe' to assume 'its responsibilities in the world of tomorrow' and 'to make a contribution commensurate with its traditions and mission' (Summit declaration). They instructed the ministers of foreign affairs to report on how progress could be made in respect of political unification by the end of July 1970. The result was the October 1970 Luxembourg Report. This set down guiding principles and convictions which revealed both cautiousness and ambivalence over the venture into foreign policy cooperation. On the one hand, it referred to 'a Europe composed of States which, while preserving their national characteristics, are united in their essential interests'. On the other hand, references were made to 'a united Europe' founded upon 'liberty and the rights of men', 'democratic States having freely elected parliaments'. Thus 'united Europe' was defined as 'the fundamental aim' to be achieved as soon as possible through 'the political will of its peoples and the decisions of their Governments'.

Aims

The aims of cooperation in the sphere of foreign policy were set out as being:

- to ensure, through regular exchanges of information and consultations, a better mutual understanding on the great international problems;
- to strengthen [members'] solidarity by promoting the harmonisation of their views, the coordination of their positions, and, where it appears possible and desirable, common actions. [Part II]

The institutional mechanisms for facilitating this were separated from the EC: the Commission was only to be 'invited to make its views known' if EPC's activities affected those of the EC; and the European Parliament was to be involved in an informal biannual colloquy to 'give a democratic character to political unification'.

Institutions

EPC's institutional arrangements included a Ministerial Council of Foreign Ministers (meeting at least every six months and whose membership could be replaced by Heads of State or Government should the need arise); and a Political Committee (comprising the directors of political affairs, meeting quarterly at least and responsible for preparing the ministerial meetings and appointing groups of experts as necessary). Each state designated a foreign office official responsible for liaising with his/her counterparts – subsequently known as the Group of Correspondents.

Evolution

At the 1972 Paris summit, the Six boldly declared that political unification was to enable Europe 'to establish its position in world affairs as a distinct entity'; and that the EC's members were 'to transform before the end of the [1970s] the whole complex of their relations into a European Union'. Political guidelines for intensifying political cooperation were drafted. The international context of these deliberations was not without significance for EPC's subsequent evolution. The communiqué stressed issues relating to *détente* and CSCE, the formulation of common medium- and long-term positions and called for EPC's refinement.

EPC was consolidated in the 1973 Copenhagen Report which strengthened EPC's institutional basis without radically changing its basis. The COREU (telex) network was set up, and operational procedures refined. Foreign Ministers were told to meet quarterly; the Correspondents' Group was codified; working groups consolidated; and arrangements made for information exchange and consultation among the embassies of the Nine in each other's capitals, as well as in third countries and international organizations. To improve the internal work of political cooperation, the Presidency's role was elaborated. Accordingly, the Presidency was to ensure the implementation on a collegiate basis of EPC conclusions; propose, on its own initiative or that of another state, consultations at appropriate level; meet the member states' Ambassadors between Political Committee meetings (if necessary at the request of one of the latter's ambassadors); and to receive member states' administrative assistance.

EPC's goals were also defined. The member states were committed to consulting each other on all important foreign policy questions and working out priorities, observing certain criteria: the purpose of consultations was 'to seek common policies on practical problems'; and the subject matter had to 'concern European interests whether in Europe itself or elsewhere where the adoption of a common position is necessary or desirable' (Communiqué, point 11). Significantly, each member state undertook as a general rule not to take up final positions without prior consultation with its partners within the framework of the political cooperation machinery.

Finally, a linkage with the EC was acknowledged although the distinction between EPC and the EC was asserted. In December 1973, the Nine adopted their document on European Identity which sought to define their relations with third states as well as their position in international affairs. EPC's progress was also reviewed again at a critical juncture in international affairs given the EC's disunity in the face of the Arab–Israeli war and oil crisis. The aims of 'determining common attitudes and ... common action' were confirmed. Further principles were set out in relation to a common policy *vis-à-vis* third countries. The Nine 'acting as a single entity' were to try to 'promote harmonious and constructive relations' with them without jeopardizing or decelerating progress towards European Union within the decade. When negotiating with third countries, they were to choose the institutions and procedures reflecting the 'distinct character of the European entity'. In bilateral relations with third countries, they were to 'increasingly act on the basis of agreed common positions'. The Nine proposed defining their identity in relation to the rest of the world and in so doing strengthening their cohesion and 'the framing of a genuinely European foreign policy', thus making easier 'the transformation of the whole complex of their relations into a European Union'. (Part III). A year later, the overlap between the EC and EPC activities was acknowledged and the Ministers of Foreign Affairs were given responsibility for ensuring consistency between the two. By then, the European Council had been set up. At the 1974 Paris summit, the Nine affirmed their 'determination gradually to adopt common positions and coordinate their diplomatic action in all areas of international affairs which affect the interests of the European Community'. They appointed the Council President as their spokesman in international diplomacy and committed him to ensuring timely 'concertation'.

EPC's organizational framework by then had six main components. At its apex was the new European Council as the ultimate forum for the coordination of foreign policy issues (Weiler, 1988: 245). It could also initiate EPC activity on any foreign policy matter or simply restrict itself to reacting to issues raised within the organs of EPC's framework. The formal head of the latter comprises the Conference of Foreign Ministers meeting in Political Cooperation. They meet formally far more frequently than the four times per annum originally prescribed. They issue declarations and prepare meetings for the heads of state and government. The highest administrative part of EPC was, prior to the permanent secretariat's establishment, the Political Committee (also known as PoCo) meeting routinely with a Commission representative and the DGs of Political Affairs from the Twelve's foreign ministries. Poco prepares the meetings of the CFM and it has been likened to COREPER. Working groups (meeting a couple of times every six months in the capital of the Presidency, and able to call on outside experts) are answerable to it. The Group of Correspondents monitors and follows up EPC decisions and declarations. Finally, embassies are associated with the EPC framework as part of a process of two-way collaboration.

Certain capitals (such as Washington) are particularly important points for collaboration and coordination. Concerted joint action by the Twelve in non-EC capitals throughout the world has become standard practice over the past fifteen to twenty years with a resultant rise in local coordination among the Twelve's embassies. To this has to be added the Troika arrangements which function at all echelons of the EPC framework, and the numerous consultations that occur on the margins of international conferences, European Councils and in international organizations.

It is clear that EPC offers little scope for parliamentary inputs, even though some association with the EP is permitted. This accords with practice in most member states where parliaments are similarly relegated to a marginal role. However, it would be wrong to deduce from this that the EP plays a minimal role in external affairs. On the contrary, MEPs see themselves as acting in the EP as the EC's international conscience. They table numerous questions on foreign affairs (whose answers are prepared in EPC) and generate a multitude of reports on an issue area that was until the SEA, strictly speaking, outside their sphere of competence. Yet, these resolutions are examined by EPC working groups and do have some impact on EPC outputs on occasion's (Lodge, 1988).

Within the space of four years in the 1970s, the essential elements of EPC had been rapidly developed. Often these reflected late recognition of the Nine's inabilities to determine and present a common position on major issues; and the Nine's intention to restrain supranational diplomacy. Negative sentiments may have inspired many of these developments but the outcome was to be a positive gain for integration. Integrative pressures were also evident in the 1975 Tindemans Report, subsequent agreements on the EP's direct election and the EC's Mediterranean enlargement. The EP itself was, through its extensive review of inter-institutional relations in 1979-81, to reveal weaknesses in and ways of strengthening EPC. It was also to broach the need for EC action on security (EPWD, 1981).

The 1980s opened with the Genscher–Colombo initiative for a European Act to link EPC and the EC. It also included cultural cooperation, a juridical union and a legal space. The Act was to be revised after five years and transformed into a Treaty of European Union. This proposal was consistently diluted and emerged in 1983 as the Solemn Declaration on European Union. In the interim, the new French government had begun a series of initiatives linked to European Union beginning with its 1981 Memorandum on promoting and guiding a renewal of EC activity; and the Commission had reported on its mandate of 30 May (COM(81)300, 24.6.81). The 1981 London Report had consolidated improvements in EPC's administration and crisis decision-making procedures. Experience had shown the impossibility of EPC working without constant Commission input and this Report noted the Commission's incorporation into political cooperation. This did not change EPC's basis, however. It merely acknowledged reality and improved the (still inadequate) link with the EP. The London Report defined EPC's goal as 'joint action' and for the first time mentioned the political aspects of security as a subject of political cooperation. It stressed the informality and confidentiality of the Gymnich meetings.[1]

The Solemn Declaration was to underscore commitment to: 'joint action on all major foreign policy questions of interest to the Ten as a whole'; advance 'prior consultation'; and the need for the Ten to give due weight to the 'adoption and implementation of common positions' when elaborating and taking national action. The idea that common positions should form the central reference point for national policy was underlined. The need for the coordination of members' positions on the political and economic aspects of security was noted. Reference was also made to enabling the Ten to act as an *interlocuteur* in third states, and to present common positions at major international conferences attended by one or more member states covering questions dealt with by EPC.

The EP was again to spur further action with the EUT's adoption in February 1984 and its wider conception of an appropriate international role for a European Union. Its foreign policy prescriptions were carefully worded to avoid raising the federal spectre (Prag, 1986). The Fontainebleau June 1984 European Council set up an *Ad Hoc* Committee on Institutional Affairs (known as the Dooge Committee after its chairman, Irish Senator Dooge). Its report was submitted in March 1985 and considered by the Milan European Council in June. Its suggestions mirrored much of the Solemn Declaration, but went further in calling for full discussion of security and defence matters including cooperation in defence technology industries and arms procurement – issues hitherto excluded (at least formally) from EC and EPC debate (except in respect of the Conference on Security and Cooperation in Europe) and pursued within NATO's Independent European Programme Group and Eurogroup. This inevitably concerned the Danes, Greeks and Irish, all of whom had different reasons for wanting to eschew common defence postures lest they compromise their own traditional foreign policy postures and interests. The Danes worried about the implications for their role in Nordic Union; the Greeks had entered reservations also against the Solemn Declaration; and the Irish adhered to a position of military neutrality although much of their recent foreign policy seemed very close if not always identical to EPC positions.

Member states' continuing ambivalence towards foreign policy issues was confirmed during the discussions leading up to the intergovernmental conference set up by the 1985 Milan European Council and the resultant SEA negotiations. The British had always affirmed a keen interest in security cooperation but eschewed supranational overtones even while advancing the idea of a permanent secretariat to assist the Presidency. Their Stresa initiative did not depart from this and their overall apparent isolation from and unguarded contempt for more visionary institutional reforms (including the stronger Presidency advocated by France) debated during this period resulted in their being easily outmanoeuvred by similar Franco–German proposals on political cooperation. Indeed, at one time the French had insisted that what was to become the SEA be known as the treaty on European Union (Lodge, 1984).

Franco–German proposals on EPC gave direction to foreign policy deliberations. However, they also fanned old fears of an emergent *directoire* which similar British proposals did little to quell. However, the idea of a permanent secretariat to assist the presidency for EPC was to find favour, but the anxiety expressed about its role and duration reaffirmed member states' concern about the relationship between EPC and the EC.

The anxiety over the relationship between EPC and the EC is reflected in the location of the Secretariat in the Council's Charlemagne premises. It is not independent of the member states. Nor is it part of them in the EC. Financially it is clearly dependent on the member states. It also depends on them for personnel and information. While this may be seen as a means whereby member states can try and contain the development of a Secretariat view of political cooperation objectives which stands *au-dessus de la mêlée*, the same dependence can be a source of strength if the practice of rapidly sharing information that comes in from one state to 'its' Secretariat administrator, prompts intra-Secretariat discussion of possibilities, options and alternative strategies. A similarly contradictory effect to the one that may have been intended by the originators of a relatively 'weak' and numerically small Secretariat is arising. Indeed, this parallels the experience of developed small states' foreign services: there is a need for specialization, for overlapping responsibilities and for working practices which allow for smooth transitions whenever new members come in under the rotating principles of the Council Presidency and EPC. Moreover, such a small staff can soon become indispensable to President depending on how they choose to develop and expand their role.

The Secretariat and the Presidency function at three levels: Political Director – head of Secretariat; European Correspondent – national (Presidency) member of the Secretariat; and working groups – national (Presidency) member of the Secretariat (Sanchez da Costa Pereira, 1988). The Presidency's personnel in these link-ups act as gatekeepers, and their position is strengthened by virtue of their importance to the various EPC working groups. The latter mirror politico-geographical divisions of responsibilities as well as functional divisions aligned to EPC foreign policy 'successes' such as CSCE, the Euro–Arab dialogue, mutually reinforcing action in the UN (where member states' positions are in harmony just under half the time) and so on.

The links will probably be developed in line with the Presidency's intentions of keeping the Secretariat in a subordinate position, performing instrumental tasks for the Presidency in EPC. In essence, the Secretariat is to assist the Presidency in the performance of tasks that the Presidency delegates to it. The extent of possible delegation is fairly open-ended in some areas. Consequently, there is room for the Secretariat to determine its own role and to make that indispensable to the Presidency. It is here that it could go beyond being an administrative vehicle for reconciling differences behind-the-scenes to becoming a real anchor for future EPC policymaking. However, it is important to remember that some of the Secretariat's functions overlap with existing ones of the Presidency and that the Presidency is unlikely to relinquish politically important functions to a body that is seen as an administrative assistant. Thus, its functions are to prepare and circulate the necessary documents, liaise with the relevant personnel and groups, provide back-up for the correspondents, prepare replies to EP questions, organize various meetings (including those of the ministers and political committee) and maintain EPC's archives and rules (EC Bull.2/86). As Sanchez da Costa Pereira points out, the latter amounts to a role as the 'guardian of orthodoxy', the preserver of traditions (Sanchez da Costa Periera, 94).

While functionally distinct from the EC and designed as an intergovernmental administrative body, the Secretariat has the potential to develop into something more than an extra (and closely controlled) arm of the Presidency. Its first head, Giovanni Januzzi, appointed by the Twelve for its first term (which expires when EPC comes up for review under the terms of the SEA), is responsible for coordinating its work, liaising with the Political Directors and with establishing high-level links with outside bodies. Januzzi's term of office and that of the five civil servants seconded from national administrations under the extended Troika arrangements (covering the two preceding and succeeding Presidencies) will inject into EPC a greater continuity and create opportunities for cohesion and the development of an 'institutional memory' and 'traditions' that have hitherto eluded EPC. Moreover, the term of office of the Secretariat is in line with that of other EC institutions' presidencies: notably, the Commission and the EP. There may come a time when not only will the Secretariat's personnel and role have to be expanded but when a coincidence of terms of office between Presidents is desirable.

At a functional level, close cooperation between the Commission and EPC is essential. Indeed, the Commission is involved in all EPC meetings at all levels from the President down. The Commission President (who has overall responsibility for EPC) is a member of the European Council. As Nuttall points out, at the European Council most EPC discussions take place among Foreign Ministers at dinner on the first evening. A Commission representative (usually a senior Vice-President) attends these. While the Commission President normally represents the Commission in EPC, he 'may be accompanied or replaced by one or more of the Commissioners responsible for external relations' (Nuttall, 1988: 106). The increasing burden on the Commission of EPC work has demanded the involvement of an increasing number of senior Commission secretariat personnel and officials in EPC organs (such as PoCo and the working groups). To facilitate its interaction with EPC machinery and the Twelve, it was directly linked into COREU in 1982, and the following year began to participate in the Troika arrangements (Nuttall, 1988: 107). In view of the expected external effects of the SEM, it is particularly interesting to note Nuttall's observation that abroad and in respect of trade issues, 'a higher degree of integration has been achieved ... than has so far been possible to attain centrally'. The practical distinctions between EC and EPC competence is being steadily eroded not through a deliberate EC ploy to augment its competence but by necessity and by the need for the Commission both to present its views and to ensure that the creeping extension of intergovernmental EPC activity does not emasculate EC competences (notably when policy is implemented). Moreover, the SEA entrusts the Commission with ensuring consistency between EC and EPC policies. This task is especially vital when EPC and EC activities overlap. Often, they do not. However, since the attainment of EPC goals may require the use of EC instruments (such as trade and aid measures and sanctions), the Commission performs extremely important functions for EPC. Its significance is bound to grow and it may well be recognized when Title III is re-examined in 1992.

EPC and the Single European Act

The SEA codifies EPC in an international treaty. However, the fact that the SEA covers EPC at all is of interest because the SEA is a series of amendments to the treaties establishing the European Communities. Accepted *in toto*, these amendments, including the section on EPC, have become part of the EC's central legal instrument. Publicly at least, few member states made much of this (with the exception of Ireland where the SEA's constitutionality was unsuccessfully contested) when called upon to ratify the SEA in accordance with their constitutional procedures under the terms of Art.236 of the Rome Treaty.

The SEA underlines member states' continuing ambivalence over the relationship between the EC and political cooperation. Only Title III (Provisions on European cooperation in the sphere of foreign policy) excludes references to 'member states' (found in EPC reports and the Rome Treaty and Parts I and II). Instead, reference is to the 'High Contracting Parties' which implies exclusive sovereignty for the signatories in the foreign policy field.

The ECJ's continuing exclusion from EPC matters similarly highlights a desire to maintain EPC agreements as a separate convention. This is, however, contradicted by the fact that Title III is presented as Art.30 of the SEA's Treaty Provisions. As Title I (Common Provisions) states, Art.30 is governed by acceptance and limited but important extension of all the practices developed under EPC and codified in declarations and communiqués from the time of the Davignon Report to the Solemn Declaration. The hotly disputed Art. 30 (6) extends commitments to security (but also safeguards closer security cooperation between 'certain of the High Contracting Parties' in WEU and NATO.

SEA Art.3(i) addresses the institutions of the EC and stipulates that they exercise 'their powers and jurisdiction under the conditions and for the purposes provided for by the subsequent Treaties and Acts modifying or supplementing them and by the provisions of Title II, (Provisions amending the Treaties establishing the European Communities). SEA Art.3 (ii) goes on to deal with EPC and to define its powers in relation to Title III as provided for by SEA Art.1(3) – the same article that states:

The European Communities and European Political Cooperation shall have as their objective to contribute together to making concrete progress towards European unity.

Moreover, the Commission and Council Presidency are entrusted 'each within its own sphere' with 'special responsibility' for ensuring consistency between EPC policies and the EC's external policies (SEA, Art.30(5)). This is given added poignancy in the context of the realization of certain aspects of the Single

European Market involving the free movement of goods and individuals. Drug trafficking, immigration and terrorism issues have been dealt with both by groups under Foreign Ministers and notably by Ministers of the Interior and Justice in the so-called Trevi (terrorism) and Pompidou (drugs) groups, (Lodge, 1988) as well as in the Five's Schengen group.[2]

The SEA confirms existing goals for EPC, and opens the door for and legitimizes discussion of other related issues (such as security and technological and industrial aspects of defence) by members in the EC as well as in EPC. Implicitly, supranational action in these 'new' areas is legitimized by the obligation imposed on the Council Presidency and the Commission to ensure consistency between the external relations of the EC and EPC. However, Title III exudes caution. New commitments in respect of security-related discussions seem to lack direct operational implications for WEU or NATO. At the same time, they do not rule out intensified efforts within EPC. Art.30(6)a states that closer cooperation on questions of European security 'would contribute in an essential way to the development of a European identity in external policy matters' and confirms the High Contracting Parties' readiness to 'coordinate their positions more closely on the political and economic aspects of security'. No direct reference is made to military aspects but these were implicit in the form of words chosen and made explicit by the Spanish Presidency in January 1989. Overall, the SEA exhibits continuity both in its content and the highly qualified presentation of EPC goals.

This unsurprising conclusion follows from the member states' experience of EPC. So far, their common external relations pursued under the aegis of EPC represent a reflexive foreign policy style. EPC has been criticized for a lack of coherent, independent, common foreign policy initiatives; and for its apparent preoccupation with declarations rather than action. Such criticism overlooks EPC's necessarily extremely limited aims, possibilities and ambiguous legal base. Even so, over the past fifteen to twenty years with, EPC the EC has conveyed the impression that the international interests of its members, while not always identical with one another, have proved sufficiently convergent to produce an image of independence and distinctiveness.

There can be little doubt that the Troika arrangements (linking outgoing and incoming presidencies with the present occupant) developed in the early 1970s have proved their worth. The current arrangement whereby three states are involved in the Troika (and a Commission representative on visits abroad) has proved particularly useful. The Troika has led to a sense of common purpose that was sufficiently deep to enable the EC to pursue a mediative role in the Middle East. Quiet diplomacy on its part was of use in this arena even when some Middle East states were pressurizing it to be more adventurous, and even though the achievements of Euro–Arab dialogue (launched on the tails of the oil crisis; see Ifestos, 1987) seemed to disappoint many.

CSCE has also proved a useful forum for concerted action by the member states. What was perhaps even more surprising was the growth in consensus among the Nine in international organizations, notably the UN. International events have helped to concentrate the minds of EC governments on what unites them in their foreign policies in a way that perhaps few would have anticipated in the early 1970s. Sharp and sometimes embarrassing differences and confrontations still occur and will persist into the 1990s as the SEA recognizes. More importantly perhaps, the sense of common purpose exhibited by the completion of the Single European Market and Title III's cautious toe-dipping into security spheres will lead to greater, but gradual, coherence in EC–EPC external relations. There is a sense in which the EC's external economic strength could be weakened unless it develops a coherent external political face.

However, in the short-to-medium term, the legal basis of external actions, agreements and policies will prove problematic. The inseparability of political and economic considerations, notably in commercial policy matters and international trade negotiations (such as GATT where the member states have progressively transferred their jurisdiction to the EC and have so conferred on it the related international rights and obligations; (Mathijsen, 1986: 234), will give rise to difficulties. The EC's institutions (especially the ECJ and the EP) may well test the limits of their authority in this field. The EP has already stalled agreements (for example on Palestine) to ensure that political considerations should be duly reflected in accordance with its wishes. Moreover, the changing international environment will make numerous demands on the EC's capacity to adapt.

Adapting to new demands and a new international role will challenge the ingenuity of the new Presidency Secretariat and the ability of the Council and Commission Presidencies to work effectively together both in the context of EPC and in international organizations such as the UN (where the Commission has observer status and the Council Presidency sets out the Twelve's positions), and related agencies; the OECD (attended by the Commission) and other IOs (Mathijsen, 1986: 242). Outside expectations of the EC in the international arena will also challenge its ability to formulate and project a coherent, harmonious image. Such expectations will often exceed the EC's ability or the Twelve's willingness to deliver.

The 1990s may well require the Twelve to reconsider EPC's aims and functions. So far, it has functioned quite well as a forum for facilitating discreet shifts in national foreign policies towards a Euro middle ground. The new Secretariat may help to define EPC aims and to bring about greater cooperation across the broad policy communities serving EPC and the EC's external relations' sectors. It must be remembered, however, that the EC and EPC have, even when they have formulated and planned action, a limited capacity to enforce it. Even with the SEA, they have to rely on national governments to formulate a view and to implement any action. The instruments available to the Twelve within the context of the EC and EPC are very limited. They are likely to continue resting on a handful of economic instruments and the politics of persuasion. The political economy of trade will present the EC and the Twelve in EPC with interesting opportunities and problems in an era where the EC is anxious to avoid creating a negative external image (or having one thrust on it) as it consolidates the SEM.

EPC and issues for the future

Fortress Europe?

Inevitably, the SEM will have major implications for EC external relations whether narrowly or broadly conceived. As Willy de Clerq said

1992 has given Europe confidence in its own destiny: Europessimism is a story of the past. This is important for Europe but not less so for the international economic system. [de Clerq, 1988]

He went on to point out that the EC is the world's largest trading partner; its exports of manufactured goods represent 26 per cent of those of the OECD compared with 14 per cent for the US and 17 per cent for Japan. Its share of world exports of services is even greater. Intra-EC trade is expected to rise by 10 per cent as a result of the SEM and exports are expected to rise by a similar level, creating a balance of trade surplus of around one per cent of EC GNP. Therefore, it has a vital interest in maintaining and reinforcing a world-wide, liberal trading system (de Clerq 1988: 10). The EC's heads of state and government confirmed this at the June 1988 Hanover Council where they stressed the need for the EC to be open to third countries in conformity with the GATT. Moreover, the EC seems keen to secure a world-wide lowering of the levels of protection through the Uruguay round scheduled for the end of 1990 – when the EC will have to have in place nearly all the proposals it wants passed to realize the SEM by 1992. While the EC opposes protectionism and the notion of Fortress Europe, it is not prepared unilaterally to extend the benefits of its own internal liberalization to third countries. Instead, the EC is negotiating (as in the services and financial services sectors) reciprocal concessions preferably on a multilateral basis but also bilaterally. As de Clerq stressed: 'We want to open our border, but on the basis of a mutual balance of advantages in the spirit of GATT'. The quest for reciprocity is, however, to be qualified in respect of developing countries, especially members of the Lomé Conventions.

1992 and the European fringe

EFTA–EC trade exceeds EC–US and EC–Japan trade. Free trade agreements exist with EFTA states. There are numerous joint ventures linking the two and overall the two economies are strongly interpenetrated. There has been growing speculation about imminent entry bids by Austria and Norway. From the EC's point of view, Norwegian accession would pose the fewest problems of any potential new European member. Greater political problems inhere in the accession of Austria which go beyond its neutral status and relationship with the USSR. Its internal makeup and leanings towards Hungary, coupled with its Germanic roots, are seen as potentially problematic as various aspects of its economy. Nevertheless, there is evidence of keen interest among neutral European states in EC developments. (Swedish observers are seen, for instance, at CSP gatherings.) Moreover, those on the EC's fringe are not entirely convinced that in the longer term their interests will be served by bilateral or multilateral arrangements with the EC or by their own adoption of legislation mirroring that of the EC as the EC insists on reciprocity in sensitive areas such as monetary union, fiscal matters and public procurement. At the same time, it is clear that the accession of states at the leading edge of some technologies could improve the EC's international competitiveness.

There is no doubt that further enlargement will not occur until sometime after 1992, and probably not before 1995. Any further enlargement will prove politically contentious in view of the Turkish entry bid tabled in 1986. Such an enlargement and the spate of further applications that this bid is expected to generate from other relatively poor fringe states (such as Malta, Cyprus and even Yugoslavia) will engender serious economic, as well as political, difficulties for the Twelve even if they are generally more prosperous by the mid-1990s. Certainly, a willingness to embrace the somewhat richer EFTA states may spark off the old allegations of the EC being a rich man's club.

The EC will also have to adapt its relations with the Soviet bloc in the coming decade. Even if the SEM's external effects are seen largely as an exercise in filling the gaps in the EC's common commercial policy, it will not be easy for the EC to unify import rules and overcome the wide discrepancies in the import regimes (and credit inducements) individual member states operate on certain products from Eastern Europe (and also from Japan). Moreover, there are several sensitive issues (notably in the high-technology sector) that may affect EC–USSR as well as EC–Comecon dealings. US sensitivities may continue to impinge on how the Twelve see their East bloc links developing.

Apart from trade, the East bloc has been an arena where the EC has tried out its capacity to respond as a unit to international stimuli where a common, identifiably Community, approach has been seen to be beneficial. The preparation for the CSCE and the signing of the Helsinki Final Act in 1975 have been applauded as a major achievement of EPC. There can be little doubt that concertation by the Twelve – begun in the CSCE set up in the early 1970s and continuing into the 1980s through CDE in Stockholm 1984-6 and through the expert's meetings on human rights and fundamental freedoms (Ottawa, 1985), human contacts (Bern, 1986) and the Cultural Forum (Budapest, 1985 – has affected bilateral and multilateral relations with the East bloc. While it did not spur the development of an EC *Ostpolitik per se*, the pattern of interaction with the East bloc through EPC concertation provided a testing ground for a variety of EC diplomatic *démarches*. These ranged from the expression of common declarations, greater homogeneity in the voting patterns of the Nine in the UN (which rose to over 61 per cent before settling at around 47 per cent) (Regelsberger, 1988: 12) to the development of EC use of traditional instruments of diplomatic persuasion. These ranged from the deployment of negative measures to positive attempts to foster trade and development with third states or regional groupings. The negative measures in particular had high political visibility even if their economic impact was questionable. An example was the EC imposition of restrictions on some Soviet luxury goods in 1982 to signal the EC's objections to Soviet policy in the wake of its invasion of Poland. Moreover, EC action to keep avenues open to the East bloc against initial US opposition following the imposition of martial law in Poland underscored the EC's credibility and independence. Even the problems arising out of Greece distancing itself from its partners over conflicts with the USSR, and the EC's material inability to follow up declarations in times of crisis with direct intervention (as in the case of the Soviet invasion of Afghanistan in 1979; the Falklands in 1982 (Edwards, 1984) and Libya in 1986, were nevertheless internally useful to the development of EPC's capacities and to the upgrading of its international diplomacy. Indeed, the opportunity for member states to respond differentially continues to be a source of strength for EPC both in allowing flexibility in its dealings with the East bloc and in matters of mutual interest, including security, and in allowing it to explore the receptiveness of outside actors to common initiatives that might be undertaken by the Twelve.

The East European arena proved a fertile ground for testing the potential for collective bargaining.

Inter-regional diplomacy outside Europe

EPC showed a penchant for inter-regional diplomacy early on. This followed on from the EC's establishment over the years of special links with the developing world, notably through the Lomé agreements, but also through ANDEAN and the younger Contadora Group *vis-à-vis* Latin America, ASEAN since 1980 (Beuter and Tsakaloyannis, 1987), the Euro–Arab dialogue and the Gulf Cooperation Council (Greilsammer and Weiler, 1987: Yorke and Truner, 1986). More recently, the Twelve have explored more active measures through EPC both to combat international terrorism (notably using Trevi) and international crime with a degree of success. It is also clear that the Twelve are developing a degree of convergence and joint purpose towards single states (like India and China) and more especially towards Australasia, the NICs and the Pacific basin. The diverse demands of these areas will inevitably require closer linkage still between the EC and EPC.

Notes

1. The London Report stipulates that no formal agenda will exist and that official interpreters and officials (except for a Presidency notetaker) will be excluded for Gymnich meetings among ministers.
2. The Schengen Group comprises the FRG, France and the Benelux Countries and aims at dismantling border controls before 1992.

References

Allen, D., Rummel, R., and Wessels, W. (eds) (1982), *European Political Cooperation*, London, Butterworth.
Beuter, R. and Tsakaloyannis, P. (1987), *Experiences in Regional Cooperation*, Maastricht, EIPA.
Bulmer, S. and Wessels, W. (1987), *The European Council: Decisionmaking in European Politics*, London, Macmillan.
de Clerq, W. (1988), '1992: the impact on the outside world', *European Access*, 1, 10-12.
de Schoutheete, P. (1986), *La coopération politique Europeénne*, Brussels, Editions Labor/RTL.
Edwards, G., (1984), 'Europe and the Falkland Crisis 1982', *Journal of Common Market Studies*, 22.
European Parliament Working Documents (1981), *Report on European Political Cooperation and the Role of the European Parliament* (Elles Report), 1-335/81.
Greilsammer, I. and Weiler, J. (1987), *Europe's Middle East Dilemma*, Boulder, Westview.
Hill, C. (1983), *National Foreign Policies and European Political Cooperation*, London, Allen & Unwin.
Hirsch, V. (1987), 'Les relations euro-arabes: à la recherche d'un nouvel équilibre', *Revue du Marché Commun*, December, 688-9.
Ifestos, P. (1987), *European Political Cooperation: Towards a Framework of Supranational Diplomacy?*, Aldershot, Avebury.

Lodge, J. (1982), *The European Community and New Zealand*, London, Frances Pinter.
—, (1984), 'The Single European Act: Towards a New Euro-Dynamism?' *Journal of Common Market Studies*, **24**, 203-23.
—, (ed) (1988), *The Threat of Terrorism*, Brighton, Wheatsheaf.
Lodge, J. (1988b), 'The European Parliament and Foreign Policy' in M.L. Sondhi (ed), *Foreign Policy and Legislatures*, New Dehli, Abhinav.
Louis, J.-V. (1983), 'La Communauté et ses états membres dans les relations extérieures', *Journal of European Integration*, **7**, 203-35.
Mathijsen, P.S.R.F. (1986), A Guide to European Community Law, London, Sweet & Maxwell.
Molle, W. and van Mourik, Aad, (1987), 'Economic Instruments for a common European Foreign Policy', in J. de Vree *et al.*, *Towards a European Foreign Policy*, Dordrecht, Nijhoff.
Nuttall, S. (1988), 'Where the European Commission comes in' in Pijpers *et al.*, *European Political Cooperation in the 1980s*, Dordrecht, Kluwer.
Pescatore, J. (1979), 'External Relations in the Case Law of the Court of Justice of the European Communities', *Common Market Law Review*, **16**.
Pijpers, A. *et al.* (1988a), *European Political Cooperation in the 1980s: A Common Foreign Policy for Western Europe?* Dordrecht, Nijhoff.
—, (1988b), 'The Twelve out-of-area: a civilian power in an uncivil world?' in A. Pijpers *et al.*, *European Political Cooperation in the 1980s*, Dordrecht, Kluwer.
Pinder, J. (1983), 'Political cooperation in Europe', in R. Jenkins (ed.), *Britain and the EEC*, London, Macmillan.
Prag. D. (1986), 'International Relations' in J. Lodge (ed.), *European Union: the European Community in Search of a Future*, London, Macmillan.
Regelsberger, E. (1988), 'EPC in the 1980s: reaching another plateau?' in A. Pijpers *et al.*, *European Political Cooperation in the 1980s*, Dordrecht, Nijhoff.
Sanchez da Costa Pereira, P. (1988), 'The Use of a Secretariat', in A. Pijpers *et al. European Political Cooperation in the 1980s*, Dordrecht, Nijhoff.
Schwarze, J. (1987), 'Towards a European Foreign Policy – Legal Aspects' in J. de Vree *et al.*, *Towards a European Foreign Policy*, Dordrecht, Nijhoff.
Taylor, P. (1982), 'The European Communities as an Actor in International Society', *Journal of European Integration*, **6**, 7-42.
von der Gablentz, O. (1979), 'Luxembourg Revisited or the Importance of European Political Cooperation', *Common Market Law Review*, **20**, 685-99.
Wallace, W. (1984), *Britain's Bilateral Links within Western Europe*, London, RKP.
Weiler, J.H.H. (1988), 'The Evolution of an European Foreign Policy: Mechanisms and Institutions', in I. Greilsammer and J. Weiler (eds), *Europe and Israel: Troubled Neighbours*, Berlin, dr Gruyter.
Yorke, V. and Truner, L. (1986), *European Interests and Gulf Oil*, Aldershot, Gower.

13 The EC: from civilian power to military integration

Panos Tsakaloyannis

Introduction

Since the early 1970s the study of the EC's role in the world has been an elusive and frustrating subject. In the 1950s and 1960s for a number of domestic and international reasons this subject was kept in abeyance. Domestically, the shock of the failure of the European Defence Community (EDC) in 1954 (Furdson, 1980), the Suez *débâcle* in 1956, preoccupation of some West Europeans (France, Belgium, the UK) with decolonization, de Gaulle's advent to power in 1958 and his bid for leadership of Western Europe in the course of the 1960s preempted any effort for even a token form of political cooperation let alone the construction of a joint West European security (von der Groeben, 1987; Monnet, 1978). At the same time the international environment was hardly conducive to undertaking such initiatives. The cold war and recurring crises in East-West relations strengthened the need for discipline and solidarity in the NATO Alliance in the face of a perceived Soviet menace.

The early 1970s can be justly viewed as a watershed for the EC and for international relations in general. In Western Europe, France's lifting of its veto on British membership of the EC at the Hague summit in December 1969 brought an end to the wrangles of the 1960s. Henceforward 'enlargement' and *approfondissement* became the EC's twin objectives not only in economic and trade matters but, perhaps of even more importance, also political matters. Moreover, since the early 1970s the fortunes of the EC have been inextricably linked with the twists and turns of the international environment, above all by the ever changing relationship of the superpowers.

In the early 1970s the seeds of superpower decline were sown although it took more than another decade before the magnitude of this decline and its international implications could be fully felt. The Vietnam war sapped the resources and the morale of the US. However, of even more far-reaching consequence for the Western world was 15 August 1971, the date US Treasury Secretary John Connally signed, unilaterally, the death sentence of the Bretton Woods arrangements. The Vietnam imbroglio and simmering crises in the Alliance ran contemporaneously. Both were symptoms of US economic and political decline and faltering morale. Since the early 1970s, therefore, the basic aim of US administrations has been to halt and if possible to reverse this decline.

The first and most determined attempt to arrest this decline came during the Nixon-Kissinger administration. The approach was to maximize the diplomatic assets of the US and to exploit the differences of its main adversaries, the USSR and China. Although Kissinger and Nixon paid lip-service to a five-polar international system which included Western Europe and Japan, for them what counted most was the American-Soviet-Chinese triangle; Western Europe and Japan were seen as auxiliaries if not irritants. Later the aim of restoring the US position was often obscured by rhetoric, as for example during President Reagan's first term, or by sidetracking the issues, as during the Carter presidency (Williams, 1988). However, all these efforts met with little success. By the end of the 1980s awareness of decline has been pervasive, if not a little overstated (Kennedy, 1988; Calleo, 1988).

For the USSR too the late 1960s-early 1970s marked a turning point. Despite appearances, that period signalled the contraction of Soviet economic, political and ideological power. Its clearest manifestation was the Soviet-led invasion of Czechoslovakia. If the suppression of the Hungarian uprising in 1956 provoked the mass exit of party members, particularly in Western Europe, the invasion of Czechoslovakia triggered the desertion of Communist parties en bloc, starting with the Italian and the Spanish. It also turned a hitherto ideological dispute with Peking into a bitter conflict. Therefore, despite Soviet advances in South-east Asia and Africa in the first half of the 1970s, the Soviet system showed symptoms of fatigue and stagnation particularly during the last decade of the Brezhnev era.

Since the early 1970s, the EC has been shaped both by the evolution of superpower relations as well as by the Community's capacity to overcome its own internal economic, political and institutional problems. This interaction between domestic developments and changes in the international environment, especially those of the superpowers, has caused profound shifts in perceptions and expectations of the EC's role in the world. The most pronounced reappraisal occurred in the early 1980s with the abandonment of the EC's traditional 'civilian power' posture and the advent of the security paradigm.

I will argue that the EC in the 1990s, for a number of domestic and international reasons to be analysed below, may have to redefine its role in the world again. This redefinition should take into account new international realities such as the decline of the superpowers and their new *détente* in the post-INF era, as well as the EC's renewed dynamism evidenced by the resolve to establish an Internal Market by 1992. It will also be contended that certain readjustments in the EC's current mechanisms will be needed if it is to respond effectively to these new challenges. The first part of this chapter outlines the EC's political evolution in the 1970s and 1980s, particularly its transition from 'civilian power' to current efforts to construct a security arm. The second part examines the kind of challenges the EC is likely to confront in the 1990s and discusses the prospects for institutional readjustments in political-security matters.

The EC in the 1970s and 1980s: from civilian power to security aspirations

Following the 1969 Hague summit the debate on political integration was reopened: in contrast to past efforts the emphasis now was on realism and on incrementalism. This was in tune with the prevailing mood in the EC which, in the aftermath of the 1965 crisis, had become more reluctant to contemplate bold steps. At the same time the approach adopted by the Nine in the framework of the Davignon Committee which laid the foundations for the setting up of European Political Cooperation (EPC) reflected to a large degree domestic and international realities (de Schoutheete, 1987; Ifestos, 1987).

Domestically, the 1950s and 1960s showed Western Europeans that that there were no anodyne shortcuts to European unity. The EDC fiasco, the Fouchet talks, Suez and Hungary in 1956, Czechoslovakia and Vietnam were all melancholic reminders of European decline in world affairs. By the late 1960s the realization had dawned that 'the European problem' had deep roots going back to the follies of the nineteenth century (Taylor, 1974; de Porte, 1979), which could not be instantly rectified by spectacular gestures.

On a more mundane level, the Anglo-French burying of the hatchet in 1969 inevitably meant that EPC would be moulded to some extent by their own predilections. Both had 'middle-power' status. Both were nuclear powers, permanent members of the Security Council of the UN and with their multiple ties with their former colonies were still in possession of a number of outposts in various parts of the world. The last factor prompted Galtung in the early 1970s to draw the rather hasty conclusion that the EC was in the process of becoming a super power. However neither the mechanism of EPC adopted in the early 1970s by the then Nine, nor their mood or predilections justified Galtung's claim. EPC, based on consensus among the Nine, was hardly the ideal instrument for constructing a 'pax-Bruxelliana' as he called it (Galtung, 1973). Irish neutrality, Danish detachment, to say nothing about the varied perceptions of the larger EC members, precluded the emergence of a new power centre.

The 'civilian power' approach adopted by the Nine in the early 1970s was implicitly a rejection of power politics. Instead it stressed western Europe's economic and cultural assets and its civilizing effects on the rest of the world. As Françoise Duchêne, a strong exponent of the 'civilian power' school, put it in the early 1970s:

The European Community's interest as a civilian group of countries long on economic power and relatively short on armed force is as far as possible to *domesticate* relations between states, including those of its own members and those with states outside its frontiers. This means trying to bring to international problems the sense of responsibility and structures of contractual politics which have in the past been associated almost exclusively with 'home' and not foreign, that is *alien* affairs. [Duchêne, 1973]

A 'civilian-power' posture was attractive for other reasons. In the climate of the early 1970s there was strong public aversion to naked military power, particularly as when employed by the US in Vietnam or the USSR in Czechoslovakia. A 'civilian power' posture, therefore, was appealing to the public at home and reassuring to those countries formerly under European domination. At the same time it sheltered the Europeans from US pressures for active European support of the US in 'out-of-area' conflicts, above all in Vietnam. As Douglas Stuart points out, 'by the end of the 1960s the US was changing places with the European colonial powers on the issue of out of area cooperation with America taking on the role of *demandeur* and the Europeans, for the most part "relieved" of their colonial responsibilities, opting for a narrow reading of Article 6 of the [NATO] Treaty' (Stuart, forthcoming).

While EPC in the 1970s was an exercise in low-profile politics, it was not devoid of substance or purpose. The fact that most of the energies of EPC throughout the 1970s were devoted to the Middle East and the Conference on Security and Cooperation in Europe (CSCE) attests to that. Both the Middle East and the CSCE were meant as exercises in low-profile diplomacy and involved, directly or indirectly, the super powers. The Middle East, since the late 1950s, had virtually become an American *domaine réservé* although Western Europeans, particularly France and UK, retained some vestiges of influences. The outbreak of the October war in 1973 was for the Nine a shattering experience, not only because of the dissension it caused in their ranks or the damage it did to their economies but also because it highlighted the degree of decline of European influence in a region traditionally regarded vital to Western Europe's security and prosperity. An early casualty of the 1973 war was the abandonment of the effort to construct an ambitious 'global' Mediterranean policy. The ensuing Euro-Arab dialogue was a damage limitation exercise which sought to cushion the effects of the oil crisis and to maintain a semblance of stability in the region.

Throughout the 1970s the overwhelming weight of the US in the Middle East and Washington's irritation with Western Europe's 'meddling' in the delicate politics of the region was the most decisive obstacle to the Nine's abortive attempts to devise a policy towards the Middle East. From the Six's innocuous 1971 attempt to tackle the humanitarian aspects of Palestinian refugees to the Nine's ambitious Venice Declaration of June 1980 (calling for the creation of a homeland for the Palestinians) Washington's reaction ranged from mounted disapproval to outright anger.

American refusal to allow the Western Europeans a degree of initiative in the Middle East has been a decisive factor in the EC's poor showing in the region. The Camp David Agreements between Israel and Egypt reinforced US predominance in the region. Since the late 1970s, therefore, West Europeans have tried to tread a cautious course in the region and avoid US accusations of recklessness. US reactions to EC political initiatives assumed more weight with the advent of President Reagan and the onset of the 'second' cold war. In the new international climate the least the Europeans wanted was to provoke US wrath. Especially during President Reagan's first term there was a temporary reimposition of US hegemony in the Alliance. The spectre of a nuclear war fought mainly in Europe had the effect of reducing Western Europeans' interest in broader issues like the Middle East; hence the unceremonious burial of the 'Venice Declaration'.

The Nine's record in the CSCE process, especially during the first phase up to the 1975 Helsinki summit, is more impressive. The CSCE offered an ideal ground for the Nine to make good use of their combined instruments: their diplomatic skills in the EPC framework with valuable Commission support in the drafting of the various 'baskets'. This experience was also indispensable in smoothing over the rather uneasy relationship between EPC and the Commission.

In the CSCE the Nine confronted mainly the USSR and, in view of US lack of interest in these talks, during its first phase (1972-5) they were allowed to take the front seat. The convening of a European security conference was Moscow's favourite hobby horse as early as the mid-1960s. The convening of such a conference was seen by Moscow as a means of legitimizing the post-1945 status quo in Europe. However, the Nine grasped the opportunity offered by the CSCE to wrest a number of concessions from Moscow on human rights, culture and trade. Coming as it did during the heyday of *détente*, the CSCE was an ideal opportunity for the Nine to display their penchant for low-profile diplomacy and to explore the possibilities of a 'civilian power' posture.

However, as with the Middle East, the Nine's low-profile, incremental approach was undermined largely by changing superpower relations, the demise of *détente* and the advent of a new cold war by the early 1980s (Wallace and Webb, 1983; Regelsberger, 1988). The debilitating effects of these events on the EC, and particularly on EPC, are known. Suffice it to say here that it took some years before the structural deficiencies of EPC and its inbuilt limits became clear. For most of the 1970s, EPC's inability to progress or, as in the case of the CSCE, to consolidate its position, were explained away as temporary setbacks.

A chain of crises from the Iranian revolution to Central America and from Afghanistan to Poland spelled the end of the idyllic *détente* of the early 1970s. At the same time, the EC drifted from one internal crisis to another unable to find solutions to its accumulated problems, or to endorse any of the proposals put forward since the mid-1970s for institutional reform. On top of all this, impending Mediterranean enlargement and the advent of a bellicose President Reagan helped darken the horizon and strengthen the prophets of an impending doom.

Against this domestic and international background by the early 1980s EPC was insufficient to cope with the new situation. Failure in institutional reform, the accession of new members not fully abiding by the *aquis politique*, squabbles over the EC budget or the British contribution to it and last but not least the spectres of superpower confrontation – probably on West European soil – had the cumulative effect of overturning earlier assumptions and calling for a reappraisal of the Community's role in the world.

The advent of the security paradigm

On a theoretical level, Hedley Bull provided the most comprehensive and authoritative critique of the 'civilian power' postulate. In view of Bull's high reputation on both sides of the Atlantic, his critique gained wide currency and set the tone for the ensuing debate which culminated in the ascendancy of the security paradigm. Bull argued that the civilian power postulate was faulty not because of institutional deficiencies but mainly because it was based on weak premises, on visionary or progressivist interpretations of international relations which were transplanted to the study of the EC in the early 1970s by economists like Andrew Shonfield and Susan Strange. Bull called for a return to the realist approach which laid emphasis on the primacy of the nation state (Bull, 1984). Above all, he rejected the idea that there was a supranational authority in Western Europe which, he felt, in itself was not a bad thing for 'even if there *were* a supranational authority in Western Europe, this would be a source of weakness in defence policy rather than of strength'. He reasoned that the primacy of nation-states in Western Europe – France, Germany and Britain – and 'their capacity to inspire loyalty and to make war' were sources of power and rebuffed the idea that Western European nations constituted a 'security community' or an area of peace as 'mere wishful thinking, if it means that war between them could not happen again'.[1]

In the early 1980s, Bull's controversial views on the EC were more or less uncritically accepted including even his questionable assertion that war between Western Europeans themselves could happen again. A weighty report published in early 1983 by five leading West European institutions argued that the concept of the EC as a civilian power had been rendered obsolete by events and that, therefore, Western Europe could no longer 'dissociate itself from the power politics of the contemporary world' (Kaiser *et al*, 1985). The return to power politics not only encouraged fragmentation but also brought about a proliferation of views and schemes about Western Europe's long-term objectives.

The ascendance of the security paradigm has had numerous political, institutional, even psychological effects on the EC in the 1980s (Fontaine, 1987). Obviously, the most pronounced was the search for an autonomous West European security structure. The reactivation of the West European Union (WEU) in October 1984, after three years of soul-searching, was the best solution under the circumstances. WEU had several things to commend it; its disadvantages were less obvious. Its most obvious advantage was that its membership was confined to seven out of the then ten Community members. Denmark, Greece and Ireland (the three non-WEU EC members) had been rather reticent about security cooperation in the EC framework (Tsakaloyannis, 1985: 5). For the other seven members this was a blessing in disguise in view of the peripheral geographical position of these three non-members. Their membership of the WEU, among other things, would make it quite difficult, if not problematic, to adhere to the Brussels Treaty which commits all WEU countries to assist any member facing aggression.[2] While falling short of a fully fledged West European security instrument, the WEU has nonetheless played a constructive role since its reactivation. First it went some way to reassure the West European public that Western Europe was not entirely at the mercy of the superpowers. Second, for the first time since EDC's failure in 1954, security entered the mainstream of the European integration process. In particular, Britain's active role in the reactivated WEU helped narrow the gap between London and the Six on security collaboration. Last but by no means least, the reactivation of the WEU raised the spectre of a two-tier Community: one comprising the seven core members of the WEU, and a wider one including the ten soon twelve or more members. Therefore, the three non-WEU countries were compelled, in varying degrees, to modify their views on the subject. It is questionable whether the Inter-governmental Conference set up in 1984 which led to the signing of the Single European Act would have made the progress it did had it not been for the agonizing reappraisal and the dilemma it posed in Athens, Dublin and Copenhagen.

On the other hand the reactivation of the WEU at a critical juncture in the EC's development was bound to create a number of institutional complications. It should be recalled that the reactivation of the WEU took place at the same time the Inter-governmental Conference was getting under way. Both initiatives were launched in 1984 and were prompted by similar considerations, namely to tackle head-on the EC's evident stagnation. Therefore, there was a degree of interaction between the two processes. In this respect, preoccupation with security in the 1980s and the resolve of some EC members to go along either in the framework of WEU, or bilaterally (the prospect of a Franco-German axis – Britain's nightmare) or multilaterally (the emergence of a Directoire – the nightmare of the smaller EC members) were contributory factors in breaking the deadlock on institutional reform.

The security dimension in the EC since the SEA

A close reading of the SEA gives the justified impression that Title Three dealing with political and security issues is a poor relative if compared to the more substantive Title Two. It is not merely the sheer disparity in length between Titles Two and Three. Of more importance is the substantive difference. Title Two makes provisions for the amendment of a number of clauses of the Rome Treaty. In contrast Title Three is largely a reaffirmation of existing practices in EPC among the Twelve. This is understandable in view of the fact that in the Dooge Committee Title Three was treated separately from the other Titles and it was discussed on a strictly inter-governmental basis by foreign ministry officials from the Twelve.

However despite the asymmetry in the SEA between the different Titles, it would be unwise to underestimate its long-term effects in the political-security field. To begin with, although in the drafting stage of the SEA there were two distinctive processes, in the final document the Twelve state as their ultimate objective 'to contribute together (that is in the EC and in EPC) to making concrete progress towards European Unity' (SEA, Title One, Article 1).

Second, the SEA abolishes the artificial separation between the EC and EPC. It explicitly stipulates that 'the Commission shall be fully associated with the proceedings of Political Cooperation' (SEA, Title Three, Article 30, para. 3(b)). This provision is very important from a legal point of view as it brings EPC within the ambit of the EC and for the first time it gives a legitimate right to the Commission to be active in the economic and political aspects of security. Since 1987 the Commission has made the most out of this provision in the SEA, and its President has declared that the Commission is determined 'to play its role to the full to ensure that future progress in the area of political cooperation keeps pace with developments on the Community front' (Delors, 1987).

Third, the setting-up of an EPC Secretariat in Brussels could in the long run have considerable effects. Given the peripatetic nature of EPC, that is following the rotating Presidency of the Council, the Secretariat may find a niche and by dint of the expertise and experience which it is bound to accumulate with time it may exert considerable influence which will go beyond its ascribed function in the SEA, to be a glorified secretary to the Presidency. The Secretariat's presence in Brussels, and not in a far away place as France had been insisting since the early 1970s, helps make it an integral part of the EC process, with easy access to the Commission and the EP. The Secretariat could become, therefore, a useful interlocutor between EPC and the EC institutions, the Commission in particular. In the years to come the Commission and the EP can count on the support of the EPC Secretariat in broadening the EC's competence in security matters. Finally the Secretariat may become a useful intermediary between the EC and the WEU and to a lesser extent between EPC and NATO.

The SEA empowers the EC to deal with the political and economic aspects of security in order to maintain the technological and industrial conditions necessary for the Twelve's security. At the same time it reaffirms the primacy of NATO and the WEU in security matters. While NATO and the WEU are lumped together, the reference made to them in the SEA stems from different considerations. The mention of the WEU is meant as a declaration of intent by the WEU members that security cooperation in the EC framework should not be to the detriment of security collaboration in the WEU. The reference to

NATO is basically a reassurance to the US and to a lesser extent to the other NATO non-EC members that security cooperation in the EC would not erode NATO's cohesion. It should be recalled that the SEA was drafted before the Reykjavik and the Washington summit meetings between Presidents Reagan and Gorbachev, that is at a time of superpower confrontation and restlessness in Western Europe especially over the issue of the siting of Pershing missiles.

The above constraints set the limits for security cooperation in Western Europe be it in the framework of the Twelve, or the Nine (in the WEU) or even in the much publicised Franco-German axis. With regard to the last, in recent years there has been remarkable progress in the political-security field – its most recent achievement being the creation of a 4,000-strong joint brigade in 1987. In October 1988 it was also agreed to set-up joint Franco-German embassies in some countries, starting with Mongolia.

However, although the significance of these advances should not be underestimated, the intrinsic value of the Franco-German axis remains controversial. Since its most potent weight is felt in EC-related matters, it tends to attract admiration even the envy of other EC members. This is particularly so in the case of the British who on occasions find it difficult to keep up with the pace set by Bonn and Paris. Mrs Thatcher, for example, had this to say about Franco-German defence cooperation: 'What I think we have to watch is that there do not grow up sub-structures in Europe which could have unwittingly, unintentionally, the effect of undermining the links across the Atlantic Alliance … I think it is important that those [Franco-German] arrangements do not take on wholly a bigger life on their own, (in an interview with the *Financial Times*, 23 November 1987). However, it seems that this concern is a little exaggerated. While there is in recent years a growing Franco-German convergence on security issues this is limited by differences on a number of fundamental issues such as:

   (i) The incompatibility of the French nuclear strategy of massive retaliation with NATO's strategy of flexible response;
  (ii) France's penchant for a world power status and independence in security matters;
 (iii) West Germany's confined scope of action and dependence on the US or its security;
 (iv) Differing views on the merits of 'out-of-area' engagements;
  (v) Last but not least with regard to the emphasis the FRG places on German reunification (see Poetering, 1986).

The strength of the Franco-German axis lies in EC-related issues. Its course also varies in accordance with the personalities holding power. Thus this relationship reached its climax between 1974-81, with the Giscard d'Estaing-Helmut Schmidt duo. Among its accomplishments were the creation of the European Council in 1974, the EMS and the first direct elections to the EP in 1979.

When it comes to fundamentals, however, common purpose holds less sway. As a sceptic has suggested, the Franco-German relationship stems from a position of weakness not strength and this sets narrow limits to its development. 'Their changed relationship', Hans A. Schmitt points out, 'remains a blessing but not the boon it would have been to the generation of our grandparents and parents'. As their descent from world power status is the most important cause of their post-war *rapprochement*, it is largely a damage limitation exercise. At the same time both sides look elsewhere for solutions to problems caused by the last war and this is more often than not a matter of concern not comfort to the other side. In Schmitt's strong phrasing, 'The ghost of reunification haunts German consciences and populates French nightmares' (Schmitt, 1987: 564-6). It is not surprising, therefore, that repeated German calls for reunification have received a cool reception not only in Moscow but also in most EC capitals. Similarly most of Germany's EC partners have displayed little enthusiasm for discussing the prospects for the EC[3] of a united Germany.

Although the climate since then has improved dramatically the American presence in Western Europe remains indispensable. It is fashionable these days to berate the US and to call for a Europe without America (see, for example Palmer, 1987) but the long-term implications of a putative American decoupling from Europe are barely touched upon in most discussions. Arguably recent events in the USSR and Eastern Europe have strengthened the case for the US presence in Europe. For while *Perestroika* and the new thinking in the Kremlin have eased bloc-to-bloc confrontation, at the same time they have undermined Moscow's grip within the Soviet bloc. These crises arising there have a strong nationalistic flavour and are reminiscent of the pre-war state of unrest in Central Europe.

Should the present fragile *status quo* break down it is highly unlikely that the EC in its present form could cope. Given the historical legacy and the unresolved issues left by the last war it is highly unlikely that Western European states in any combination could cope effectively on their own with crises of such magnitude. At the heart of the matter, of course, lies the division of Germany. Thus whereas France, Britain and other Western powers can talk about a policy towards Eastern Europe, the FRG is directly affected by developments in Eastern Europe (see Gordon *et al.* 1987).

The EC in the 1990s: a civilian or security power?

The EC's new dynamism, after years of stagnation, coincides with profound and unexpected changes in the world scene whose main features are the termination of 'the second cold war' and a rapid *rapprochement* between the superpowers. The signing of the INF Treaty in December 1987, was hailed as a landmark. While many thorny problems still remain, the temperature of superpower relations nevertheless changed dramatically. The signs are that this process will continue and gain further momentum in future. What are the implications of this for Western Europe in general and the EC in particular? A key theme in this chapter has been the close interaction between domestic EC developments and superpower relations in the past two decades. A fundamental problem for West Europeans is their difficulty in deciding what kind of relationship the US and the USSR should develop. This is understandable, of course, considering the overwhelming weight of both powers on Europe, and West Europe's limited leeway. This situation feeds recurring European suspicions about superpower collision or collusion which, it is felt, invariably impedes European integration. In the early 1970s, for instance, President Pompidou confided that the West Europeans had to be cautious lest the Russians and the Americans neutralize them by thwarting total integration in the EC (Brandt, 1978).

Similar warnings have been heard again recently. However, while there are certain similarities between the early 1970s and early 1980s, there are also marked differences. First, the EC is today much stronger than fifteen years ago. The creation of the Single Market marks a qualitative leap forward that is capable of generating spillovers in other areas. By contrast, in the early 1970s there was plenty of euphoria in the wake of the first enlargement but little substance. Indeed lack of progress in EC policies prompted Jean Monnet to press for closer cooperation on international political issues so that there would be a semblance of momentum (Monnet, 1978). In the late 1980s the situation has arguably been reversed. Moreover, despite remaining vestiges of opposition to full integration, the EC nowadays is more confident in itself and less uncertain about its future. Without being complacent, therefore, it is valid to assume that the Twelve would be able to confront a major crisis, such as the 1973 Middle East war, more effectively than in the past. A second difference is the decline of the superpowers. This in turn will have considerable impact on their capacity to act. Moreover, preoccupation with economic problems at home will weaken their inclination to undertake costly actions abroad. It should be remembered that in both the US and the USSR present problems are attributed to 'over-stretching' (Kennedy, 1988) which implies that 'contracting' might not be a bad thing after all.

It would, of course, be simplistic and unrealistic to assume that we are on the eve of a peaceful superpower disengagement from Europe which would end the legacy of Yalta. Both superpowers, particularly the US, have a number of options available. For the US economic decline most probably will make tempting protectionism combined with a more unilateralist approach to security. Above all, it may foster the 'specter of American strategic decoupling from Europe' (de Santis 1988) which has been a recurring theme since the early 1970s. Similar warnings in the past proved unfounded and there is the reassuring counter-argument that the US presence in Europe serves American interests just as much, if not more, than those of the Europeans. Yet American economic decline compounded by rising trade friction with Western Europe might occasion a major shift in US policies. As Phil Williams points out, 'the policy framework that has prevailed since 1951 was predicated upon certain assumptions about American primacy. As these assumptions become increasingly inappropriate to a declining superpower, so the policy itself, or what is left of it, will appear outmoded or unsustainable' (Williams, 1988).

However, while US withdrawal from Europe is a more likely prospect than in the past, it is neither inevitable nor imminent. The US dilemma is that a diminution of its influence in Western Europe, especially if combined with a loosening of the Soviet grip on Eastern Europe, might lead to greater political assertiveness in Eastern Europe and a drive for military integration in Western Europe. This could be a recipe for regional instability and detrimental to all parties concerned. After all, few would like to see an inherently troublesome Europe returning to its turbulent pre-war past.

If decoupling from Western Europe is not an attractive option for the US, a reshuffling of the international economic system, which is presumably within its reach, may be more appealing. Such reshuffling is canvassed in Washington and it seems to have strong advocates including Brzezinski. He has argued that US global primacy in the world is challenged not by the Soviet Union but by the erosion of its own economic position. A way out favoured by Brzezinski is a turn to the Pacific and the construction of a global partnership between the US and Japan. The creation of an *Amerippon* free trade zone could provide leadership in tackling international economic problems, curb the trend to protectionism, and enhance global political consultations and joint (US–Japanese) 'strategizing' (Brzezinski, 1988). Although Brzezinski does not refer to West Europe, his scheme contains a thinly veiled warning to West Europeans. Similar views are in vogue in the US and are not confined to a particular section of public opinion. Wallerstein, for example, has called for 'a reshuffling of alliances under American guidance' which he believes to be politically possible. While it is difficult to foresee who would end up where in the event of reshuffling, he too sees as a likely outcome the creation of a Pacific zone under US, Japanese and Chinese leadership. Western Europe might end up worse off considering its perennial problems and the inadaptability of its institutions (Wallerstein, 1988). Whether the US will press ahead with the Pacific option or seek alternative strategies in the years to come, is hard to say. Much will depend on its domestic politics in the post-Reagan era, on its capacity to reinvigorate its economy and on the shape of the international economy. One thing is clear, however. Whereas in the 1970s and 1980s Washington tried to maintain its global primacy by making more use of its diplomatic-military assets and by concentrating on the USSR and China, in the 1990s it will have to pay more attention to economic and trade issues. Arguably, therefore, a reshuffling of the present international economic arrangements and attainment of a new equilibrium with Western Europe and Japan, more favourable to the US, would be more attractive than tinkering with military-security imperatives, a risky exercise with unpredictable results.

Issues that will figure prominently in the 1990s will be of a different nature to those of the early to mid-1980s. Economic and trade issues particularly among the US, Japan and Western Europe will become more politicized. Similarly, although Third World crises will continue to flare up due to unsurmountable economic and social tensions, they will not endanger international stability to the degree they did in the 1970s and 1980s. The end of the Gulf war, the manifest fatigue of the Iranian revolution, the Soviet withdrawal from Afghanistan, moves for a settlement in Kampuchea, Southern Africa, Cyprus and elsewhere are encouraging trends. At the same time, the United Nations' role in resolving disputes is experiencing a spectacular revival which is gathering momentum. It is in the EC's interests that this process is strengthened.

If the above assessment is sound, then what are the options for the Community? Is the concern of the early 1980s with security still valid or should there be a return to the civilian power stance of the 1970s? The answer depends largely on the exigencies of the international system and on the capacity of the EC to resolve remaining institutional and political problems in the coming years. With regard to the former point, while the international climate is more relaxed today than in the early 1980s, it would be unwise for the EC to be complacent and turn its back on its security requirements. The latter point deserves more detailed elaboration.

Title Three of the SEA on the political and economic aspects of security is a move in the right direction. From now on, as many, notably MEPs, argue all possibilities should be explored to widen the EC's mandate in political and security matters (Januzzi, 1988). At the same time a more difficult task would be to bring the WEU closer to the EC. The ultimate objective should be to bring the WEU within the orbit of the EC[3] (Heath, 1988), an admittedly difficult task in view of Irish neutrality and the Danes' lack of enthusiasm. The WEU's adoption of a security platform in October 1987 is an encouraging development. Another encouraging sign is that the WEU, after years of hesitation, decided last year to start negotiations with Spain and Portugal for their accession to the modified Brussels Treaty.

Spanish accession to the WEU might also have beneficial effects in facilitating a compromise to the Gibraltar dispute with Great Britain. It should be recalled that intra-EC disputes like Gibraltar or Northern Ireland are excluded from EPC deliberations. On the other hand the modified Brussels Treaty (WEU) stipulates that disputes among its members should be referred to the International Court of Justice (Article 10). This procedure was designed in order to resolve stinging disputes among WEU members who in case of war would have to fight side by side. The problem with this procedure, however, is that it draws unwelcome publicity and it may be a hindrance to quiet diplomacy. Therefore it was agreed by Madrid and London that Gibraltar would be exempted from this procedure and only disputes which might arise after Spain's (and Portugal's) accession to the WEU would be referred to the Hague. Nevertheless the WEU is considered as the most appropriate forum to work for a setlement of the Gibraltar problem (*Financial Times*, 25 October 1988).

Eventually the increased overlap in the membership of the EC and WEU might help to overcome a number of institutional problems, including the seat of the WEU's scattered bodies, the Assembly's composition and problems of coordinating the work of the EC and WEU Councils (Tsakaloyannis, 1988).

The experience of the past two decades or so is that the separation of the EC's economic from its political objectives has been detrimental to its development. At least implicitly the SEA recognizes this. The future policy implications are that the EC should refrain from taking any steps which might dilute its cohesion, political and economic. At present its new economic dynamism and '1992' have aroused considerable interest in the outside world not least in Europe, East, North and South. The recent agreement with COMECON (and the latter's recognition of the EC) is evidence of this. However, equally important, has been EFTA's considerable interest in the EC.

While the EC would gain substantially from an enlargement to the North, political considerations cannot be ignored. This means that a further EC enlargement should not undermine its recent advances nor should it impede its future development. For example, EFTA countries exploring prospects for EC membership should not use Irish neutrality as a precedent. It is worth pondering the effects on the EC if Switzerland, which is against membership of the United Nations on grounds of neutrality, ever joined (Saint-Ouen, 1988). The EC's economic muscle, especially after 1992, will have a greater and more direct bearing on the outside world. Therefore the EC cannot be confined to a passive role merely reacting to outside pressures in a reflexive, disorderly manner. This, of course, opens new possibilities but at the same time creates more responsibilities. It means that the EC will have to pay more heed to the effects on the outside world of its domestic policies, notably those of the Single Market. It may be argued that the Community has to put its own house in order before it can address these questions. Nevertheless, until now it has been rather reticent to tackle this issue. Moreover, statements attributed to EC officials have fed existing anxieties and apprehensions in the Third World and have caused suspicions and irritations in Washington. The image of a 'fortress Europe' therefore, could be very harmful to the EC's long term economic *and political* interests. The problem is compounded by the fact that the creation of an internal market will affect EC-US relations in the security field. Already the EC Commission has put forward proposals for the legal extension of the EC's external tariff to cover military imports from third countries, mainly from the US. Although the practical effects of this move are, for the time being at least, limited, its long-term implications are considerable. As a Commission official noted, this could be 'the thin end of a big wedge', for it could facilitate an historic extension of Community competence to cover European defence industry, if not policy (*Financial Times*, 1 August 1988).

Concluding remarks

As the 1980s draws to a close, the European Community seems to have come full circle. After the erratic 1970s and early 1980s, it has entered a period of consolidation. The Single Market and the SEA's endorsement hold prospects for qualitative leaps and spillovers undreamt of since the early 1960s. If there is an imbalance in need of correction it is on the political security side where the possibilities offered by the SEA in generating progress are rather confined. As we enter the 1990s, therefore, the EC finds itself at a critical juncture. Internal and external events have rendered the 'civilian' or 'security' dilemma obsolete. Therefore, the EC will find it increasingly difficult to separate economic and trade issues from security questions. To put it another way, what might appear to the Twelve as 'low' politics could be viewed as 'high' politics to outsiders and vice versa. This implies that the Twelve will have to use their economic clout prudently and with circumspection, and that they will be compelled to do more for their own security. The EC's overriding objective should be to steer the international system towards a course of evolutionary change and ensure that the transition to a multi-polar world takes place in an orderly manner. To do so, however, the Twelve need a common purpose and a clearer perspective of their position in the world.

Notes

1. For an informative account of the Franco-German record in the EC see Walter Schütze (1987), 'Franco-German Relations and European Cooperation', *European Affairs*, no.4. On the historical evolution of the Franco-German relationship see Haig Simonian, (1985), The *Privileged Partnership*, Oxford, OUP; also Werner Weidenfeld (1988), '25 Years After 22 January 1963: The Franco-German Friendship treaty', *Aussenpolitik*, **39**, no.1.
2. For a more extended discussion on this subject see P. Tsakaloyannis (1987), 'Political Constraints for an Effective Community Foreign Policy', in J.K. De Vree, P. Coffey and R.H. Lauwaars (eds), *Towards a European Foreign Policy*, Dordrecht, Martinus Nijhoff, esp. pp.151-4 and comments by Peter R. Baehr, pp.157-60. On German reunification and the EC see S. Schulz (1984), 'Unfinished Business: The German National Question and the Future of Europe', *International Affairs*, **60**, no.3.
3. This is the view of the Vredeling. Report on the IEPG (1986), *Towards a Stronger Europe*, Brussels, December, especially volume one, pp.13-15.

References

Brandt, W. (1978), *People and Politics*, London, Collins.

Bull, H. (1984), 'Civilian Power Europe: A Contradiction in Terms?', *Journal of Common Market Studies*, **21**, nos 2-3, 1982. 'European Self-Reliance and the Reform of NATO', *Foreign Affairs*, **66**, no.4.

Brzezinski, Z. (1988), 'America's New Geostrategy', *Foreign Affairs*, **66**, no.4.

Calleo, D (1988), *Beyond American Hegemony: The Future of the Western Alliance*, Brighton, Wheatsheaf (for the Twentieth Century Fund).

Delors, J. (1987), 'SEA: A New Frontier, Programme of the Commission for 1987', *EC Bulletin*, **1**, 60.

Duchêne, F. (1973), 'The European Community and the Uncertainties of Interdependence' in M. Kohnstam and W. Hager (eds), *A Nation Writ Large? Foreign Policy Problems Before the European Community*, London, Macmillan.

Fontaine, P. (1987), La Défense Européenne: les occasions manquées et les chances de renouveau, *Revue du Marché Commun*, no.307, May-June.

Furdson, E. (1980), *The European Defence Community: A History*, London, Macmillan.

Galtung, J. (1973), *The European Community: A Super power in the Making?* London, Allen and Unwin.

Gordon, L. (1987), *Eroding Empires: Western Relations with Eastern Europe*, Washington, The Brookings Institute.

Groeben, H., van der (1987), *The European Community. The Formative Years: The Struggle to Establish the Common Market*, Brussels, The European Perspectives Series.

Heath, E. (1988), 'European Unity Over the Next Ten Years: From Community to Union?', *International Affairs*, **64**, no.2, Spring.

Ifestos, P. (1987), *European Political Co-operation: Towards a Framework of Supranational Diplomacy*, London, Gower.

Januzzi, G. (1988), 'Political and Economic Aspects of European Security', *The International Spectator*, **23**, Jan-March.

Kaiser, K., Merlini, C., de Mondbriant, T., *et al.*, (1985), *European Community Progress or Decline?*, London, RIIA.

Kennedy, P. (1988), *The Rise and Fall of the Great Powers: Economic Change and Military Conflict from 1500 to 2000*, London, Unwin Hyman.

Luif, P. (1989), 'The European Neutrals and Economic Integration in Western Europe', *Annuaire Européen*, **34**.

Monnet, J. (1978), *Memoirs*, London, Collins.

Palmer, J. (1987), *Europe without America?* Oxford, Oxford University Press.

Poetering H-G. (1986), 'Germany's and France's Interest in European Security Policy', *Aussenpolitik*, **37**.

Porte, A.W. de, (1979), *Europe between the Superpowers: The Enduring balance*, New Haven, Yale.

Regelsberger, E. (1988), EPC in the 1980s: Reaching another Plateau?' in A. Pipjers *et al.* (eds), *European Political Cooperation in the 1980s: A Common Foreign Policy for Western Europe?*, The Hague, Nijhoff.

Saint-Ouen, F. (1988), 'Facing European Integration: The Case of Switzerland', *Journal of Common Market Studies*, **26**.

Santis, H. de (1988), 'The New détente and Military Strategic Trends in Europe', *SAIS Review*, 8.

Schmitt, H.A. (1987), Journal of Modern History, **59**, 564-6.

Schoutheete, P. de (1987), *La coopération politique Européene*, Brussels, Labor.

Stuart, D. (forthcoming), 'Hegemonic Decline and NATO', *Armed Forces and Society*.

Taylor, A.J.P. (1974), *The Struggle for Mastery in Europe: 1848-1918*, London, Oxford University Press.

Tsakaloyannis, P. (1985), *The Reactivation of WEU: The Effects on the EC and its Institutions*, Maastricht, EIPA.

Tsakaloyannis, P. (ed.) (1988), *Western European Security in a Changing World: From the Reactivation of the WEU to the SEA*, Maastricht, EIPA.

Wallace, H. and W. and Webb, C. (eds) (1983), *Policymaking in the European Community*, Chichester, Wiley.

Wallerstein, I. (1988), 'European Unity and its Implications for the International System' in B. Hettne (ed.), *Europe: Dimensions of Peace*, London, Zed Books and the UN Universities.

Williams, P. (1988), 'West European Security and American Troop Withdrawals', *Political Quarterly*, **59**.

14 US–EC relations

Roy H. Ginsberg

Introduction

The EC–US relationship of the 1990s will be vastly different from any period since the 1950s. The difference is in the two sides' relative strength, in tenor and emotive quality, in sea changes internationally and in the extent to which both must walk a tightrope, a tightrope that may unravel at any time given the delicate balance on which their sensitive relationship depends. Above all, the biggest change has less to do with the US than with the EC.

The EC has come of age. It is no longer as dependent on the United States as it once was. It has a sense of self-worth and mission in the world. Its view does not always gel with America's. Its foreign policy actions give it an independent foreign policy personality that often put it at odds with its old patron, adding grist to the maturing, less harmonious bilateral relationship (Ginsberg, 1989). The EC's foreign policy actions in Central America, the Mediterranean and the Middle East differ from those of the US. It has become more self-assertive. Through EPC, the EC states have extended foreign policy activities into the realm of security politics. EC members of WEU, a collective self-defence arrangement dating back to 1954, have sought to revive a European security identity distinct from America's.

The EC has become an economic giant, and in many respects a much larger economic entity than the United States. With its 320 million people, the EC has a larger GNP and a much larger share of international import/export trade than the US. It is the largest trader in the world. The EC is an economic competitor of the US. It has had a merchandise trade surplus with the US since 1983,(then only $1.3 billion) rising to $23 billion in 1987, representing 14 per cent of the US total merchandise trade deficit of $158 billion (USITC, 1988). Behind the EC trade surplus with the US is the superior performance of the West German economy. In 1987, West Germany had a trade surplus with the world of $70 billion, putting it ahead of the US as the world's largest single exporter. In the most divisive issue in bilateral relations, the EC has stood up to US pressure to reform the CAP by refusing to eliminate export subsidies and other farm aids the US views as damaging to its trade. Nothing is more exasperating to US policymakers as the EC's massive entrance into international farm export trade, by using export subsidies to garner new shares of foreign markets at the expense of US farm exports. The EC and the US have the world's largest two-way trading relationship, which in 1987 amounted to $137 billion (USITC, 1988), indicating the stakes each side has in the other.

Turkey has applied to become the EC's thirteenth member. Others in Europe are expected to apply in the 1990s, perhaps even one or two of the European neutrals. Expansion from six in 1951 to possibly thirteen or fourteen members in the 1990s points to the enduring notion of European unity. Other European states are contemplating membership just as a new self-confidence underlies the EC states' commitment to complete the internal market. Many informed observers anticipate that during the 1990s the EC will generally succeed in its quest to finish what it began in 1958.

As the EC and US enter the 1990s, the relationship is based more on equality and interdependence and less on inequality and dependence. As increased symmetric interdependence can trigger differences, since both have much at stake in one another, transatlantic relations can be expected to remain on a rocky, or move to an even rockier, course. As we are, and hope to remain, in global peacetime, the sense of urgency that once served to cement bilateral ties has given way to the competition and rivalry expected in peacetime as all states, friends and foes, attempt to function in a complex, multi-actor, fast-changing world.

The political implications of a more economically vibrant Western Europe after 1992 for EC–US relations are not difficult to fathom. To the extent that a stronger European economy will build European political self-confidence and thus encourage further assertion in world affairs, more confrontation in relations with the US is likely. There is now a need, more than ever before, for the two sides to arrive at a new *modus operandi* to manage relations into the 1990s. Without better management of the world's largest two-way trade relationship, of the Western world's economic and trading system and of the military deterrent that protects the bread and butter of over a half billion EC and American citizens, we can expect unchecked divisions to weaken Western civilization and the political and economic system that derives from it.

Table 14.1, shows that several common aspects order EC–US relations: – historical and trade ties; security links through NATO (all EC states except Ireland are tied to NATO); and similar political and economic systems based on common civilization. Yet for each aspect of the bilateral relationship, there is a tug between centripetal forces – that hold it together, such as trade – and centrifugal forces that pull it apart, such as foreign policy differences. There was a time in the early post-war era when the centrifugal forces were either nonexistent or underplayed for the sake of broader amity. After post-war reconstruction, when the glow of allied victory and any urgency beyond containment of communism receded, centrifugal forces challenged the assumptions behind the centripetal forces and the depth of commitment beyond trade and investment flows. Centrifugal forces produced petty differences that threatened broader ties. The existence of the relationship now depends on a balance struck between those contending forces by politically strong and committed Atlanticist leaders, leaders committed to nurturing European–US relations. Domestic and international pressures that work against transatlantic accord must not be underestimated. The centrifugal forces have grown in number and substance since the 1960s, as the US, the EC and the surrounding international system have changed. So far, Atlanticist leaders have been able to maintain balance by underscoring the importance of the centripetal forces. However, a gradual transition in the EC's American relationship has been at work since the 1970s, causing inevitable frictions in the bilateral relationship. Whether the triumph of centripetal over centrifugal forces will continue remains the most critical question facing bilateral relations today.

This chapter briefly examines four periods in bilateral relations as they developed over four decades. Historical examination enables us to explore

Table 14.1 EC–United States relations: the balance sheet

Aspect of relationship	Centripetal Forces	Centrifugal Forces
Civilization	common Judeo-Christian heritage	different political cultures
Historical experiences	wartime and post-war cohesion; ethnic and trade links	end to post-war cohesion in 1970s; divergent historical ties with LDCs and Soviet bloc have led to foreign policy disputes; growing proportion of Americans of Asian and African descent relative to those of Anglo-Saxon descent, diluting ethnic ties
Political-economic systems	pluralist democracies, mixed capitalist, developed economies; mutual commitment to human rights and democratic practices around the world	mixed pluralist political-economic systems allow such special interest groups as producers to demand protectionist action by the state that when taken can disrupt overall ties; different views on social welfare and state intervention in society
Strategic security	collective self-defence through sister organization, NATO; equal stakes in the defence of Western democracies against the common enemy	EC states are ultimately dependent on US for strategic security; concern about superpower nuclear accords affecting European security; existence of pacifist-neutralist sentiment in West Europe that calls into question efficacy of nuclear deterrence; rising number question about US reliability in wartime; declining spectre of Soviet invasion of West Europe that points to differing perceptions of the common enemy; rising number question urgency behind the alliance; EC's geographic proximity to the East makes it more vulnerable and sensitive to pressure
Interdependence	symmetric trade, investment, and political inter-dependence	asymmetric monetary and strategic security inter-dependence

International trade	common stakes in liberal world trade order; huge stakes in world trade	politicization of world trade has led to rise in area and number of EC–US conflicts; EC's heavy dependence on import/export trade makes it more vulnerable than US to pressure; differences over export subsidies/credits to garner shares of markets
Bilateral trade	heavy dependence on each other's huge markets	bitter commercial rivalry in one another's markets; US merchandise trade deficit with EC; differences over scope and level of state aid to industry; use of non-tariff barriers to protect domestic producer
bilateral investment	heavy dependence on each other's huge investment markets	barriers to trade in services and investment
leadership	committed and politically strong leaders capable of balancing bilateral relations so that no one dispute poisons broader ties	uncommitted or weak leaders susceptible to producer group protectionist calls; less capable of providing balance to overall relationship
international system	members of a small group of two dozen advanced, developed, mixed capitalist democratic states in an international system of 170 states, many hostile to the West	changes in the international system from bipolarity and US hegemony to multipolarity and interdependence complicate bilateral relations, ease relations with other partners, reduce US influence over EC, and give the EC the environmental incentives needed to develop its own interests in the world
Foreign policy	broad accord on long-term Western goals; mutual sensitivities to pressures from the non-Atlantic outside world	broad discord over the means to achieve common goals; EC foreign policy independent of, and conflicting with, US; disagreement over foreign policy methods; lack of mechanism to coordinate foreign policy outside NATO and EC institutional constraints; lack of coherent policies toward one other; lack of division of labour in conduct of Western foreign policy interest

themes, trends and patterns as we search for root explanations of the problems in bilateral relations today. Enough time has passed since the early post-war era to look back more dispassionately – without cold war rhetoric – to determine what brought the two sides together and why. If we examine the EC–US relationship shorn of previous biases and normative judgements, we are more likely to unveil the truth about its bases and origins. This chapter also identifies and analyses some of the outstanding issues and suggests prescriptions for improvement. Three central themes underlie bilateral relations.

First, although bilateral trade differences have always been as variable as the wind, the root of today's trade problems is no different than the trade problems of the early 1960s when the effect of the CAP began to harm American farm exports to the EC. To achieve food self-sufficiency the Europeans poured large sums of public funds into the agricultural economy. As farm production rose through state intervention, certain US farm exports to the EC declined. Increased farm production led to large surpluses which the EC then exported with subsidies to garner new markets. The effect in some instances has been to undercut world market prices and thus US farm income. US shares of food markets in certain foreign countries dropped as EC shares rose, embittering the US farm community. What has not changed is:

- Sharp disagreement over each other's farm support practices to protect domestic producers from outside competition and gyrations of world market conditions. Both interfere with market forces to support farming, but do so differently (Gardner, 1982). Disagreement persists over the scope and level of state farm support.

- Bitter competition for scarce foreign import markets continues. EC heavy dependence on import/export trade puts it at a disadvantage as this restricts action and renders a *modus operandi* with the US on the politics of world trade difficult if not impossible to reach.

- The effect on the European economy of swings in the value of the US dollar and interest rates set by the US Federal Reserve Board continue to render the EC dependent on US monetary policy and economic performance.

Second, unlike the persistence of trade and monetary problems that have always haunted relations, political, diplomatic and security problems have cropped up in the past two decades that were nonexistent or dormant in the 1950s and 1960s.

These problems have materialized as the EC–US relationship has become more politicized; as the EC continues to assert itself in international diplomacy and translates its global economic power into political clout abroad; as European and US approaches to international problems diverge; and as world politics and commerce fuse to make their distinction illusory. The extent of disagreement may be no greater than it was before. However, it causes greater disruption as a stronger Europe faces a relatively weaker America in the 1980s and beyond. What makes the current crisis of confidence historically dangerous is that the two-way economic and trade problems are compounded by serious differences over international politics and security. If such differences are left unchecked by apathy or ignorance they may disrupt the normally stable, but mutually inclusive, NATO alliance as the bases that underpinned relations in the 1950s weaken in the 1980s and 1990s.

Third, the EC–US relationship does not function in a vacuum. The international environment exerts an enormous influence over bilateral relations. EC–US problems must be viewed in relation to US and European ties to the USSR, China, the LDCs, and the advanced developed states and the international economic system. The international environment could be conducive to good relations in times of economic prosperity and regional peace; spur joint action in the face of a Soviet threat to West Europe; or sour relations in times of world recession and with differing perceptions of how to handle relations with the non-Atlantic outside world. The international environment is the more problematic as it is frequently viewed differently from each side of the Atlantic. The strife in Nicaragua comes to mind. What appears to the US government as a threat to national and hemispheric interests appears to the Europeans as an insignificant domestic affair of an obscure banana republic not worthy of superpower intervention.

Definition, structure and function of bilateral relations

EC–US relations are an important part of broader transatlantic relations. Transatlantic relations refer to all multilateral ties – military (NATO); economic (OECD), Western Economic Summits; trade (GATT), United Nations' commodity agreements, the EC–US annual ministerial, Quadrilateral talks, energy (IEA); and monetary (IMF and the World Bank) – among the countries of, and institutions, common to, North America and Western Europe. The term 'Western Alliance' in its broadest sense refers to the host of economic, political and social links among the advanced developed capitalist Western democracies that set them apart from the rest of the world. Their number at twenty-four is small, roughly 14 per cent of the world's 170 states. Transatlantic relations also refer to the spirit of shared beliefs and understanding among these states based on a common civilization and similar political, economic and social systems.

Somewhat different is the European–US relationship which refers to all multilateral and bilateral links – economic, political, diplomatic and security – between the West European states and the US. More limited is the EC–US relationship which centres on bilateral trade. However, one can no longer limit EC–US bilateral relations to trade as political, diplomatic and security issues have infiltrated them to make the distinction between what is commercial and what is political purely an illusion. The politicization of trade relations mirrors politicization of economic and trade relations worldwide. The ability to trade, and the importance of economic questions to national security, point to a broader concept of state security – one that does not rely solely on the military aspect. After all, in global peacetime, in a highly interdependent international system, the ability of a state to provide for the welfare of its public and to protect it from commercial threats from the outside, such as an embargo, is as much a question of physical security as an outside military threat. The politicization of international commerce, and the heightened importance of commerce to the question of national security, points to problems for NATO and the EC as organizations unable to cope adequately with some of these developments. Outside NATO's regionally limited purview (the North Atlantic) and the EC's legal purview (trade and civilian politics), there are no mechanisms to coordinate the EC's and America's foreign policies. This becomes painfully clear when threats to western commercial interests in the Persian Gulf require but do not enjoy collaboration.

The dividing line between EC–US and European–American relations is now more difficult to draw than at any other time in the past forty years. Of the twenty West European states, twelve are in the EC; the rest are affiliated to the EC through an industrial free trade area (EFTA) or by associate membership (Turkey, Malta, and Cyprus). Trade relations interface with political-diplomatic-security issues. Of NATO members, all but the US and Canada are either members of, or closely affiliated to the EC. A controversial overlap between the EC (in EPC) and NATO, much to the chagrin of the US is the discussion within EPC of certain aspects of Western security which in the past would have only been discussed in NATO. Continued EC–US discord on foreign policy questions in the 1990s and beyond can be expected. Some leading scholars of bilateral relations have suggested that we ought to view Western Europe as a whole configuration of economic, trade, political and security relationships, rather than splitting up our examination of West Europe into the EC, EFTA, NATO, WEU etc. The logic here points again to the inextricable overlap between the membership and function of these bodies to make their distinctions less and less critical as dividing lines blur.

To handle diplomatic and commercial relations, the US and the EC exchange diplomatic missions and heads of delegations who have ambassadorial rank. The staffs of each delegation enjoy full diplomatic immunity. Senior EC and US officials used to meet biannually to consult on economic and some political issues. However,with the frequency of official high-level meetings between the two sides in recent years, in such forums as the OECD, Economic Summits and the UN, they have been replaced with ministerial meetings every December. Members of the European Parliament and US Congress exchange regular official visits to discuss mutual political and economic problems, although how much substance in bilateral relations is dealt with, and how much common ground is found, is questionable. A crisis management mechanism under the EC's 'Gymnich formula' has been set up to handle EPC foreign policy deliberations that affect the interests of the US (and other close partners). When EC members in EPC discuss or act upon an issue of vital interest to the US government, the EC Council Presidency consults the US government.

At the commercial level, there is no EC–US cooperation accord. Trade is regulated by the GATT where the EC negotiates for its members. There are six multilateral forums through which the EC bodies and/or members and the US intersect, but that are not directly linked to the EC–US relationship: economic cooperation and development among the Western developed states is promoted through the OECD; energy cooperation is attempted through their mutual membership, as large energy consumers and importers, in IEA (although France is not a member); discussions of trade and payments' problems and international politics are conducted at the annual Western Economic Summits where the EC Commission and Council Presidents join the US President and leaders of the other major industrialized states (and at the less regular meetings of the Trilateral Commission); multilateral commodity trade is governed by several UN international agreements to which the US and the EC adhere; and consultations between the EC and the US at the follow-up meetings of the Conference on Security and Cooperation in Europe (CSCE).

Why study these relations? It is both significant and timely to study EC–US relations because:

(1) both have huge stakes in world trade accounting for nearly half of all world imports and exports. Both have favoured a liberal world trade order to varying degree by concluding various GATT rounds of multilateral trade negotiations (MTNs) to reduce tariffs.
(2) Both have huge stakes in the defence of the Western political and economic system against the Soviet military threat. NATO is weakened when trade disputes disrupt it. Both have equally vital stakes in the balance between their trade and strategic security relationships as there is much more to lose than to gain from a rupture in civil, balanced and mutually beneficial relations.
(3) Both face essentially similar economic and social problems as the Western world's largest advanced industrialized states, so that their collaboration at all levels is mutually advantageous and vital to solving common problems.
(4) Both share an intense economic and political interdependent relationship and are the two main pillars of the Western politico-economic system. Without the two there would be no GATT, no liberal world trade order.

The security of the developed capitalist-democratic states outside NATO hinges on amicable transatlantic relations and prosperity. The EC–US trade relationship deeply affects the broader Western international economic system. Any cracks in the economic wing of the Western alliance could send the wrong signal to the USSR and provide opportunities to test Western military resolve even in this current era of 'new thinking' in foreign policy proferred by President Gorbachev. To the less developed states (LDCs), EC–US cooperation and accord on how best to assist their development needs is of paramount importance if the LCDs are to move ahead economically.

EC–US relations have undergone fundamental change with the closing of the post-war era in the 1970s. In the 1980s and 1990s, the relationship is characterized by a paradox: commercial rivalry and competition on the one hand, and military and economic cooperation, on the other. As the following historical account shows, the very nature and process of European as opposed to transatlantic integration made EC–US conflict inevitable.

Historical evolution of EC–US relations

Relations may be categorized into four distinct periods with definitive historical contours: 1948-62; 1963-70; 1971-80; and 1981–present. Examination of these periods points to the root of today's differences between the two parties and illuminates some of the reasons behind Europe's quest for foreign policy actions independent of the United States. Six observations may be made about the relationship that apply to all four periods:

(1) The US has been a fairly constant supporter of the idea of European unity in a general sense, first as an active proponent even when EC policies negatively affected US trade interests, and later in much more rhetorical and less convincing terms with less patience in accepting costs of discriminatory EC trade policies. Yet beyond the rhetoric of support, the US does not have a coherent, much less an effective, 'EC policy'.

(2) The US assumed that a united Europe would share its burden of defending the West and managing the international economy. Because the US viewed the EC as a component of its post-war policy, it has been unable to credit the EC with its own separate interests (Warnecke, 1976).

(3) The relationship has a turbulent history. An incompatibility has always existed in US policy between its goal of a post-war multilateral liberal economic order and support for EC integration, which called for some trade discrimination against non-members.

(4) The EC has generally not formed a coherent, much less an effective, 'US policy', even though the EC has well-formed policies toward many of the world's states and regions. Lack of a 'US policy' points to the members' varying views of how to conduct relations with the US and to the way in which the US has treated the EC, gyrating as it has between grand schemes of cooperation and 'divide and rule' tactics.

(5) As a general rule, most European and American leaders favour close and amicable trade ties. Their biggest difficulty is to ensure that divisive trade disputes do not affect the more consensual military security relationship in NATO. It is usually when influential domestic producer groups raise their voices in response to loss of trade in one another's markets that the relationship boils over into hostile words and actions.

(6) What sustains the EC–US trade relationship is dependence on one another's vast internal markets; common democratic beliefs; increasing isolation in a hostile anti-Western world; the common goal of a liberal world trade order given their large stakes in it and the calming effects of the less divisive military security alliance. The delicate balance struck between mutual trade and security interests constitutes the dynamic behind the relationship.

During the 1948-62 period, the US was a driving force in European reconstruction and integration. With exceptions (such as the 1956 Suez War when the US reacted very strongly against British and French involvement), both cooperated as allies and partners. Differences existed but both understood that what they had in common was more important than what divided them.

The roots of some current problems go back to this period. The US envisaged a unified EC partner – not a competitor – in its plan for a post-war, Atlantic-centred world trade and political order. The US sought to rebuild Europe as a major market outlet and to incorporate it into a new liberal, nondiscriminatory world trade order. Sensitive to the economic nationalism and trade protectionism of the inter-war years, the US sponsored the creation of GATT in 1947 to codify rules providing for fair and equal trade among members. Support for a revitalized Europe as a bulwark against the spread of communism and as an indispensable participant in the emergent liberal world trade order became the cornerstone of post-war US foreign policy.

The EC was partly a by-product of US support for European reconstruction based on the 1947 Marshall Plan – a massive injection of US economic aid (Johnson, 1980). Establishing the OECD in 1948, the US encouraged European governments to work together for economic reconstruction. The US also lent moral and diplomatic support to the European Payments Union (1950), the ECSC (1951), the European Defence Community (vetoed by France in 1954) and the European Economic Community and the European Atomic Energy Community (1957). Barred from East European markets, EC members were thrust into a more intense trade relationship with the US. Later, when the EC pursued its own commercial interests in Eastern Europe, fears were aroused in Washington of West European 'appeasement' of the communist East.

In return for a rebuilt and prosperous European partner, the US tolerated – perhaps underestimated – the costs to its foreign commerce of the high EC tariff barriers, export subsidies, EC tariff reductions for privileged non-members in the Mediterranean and elsewhere and competition with EC members in third markets. The seeds of future misunderstanding were sown with the EC's founding: the very notion of a common market – with its customs union and common external tariff (CET) – inevitably discriminates to some extent against non-members. It was thus no surprise that the EC would to some extent work against the US vision of the post-war world liberal economic order. What brought the two sides together in the 1950s – a mutual fear of Stalinist Russia, Soviet rejection of US reconstruction aid and the GATT, and the need for one another's markets – began to unravel in the 1960s as they began to find other lucrative markets, as the Soviet threat lessened, as *détente* took root and as long as the EC did not challenge US leadership of the world economy and the Atlantic Alliance.

By 1962, the US had begun to lose its influence over EC integration. Realizing that the EC could become a strong economic power in its own right and promulgate an independent foreign policy, President Kennedy announced his so-called 'Grand Design' in July 1962. The Grand Design was an overambitious attempt to redefine US–European relations, calling on the EC to be an equal partner of the US in managing bilateral relations (Kraft, 1962). The Grand Design endorsed EC integration and called for British accession to the EC. However, the EC was not ready to shoulder the burdens the US was attempting to place on it. General de Gaulle opposed the Grand Design as he favoured the EC developing into a French-led 'third force' in international relations. As the United States erred in expecting a cogent European response, its high hopes for the Grand Design quickly faded as the two sides entered the tumultuous 1963-70 period.

During 1963-70, the US and EC gyrated between insensitivity and hostility as they tried to adjust to their changing relative positions in the world. Little mutual cooperation and understanding developed. By the end of this period, other centres of international economic power had begun to emerge (Japan, OPEC, and the EC); the US was no longer in a position to dominate world trade. The strictly bipolar world configuration of the 1960s necessitated and simplified EC–US cooperation. The multipolar interdependent world configuration of the 1970s and beyond complicated, and added new pressures to, the relationship. The US found that outside NATO, its European allies had become competitors and, in some cases, even adversaries. Memories of wartime camaraderie and early post-war collaboration faded with the new generation of European youth; relations began to give way to what might be considered normal competition between states in global peace-time.

By the late 1960s, the US had begun to feel threatened by the EC as it grew in strength and function. Before then the EC had been too preoccupied with internal developments to challenge the primacy of US foreign policy leadership. EC integration reached a plateau by the late 1960s by which time the EC had secured the structural base upon which to assert itself in the outside world and became the vehicle through which its members projected both their policies for attaining competitive equality with US industry, and remnants of their former world roles. From the time the US balance of payments went into deficit in the late 1950s, the US began to focus on its own economic problems and less on Europe's. All along, the US calculated that any damage from EC integration to its producers would be compensated by the political advantages of an EC ally.

US support faltered in the 1960s as the EC was perceived to threaten US trade interests without political advantage (Morgan, 1976). In retrospect, six 'sore points' emerged during the period.

(1) In the early 1960s, the EC began to grant tariff reductions on certain imports from close trade partners in the Mediterranean and Africa. The US claimed this discriminated against its exports of like products to the EC and opposed the intent of nondiscriminatory world trade enshrined in the GATT.

(2) In 1963-4 the notorious Chicken War broke out between the EC and the US, presaging trade wars to come in the 1980s. The new CAP poultry policy in 1963 enabled the EC to set high import levies to protect the infant European industry from outside competition. This had a devastating effect on US shares of the EC market. Pressed by producer groups, the US retaliated by imposing high tariffs on imports of high-priced brandy, Volkswagen pick-up trucks, dextrine and potato starch from the EC (Talbot, 1978).

It became clear by 1967 when the CAP was extended to cover most major farm products that the Chicken War was less an issue in itself and more an early warning of bitter trade disputes to come. US exports of items covered by the CAP fell by nearly half in the last half of the 1960s as intra-EC trade and production rocketed. The punitive duties imposed by the US during the Chicken War remain testifying to the beginning of the end of a time when the US was willing to pay a heavy price for European integration.

(3) France's veto of US-supported British bids to join the EC (1963 and 1967), its break with the military command of NATO (1966), its boycott of the EC (1965-6) and its snub of membership in IEA quickened US disenchantment with EC integration and severely reduced its role in it.

(4) The Kennedy Round of MTNs proved the EC's ability to be tough and united in negotiations with the US; EC resolve caught the US off guard.

(5) EC members' silence over, or condemnation of, US participation in the Vietnam War heightened US resentment toward the European allies, awakened America's realization that EC members had their own foreign policy interests, and hastened the rift between European and US foreign policies.

(6) In the late 1960s, *détente* caused further division. Some EC members generally perceived the benefits of *détente* in terms of new market opportunities in Eastern Europe, whereas the US generally viewed it in terms of SALT and other areas of international politics. Europeans were anxious and felt helpless and inadequately informed about the US–Soviet dialogue and resented superpower talks on arms limitations that left their fate hanging in the balance.

The Nixon administration broke traditional US support for EC bodies, preferring instead bilateral ties with member governments even on affairs that clearly fell under the EC legal purview. It avoided dealing directly with the EC which seemed to it to be 'as mystifying as the Tibetan theocracy' (Schaetzel, p. 14). During this period, what the US assumed about the EC affected what the EC did (Diebold). A consistent US error has been to force relations with the EC into two familiar patterns: to treat it as if it were a nation-state or just another international organization (Schaetzel, 1975: 95). Coolness and indifference marked and marred the relationship after the 1967 Kennedy Round until the early 1970s.

In the 1971-80 period, US policy moved between unilateral neglect and bilateral cooperation, while the EC's relationship to the US shifted from client status and toward more independent foreign policy action. The pressures of coping with global interdependent life also bore on the need for the EC to act for itself in foreign affairs. A gradual transition began in the 1970s that led the EC's US relationship from one where it was a passive or reactive actor to one where it was more inclined to activate policies of its own toward the outside or to respond to external stimuli differently than would the US.

In the 1960s, the US ran increasingly large balance of payments deficits due in part to massive economic and military aid to allies, European accumulation of dollar holdings and a gold drain caused by their conversion into gold. US deficits helped generate an economic boom in the Atlantic world by constantly increasing liquidity in the international monetary system (Calleo, 1974). The US payments' crisis led the Nixon Administration to take unprecedented unilateral measures between 1971-3 to strengthen the dollar and combat domestic recession, without much prior consultation of the EC. It suspended gold payments for dollars; abandoned fixed exchange rates between the major currencies, leaving them to float freely in response to market forces; imposed temporary import levies on products not already subject to quotas; and temporarily embargoed soyabean exports. The Nixon actions shocked the Europeans because they abruptly ended the 1944 Bretton Woods agreements and altered the post-war multilateral cooperative approach to international monetary and trade relations. The Bretton Woods agreement set up an international monetary system in the form of a gold exchange standard based on the dollar (Calleo, 1974). The US functioned as the central banker. Suspension of dollar convertibility caused upward revaluation of the European currencies against the dollar. For the first time since 1945 a US administration treated the EC 'as it would a hostile state' (Schaetzel, 1975: 78).

This historical juncture marked an important turning point as the Europeans were spurred towards greater trade, monetary and political independence from the US. In a sense, the US again, although inadvertently, was helping the Europeans to integrate. However, this time it was not out of paternalism and sacrifice for the Europeans but out of pure self-interest and annoyance with the Europeans.

Britain's 1973 accession to the EC – long-encouraged by the US – was another indicator of change in European–US relations. Britain joined the EC in part to enhance is foreign policy interests just when the EC had begun to develop EPC as a forum for foreign policy coordination and consultation in areas that fell outside the Rome Treaty. Since the US was sceptical of EPC, the effect of EPC on both the broader transatlantic relationship and US leadership in the Western alliance, British accession heightened concern that the Europeans were moving away from an Atlanticist foreign policy orientation, even though the US and Britain did not really have the kind of 'special relationship' they once did. The proximity of British accession to the US announcement of the infamous 'Year of Europe' was not totally coincidental.

In 1973, there was a surprising, almost impetuous, brief turnabout in US attitudes toward the EC and NATO members. With the end of US involvement in Vietnam and new US relations with the USSR and China, the Nixon administration suddenly tried to reverse years of neglect of the European allies by announcing a Kennedy-like Grand Design – this time dubbed 'The Year of Europe'. Articulated by Secretary of State Kissinger, the US called for a new 'Atlantic Charter' to revive US–European relations. The US sought to redirect the development of EC foreign policy activity back to an Atlantic-based centre. Anticipating EPC's potential to challenge US leadership of the Western alliance,

Kissinger insisted that the US should be consulted on EC foreign policy actions or declarations before they were taken or made. The compromise came in June 1974 'Gymnich formula' whereby the EC agreed to inform friendly governments of EPC deliberations affecting them.

The Year of Europe was put forth just at a time when the former client was beginning to stress its own foreign policy identity, distinct from American patronage. Kissinger's inference that European interests were largely regional compared to US interests which were largely global struck an offensive chord. The net effect of unilateral and unfavourable US actions toward the EC during the 1971-3 period was to reduce European trust in the US. Europeans viewed the Year of Europe with suspicion and saw the US as patronizing and clumsy. Instead of the new Atlantic Charter called for by the US, the EC responded belatedly with a statement of principles that fell short of US hopes. The Grand Design and the Year of Europe were similar in that the US treated EC members as if they comprised a unified nation-state. Whereas Kissinger wanted to restore to the West a sense of common purpose, he only succeeded in highlighting its absence (Aron, 1977). The controversy was quickly overtaken by events in the Middle East in 1973-4.

Perhaps the most serious foreign policy split between the EC and the US was over divergent responses to the Yom Kippur War and the subsequent OAPEC embargo and OPEC price actions. US commitment to Israel conflicted with the EC's attempt at a more even-handed – some would say pro-Arab – policy. EC dependence on oil imports has always made it more vulnerable than the US to embargoes and price increases. The EC has taken special care not to offend Arab League members. What especially complicated European–US relations in this arena was the lack of institutional mechanisms for consultation and coordination when possible. The Arab-Israeli conflict fell outside NATO's limited regional purview and the EC's limited legal purview. In 1973-4, the US was angered by the EC's independent actions – and in some cases inactions – with regard to the Middle East crisis. Some EC actions that openly conflicted with US moves included:

(1) EC members' refusal to put their air bases at US disposal in its effort to resupply the Israeli war effort in October 1973.
(2) The EC communiqué of 15 December 1973 that called on all sides to take into account the legitimate rights of the Palestinians.
(3) French refusal to join the other eight members and the Commission in membership in the International Energy Agency in 1974.
(4) EC and Arab League members' creation of the Euro-Arab Dialogue in 1974.
(5) EC unity and resolve dissolving in its response to the oil embargo of the Netherlands.

Never before had EC members failed so miserably to act with resolve and unity on a trade issue (oil) that clearly came under the legal purview of the Rome Treaty. Treaty trade rules were violated by some EC members as they rushed to conclude bilateral trade accords with Arab oil producers. All members were bound by EC law to work within EC rules and regulations. Commission proposals for a joint response to the embargo were rejected by two member states. Any last minute hope for a common front fell apart at the Washington Energy Conference in 1974. Establishment in 1974 of the Euro-Arab Dialogue to forge economic, financial, technical and cultural links between the EC and Arab League members met harsh American criticism. However, the EC bowed to US pressure to keep discussions with the Arabs on a nonpolitical level. Yet, given the politically charged currents of the Middle East crisis, it would be naïve to believe that politics do not enter into discussions.

Two bright spots emerged in 1975 that foreshadowed improved relations for the rest of the decade. Cooperation between the two led to the conclusion of the Helsinki Accords and showed how receptive they could be to working together in an area of mutual concern and on an equal basis. In the 1975 Lomé Convention, the EC eliminated reverse preferences which pleased the US. In earlier trade accords with African associates, the EC not only offered tariff reductions for the signatories but itself received preferences. Bitterly attacked by the US as discriminatory against its trade, the Lomé Convention included only tariff reductions for the ACP states.

The Carter administration in the late 1970s took measures to improve political ties with the EC. Since many Europeans felt Carter's foreign policy lacked resolve – despite efforts to revive good relations with the EC – the EC continued to move along a more independent foreign policy course. Certainly differences between the two over the Middle East and other areas persisted. Sceptical of Camp David, the EC called in 1980 for a Palestinian homeland, Palestinian participation in peace talks and international guarantees of mutually recognized borders. Injection of a unified EC position – representing a break with US policy – continued to exacerbate relations well into the 1980s. One bright spot occurred in 1981 when EC members endorsed a plan to provide troops for a US-supported multilateral force to oversee Israeli disengagement from the Sinai – considered, by the way, as an integral part of the Camp David process. The EC itself backed participation of troops from four of the members. Without their participation, the multilateral force would have lacked a genuine international (certainly European) credibility.

In contrast, the EC's reluctant response to the Iranian hostage crisis in 1979-80 angered the US which expected more immediate and cogent sanctions. Divergent EC and US approaches to East-West relations were made more acute by their different reactions to the Soviet invasion of Afghanistan in late 1979. Again the US was disturbed by the EC's reluctance to impose more forceful and comprehensive sanctions against the USSR. In spite of these differences, the Carter administration took several actions to improve bilateral relations. In addition to concluding the tough-going Tokyo Round of MTNs and signing SALT II – both welcomed by the Europeans – President Carter lent support to the EC by:

(1) Paying an unprecedented official visit to the EC in 1979; although largely symbolic, it went a long way to reconfirming US backing of EC institutional development. It showed US capacity to facilitate EC institutional integration by dealing directly with EC bodies on a more equal footing.
(2) Directing the official foreign agricultural bureaucracy in Washington to accept the CAP as a *fait accompli* and to work with it.[1]
(3) Approving participation by the EC Commission President at the annual Western Economic Summits beginning in 1977.
(4) Assigning importance to the new biannual high-level EC–US consultations.
(5) Being the first US administration to give its blessing to EPC, previously considered anathema to America's grip over Western policy formation.

A new phase in EC–US relations began in 1981. The US began to emerge out of the introspection and neo-isolation of the post-Vietnam war era with a 'rambo-like' commitment to rebuild its own military strength *vis-à-vis* the USSR. The first Reagan term took a hard line on relations with the USSR and a dim view of international *détente*, particularly after the Soviet invasion of Afghanistan. It linked Soviet actions throughout the world to progress made in East-West trade liberalization and arms control negotiations. It was willing to use trade, when necessary, as a tool of foreign policy in confronting its adversaries. Concomitantly, the EC emphasized fashioning its own foreign policy actions independent of, or even complicating, US foreign policy actions. Committed to 'European *détente*' unlinked to Soviet actions elsewhere in the world, the EC did not generally share the US view of *détente* as a global matter linking all facets of East-West relations. More sensitive to export trade for a variety of historical and contemporary economic reasons, the EC was much less inclined to consider using trade as a lever in East-West relations. In addition to other foreign policy disputes over Central America, Poland and the Middle East, the trade relationship sank to an all-time low. With the most intractable recession since the Great Depression having wreaked havoc across the Atlantic in the early 1980s, the expanding number of calls from producers and workers on both sides for beggar-thy-neighbour trade policies – reminiscent of the interwar years – was taken seriously.

What goodwill the Carter administration tried to generate toward the EC was replaced by old economic antagonisms and heightened foreign policy differences as the Reagan administration took office. Whatever administration took office in 1981, EC–US relations were likely to have worsened because the bilateral relationship was going through historical changes. Like its predecessors, the Reagan administration supported the concept of a united Europe and a strong Atlantic alliance, but had also shown itself to be a formidable, no-nonsense protagonist of US producer interests *vis-à-vis* the EC and vociferously attacked the discriminatory effects of EC internal and external trade policies.

The first Reagan administration revived a catalogue of complaints against the CAP. It hoped to change EC farm policy through direct pressure and/or official complaints at the GATT, a development some in Europe believe will be the only way to achieve CAP reform. Others maintain that any frontal attack on the CAP will meet stiff resolve not to negotiate an article of faith of European integration. The main bones of contention in the 1980s centre on:

(1) Export subsidies. The US claims that the EC dumps surplus produce on to the world market using subsidies that cause gluts, depress prices and put US exporters at a relative disadvantage. The EC rejects US allegations, resists efforts by the US at the GATT to reach international agreement on the matter and accuses the US of subsidizing its own grain sales abroad as part of its foreign assistance effort;

(2) Export credits. Subsidized EC export credits to keep interest rates on export financing are kept low to promote foreign sales. The US has joined the EC in using export credits to grab larger shares of foreign markets, with an export credits war costing each side hundreds of millions of dollars.

(3) High variable import levies. These levies shield the EC market from world market forces and effectively raise the cost of US food products for European consumers and produce high support prices that encourage European surpluses of many farm products.

(4) EC tariff cuts on imports of Mediterranean citrus fruits as part of the EC's Mediterranean policy.

During the early 1980s, the EC and the US were on the brink of trade wars. The biggest problem areas – agriculture and steel – are as old as the EC–US relationship itself. Unless resolved so that no one side gains too much relative advantage, the trade disputes may embitter the broader set of European–US relations. Steel, farm and many other trade disputes will remain unresolved so long as both sides produce the same kinds of products, compete for the same market outlets, support industry and agriculture in different ways and follow contradictory economic and monetary policies. Trade problems will therefore always exist. They most often become confrontations during periods of economic recession when producer groups, claiming unfair competition from outsiders, press their governments into taking unilateral protectionist measures. Improved economic conditions on both sides of the Atlantic may ease trade tensions until the next economic downswing.

During the second Reagan administration, several trade disputes were settled only after the US and EC imposed or threatened to impose punitive duties and quotas against one another. The period was the most confrontational since the 1963 Chicken War. Disputes centred on continued US complaints against the CAP, although disputes over access of EC steel to the US market and EC members' subsidies to Airbus Industries plagued relations as well. The US continued to claim that EC tariff preferences for imports of Mediterranean states' citrus fruit discriminated against its citrus growers' access to the EC market. The US also claimed that EC export subsidies and credits for wheat flour gave the EC new third-country markets at the expense of its historical shares in them (USITC, 1988).

When the two were unable to agree on mutually acceptable positions on EC Mediterranean tariff preferences in 1985, the US imposed increased duties on pasta imports and the EC counter-retaliated with increased duties on imports of US lemons and walnuts. EC action indicated increased confidence in dealing with the US. The US retaliated on EC pasta sales in the US to protest at EC export subsidies of the durum wheat component of pasta. The EC countered by raising such subsidies.

In response to the EC's increased use of farm export subsidies, the Reagan administration launched the Export Enhancement Program of 1985, that gave free surplus farm products held by the US Department of Agriculture to US exporters to enhance their sales to targeted third-country markets. The EC challenged the programme under the GATT Subsidies Code (USITC, 1988). By 1986, the two ended the citrus conflict. Punitive duties were lifted on EC pasta and US lemons and walnuts. The EC agreed to improve access of imports of US grapefruit, lemons, certain oranges, almonds, ground nuts and frozen orange juice while the US agreed to improve access of imports of EC anchovies, some cheeses, certain oranges, olives, capers, cider, paprika and olive oil (USITC, 1988). The US agreed not to challenge in the GATT the legality of the EC's preferential trade accords with the non-EC Mediterranean states. Legal settlement of the EC pasta subsidy question was postponed. Negotiations opened later in 1987 over the amount of the subsidization.

Spanish and Portuguese accession in 1986 triggered one of the nastiest rounds of US–EC disputes. While settled in early 1987, the tenor of future bilateral relations is bound to suffer because the two came to the brink of a full-scale trade war. Threats of punitive action, counterthreats, actual punitive action and more retaliation are bound to unleash the kinds of centrifugal forces that could throw the relationship off balance, perhaps to the point of no return. The point of no return would be a fundamental break in the bilateral status quo, including an end to, or a scaling-back of, cooperation in such areas as defence and economics. States engaged in trade war hardly make good military allies in peacetime to deter real war, or in wartime to wage battle.

Under the terms of accession, Spain and Portugal imposed measures that the US claimed would restrict its trade. First, the EC required Portugal to purchase about 15 per cent of its grain from other EC members. Second, with Spain's transition from its own lower tariff scheme to the EC's much higher CET, Spanish imports of corn and sorghum rose from 20 to 100 per cent. US officials estimated that the higher Spanish duties would cost the US $400 million in corn and sorghum exports to Spain annually (USITC, 1988). US officials were responding to the question of access to the Spanish corn and sorghum market with an eye to the future. The heated response was to put the EC on notice that should it also restrict imports of US soyabeans, other oilseeds and corn gluten feed which enter the EC duty-free and comprise a large proportion of total US sales to the EC, the US would be quick to retaliate. The EC has been considering the renegotiation of the duty-free import of these products, a commitment it made to the US during GATT's early days.

When the EC insisted that its actions would not harm US trade and it appeared that the EC would not offer adequate compensation to the US for the expected trade loss, the US imposed quotas on EC exports of white wine, chocolates, candy, apple and pear juices and beer in retaliation for the Portuguese grain action (the quotas were set high so as not to obstruct the flow of trade but to send a signal of more painful actions to come). In response to the jump in tariffs involving the Spanish market, the US drew up a list of EC products whose access to the US market would be restricted if adequate compensation were not forthcoming. The EC countered with its own list of US products whose access to the EC market would be restricted if the US took punitive action against it. Negotiations broke down in late 1986 and the US announced its intention of imposing 200 per cent duties on imports of several EC farm products, amounting to about $400 million in annual sales in the US. The EC indicated it was prepared to retaliate on imports of US farm products. However, the posturing ended in early 1987 when the EC granted the US adequate compensation by ensuring that Spain import 2 million tonnes of corn and 300,000 tonnes of sorghum from non-EC suppliers over each of the next four years. The EC withdrew the requirement in Portugal's accession treaty that the country purchase 15 per cent of its grain from EC members. The EC provided further compensation in the form of lower tariffs on over twenty industrial and farm products.

Trade disputes are expected to continue well into the 1990s. In 1987, the US filed a complaint with the GATT over a new EC programme to aid rice production, claiming that the EC was in breach of a GATT accord not to add new subsidy programmes during negotiations for a new round of MTNs begun in Uruguay in 1986. EC subsidies to Airbus Industries, US access to the EC telecommunications market and US charges of unfair EC oilseed subsidies were also on the trade agenda in 1987 and 1988.

Why the outbreak of hostilities? In the late 1980s, both have internal economic and political problems that are reflected in trade policies. The soaring US trade deficit fuelled Congressional pressure to enact protectionist legislation to assist such depressed industries as agriculture, textiles and steel. For its part, the EC went on the offensive to find foreign outlets for farm surpluses. The EC also went on the defensive as the US and other major farm exporters protested against its growing share of world food markets and the methods used to support this expansion. In late 1985, the EC began an annual practice of presenting the US trade representative with a list of US trade practices it claimed impeded exports to the United States including 'Buy America' regulations, the Export Enhancement Programme, research and development expenditures by the US Department of Defense and export controls related to national security.

The two differ on interpreting GATT rules on farm export subsidies. Gatt permits farm export subsidies if they do not take more than an 'equitable share' of the market and do not undercut world market prices. The EC invoked GATT rules to legitimize its export subsidies just as the US invoked those same rules to challenge EC practices. The number of US-EC trade disputes has risen as the EC has grown from a food-deficit region to one of the world's largest exporters of cereals, dairy products, meat and sugar. Farm trade problems between the two trading giants in the late 1980s are likely to persist, and could, if mismanaged, worsen.

The US views the Uruguay Round, designed to reduce barriers to international trade, as the last hope of diffusing such disputes with the EC. It wants to fine tune GATT rules on export subsidies and other farm aids. It seeks to place limits on all GATT members' financial support for food production. For its part, the EC has categorically stated that the CAP is not subject to negotiation. However, given the CAP's high cost, the EC may be hard pressed not to agree to some international agreements limiting costly practices. Some of the CAP's critics within the EC encourage foreign pressure on the EC to reform. Efforts at CAP reform have begun but are painfully slow. The US and the EC at the Uruguay Round will either hammer out a new agreement on agricultural support or the talks will break down, and with it the benefits of four decades of liberalized global trade. The stakes are high. The great irony is that compared to the amount of two-way trade – $137 billion – the amount of trade subject to dispute seems rather small.

Politicization of trade relations in the 1980s

Many aspects of EC-US trade relations have become politicized in recent years, a function of the interdependent world order. In many cases, international trade and politics have become so interlocked that conduct of one may affect the outcome of the other. Each has implications for the other in a world where trade joins politics in the formulation and execution of broad-range foreign policy. Differing, often opposing, positions on East-West and North-South relations affect the way the EC and the US choose to trade with one another and with others. The politicization of EC-US relations is problematic from an institutional point of view: there exist no bilateral organizational mechanisms to coordinate their policies. NATO's purview is regional and excludes economic affairs. The EC is limited so as to exclude military affairs. Disputes often fall between the two.

In addition to bilateral trade disputes, the EC and US are at loggerheads over trade and other ties with the Soviet bloc. European and US attitudes toward the Soviet Union and its satellites are shaped by their different historical experiences and contemporary needs. Despite recent improvements in superpower relations, there exists a deep difference between the two sides on how serious the Soviet danger is to West Europe – how it should be met and by whom. That they bicker over the common enemy that once united them underscores the poignancy of the current dispute over the course of East-West relations.

The US and the Soviet Union had been historical rivals long before the founding of NATO and the EC. Hostility is based on their opposing political cultures; simultaneous consolidation and expansion of the nation-state and of national identity in the nineteenth century; and simultaneous rise to superpower status in the twentieth century. In 1949, West Europe by default joined the US in its animosity toward the USSR. When *détente* became discredited by the early 1980s in response to hostile Soviet actions around the world, for most West Europeans, it was still business as usual with the USSR – with minor exceptions – based on the belief that European *détente* was unlinked to superpower *détente* in areas outside Europe.

Most US trade links with the Soviet bloc, barring grain and high-tech sales, are generally limited. The US appears more willing to use trade as a lever over Soviet actions. Although the Soviet bloc takes only 2 per cent of its total exports (6 per cent for West Germany), some EC members would like to increase market opportunities in the East. While trade with the Soviet bloc is small, some key industries that together employ over 150,000 in West Germany alone are dependent on business with the Soviet bloc. The FRG's *Ostpolitik* has been generally supported by the EC. The likely establishment in 1989 of diplomatic relations between the EC and the Council for Mutual Economic Assistance may facilitate new trade accords between the EC and individual CMEA states, an EC goal the USSR opposed prior to Gorbachev's era.

The EC's import dependence on energy supplies, dependence on export markets, and geographic proximity to the Warsaw Pact explains why the West Europeans seek low-key cordial relations with the Soviet bloc. While the EC has been slow in formulating a coherent policy toward Eastern Europe, there can be no doubt that EC members have resisted US attempts to permit the downturn in superpower *détente* to poison European *détente* and prospects for increased trade between the two halves of Europe. The EC has been very reluctant to use trade as a lever to influence Soviet actions. West Europeans tend to take a longer-term view of East–West relations than do Americans. The following aspects of East-West relations in the 1980s are those over which the two sides are most at odds. The US and EC differ not so much on the outcome of East-West relations – security for the Western States – but over the methods.

(1) *1979 Soviet invasion of Afghanistan.* The US responded forcefully by imposing a partial grain embargo on the USSR and boycott of the Moscow Olympics. The EC responded less speedily with milder sanctions by preventing its own exports to the USSR from replacing suspended US supplies. The EC disregarded EP resolutions for broad economic sanctions and an EC-wide boycott of the Moscow Olympics. The US saw the EC response as indifferent.

(2) *1981-82 Soviet-instigated imposition of martial law in Poland.* The US responded quickly by imposing mild sanctions against Poland – including suspension of official food aid, commercial credits for non-food sales and Polish fishing rights in US waters; it postponed talks on rescheduling Poland's official debts. Slow to respond to the

crisis, the EC bowed to US pressure and members adopted NATO sanctions previously imposed. It continued to provide emergency food aid through non-official channels.

(3) *1981-2 Soviet role in the Polish crisis.* The US banned sales of GE turbine parts and Caterpillar pipelayers already earmarked for use in building the Siberian gas pipeline following Soviet interference in Poland's domestic crisis. The EC responded belatedly by imposing mild symbolic sanctions. It imposed import quotas on about half of all imported luxury and manufactured products from the USSR, amounting to two per cent of all Soviet exports to the EC. The US was angered by the EC's initial hesitation to impose sanctions which it felt would press Moscow to influence the Polish regime to moderate its actions against Solidarity. Most EC countries took a less Soviet-orientated view of the Polish crisis and preferred to view it more as a European than a superpower problem.

(4) *1981-2 construction of the Soviet pipeline linking Siberian natural gas to West Europe.* Participation by some EC members in manufacturing parts for construction of the pipeline and in arranging long-term contracts for the sale of natural gas was resisted by the US who believed it would make part of the EC dependent on the USSR for natural gas supplies; and it would earn the USSR hard currency to expand military spending. The US claimed that by denying the USSR the needed bank credits, equipment and technology it would be forced to divert its own huge resources away from defence. The EC claimed the US was overreacting and interfering in its internal affairs.

In mid-1982, the Reagan administration extended its pipeline-parts embargo of the USSR to foreign subsidiaries of US firms and to foreign companies granted licenses to produce pipeline equipment with US technology. The action angered the Europeans who claimed that they were illegal under international law. The US export ban hurt allied interests. EC and US views on the pipeline suggested a much wider chasm in approaches to relations with the USSR. The ineffective and divisive ban was lifted by a somewhat embarrassed Reagan administration a short time after implementation. It was ineffective and divisive to allied relations from the outset.

(5) *Civil war in El Salvador.* Material and political support by the US for the anti-communist El Salvadorean government in its war against leftist guerrillas is strongly opposed by the EC over the oppressive nature of that country's current regime. The US views the conflict within the context of the broader East-West confrontation and is angered by hostility or ambivalence among the European allies for its efforts to bolster the pro-Western government in power.

Bilateral relations by the late 1980s have become even more complex and divisive. From the US perspective, the EC began in 1982 to initiate a dialogue with Latin American and Caribbean states which has resulted in annual endorsements of the Contadora peace process. Not only was the EC action viewed by the Reagan administration as an intrusion in its traditional backyard but it ran counter to US policies to destabilize socialist dictatorships there. Similarly, repeated EC condemnations of Chile for human rights violations collided with the Reagan administration's priorities in supporting the Pinochet government as a bulwark against communism in South America, despite the human rights' violations in that country.

From the European perspective, the US has stepped up involvement in its backyard. In response to bitter contests with the EC to retain historical shares of the Egyptian and other Middle Eastern agricultural markets, the US concluded a trade agreement with Egypt and subsidized wheat flour sales to the Egyptians (and to the Algerians).

In the US-Libyan confrontation over Libyan terrorist acts in Europe the

Europeans reacted very negatively to the US bombing raid and actions as they discouraged the flow of American tourists to Europe, and increased the fear of terrorism; US support for Israel in Lebanon throughout the 1980s did not meet with EC approval, thus further straining EC–US relations in the Mediterranean. These confrontations suggest that the EC has gone beyond America's junior partner in international relations and that the logic behind the EC's relationship with the US has changed from one explained by dependence to one explained by interdependence. However, there are limits to the EC's ability to break fundamentally with US policy in most instances. For example, the US bombing of Libya – while engendering a negative response throughout most of the EC – did not evoke an EPC response one way or the other. The EC's silence may be found in the member governments' inability to come to grips with the issue and the members' reticence to confront the US directly. In other differences, EC actions were either less antagonistic (support for Contadora or condemnation of Chilean human rights' policy) or tied closely to vital interests of the EC on its own periphery (Mediterranean tariff preferences). While there are limits to what the EC can do to challenge the US in most foreign policy areas, the EC of the 1990s will chart an increasingly independent foreign policy course, one that will differ, and likely confront, US policies.

Growing EC independence underscores changes in the international system since the 1970s. The US is still one of two military superpowers. However, in the global political economy, its capacity to dominate others, such as the EC and Japan, is on the decline. The EC, despite its economic power, cannot assume leadership of the international political economy, currently filled by the United States, because of its current structure, composition and mission.

Prospects and prescriptions

We have shown that the tenor of the EC–US relationship has changed during the last four decades from a client-patron to a more symmetric interdependent relationship. On both sides, policy adjustment to changes has been very slow, a belated reactiveness which seems to plague the policymaking process of advanced capitalist democracies. Both must come to grips with each other's new relative positions in transatlantic and international relations. Both most formulate and execute new trade policies to manage the bilateral relationship better if they continue to value the benefits of cohesion over disarray. The Uruguay Round of MTNs is a good place to start. If the two sides fail to reduce barriers to international trade during the course of these negotiations, many, including this author, fear the decline of multilateralism that served to open the floodgates of international trade for four decades.

The rise of bilateralism, that is the division of the world into powerful trade (and to some extent political) blocs – North America, Japan and south-east Asia, and Europe and its associates – cannot coexist with multilateral cooperation as we have known it. However, if the international trade order divides into trade blocs, then the US and the EC must quickly learn how best to manage that new reality without losing what was gained from multilateral cooperation. We can expect the EC to strengthen economically as a result of the completion of its internal market sometime in the 1990s. A more confident EC is likely to be a more formidable actor in transatlantic and international affairs. The US must quickly adjust and learn how to work with the EC in more effective ways. Trade brinkmanship – bringing the two sides to the precipice of trade war and then stepping back from the abyss – is dangerous and may set the international trade order back to the days of Smoot-Hawley in 1930, when the US Congress took protectionist measures that triggered worldwide protectionism. Appointment in the US of an Assistant Secretary of State for European Community affairs might help the country to focus better on a coherent and effective 'EC policy'.

Likewise, the EC must learn to deal with the US more effectively by forming a more cohesive unit and by more closely considering the effects of its internal policies on its old patron before taking action that is likely to trigger a heated response. An EC 'US policy' is more problematic since the EC is an organization of twelve states, and growing. When one compares the lack of an EC 'US policy' to well-formed EC policies toward many other states (and regions) in the world, it is apparent that the EC states have the potential to come together as one if the political will is there.

That the two sides lack coherent foreign policies toward one another is not reasonable given the enormity of what is at stake: the world's largest trading partnership – which largely goes untouched by dispute but is not well managed, and one of the world's two largest military partnerships – NATO. Without coherent policies to guide relations, both sides are more prone to narrow domestic interests which could dominate the bilateral agenda. With coherent policies to guide relations, Atlanticist leaders can better place commercial interests within the broader framework of bilateral relations provided for in such policies.

Political and security relations will always be captive in part to the mercantile interests of powerful domestic producer groups so long as the US and the EC remain open, mixed-capitalist democracies. Narrow commercial interests often conflict with broader national and international interests. The two sides must strike a new *modus operandi*. NATO has, with some exceptions, kept the trade peace for four decades. As political malaise deepens in the Atlantic alliance, the trade relationship – controversial since the Chicken War – will be subject to further costly disruptions.

What distinguishes the current crisis from previous ones is that both sides differ over concomitant trade and foreign policy (earlier foreign policy discord was less pronounced) and that both appear willing to bluff, coax and bully one another into submission at the expense of broader political amity. Both take for granted the positive aspects and stress the negative ones in bilateral relations. They disagree more often over means rather than ultimate goals. That the two complain about one another so ferociously underscores the extent to which they are mutually dependent. The more interdependent the relationship, the more each side is affected by what the other does and says, making trade brinkmanship so very dangerous. Seen from this perspective, there is much more to the depth of the relationship than we sometimes realize.

Yet this should not hide two facts. The relationship has undergone fundamental change in the 1970s and 1980s and the two sides will be hard pressed to find the same kind of unifying missions to keep them as closely bound as they once were, short of a military threat to NATO. Since change is constant, the institutional and policymaking framework of transatlantic relations continues to be anachronistic and ought to be reformed. If both sides value the depth of relations, and the mutual benefits derived from them, then new policies toward one another must quickly develop. This may mean creating a new forum or revising old ones to encourage clearer lines of communication and consultation in foreign policy questions that fall outside the NATO area. This may mean a closer political dialogue between the two sides with improved mechanisms for crisis management; closer coordination between heads of government and state and their ministers assigned to NATO and the EC; and an intentional strengthening of the mechanisms of coordination and consultation between the US and EC institutions. However, new or revised institutional mechanisms themselves are not enough. The two sides have to want to improve relations, have to learn to agree to disagree and still function in partnership, and have to avoid taking for granted the depth of relations, lest what has been gained during forty years be neglected and eventually lost. Surely US-EC relations are worth strengthening to accommodate changing times.

Note

1. Observation based on own experience in the international trade policy division of the Foreign Agricultural Service, US Department of Agriculture, 1977-9. While Carter directed farm trade bureaucrats to accept and work with the CAP as it is, a built-in institutional bias against the CAP remained.

References

Aron, R. (1977), 'Europe and the United States: The Relations between Europeans and Americans in D. Landes (ed.), *Western Europe: The Trials of Partnership*, Lexington, D.C. Heath.

Calleo, D. (1974), 'American Foreign Policy and American European Studies: An Imperial Bias?' in W. Hanrieder (ed.), *The United States and Western Europe*, Cambridge, Winthrop.

Diebold, W. (1974), 'Economics and Politics: The Western Alliance in the 1970s' in W. Hanrieder (ed.), *The United States and Western Europe*, Cambridge, Winthrop.

Gardner, B (1982), *Agricollision'*, *Europe*, January.

Ginsberg, R.H., (1989), *Foreign Policy Actions of the European Community: The Politics of Scale*, Boulder, Lynne Rienner.

Johnson, H. (1980), 'EC–US Relations in the Post-Kissinger Era' in L. Hurwitz (ed.), *Contemporary Perspectives in European Integration*, Westport, Greenwood.

Kraft, J. (1962), *The Grand Design: From Common Market to Atlantic Partnership*, New York, Harper.

Morgan, R. (1976), 'The Transatlantic Relationship' in K. Twitchett (ed.), *Europe and the World*, London, Europe.

Schaetzel, R. (1975), *The Unhinged Alliance: America and the European Community*, New York, Harper & Row.

Talbot, R. (1978), *The Chicken War: An International Trade Conflict between the United States and the EEC*, Ames, Iowa State University Press.

US International Trade Commission (USITC) (1988), *Operation of the Trade Agreements Program*, 39th Report, Washington, July.

Warnecke, S. (1976), 'The Political Implications of Trade for European–American Relations' in Czempiel, E -O. and Rustow, D. (eds), *The Euro–American System*, Boulder, Westview.

15 EC–Japan: past, present and future

Gordon Daniels

When the leaders of six West European states signed the Treaty of Rome in 1957 Japan had virtually no place in their political and economic consciousness. Since 1949 the United States had provided their military shield, and Marshall aid had sustained their economic reconstruction. Equally significant had been the encouragement which Washington had given to the beginnings of West European integration. Then, as now, the United States was the most powerful and positive element in the EC's external relations. In contrast, a negative force, the Soviet Union, was of almost equal significance. Moscow's military power, and her control of Eastern Europe, had culminated in the re-invasion of Hungary in 1956, and a steady stream of refugees from the East frequently reminded Western Europeans of the austerity and inhumanity of life in the People's Democracies.

When European statesmen looked beyond North America and their own continent their interests lay principally in Africa and the Caribbean where France, Belgium and the Netherlands still ruled colonial empires. Thus the new Community's extra-European policy was largely based upon schemes for economic aid, imperial preference and colonial or semi-colonial development. Indeed many writers would argue that the prejudices of empire still dominated European attitudes to Africa, Asia and the non-European world.

If Japan had any place in the contemporary European world view it was a particularly unfortunate one. Memories of pre-war trade were deeply unfavourable. The pirating of European designs, the dumping of inferior articles and the exploiting of cheap 'Asiatic' labour were all considered typical of Japanese commercial behaviour. Japan's wartime alliance with Nazi Germany and Fascist Italy evoked equally unhappy memories. Her military occupation of French Indo-China and the Netherlands Indies and her ill-treatment of Dutch civilians in Java and Sumatra had engendered antipathies which were to last for almost half a century.

In contrast to European attitudes of suspicion and hostility, the United States had demonstrated remarkable benevolence towards her defeated enemy. As early as 1948 American statesmen had viewed Japan as a potential bulwark against Communism and supported her economy with financial aid and technical assistance. In 1951 this relationship had been reinforced by the United States–Japan Security Treaty which provided American military protection for a democratized and virtually disarmed Japan. America's sympathetic attitudes were also evident in her support for Japanese membership of major international organizations. In 1956 Washington sponsored Japan's entry into the United Nations, and eight years later she ensured Japan's membership of the OECD.

The gulf which separated American and European policies was particularly evident in the sphere of international commercial agreements. British and Commonwealth obstruction delayed Japan's accession to the GATT until 1955, and even then Britain, France, Belgium and the Netherlands gave only grudging acceptance. More specifically, all invoked Article 35 of the GATT which permitted selective non-application of the Agreement, should a signatory desire it. In 1959 and 1962 Japanese prime ministers visited Western Europe and sought concessions, but it was only in 1963 that Britain abandoned her adherence to Article 35. In the following year France and the Benelux countries belatedly followed suit.

If European hostility to Japan softened in the 1960s there remained little positive affection. In 1964 the Tokyo Olympics did much to improve Japan's international reputation, but President de Gaulle still characterized Prime Minister Ikeda as a 'transistor salesman' – rather than an architect of remarkable policies of economic growth. Indeed serious European interest in Japan and recognition of her importance only emerged when Community countries began to experience significant trade deficits with their new competitor.

In the early 1960s Euro–Japanese trade had been in general equilibrium, but from 1969 the Community experienced annual deficits. It was this issue, combined with a new awareness of Tokyo's economic importance, which inspired the EEC's first attempt to negotiate a Community-wide commercial agreement with the Japanese government. In 1970 and 1971 Commissioner Dahrendorf embarked on treaty negotiations and achieved a wide measure of agreement. Both Europeans and Japanese favoured trade liberalization and frequent meetings, but European policies were still too restrictive to secure full Japanese agreement. The EEC feared a sudden inrush of low-priced Japanese products and demanded that any treaty should include a 'Safeguard Clause'. Such a provision would permit the imposition of emergency controls in times of crisis. However, Tokyo countered by claiming that Article 19 of the GATT already provided for such emergencies. Japan refused to countenance the possibility of any new restrictions upon her exports and Dahrendorf's negotiations ended in deadlock. Once again, European attitudes had appeared unsympathetic and inflexible.

Soon worse was to follow. The rise in oil prices which followed the Yom Kippur war generated recession and unemployment in Europe and calls for protection against Japanese exports. European alarm was further deepened by the changing character of Japanese products. Increasingly textiles, pottery and light industrial goods were giving way to steel, ships, electronic goods and bearings. These were not only the products of heavy and advanced industries, they often outclassed their European equivalents. European criticisms of Japanese economic policies were understandable, but they were often characterized by ignorance, prejudice and serious misconceptions. European writings which equated Japanese marketing with 'aggression' and corporate planning with 'conspiracy' were not only common but surprisingly influential in major Community countries. Such ill-informed attitudes often obstructed constructive European responses to Japanese competition. These European fears had their most potent impact in October 1976 when Mr Doko and a delegation of Japanese industrial leaders toured Western European capitals. Even in West Germany, which was a bastion of economic liberalism, Doko and his colleagues were subjected to strident criticism. European threats of protectionism were alarming, but even more disturbing were simplistic criticisms of 'Japan Incorporated' which suggested that the Japanese state was omniscient and omnipotent in economic policy. Doko's bitter experience in

Europe was later to be termed the 'Doko Shock'. This exerted a marked influence on Japanese governmental and company attitudes.

In short, Japan now sought to implement measures which would defeat protectionism and simultaneously make some concessions to European demands. Now 'Voluntary Export Restraints' became an increasingly common device to avoid the dangers of market saturation. Doko also sought to encourage a measure of domestic reflation. It was hoped that this would moderate foreign criticism and the need for relentless exporting.

In the aftermath of the Doko visit Europeans and Japanese developed strategies of conflict and compromise which avoided the excesses of both protectionism and *laissez-faire*. In part these new solutions were the product of greater knowledge and more sophisticated negotiation. In 1975 the European Community established a permanent delegation in Tokyo, and Japan founded its own mission to the European Communities. Furthermore, from the autumn of 1975 both Europeans and Japanese participated in the annual seven-power summits of advanced industrial nations where the common political interests of the participants were increasingly recognized. All these changes were reflected in a broad ranging series of discussions, and an increasingly subtle blend of rhetoric and persuasion.

By 1980 Japan's ever-growing surplus appeared likely to stimulate drastic protectionist measures, and EC representatives criticized Japan with particular intensity. But by the end of the year crisis was averted – both parties sought opportunities for compromise. Such complex patterns of negotiation were not without considerable political value. Harsh language could mollify angry pressure groups and compromise could avoid the erection of barriers which were likely to impede the growth of trade. This new mood of qualified harmony was also the by-product of an important new direction in Community diplomacy. In 1976 European criticism had concentrated upon the damage which stemmed from Japanese exports. Soon after, the Community turned its attention to the promotion of its own exports and the opening of the Japanese market.

One of the most imaginative aspects of these new policies was the establishment of the Executive Training Programme (ETP) which provides scholarships for young European businessmen to spend a year in Tokyo, studying Japanese. This is followed by a further six months of 'in-house' training in a Japanese company. By 1987 over 170 such trainees had successfully completed this programme and constituted a corps of young 'Japan hands' able to assist in the promotion of European exports.

Needless to say Community attacks on perceived obstructions to European exports formed an even more crucial element in EC policy towards the Japanese market. Here issues were often a complex weave of reality and imagination. In the 1960s the Japanese market had been highly protected and many European companies had found it uneconomical to establish expensive sales networks in Japanese cities. However, by the 1970s Japanese ministers were commited to a serious policy of liberalization which received far too little attention in European business circles.

Unfortunately Japanese measures to reduce tariffs and increase quotas were no more than a partial solution to European difficulties. Japanese inspection procedures were often cumbersome and lengthy and at times constituted protectionism in disguise. Yet Europeans could sometimes attribute bad motives to creditable acts. When Japan attempted to reduce air pollution in her cities by imposing rigorous emission controls on all passenger cars many Europeans mistakenly saw this as a means of obstructing the importation of British, German or Italian vehicles.

Year after year European negotiators, like their American equivalents, claimed that the Japanese market was also protected by a complex network of cultural and organizational barriers. Some attacked Japan's inefficient distribution system. Others criticized the high level of Japanese savings, and some businessmen termed the Japanese language a non-tariff barrier. Such social and cultural phenomena may have constituted barriers to European exporters but they were difficult barriers for Japanese leaders to remove.

In fact, by the early 1980s Japanese governments were resorting to a remarkable range of measures to appease their European and American adversaries. Import promotion missions were despatched to European factories. Foreign laboratories were permitted to carry out inspection procedures, and the Office of the Trade Ombudsman (OTO) was established to resolve foreign complaints. Some of these measures were clearly tactical – particularly those which preceded international conferences – but conditions for foreign exporters eased with the years. However, these changing conditions rarely made a significant impact on the scale of Japanese imports. At the heart of this problem lay the uncomfortable fact that few European manufactured goods could outclass their Japanese rivals. Furthermore, the expense of establishing an effective sales operation in Tokyo was often a major deterrent to potential exporters. Consequently the technical opening of the Japanese market was slow to influence the scale of Japan's trading surplus.

The scale of these many problems may suggest that the European Community posed no difficulties for Japanese exporters. However this was hardly the case. European states were in general more open and accessible than Japan but there were marked exceptions. In 1983 the French government decided to impede the importation of Japanese video cassette recorders by channelling them through a single inspection point at Poitiers. This measure was abandoned some months later, but its spirit was clearly at odds with the liberal principles proclaimed by Commissioners in Brussels. Italian obstructions have been far more resilient. For many years Italy has had an import quota for Japanese cars of little over 2,000 per year. Such policies have provided ready ammunition for Japanese who wish to question the Community's commitment to free trade and liberal internationalism.

Despite many Euro–Japanese frictions, the years 1976-85 have been marked more by flexibilities than rigidities. In particular European attitudes to Japanese manufacturing investment in the Community have undergone a significant transformation. In the 1970s Japanese plans to establish assembly plants or factories in Europe were often the objects of heated criticism. Some saw them as threats to local companies and workers while others were hostile to the introduction of new industrial methods and mores. Nevertheless, the success of Japanese factories in providing employment, however small, has done much to dampen local criticism. Support for such factories has been particularly evident in regions which have suffered from profound problems of industrial decline. Equally important has been the broadly educational role of such factories in introducing patterns of training, industrial relations and quality control which are often superior to local models.

The late 1970s and early 1980s have also seen significant changes in European attitudes to other forms of industrial collaboration. The Rover Company's links with Honda clearly aided an ailing British car producer; while ICL's links with Fujitsu were also of mutual benefit. Clearly all such arrangements embrace rivalry and struggles for advantage, but the notion that both Europeans and Japanese can gain from such arrangements was far less widely accepted in the early 1970s.

Despite all these major developments in industry and commerce political changes may have been the most significant new elements in Euro–Japanese relations in recent years. Since 1980 Japan has not only given general support to the concept of European integration but has supported the Community's stance on significant political issues. In 1980 and 1981 Tokyo supported the Community's opposition to Soviet policy in Afghanistan and Poland, and Japan has taken economic initiatives which have complemented European interests. Japanese financial aid to Turkey and food aid to Southern and East Africa has been helpful to Europe – in areas which are distant from Japan's main spheres of interest.

This convergence of political attitudes has also been symbolized by the annual meetings of members of the European Parliament and the Japanese Diet. Although these gatherings may be criticized for their high ceremonial content, their working sessions have considerable significance. In specialized discussions, debate ranges over issues which extend well beyond trade and industry. Both domestic and international problems appear on these inter-parliamentary agenda and encourage a sense of shared interests and objectives.

If the Doko shock inaugurated one era in Euro–Japanese relations, Japan's trade liberalization measures of 1985 may have inaugurated another. After repeated criticism from European and American negotiators the Japanese government launched its major Action Programme for the de-regulation of trade. This plan not only embraces tariff reductions and the simplification of inspection procedures but proposes the liberalization of financial markets and government contracts. The ultimate impact of these measures is difficult to judge, but some European companies have already been awarded small symbolic contracts for the design of the new Kansai International Airport. These Japanese moves towards a more open economy were further reinforced in autumn 1985 when the Plaza Agreement permitted the Yen to float to higher levels. As a direct consequence of this strengthening of the yen the European Community's deficit with Japan has fallen by small but significant amounts in 1987 and 1988.

These recent steps which seek the greater internationalization of the Japanese economy were given greater impetus in 1986 with the publication of the Japanese government's Maekawa Report. This major strategic document calls for increases in imports, increases in domestic consumption and less dependence upon exports for Japan's prosperity. The implementation of the Maekawa Report will be a slow and complex procedure but its proposals show a profound understanding of the political and economic dangers which emanate from recurrent trade surpluses with the United States and the European Community.

In conclusion, what steps should the European Community take to secure a stable and rewarding relationship with contemporary Japan? First must come an appreciation of the realities of relations with the world's second largest economy. Whatever the fate of Europe's own scientific strategies, Japan is likely to dominate an increasingly broad range of major industrial technologies. Thus any attempt to exclude Japan from close relations with Europe is likely to prove destructive rather than creative. Even the United States, which has close defence ties with Japan, has difficulty in keeping abreast of the most advanced Japanese technology. Hence the problem for Europe is even more serious. Given these realities, Europeans should seek closer relations with Japan in a wide range of scientific, cultural and commercial fields. Joint Euro–Japanese projects in such fields as health, social science and technology would not only create an intrinsically closer relationship but would help to lay the spectre of anti-Japanese prejudice which still haunts the corridors of Euro–Japanese negotiations.

Furthermore, if Europe is to monitor the rapid social, scientific and economic changes which characterize contemporary Japan, much greater attention must be paid to the teaching of the Japanese language in the member states of the Community. Of equal importance is the creation of some pan-European institution for the study of the Japanese economy and its social foundations. It is similarly important that such bodies as the European Parliament have at least a minimum of Japanese-speaking staff so that cooperation with the Japanese Diet may be further developed.

Finally, one must note an obvious truism regarding the future of all Euro–Japanese relations. In matters of trade, culture, politics or technology, Japanese leaders will always compare the power, unity and achievements of Europe with those of their formal ally, the United States. The more unified, integrated and prosperous Europe becomes the more power it will command in its relations with Japan. In the future as in the past Europe will find competition with Japan arduous and daunting. To meet this challenge a single currency, a single foreign policy and an educational strategy are no more than essential beginnings.

16 ACP and the developing world

Adrian Hewitt

Background to the Lomé Conventions

The first Lomé Convention was signed in 1975 between the EC and forty-six African, Caribbean and Pacific (ACP) states. Hailed as a new departure in North–South relations, it grew out of the twin roots of the Six's existing relationship under the Yaoundé Convention with their former colonies, and of the need to make provision for some of Britain's former colonies after the first enlargement of the EC. The 'seven outside' – the bigger or more industrially advanced Commonwealth countries in South and South-East Asia – were not offered membership of the exclusive Lomé club. The Lomé Convention was notable both for what it contained and for the way it was negotiated, with the ACP establishing an impressive degree of unity. This was the time (1973-5) of commodity power and increasing Third World solidarity. Developing country growth rates had been impressive – at least up to the 1973 oil price disruptions – and for years thereafter many of the middle-income developing countries were deemed highly creditworthy and were offered large amounts of lending at commercial rates.

The Convention included: a trade regime that was more preferential, at least superficially, than that accorded by the EC to any other group of states; a five-year aid programme that was presented as giving the recipients an unusual degree of freedom in determining priorities; a novel scheme, Stabex; and an array of consultative institutions. The sentiments running through the Convention were 'partnership' and 'contractual obligations'.

When the second Convention was signed in 1979, again in Lomé, to cover 1980-5, the atmosphere was much less harmonious. This was partly because the first Lomé agreement had failed to fulfil its promise and, related to this, because there had been a subtle shift in the bargaining power of the two sides. When Lomé I was negotiated, the ACP had some freedom of manoeuvre; most states had a pre-existing aid/trade relationship with some members of the enlarged Community, and a number openly took the view that they could afford to see the negotiations collapse. By the time of Lomé II, however, the ACP were the prisoners of their own success; the risk of collapse was perceived by them to entail the loss of a fresh source of aid. Moreover, their negotiating stance was somewhat muddled and, because of the recession, the EC adopted a restrictive negotiating mandate which the Commission presented with a blunt, take-it-or-leave-it style. As a result, Lomé II resembled its predecessor and contained few innovations.

Lomé III was signed in December 1984 and entered into force after belated ratification on 1 May 1986; however, it remains current until 1990: all Conventions have been of five years' duration so far. By this time, many ACP states were in severe balance of payments' and budgetary difficulties. They were largely forced into the role of supplicants for the negotiating process of Lomé III. The negotiating calendar, however, meant that by Autumn 1988, negotiations between the EC and the ACP had already started to prepare the fourth Lomé Convention. By the time these negotations started, the ACP Group numbered sixty-six states – virtually half the countries of the developing world by number, though a smaller share of its population. Angola was the latest member to sign on the ACP side, while an independent Namibian state would be eligible to apply. By mid-1989, decisions had not yet been arrived at regarding the candidacy of Haiti and the Dominican Republic. Significantly, the EC side of the relationship had expanded since Lomé III to include two states, Spain and Portugal, with powerful Latin American connections and cultural interests, which contrasted with their rather mixed experience in Africa. The fourth Convention will moreover cover the period 1990-5 or beyond, when completion of the internal EC market by 1 January 1993 is due and when the Uruguay Round of the multilateral trade negotiations of the GATT will be implemented. Both developments are likely to alter the trade preferences currently enjoyed by the ACP: without safeguards they are likely to be reduced. As in the 1983-4 negotiating period, the ACP economies were hardly in a robust state by the end of the 1980s. ACP government ministers faced their EC counterparts with an uncomfortable baggage of debt (much of it owed to governments and international financial institutions, rather than banks as would have been the case for non-ACP third world debtors), balance of payments' problems, poor growth performance, increasing income inequality and decreasing social service provision. Their bargaining power did not have the economic strengths it knew in the mid-1970s, though it could still call on significant political forces. For complex historical reasons, both parties to the arrangement appeared content to regard the nub of the Lomé arrangements as a special and durable relationship between Europe and Africa in which the Bretton Woods' institutions, the World Bank and the IMF, were supposed to be cast as transatlantic interlopers – who could nevertheless be called on for support – while the globalization of the EC's development assistance policy to Asia and Latin America would still have to await future developments. The concept of 'Eurafrica' and the challenge of structural adjustment policies prescribed by the Washington institutions remain the two key elements over which policy tensions arise.

Lomé as a manifestation of 'Eurafrica'

The European Community as a regional grouping has links with Africa which are almost as old as the EC's own internal bonds. As part of the bargain struck in 1957 in establishing the Treaty of Rome, France insisted that a special relationship be established, under part IV of the Treaty, with selected African states and Madagascar, almost all of whom were then still French dependencies, though shortly afterwards destined for independence in 1960.

Over the succeeding thirty years, the relationship has been both expanded and diluted. With the increase in EC membership from six to nine (1973) and eventually to twelve, the admixture to the Community's own putative external relations' policy of components of the foreign policies of the new member states, traded against the entrenched interests of the original members, has resulted in sub-Saharan Africa remaining the firm focus of the EC's development assistance policies, though hardly an important item in its global trading and economic relationships. By the time of the Lomé Conventions, starting in 1975, the EC had drawn into this special cooperation relationship all the independent states in sub-Saharan Africa. Even Mozambique and Angola eventually joined, while neither Ethiopia nor Uganda, during their worst disputes with governments of European member states, ever withdrew their membership. Save for Namibia and South Africa, neither enjoying a representative government, the EC's African jig-saw puzzle was complete by the 1980s. (The North African countries had separate agreements with Brussels outside the Lomé Convention arrangements.)

Effects of enlargement

New EC members have signalled a dilution in the single-minded concentration on giving substance to the invented concept of 'Eurafrica' which was so dear to the French policymakers who numbered themselves among the founding fathers of the EC. With the accession of the United Kingdom (plus Denmark and Ireland) in 1973, the EC's Yaoundé agreements, which had until then been limited to Africa and made almost the exclusive preserve of francophone states, were transformed into a more liberal Lomé Convention which embraced both francophone and anglophone Africa (and much else on the continent besides) and which also extended to Commonwealth and a few other countries in the Caribbean and the Pacific. By 1989 there are sixty-six developing country signatories of the (third) Lomé Convention and so members of the ACP (Africa, Caribbean and Pacific) Group. Only about forty of them are in Africa. Although because almost all the Caribbean and Pacific members are small islands (membership of the group was not allowed to be extended to the big Commonwealth countries of mainland Asia like India, Bangladesh, Sri Lanka and Malaysia), Africa remains preponderant in the ACP Group in terms of its share of population, output and also in the amount of EC funds it absorbs. The latter accession to EC membership of Greece and, more importantly, Spain and Portugal has yet to alter this balance. Sub-Saharan Africa remains at the apex of the 'pyramid of privileges' which the EC has erected for its relationships with Third World countries. While some see it as a relationship which has failed to mature over the last thirty years (some African countries are now poorer than when the relationship began, in contrast to the excluded Asian countries), others can see a fruitful partnership which can be built on for the future, an alternative for African governments to the blandishments of the superpowers. Yet others see the EC – a community of 320 million people not dissimilar in population size to Africa – as a future superpower itself.

Colonial roots of the 'Eurafrica' concept

EC–African links are almost as old as the Community's own institutions. Yet thirty years is little more than a twinkling of the eye in Africa's rich history, and even if we date the most concerted European involvement in the depths of the African continent from the 1885 Congress of Berlin, that means that European (as opposed to EC) links with Africa are well over a century old. This is a crucial distinction. While the EC *qua* Community has no colonial past and no relationship with Africa dating back beyond 1957-8, the countries which are its member states obviously do. The colonial connection is obviously most important for Britain and France because it was most durable, but it should not be overlooked in the cases of West Germany, Italy and Portugal (historically cast as particularly negative experiences for Africans) or even in the minor colonial forays into Africa of Belgium and Spain. Thus seven countries – over half of the EC's twelve member states – had colonies in Africa. In fact only the small EC members – Denmark, Luxembourg, Ireland, Greece and the Netherlands – did not. The contrast with the other superpowers is striking, notwithstanding the EC's own absence of a colonial past. For the USA[1], the Soviet Union, Japan and China never had any colonial possessions on the Continent; indeed, until the mid-twentieth century, none of these major countries had any significant economic, cultural or political activity in Africa at all, with the partial exception of some American business penetration. In other words, until recent times Africa, when it was not the preserve of the Africans, was encroached upon only by Europeans (and Arabs), but certainly not by emissaries of the other major world economic powers.

The three pillars of the EC's Africa policy

An objective assessment of the EC's relationship with Africa would conclude that it rests on three main supports:

– the legacy of colonialism, some of which is positive, for familiarity does not only breed contempt, it can foster understanding and mutual respect;
– a belief in the complementarity of the two blocs – one temperate, the other mainly tropical; one natural-resource-rich, the other skill-intense; one densely populated and urbanized, the other enjoying vast open spaces and so on;
– an assertion that Europe has more to offer in terms of culture, the benevolent promotion of development, disinterested assistance and political cooperation than the newer, brasher superpowers ever could.

None of these supports is of course totally solid; closer scrutiny will show definite flaws in their construction. Furthermore, a tripod, though reputed to be a very stable construction, is not actually used very often, for the best practical reasons. Yet each of these elements bears closer examination as an explanation of the present EC–African relationship and as a potential mainspring of its future dynamics. Each of them figures prominently as an underlying theme of the Lomé Convention relationship. Selectivity, and hence exclusion from the Group at the EC's behest, relates to colonial history; the exchange of raw materials for manufacturers underlies the trade, commodity and Stabex arrangements; while a cultural chapter has recently been added to the Convention, which had always been a political treaty. The final question to be addressed, however, is whether each column of the tripod is not unduly backward-leaning and so incapable of supporting either the changing dynamics of the European Community itself or the responses which Africa needs and expects in a global context.

Role of the Lomé Convention

The roots of the Lomé Convention lie in the special trading arrangements negotiated in the post-colonial period. France in particular wished to maintain a close relationship with her ex-colonies which would keep open a potentially lucrative market for her exports. West Germany, politically weakened, was prepared to do a deal. For their part, the newly independent African nations hoped in the 1960s to benefit from aid and trading concessions. The Yaoundé Convention of 1963 formalized preferential trading arrangements between the original six members of the EC and most of the ex-French colonies. The entry of Britain to the EC in 1973 led to the replacement of the Yaoundé Convention by a new treaty incorporating the ex-British colonies of Africa, the Caribbean and the Pacific, plus some others. In this way, the Lomé Convention was born: Africa was always dominant.

The establishment of the first Lomé Convention in 1975 was heralded by African, Caribbean and Pacific and European governments as a landmark in the evolution of North–South relations. Even the United States later launched a Caribbean Basin Initiative (CBI) which borrowed some elements from the Lomé Conventions.

Lomé I was, perhaps fortuitously, negotiated at a time of brief Third World commodity power, just after the quadrupling of OPEC oil prices and the emergence of world shortages in certain raw materials (sugar, phosphates, foodgrains). In UNCTAD and pervasively throughout the United Nations system, the call was for a New International Economic Order (NIEO) in which Third World nations – and particularly their governments – would seize a stronger position in negotiating and determining both global economic relationships and their own development patterns.

The EC responded to this new climate with considerable alacrity and a measure of presentational aplomb. The Lomé Convention was put forward as a path-breaking 'partnership of equals', hitherto unknown among rich–poor global relations. It was claimed to represent a new way of organizing economic and trade relations, negotiated by two groups of countries on a basis of equal partnership. For the first time ever, the interlinkages between aid and trade appeared to have been formally recognized. The interest which developing countries showed in the Lomé – an interest that stood in strong contrast with the sharp criticism repeatedly levelled at the Yaoundé Convention – was doubtless due to the fact that many governments regarded the new framework as a possible precedent and a model for future relations between industrialized and developing countries. The provisions of the Convention offered some major innovations, the most important being the stabilization of export earnings – the Stabex system – and the removal of reciprocity in the EC's trade preference-giving. ACP states could in theory develop manufacturing export lines and gain free access to the Community's vast market, over that accorded to their Third World competitors in Asia and Latin America as well as to industrialized countries, without having to accord the EC countries similar tariff concessions in return.

Above all, the Lomé I Convention offered 3 ECUS billion worth of aid, most of it to be allocated to Africa. The Lomé Convention, like its predecessor agreements, uniquely enjoyed its own special fund, the European Development Fund, replenished every five years for this purpose. The EDF was and is mainly grants. Other countries outside the ACP could not have access to this Fund; moreover its allocations to each individual country were made in advance but programmed only loosely ('indicatively'). The EDF, again uniquely, was funded directly by the EC member states (the UK, for instance, contributes a fixed 16.6 per cent of the current sixth EDF) and does not form part of the general EC budget. That is why African governments have held the Lomé arrangements with the EC in such high esteem. They regard EC aid as additional to the aid they receive from France, Britain, West Germany or any of the member states. In fact this cannot be the case, though the illusion is powerful. On the other hand, they are correct in judging that EC aid is generally 'softer', both in financial terms and in general conditions than that of the other donors or of the international financial institutions. That is a phenomenon which seems ripe for modification as the Lomé IV negotiations start (see below). Lastly, they are also partially correct in setting great store by the predictability of the EDF aid. African governments know at the beginning of each five-year Lomé period the amount earmarked for them, and at least the broad sectors or operations in which the aid is to be used. In fact EDF spending is still quite slow compared with that of other donors, and the benefits of 'five-year indicative programming' are at best arguable as against the three-year rolling programmes or similar used by many other aid donors in their main partner countries in Africa.

Perhaps Lomé I raised unrealistic expectations, as hindsight confirms the scale of resources available, and the implementation mechanisms established, were not sufficient to bring about significant economic and social development of the ACP countries. Neither Lomé I nor its successors reduced poverty levels or improved living conditions for the mass of urban and rural families in ACP countries. Indeed, Africa is facing crisis, and African per capita income and per capita food production are lower now than before the start of Conventions I and II, even though the EC's role has been to help not to harm, on balance.

ACP states have not greatly diversified their production or exports. African exports are still highly concentrated in a few products. Primary products still constitute over 95 per cent of the EC's imports from ACP countries, with oil from Nigeria and Gabon the major single item. The ambitious industrialization targets of the Lomé Convention have not been met. The reality of the Convention has been that both aid and trade provisions have acted to confine ACP countries to the export of certain primary commodities. Manufactured and semi-manufactured goods have a very small share of EC imports from ACP countries, barely 3-4 per cent, and are hardly rising. Only Mauritius is a significant exception to this rule.

In absolute terms, aid has increased with each Convention. But when inflation and population growth are taken into account, it can be seen that over 1976-85 (Lomé I to Lomé III), European Community real per capita transfers to ACP states fell by 40 per cent. This was at a time when ACP states' needs for resource transfers were increasing. The African ACP grouping comprises the bulk of the UN's list of forty-one least developed countries (LDCs), hence the least viable in commercial terms and the least able to secure commercial bank credit. Lomé III provides for a total allocation of *ECU* 8,500 million over 1985-90. This barely covers the rise in prices and, with the number of ACP states now sixty-six, represents a further decline in real per capita transfers. According to calculations made by the UN Economic Commission for Africa (see Table 16.1)

Table 16.1 Resources under Lomé I (1979-84) and Lomé II (1985-90) Conventions

	Value of resources allocated (ECU 000,000)			(%)
	Lomé II	*Lomé III current prices*	*Lomé III at constant (1980) prices★*	*Change in real expenditure of Lomé III over Lomé II*
I. EDF				
Grants	2,998	4,860	3,371	11.24
Soft Loans	524	600	416	−20.61
Risk				
Capital	284	600	416	46.48
Stabex	557	925	641	15.08
Sysmin	282	415	288	2.13
Total	4,645	7,400	5,132	10.48
II. EIB†				
Subsidised loans	685	1,100	763	11.39
Ordinary loans	200	—	—	—
III. Total resources	5,530	8,500	5,895	6.60

★ deflated to allow for inflation over 1980-7
† European Investment Bank

Source: United Nations Economic Commission for Africa (ECA); Statistical Office of the European Communities.

while Lomé II was already a worse deal than Lomé I for the ACP, the aid allocation under Lomé III increased only 10 per cent in real terms (EDF only) or 6.6 per cent overall at a time when population increases and expansion of the Group to sixty-six more than offset this in per capita terms. In nominal terms, of course, the figures look more impressive (See Table 16.2). The financial contributions of the Member States are shown in Table 16.3. The reality already for Lomé III was that Africa's and the ACP's negotiating power was so weakened by the rude economic shocks of 1979-81 and the recession which followed, that they were unable to negotiate hard and coherently with the EC: Africa was already on its knees.

Lomé III

Lomé III was signed on 8 December 1984. The trade benefits offered by the Community were substantially the same: strict rules of origin and other non-tariff barriers still applied. There was a change in the distribution of aid, the amount allocated to soft loans declining in favour of more grants and the Stabex fund – for soft commodities – being boosted considerably more than the mining loan facility, Sysmin. The third Convention contained a number of

Table 16.2   Lomé Convention financial resources (ECU 000,000)

Convention (Fund)	Date of entry	Number of countries	Total population 000,000	Total Aid (ECU 000,000)	
				EDF	EIB own resources
Lomé I (4th EDF)	1.4.76	46	250	3.072	390
Lomé II (5th EDF)	1.1.81	57	348	4.724	685
Lomé III (6th EDF)	1.5.86	66	413	7.400	1.100

Convention total	Lomé I 3,462	Lomé II 5,409	Lomé III 8,500
EDF	3,072	4,724	7,400
– subsidies	2,150	2,999	4,860
– special loans	466	525	600
– venture capital	99	284	600
– STABEX	377	634	925
– SYSMIN	—	282	415
EIB, loans on owns resources	390	685	1,100

Source: Ten years of Lomé (Europe Development Information)

minor innovations: the principle of self-reliant agricultural development involving the full participation of rural populations and the general assertion of priority for agricultural and rural development; a cultural chapter; and for the first time, a general undertaking by *all* signatories – EC governments as well as ACP – to work towards the eradication of apartheid.

Many negotiators, not least many of those in the European Commission, felt this element – and indeed the 'cultural chapter' too – sat uneasily in an agreement which had been at base an arrangement for economic cooperation. Others argued that the apartheid system on the continent of Africa was so pernicious that its continued existence – and worse, the tacit countenancing of it – negated the constructive works of the economic and social sectors of the Convention, particularly in the Frontline States, if it were not going to be addressed and actively tackled in this manner. In a sense, the Lomé III outcome reflected the feeling of relatively little progress achieved by the African ACP members from the relationship over the previous decade in economic terms, and it thus both permitted and justified harder bargaining on the political and cultural fronts.

The Lomé III Convention is the longest to date and contains five parts. Part One provides a guide to the general objectives and expectations of the contracting parties. Part Two outlines the areas of cooperation: agriculture, industry, transport and so on. Part Three describes the operating mechanisms of cooperation: this section details the arrangements regarding trade, Stabex and

Table 16.3a   Member states' contributions to 4th, and 5th EDFs (for Lomé I and II, respectively). (ECU 000,000)

	4th EDF		5th EDF	
	ECU	%	ECU	%
Belgium	196,875	6.25	273.524	5.90
West Germany	817,425	25.95	1,311,988	28.30
France	817,425	25.95	1,186,816	25.60
Italy	378,000	12.00	533,140	11.50
Luxembourg	6,300	0.20	9,272	0.20
Netherlands	250,425	7.95	343,064	7.40
United Kingdom	589,050	18.70	834,480	18.00
Denmark	75,600	2.40	115,900	2.50
Ireland	18,900	0.60	27,816	0.60
Total	3,150,000[1]	100.00	4,636,000[2]	100.00

Notes: 1. 3,000 million ECU for the ACP and 150 million ECU for the OCT
       2. 4,542 million ECU for the ACP and 94 million ECU for the OCT

Table 16.3b   Breakdown of contributions to the 6th EDF for Lomé III (ECU 000,000)

	ECU	%
Belgium	296,94	3.96
Denmark	155.82	2.08
West Germany	1,950.40	26.06
Greece	93.03	1.24
France	1,768.20	23.58
Ireland	41.30	0.55
Italy	943.80	12.58
Luxembourg	14.00	0.19
Netherlands	423.36	5.64
United Kingdom	1,243.20	16.58
Spain	499.80	6.66
Portugal	66.15	0.88
Total	7,500.00[3]	100.00

Note: 3. Of which 7,400 million ECU for the ACP States and 100 million ECU for the OCT

Sysmin, aid programming and investment. Part Four describes the functioning of the institutions of Lomé. Part Five contains a number of minor provisions concerning accession, and is followed by the special protocols, making specific arrangements for protected markets with uncompetitive ACP imports such as cane sugar, bananas, beef and rum, which are generally of minor interest to Africa, though important for a few countries. These five parts are followed by the Final Act of Lomé III, containing a number of annexes of particular interest such as provisions on migrant workers.

Significantly, special provision is made under the Lomé Convention to channel aid and Stabex benefits disproportionately towards the least developed country (LDC) members of the ACP who are mainly in Africa. Annoyingly, however, the EC uses its own classification of 'least developed', and its own list, though limited only to the ACP, already exceeds the UN's definitive list of forty-one LDCs (which includes Bangladesh, Haiti, Laos etc., outside the ACP grouping). Under Lomé III the EC's own list of ACP LDCs has risen to forty-three, accounting for 40 per cent of the total ACP population and accorded twice the amount of programmed aid given to the other ACP states. This is a 'bias towards the poor' which could serve the EC well in its future relations with Africa, if it were not for the fact that programmed aid, for example to Ethiopia, has not in practice always resulted in commensurate disbursements when political controversies (in Ethiopia's case, over agricultural policies, resettlement and the prevailing economic doctrine) intervened, allowing the EC to suspend aid on the insistence of its hard-line member states.

Despite these occasional lapses, and the disappointing economic performance of sub-Saharan Africa – the EC's chosen partners for cooperation – more generally, there is much to appreciate still in the list of general principles which the then European Commissioner for Development, Lorenzo Natali[2], set out in his guidelines for the negotiations of Lomé IV starting in 1988:

The unique, innovatory character of the ACP/EEC relationship, steadily built up over more than a decade of joint experience, comes first and foremost from its approach and general principles.

The ACP–EEC Lomé Convention is not only the main pillar of the Community's development policy but also, in the broader context of overall North–South relations, the most comprehensive contractual instrument linking a regional grouping of industrialized nations and developing countries. The number of Contracting Parties, the scale and diversity of areas of cooperation covered, the volume of financial resources involved and the innovatory nature of some of its mechanisms – such as policy dialogue, Stabex or the regional cooperation instruments – make the Lomé Convention today a model for and witness to North–South relations which plays a large role in promoting the Community's image in the world. Its main characteristics are:

  (i) respect for the sovereignty of States and their economic and political options;
 (ii) institutionalized group-to-group cooperation, preventing political discrimination between recipients;
(iii) security and foreseeability of aid and trade advantages, based on binding international commitments covering the duration of the Convention: this is the often-cited advantage of the contractual nature of Lomé;
(iv) comprehensive cooperation arrangements covering a wide range of areas and instruments;
 (v) permanent dialogue both at technical level (aid programming and policy dialogue) and at political level, in the joint institutions (ACP–EEC Council of Ministers, Committee of Ambassadors, Joint Assembly).

It is, at the very least, a package whose *potential* would be highly appreciated as a basis for relations with Africa by other superpowers such as the US or Japan, who do not enjoy such an elaborate network of arrangements and who cannot draw on such a history of European colonial links at its base. It is potential which however has yet to be realized given the changed circumstances of Africa today. That is why substantial reforms will be in order for Lomé IV.

The changes afoot for the 1990s: Lomé IV

Negotiations for the renewal or reformulation of the Lomé Convention (all such treaties have been signed in the Togolese capital so far) began in September 1988 although the 'fourth Lomé' Convention will not take effect until 1990 at the earliest. There has to be a common European position established before serious negotiations with the ACP can start, and the same applies vice versa. For the EC, the main issue is how to use Lomé to retrieve some semblance of influence over the structural adjustment policies of the World Bank. For the ACP, with the dominant role of Africa, deals are struck among senior government representatives at ministerial and ambassadorial rank, with the Brussels-based ACP Secretariat as clearing-house, intelligence HQ and think-tank. For the EC member states, the position is as varied as national parliamentary and executive procedure. It is however significant to note that in the past, on development issues, the EC (despite the Commission's key role in proposing innovations) has tended to travel at the speed of its slowest major member; or else France has asserted its primacy over EDF and development matters in its own subtle way. This time round, the British and the Dutch are much more openly supportive of World Bank/IMF policy-based lending in ACP countries, and want the EDF to give up its 'specificity' in favour of creditor solidarity.

In the view of many observers, the European Community's relations with the Third World, though apparently dynamic and innovatory in the Cheysson years in the mid-1970s, before Lomé I was put to the test, had by the late 1980s become something of an anachronism, a style of operation frozen into a past of paternalistic project aid and few usable trade stimuli or concessions, and a cooperation programme which, under Lomé III and particularly Lomé II, failed to address the leading issues of concern to Africa, viz:

– the impossibility of servicing debt, including for many African countries government-to-government debt;
– facing up to the demands of the Washington-based financial institutions to submit to tough political changes in the economic and social policies of African governments;
– resolving the problems of turmoil, destabilization and apartheid in Southern Africa.

On debt problems, the EC, at least in its Lomé Convention guise, was almost totally silent until 1988 (the debt crisis 'broke' with Mexico in summer 1982). This was because the EC Commission had chosen to believe that debt problems were somewhat separate from the project-based approach to aid and development the EDFs had espoused from the beginning almost without change. Stabex was supposed to tide over dependent commodity exporters during the bad years (though it has repeatedly proved to be underfunded, especially in 1981 and 1988), but otherwise Brussels chose to regard the inadequacy of export earnings to service even debt interest let alone repayments as a problem for the IMF and World Bank. This proved increasingly untenable as successive governments of the EC's own member states produced the Lawson plan, the Balladur plan, the Mitterrand plan etc., all to address African debt problems in particular. Thus belatedly in 1987-8, the EC agreed to provide – mainly from recycled funds and unused Lomé–EDF contingency reserves – balance of payments' support to ACP states as a help towards debt relief, initially at the level of ECU 100m of import finance, now increased to an ECU 500m pledge. There is now firm agreement that a quick-disbursing sectoral support fund should be offered under the Lomé IV Convention, in addition to the traditional EDF project aid.

The EC always prided itself on not exercising any political discrimination among the ACP. The EC's hardliners now insist that strings have to be attached to such balance of payments' support programmes and in the interests of policy effectiveness and of Western coordination and solidarity, the conditions must be those of the World Bank and IMF or at least 'implemented in close coordination with the World Bank and IMF'; moreover, that the receiving governments must show evidence of a commitment to undertake 'significant efforts to carry out economic adjustment' in the form of macroeconomic programmes which are 'deemed sustainable'. While the ACP governments are concerned that they are about to lose their tradition of 'soft aid' from Europe and that the donors now appear to be 'ganging up' on them, in Europe too, dissenting voices are already heard. Not only would this prescription for future Community relations on development issues eliminate much of the distinctive European contribution which has been offered in the past and on which a better future of cooperative relations was to build, but in particular, it casts the IMF – a body firmly devoted to short-term world monetary and payments management and without a vocation for promoting longer-term development – in the driving-seat, and with its own short-run conditions overwhelming those of all the other partners who are persuaded to coordinate. Thus while the EC is now prepared to help constructively with African debt problems, the final design and implementation of that contribution has yet to be resolved politically. The EC has already agreed to help African countries with the World Bank's 'Social Dimensions of Adjustment' (SDA) project, to mitigate the ill-effects of enforced public spending cuts and liberalization, but does not want to be relegated to the role of 'social fire brigade' among other donors.

The other major political issue facing the Lomé IV negotiators – and all future EC relations with Africa – is the problem of South Africa and the effort to be put behind generalized sanctions against Pretoria. The EC is held back mainly by the UK and West German governments, who were staunchly opposed to sanctions and who strongly supported Reagan's policy of constructive engagement instead. With condemnation of apartheid already written into the text of Lomé III, a small (almost nominal) aid allocation already made for the victims of apartheid within South Africa from EC funds and assent indicated by the ACP Group to a proposal to welcome an independent Namibia into the Lomé arrangements, it now seems that the EC has considerable scope for movement on its South Africa policies in the 1990s, and for Lomé IV in particular. Already the EC has begun to show considerable constructive support for the regional SADCC grouping, and this will be taken further.

Five further areas of potential reform can be identified. First, there is great concern that the Lomé trade provisions have failed to stimulate trade and investment (we earlier cited Mauritius as a minor exception which helps to prove this rule). Given that the leading declared aim of the Lomé conventions has been to promote and diversify trade between the EC and the ACP states, the performance of this instrument has of course left much to be desired. In addition, Africa and the other ACP economies were affected at least as badly as the rest of the Third World by the collapse in commercial bank lending in the early-to-mid-1980s (not offering many 'bankable' economies, they had perhaps less to lose than Latin America and Asia, but also felt the draught of debt-saddled bankers leaving for safer portfolios). ACP countries have not yet provided many attractions for direct investment, including by the multinational corporations, except in the undiversified plantation sector. This is partly because of high labour costs and small national markets, but partly also because of the lack of guarantees of both political and economic stability. As a result, the trade and investment provisions of the EC's package have performed poorly to date. The EC will now suggest that Lomé IV could be of indeterminate duration (that is permanent) as regards its trade provisions, instead of being tied to a five-year renegotiating cycle. The idea behind this proposal, which African governments will treat gingerly, is that longer-term guarantees of trade access will attract more investment and more investors of the non-footloose variety to the benefit of African economic stability and export expansion. While the EC market access arrangements would not in future end, subject to renegotiation, after five years, this would not of course apply to the financial arrangements. It is still proposed to replenish the EDF only for a five-year period and indeed as before, the size of the next European Development Fund (it will be EDF VII for Lomé IV) is to be a closely kept secret, ostensibly not for negotiation with the ACP, to be unveiled as the 'carrot' at the end of the negotiating period as an incentive for ACP governments to sign the new political treaty. Any increased funding will inevitably be tied to undertakings on policy reform. Indeed, the amounts of EC aid earmarked for each state will not be known formally until *after* the Convention is signed, though it takes little imagination to conclude that such amounts are eagerly discussed in private and bilaterally between individual governments and the EC authorities during the negotiating stage.

Second, a new element is introduced by the EC's internal politics. In 1992, physical, technical and fiscal barriers within the Community are supposed to be finally disbanded. This will occur midway through Lomé IV; provision has to be made for its effects now. Perhaps most salient of these are the following:

- technical standards harmonization could mean more demand for tropical products such as cocoa, butter and vanilla in chocolate and ice cream if standards are raised, but less if they are lowered.
- harmonizing excise duties and value-added taxes could stimulate demands for imports if the incidence of taxation on developing country products is decreased.
- for banana producers – including African and Caribbean states at present heavily dependent on exports – the present marketing arrangements whereby Somalia supplies Italy, Cameroon and the *DOM/TOM* supply France and the Windward islands supply the UK will collapse, letting in the cheaper and higher-quality 'dollar bananas' from Central and South America which will dominate the wider and unrestricted EC market.
- the EC authorities and the Cecchini Report promise growth of up to 70 per cent resulting from completion of the internal market. Will this be translated as demand for developing country goods and services? The locomotive effect of growth may well have second-round effects on external demand, but it must be remembered that its first-round intentions are to internalize demand within the EC.
- if 1992 is also taken to mean monetary unity, with full membership of the European Monetary System, this means that European Central Banks will effectively jointly adopt the monetary burden (and benefits) of the Franc Zone (the African currency arrangements through the CFA Franc which are presently shouldered only by France); logically, this might even become the 'Ecu Zone'. However, France and the African

Franc Zone member governments are already under pressure to delink their currencies, and devalue the CFA Franc against its 50:1 parity with the French Franc for the first time in forty years.

Africa can also see some major changes on the horizon in terms of its own position in the EC's constellation of relationships with the Third World. While the EC has always made clear in the past, and on French insistence, that Africa is the heart of its development assistance efforts, and rejected proposals to globalize Community policies in this field, two partly unrelated phenomena are now blossoming, both arguably to Africa's short-term disadvantage. It is interesting that *Le Monde* published on 18 March 1989 an editorial entitled 'French Disengagement from Africa'. Only a few weeks later on 20 April 1989 the French Ministry of Cooperation paid for a full page advertisement in *Le Monde* in an attempt to refute this.

On the one hand, and through UK and European Parliament pressure and action, there now exists an emerging EC aid programme for the so-called 'non-associates', shared equally between Asia and Latin America. Though it has nothing like the size of the EDF, it is growing faster and has none of the awkward 1960s' baggage which has in the past made EDF aid so disappointing in practice. On the other hand, there are pressures for the EC to admit new members outside Africa to the Lomé Convention, and hence effectively to the ACP Group. While Namibia is a future prospect when political obstacles are overcome, the candidacy of Haiti and the Dominican Republic is already a reality. The EC would be able to find some grounds to refuse entry to Haiti, if only for its undemocratic record (*Toussaint l'Ouverture* notwithstanding!), though such grounds were not applied to expel Uganda or the Central African Republic in the Amin or Bokassa years. On paper Haiti would be a prime candidate as a very poor, least developed, Caribbean state which was once a colony of European states. The Dominican Republic, a major sugar exporter, might be easier to reject – though it was once Spanish – if Haiti's membership were not granted: they after all share the same island and face fundamentally similar development problems. The Dominican Republic's entry without conditions would however open the floodgates to generalized Central American entry (Belize on the mainland is already an ACP state) if not Latin American membership. If any of this were to happen Africa's strength in the special relationship will be diluted.

Part of this question reflects the shifting point of gravity of the EC itself. While the Franco–German axis dominated, and while France was fully in control of Third World policies, Africa was unquestionably put at the apex. British entry failed to disrupt this completely: Asian entry to the special relationship was prevented, and only small far-flung islands were brought in to dilute African dominance. The delayed effects of Iberian entry – even Portugal's interests are effectively now more with Brazil than with its former African provinces, and Spain is firmly committed to Latin America – have yet to come. Though the French resist this, neither West Germany nor Italy (nor, arguably the UK too) would be averse to a shift of aid and concessional resources towards Latin America over the medium term, though they are concerned that Africa should not suffer.

A fourth phenomenon is already present. With Iberian enlargement, plus the earlier membership of Greece, the EC in the 1980s has already developed a southward tilt. This has been to the benefit of the Mediterranean, hence also of the old concept of 'Eurafrica', though mitigated by the Latin American connection outlined above.

How will the next enlargement affect Africa? Turkey, long an applicant state, may not become the thirteenth member state of the EC. It might be Cyprus or Malta in the Mediterranean; it could be Norway following another referendum; but more likely, it could – despite protestations of neutrality – be almost any of the remaining EFTA states such as Austria or Sweden. Thus it is quite possible that after the last southward tilt of the EC, the next movement could be a Nordic shift, with complex implications for Africa. A later shift could even take in East European countries, further diminishing the Community's interest in the Third World.

Developing countries in the 1990s will still confront an EC of member state governments, however cohesive the Community and its dismantled economic barriers is by then. For much of the 1980s, the key EC governments (of the UK, West Germany and France under Chirac) were conservative administrations closely attuned to the Reagan line on economic liberalism, monetarism and international affairs. Though this affected direct EC–ACP policies less than it might (itself proof of the institutional strength of parts of the Lomé arrangments), it did severely affect the world economic climate in which ACP economies had to be managed. Moreover, only at the end of the 1980s did East–West proxy wars in the Third World begin to be run down. Although one cannot accurately describe what the alternative 1980s world economy would have been, given that in any case it needed to recover from the energy turmoil of the 1970s and the recession starting in 1979, it is clear that the actual 1980s' policies have not been kind to Africa. It follows that European governments in the 1990s might offer Africa and the ACP a better deal. The EC as a budding superpower is thus well placed to capitalize on such changes and update its policies, instruments and institutions.

Conclusion

We asserted at the outset that EC policies towards the ACP rested on three supports: the legacy of colonialization, the mercantilist idea of exchanging raw materials for manufactures and the belief that European culture and civilization could be bestowed as part of development. In the course of this chapter, all three have been shown to be found not only wanting, but excessively backward-looking. The colonial legacy is the legacy of member states – not even governments let alone the European Community itself – which did the colonization. These relationships could however still be the basis for doing better in future, as knowledge and understanding need never be lost. Even if the idea that raw materials should be exchanged for manufactures for mutual benefit (an excessively two-dimensional model even for Ricardo) were persuasive, it would no longer be relevant for the future. Not only do developing countries need desperately to diversify out of commodity dependence, Europe is already shifting out of commodity-using manufacturing into services. Lastly, although culture has obviously a part to play in relations with Africa, it is not at all obvious that a sterile administrative body like the European Commission – hitherto no guardian of culture – should be empowered to be the vector for it or allowed to negotiate on behalf of the cultivated population of Europe a deal with Africa in this non-economic area. These three iconoclastic remarks mean simply that if the EC currently sees itself as a world power in the future, on a par with the US, the USSR and Japan, it needs to begin establishing now a global programme of foreign relations and a balanced agenda for the Third World in which its traditional links with Africa will form just a part. As such, the Lomé Conventions will provide some good building-blocks.

Notes

1. Liberia was never a colony.
2. He was replaced on 1 January 1989 by Manuel Marin.

References

Boardman, R., Shaw, T.M., Soldatos, P. (1985), *Europe, Africa and Lomé III*. University Press of America.

Cornell, Margaret (ed.) (1981), *Europe & Africa. Issues in Post-colonial Relations*, texts of the Noel Buxton Lectures 1980, London, ODI.

Cosgrove, C., McLeod, J., (ed.) (1987), *Trade from Aid: A guide to Opportunities from EEC funding in Africa, the Caribbean and the Pacific*, Reading, CTA Economics & Export Analysts Ltd.

European Communities (1973), *Treaties Establishing the European Communities*, Luxembourg, Office for Official Publications of the European Communities.

European Communities (1975), *ACP–EEC Convention of Lomé and Agreement on Products within the Province of the European Coal and Steel Community*. Presented to Parliament by the Secretary of State for Foreign and Commonwealth Affairs, September, HMSO, London.

Faber, Gerrit (1982), *The European Community and Development Cooperation*, Van Gorcum, Assen.

Federal Trust for Education and Research (1988), *The European Community and the Developing Countries: A Policy for the Future*. A Federal Trust Study reviewed by an international conference held jointly with the Institut d'Etudes Européénes, February, London, Federal Trust for Education and Research.

Hewitt, A.P. (1984), 'The Lomé Conventions: Entering a second decade', *Journal of Common Market Studies*, December.

Hewitt, A.P. (1987), 'Stabex and Commodity Export Compensation Schemes: Prospects for Globalization', *World Development*, May.

House of Lords Select Committee on the European Communities (1981), *Development Aid Policy. Observations by the Government*, Session 1980-1. Presented to parliament by the Minister for Overseas Development, August, London, HMSO.

Killick, Tony and Stevens, Christopher (1989), *Development Cooperation and Structural Adjustment: The issues for Lomé IV*, London, ODI.

Lister, Marjorie (1988), *The European Community and the Developing World*, Aldershot, Avebury.

Ravenhill, John (1985), *Collective Clientelism: The Lomé Conventions and North–South relations*, New York, Columbia University Press.

Stevens, Christopher (ed.) (1984), *EEC and the Third World: A Survey 4. Renegotiating Lomé*, London, Hodder and Stoughton.

Part IV Future perspectives

17 Social Europe: fostering a People's Europe?

Juliet Lodge

Completion of the internal market, a central element of European integration, will become really meaningful only if it brings balanced economic and social progress within the large frontier-free area ... [These] will not be enough to make Europe a tangible reality. Each and every Community citizen needs to feel bound by the links which unite European society.

Jacques Delors, Strasbourg, January 1988

Introduction

The creation of a European social space is bound to lead to major confrontation between the EC (epitomized by the Commission and the EP) and the member governments. It is this area that underscores the potentially all-embracing scope of EC competence. Issue areas formerly deemed the exclusive preserve of domestic ministries are being brought into the EC arena. They include health, education, industrial relations and inviduals' rights as citizens of the EC. A highly politically charged agenda for the future has been presented by the Commission.

Many of the areas subjected to greater EC scrutiny than hitherto and earmarked for EC action – mainly via directives and measures to advance harmonization of standards and provisions (not to be confused with uniformity) – were identified at the EC's creation. Their importance has been underscored for two main reasons: first, because they are deemed to be important incentives to and pre-conditions for achieving labour mobility; second, because the SEM's realization will have unequal regional economic costs and benefits. In agreeing to the SEA, member governments accepted that measures would have to be introduced to attempt to redress the balance. The creation of an integrated economic and social area and the promotion of economic and social cohesion demand EC-level intervention. Moreover, as progress on the removal of physical and technical barriers to trade has occurred, the Commission has stressed the need for balance: the SEM is not simply to benefit commerce. It is part of a wider strategy for the achievement of European Union in which ideally there is to be a balanced distribution of the advantages of the SEM. This could remain a pious hope for years to come.

Estimates suggest that the SEM will increase EC GDP by 5 per cent (using the 1988 baseline) and create an extra 5 million jobs (Cecchini, 1988) assuming that conditions are right and are matched by appropriate economic policies. This major assumption has critical implications for EC economic and industrial policies broadly seen (Swann, 1983) as well as for a wide range of microeconomic areas (such as rural policies, structural and financial instruments, R & D, consumer protection, environmental and competition policies, company law, taxation, intellectual property and so on). Above all, it implies a degree of macroeconomic coordination that has so far proved elusive, and also appropriate instruments to combat difficulties. All kind of national practices (having protectionist intent) can distort competition. The SEM programme has addressed such problems as standards, NTBs, state aids, public procurement, fiscal issues, mergers, cartels, barriers to the free movement of capital and financial services and so on. It has also raised awareness of factors that both inhibit labour mobility including, for example, the nature and level of education, training, wages, employee protection and rights, health and safety provisions and industrial codetermination.

Commission action on the social front is deemed justified to avert distorting competition. It can be presented with a 'human face' and legitimized on the grounds of 'social justice' and 'equal treatment' for EC citizens. However it is presented, its application impinges on national practices from the shop floor to the board of directors, from unemployment offices to health and safety bodies, from small businesses to MNCs and R & D establishments. Since the EC wants standards and provision to be raised to generally higher levels, member states with lower levels will face economic and political pressures to upgrade traditional practices. Already, the potentially distorting patterns of 'social dumping' (that is de-investment to states with the lowest, and implicitly cheapest, standards and regulations) have aroused great concern in states like FRG and Denmark which have developed higher standards in some cases. In the short term adverse effects may well arise from dumping which will reduce economic activity in richer states and increase it in poorer states with less oversight over and restraints on economic activities. Many of these may very well be environmentally damaging or may simply have been shifted to a given state in order that advantage can be taken of slacker standards and poorer wage, labour and social provisions. This shift is usually presented in terms of the benefits of a liberal, free and de-regulated market. Viewed in broader perspective, the argument is less than watertight. Moreover, Commission intervention will be demanded and states will be unlikely to be able to defend lower standards indefinitely given the high profile the Commission is attaching to a 'social space' and principles of social justice. The EC's credibility would be seriously eroded if it were to fail to go beyond the very limited aims it has set itself so far.

What differentiates current Commission aims in the social arena from past policy is the existence of an over-arching goal – whose achievement can be plotted with reference to short- and mid-term targets in microeconomic sectors – coupled with a commitment to a People's Europe and common rights for EC citizens whether in the political, social, economic or educational realms. The idea of a Bill of Rights and an EC Freedom of Information Act (EPWD A2-208/87) has been raised and will continue to preoccupy many. While many goals realistically cannot be realized by 2000, others could be and Commission intervention aims to foster the kind of environment that will make them possible and to show that the EC 'cares' for its citizens: it has a human face.

The preoccupation with what might loosely be termed a 'Social Europe' during the 1990s requires explanation, however. It represents a departure from the original idea that the way in which any enlarged EC cake was to be distributed was largely a matter for the member states. The economic, political and psychological dynamics behind this change warrant brief comment as their interlinkage and recurrence over the years is telling.

Economic considerations derived from the view that the EC needed rapidly to reform many of its practices if it were to maintain let alone improve its position in world markets. This point had been made repeatedly since the end of the 1970s and began to hit home when concurrent pressures for political reform grew.

Contributing economic considerations included continuing attempts to advance integration beyond the customs union (see Swann 1988, chap. 4) to promote monetary integration and 'economic and monetary union'. The terminology is telling since it highlights the idea that 'economic' issues are separable from 'monetary' matters. Practice, however, shows their intermeshing and in the EC's context, some monetary integration was seen in the late 1960s as a precondition to the integration of domestic policies over a broad area. It is true that the end of the Bretton Woods system gave impetus to the move but the political goals of integration provided a major impetus then as now.

The Rome Treaty (Arts.103-9) does not refer to an economic and monetary union, but it does imply a far greater degree of coordination and convergence between the members states' conjunctural, monetary and economic policies than had been achieved with the help of the special advisory Monetary Committee (eventually responsible to the ECOFIN Council set up in 1969) and the Committee of the Governors of Central Banks eventually set up in the mid-1960s to assist cooperation between the member states' central bank governors. The commitment to economic and monetary union was reasserted in the SEA (Subsection II – monetary capacity) through the insertion into the EEC Treaty of a new chapter 1, 'cooperation in economic and monetary policy: (Economic and Monetary Union)'.

EMU itself was put firmly on the EC's agenda at the 1969 Hague summit (after years of inadequate Council response to Commission pressure)[1] and consolidated, significantly on the eve of EC enlargement, at the 1972 Paris summit which committed the EC to realizing EMU by 1980. This is not the place to rehearse the division between economists and monetarists (Swann,1988: 180). Suffice it to note that the EMU deadline was the product of the work of the Werner committee which reported in 1970 and which pointed to the need for greater monetary integration (notably *vis-à-vis* the outside world), a central EC banking system and institutional reform.[2] It was partly applied and was, like the 'Snake' set up in April 1972, overtaken by events – oil crisis, inflation, international monetary crises – all of which encouraged the member states to pursue very independent national economic policies to the neglect of their commitment under EEC Arts. 103-9.

In 1975 as pressure for political reform and European Union grew (note the confluence with the Tindemans Report and the decision on direct elections), a Commission study group chaired by M. Marjolin reported on EMU. In 1977 EC Commission President Jenkins called for monetary union and a single EC currency and monetary authority. The idea was taken up at the 1978 European Councils and pushed by West German Chancellor Schmidt and French President Giscard d'Estaing. The result was the creation of the European Monetary System designed to combat the destabilizing effect of the dollar on European currency movements. EMS was not linked up to the more grandiose European Union schemes though it may be argued that it was seen as being instrumental to it (as Art.102 SEA underlines). EMS was, moreover, a tool to minimize currency fluctuations and their attendant destabilizing effect on domestic and EC policy (notably the CAP and the problems arising out of the need for monetary compensatory amounts to offset problems over the unit of account and European unit of account). To this end, in 1979 the European Currency Unit (ECU) was introduced. It is a composite currency whose international, public and private use has grown rapidly.

Allied to the EMS was the exchange rate mechanism (ERM) which allowed currencies to fluctuate against each other within flexible margins; and the New Community Instrument. The latter, with the EIB, was to make cheap loans available to weaker EMS members. In addition, it must be stressed that in setting up the EMS the member states recognized the growing disparity between the prosperity of the core and periphery states and their economies. They even called for coordination of their national macroeconomic policies with a view to promoting a convergence of economic performance. This presaged the emphasis on economic convergence and 'cohesion' in the SEA and SEM deliberations. Moreover, the SEA's 'Final Provisions' contain a declaration by the Presidency and the Commission on the EC's monetary capacity to the effect that the SEA's provisions on this 'are without prejudice to the possibility of further development within the framework of existing powers'. This signal that this sector was incomplete and open to development not just by treaty amendment is highly significant. It hints at the sometimes furious disputes during the Dooge processes over EMU issues raised by the EUT and a growing role for the European Monetary Cooperation Fund presaging an EC Central Bank.[3] The political implications of such a move, while often presented as a major restriction on national sovereignty, imply commitment to the EEC Treaty's goals concerning economic policy integration. This in turn presupposes a greater degree of convergence among EC states' policies not only in respect of exchange rate fluctuations but across the range of economic activity subject to state intervention, and including social policy.

Political factors impelling a reappraisal of economic issues from the 1970s onwards arose both out of domestic concern over the management of stagflation and rising unemployment but more instructively out of the EC's desire to highlight and fix new goals for integration before EC enlargement. This in effect committed acceding states to a series of priority goals pre-determined by the EC's core in advance of their membership. Other political impulses were prompted by international events as shown above. Further pressures emanated from quarters concerned with realizing a European Union, Euro-elections and the EC's 'democratization'. They in turn were bolstered by internal policy developments (as in respect of the budget) and the decision to give the EC 'a human face', to make its work relevant in a direct way to the EC's citizens. This goal was itself loosely linked to the longer-term need to make the EC comprehensible to those who would be called upon to elect its Parliament.

Underlying the political impulses are psychological factors which relate to swings in public attitudes to the EC and to the goal of European Union. The concern over the impact of a disaffected public on member states' willingness to promote further integration (in whatever sphere) might have been seen as of minimal interest given citizens' marginalization in EC decisionmaking, but it did spur the refinement and broadening of the scope of EC activity in the social sphere (Lodge, 1978). That such action resulted from negativism suggests that the low priority accorded social policy measures might not have been confronted had not the EC's first enlargement and generalized stagflation led to sharp criticism of the EC's policy preoccupations and the limited impact of its social instruments (Taylor, 1983: 209).

Not until Mediterranean enlargement became a real possibility did a number of economic, political and psychological factors coalesce to stimulate a more adventurous approach to the EC's social policy and social obligations *vis-à-vis* its citizens. It was clear that Mediterranean enlargement would profoundly alter overall measures of EC prosperity, the respective status of Ireland, Italy and the UK and with it, their claims on EC funds having a redistributive intention. Such enlargement was also bound to lead to pressure to alter spending priorities and key aspects of established policies (notably the CAP). In addition, not only had the publics in the Mediterranean states to be convinced of the economic benefits of EC membership over the medium to long term, but public disillusionment was apparent in the core even in states whose pro-integration sentiment had long been taken for granted (for example the FRG). These issues collided on the eve of the second elections to the European Parliament (*Eurobarometre*, 20).

Moreover, the idea of European Union had been revived with aplomb and had found sponsorship not only in overtly pro-federal Italian government circles but tactically more importantly in President Mitterrand. The Spanish and Portuguese governments' support for many EUT ideals and for the more federal ideas that the Dooge committee assimilated from the EUT presented two core members with a vision of the EC being given direction from the Mediterranean flank. There were, of course, misgivings about the resource redistributions wanted by the Mediterranean states but these were seen as flowing with the tide and being a legitimate demand in the context of the overall thrust to realize the internal market. As in the Jenkins-Schmidt-d'Estaing era, the fact of a useful coincidence of view on some major issues between President Delors and influential governments (notably in France, Belgium, the FRG and Italy) facilitated the launching of initiatives in the socio-economic spheres to complement the SEM's politico-commercial aspects. In order to appreciate how Delors's Social Europe fits in with this, it will be helpful briefly to outline how the EC's social policy has evolved. The likely effects of the 'Social Europe' endeavour must not be exaggerated. Their immediate importance lies perhaps more in the high profile and legitimacy they give to EC intervention in this area and in the signals given relating social policy to EC economic policy and hence to economic and monetary union.

Background to the EC's social policy

Social policy has a very restrictive meaning in the context of the ECSC, EEC and EURATOM treaties. Essentially, it is conceived as instrumental to the improvement of living and (in the ECSC and EEC treaties) working conditions. EURATOM refers to health and safety matters and this, according to Collins (1983: 97) means that basic standards of health care are to be laid down in the EC area. She goes on to point out that while the EC is not entrusted with a full blown capacity to redistribute wealth in order to improve living conditions, it is given particular obligations. Art.117 urges member governments to promote improvements to enable workers to share in the expected benefits of economic integration. The SEA goes further, however, in giving the Commission responsibility for drafting comprehensive proposals to use the Structural Funds (including the Social Fund) to reduce regional disparities and the backwardness of the least-favoured regions (SEA Title V, Arts.130A-E).

In July 1988, the Commission adopted four new implementing regulations to simplify and reform the structural funds. They define the areas of work of the three funds (ESF, ERDF, and FEOGA) and coordination between them and the European Investment Bank. All three funds are important instruments in their relevant sectors, but the sectoral policy division between them has undermined their potential effectiveness. It was therefore important both to interlink their respective networks and to take steps to rationalize and focus their activities on a coordinated basis to bring the maximum amount of aid available to bear on the problem addressed.

The funds have suffered over the years from chronic underfunding. The need for reform was heightened by the accession of Greece, Spain and Portugal; appreciation of the effects of economic recession; and growing long-term unemployment and recognition of problems associated with the impact of steps to complete the Single European Market on areas of industrial decline and relative deprivation. Political factors (notably the demands from the periphery for at least a doubling of the funds' resources) coupled with awareness of the complexities of administering and obtaining assistance from the funds impelled reform. In particular, there was concern that the funds' respective regulations and the multiplicity of rules governing their use were cumbersome, contradictory and diverse. Public-sector bodies often found it difficult to access them for reasons associated both with administrative requirements and the interventions and limitations placed on them by national governments.

The funds themselves, and notably the ESF, had repeatedly tried to maximize their potential by setting out short-term priorities. The core problem of underfunding was not addressed effectively until February 1988 when the European Council agreed to double the Funds by 1993. By then, the Commission had already put forward a set of coordinated goals for the funds, earmarking five major areas of concern. These are:

1. structural development and adjustment of the poorer regions;
2. reconversion of the regions including employment areas and urban communities seriously affected by industrial decline;
3. combating long-term unemployment;
4. professional integration of young people;
5a. adjusting agricultural structures;
5b. developing rural areas.

The ERDF is to intervene under objectives 1, 2 and 5b and is to co-finance productive and infrastructure investment programmes as well as measures designed to develop the indigenous potential of the regions, including transfrontier cooperation and information exchange.

The ESF is charged with intervening under objectives 3 and 4 and in liaison with other funds under 1, 2 and 5b. The aim is to ensure that the ESF contributes to the promotion of employment and the development of new jobs for the unemployed and those threatened with unemployment. It is important to recall that the Cecchini Report forecast medium- and long-term unemployment rising by around 225,000 before falling sharply. FEOGA is to concentrate on 1, 5a and 5b.

The overall aim is to ensure that assistance is directed to areas of greatest need in an effective and integrated manner. This implies not only better coordination between the various funds and combined use of subsidies and loans, but also the selection of fewer, but bigger, programmes as recipients of EC aid. The signs are that industrial counterparts to the large-scale IMPs are being developed.

While the Social Fund is the prime instrument of EC social policy, it is by no means the only one to be used for promoting economic and social cohesion. Moreover, over the years, its preoccupations and role have changed. Initially, the ESF was a source of funds to assist with the retraining and relocation of redundant workers. Its greatest beneficiary was the FRG which maximized the receipts from the ESF both by adroitness and by fulfilling the eligibility criteria regarding the re-employment of workers. Italy's less buoyant economy at that time meant that even though it had a higher unemployment rate, it did not benefit as much.

The ESF has been reformed over the years to enable it to address, albeit on a very limited scale, the major socio-economic problems facing the EC. The second ESF came into force in 1972. It was to try and ensure that its resources went to areas of greatest need. Once again, it failed to meet its much broader goals through want of adequate resources and the EC's lack of competence for macro-economic matters. By 1978, its role had been refocused as an instrument of the labour market.

By the early 1980s, the Commission was insisting that it address priority issues and the EP had argued for funds being directed to specific groups of workers as well as to specific sectors – textiles, workers leaving the land, technological progress and re-tooling. In 1983, the Council of Ministers decided that over 70 per cent of ESF funds should go to unemployed workers aged under twenty-five. Since then the Commission, which is responsible for determining the ESF's guidelines on a three-year basis, has emphasized technological concerns and has ensured that funds are more focused and directed to areas where they are likely to have greatest impact. In 1987 and 1988, it introduced new guidelines to ensure that resources went to areas of the highest unemployment and lowest GDP and areas of industrial restructuring. It also made eligible for ESF aid long-term unemployed adults, those in SMEs and those in training posts.

The ESF's area of activity has widened over the years. The ESF has also shown itself to be a flexible instrument of EC social policy. Nevertheless, its impact has been constrained by limited resources and by the fact that its terms of operation continue to reflect a narrow range of preoccupations at the heart of EC social policy.

EC social policy

EC social policy has not been directly concerned with the range of issues that the term 'social policy' connotes in many West European states. It is not a generalized scheme for the provision of social welfare. Nor is it designed as a means of harmonizing social security systems or levelling out social security burdens between the states by a set deadline as France had requested at the inception of the Communities; (Swann, 1988; Collins, 1983). Rather, it was initially tailored to the precise and immediate concerns of the three Communities and focused, from the outset, on employment (including re-deployment and training).

EC social policy is set out in Articles 117-22. The role of the Social Fund is specified in Articles 123-8. The ECSC treaty (Articles 46-8, 68, 51, 54-6) did, however, bring in measures affecting social well-being and these ideas were to influence the EC's provisions. Article 104 states the EC's commitment to maintaining a high level of employment, and Articles 48-66 outline EC goals in respect of labour mobility, right of establishment and freedom to provide services (see chapter 6).

EC social policy has two broad components. One relates to technical matters, the other reflects the EC's social conscience. The first relates to factor mobility, labour mobility, industrial relations and technical aspects of social security necessary to foster labour mobility in a customs union, and the second to social improvement and social harmonization. Operationally, this relates to the interpretation and implementation of measures to realize the commitment to improving living and working conditions. There is no commitment to achieving uniformity in social provision by set deadlines. Rather, the aim is to deter states from maintaining provisions inhibiting labour mobility (for example to ensure non-discriminatory treatment of EC nationals in employment matters ranging from pay to working conditions and so on. Migrant workers' issues were not comprehensively addressed until the mid-1970s, and to encourage a progressive raising of standards partly through the approximation of laws.

Objectives

EC social policy has proved flexible and adaptable. It is supposed to be more than a cosmetic adjunct to the EC. Commission and Council reports over the years have identified new priorities and refined the social policy's main instrument, the Social Fund, to augment the policy's responsiveness and impact on employment. The overall aim is to alleviate and minimize hardship arising from structural change. To that end, its main objectives are the improvement of living and working conditions; promotion of cooperation among members on employment, labour law and working conditions; basic and advanced vocational training (OJL199, 31.7.85); social security; prevention of occupational accidents and diseases; occupational hygiene; and the right of association, and collective bargaining between employers and workers (Article 118); equal pay (and other considerations 'in cash or in kind': Article 119); and fostering equivalence between existing paid holiday schemes. The Social Fund's operations are geared to these goals and specific schemes have been set up over the years to direct funds to certain groups of underprivileged workers including women, the underqualified, under-twenty-fives, long-term unemployed, those in need of vocational rehabilitation and the handicapped. A series of programmes were implemented for the last group beginning in 1974 and culminated in the 1980s, following the 1981 International Year of Disabled People, with the Council's adoption of the Commission's communication on the Social Integration of Disabled People (OJ C347, 31.12.81). In principle the EC remains committed to social integration, but progress remains slow even though the EC is coordinating research programmes (the first in 1982-6, and others running into the 1990s).

The Social Fund also aims to promote training rather than just the readaptation and reinstallation of workers; to retrain those unemployed through technological progress; and to combat underemployment in the periphery. In addition, the operation of the Fund has been altered to direct funding to areas of greatest need and to properly coordinated projects rather than to states most adept at making claims (ESC, 1973).

Not until 1969 did the Commission begin to confront the problem of a lack of coordination between social policy *per se* and other relevant sectoral actions. It took a political initiative to revitalize social policy in the 1970s. (Note its juxtaposition with the first enlargement.) Chancellor Brandt submitted a memorandum on social policy to the 1969 Hague summit arguing that coordination of related sectors was vital and that progress in economic integration (and specifically towards EMU) demanded a corresponding progress in social matters. The Commission, echoing this view, insisted that social policy affected people both as producers and consumers and thereby widened the policy's potential scope. In response to the 1972 Paris summit's decision to promote EC initiatives in social, environmental and consumer policies, attention turned to the problems of migrants, poverty and unemployment. In 1973, the Council adopted a Social Action Programme (SAP) which the Commission welcomed as 'the first attempt by the [EC] to draw up a coherent social policy setting out in a purposeful way the initial practical steps on the road towards the ultimate goal of European Social Union' (Commission, 1972). The SAP had three broad aims: (i) full and better employment; (ii) improvement of living and working conditions; and (iii) greater participation of the social partners in the economic and social decisions of the EC.

The SAP was full of good intentions and did have some concrete results in very troubled economic times (Shanks, 1977; 16ff). Brief highlights concerned the involvement of the ministers of education who in 1976 adopted a resolution on measures to improve young people's preparation for work and their transition from school to work. The same year saw the setting up of the European Foundation for the improvement of Living and Working Conditions in Dublin, and 1977 the opening of the European Centre for Development of Vocational Training in Berlin. The 1978 Bremen European Council endorsed the Social Fund's extension of activities to work creation schemes for unemployed under-twenty-fives.

Evaluating the impact of the EC's social policy on the member states is outside the scope of this survey. Suffice it to note that it has always suffered from underfunding (securing well under 10 per cent of the EC's expenditure). As its scope has expanded it has become unable to meet the demands on it. Moreover, whereas in the mid-1970s a number of Commissioners saw the social policy as a vehicle for promoting the EC's 'human face', member states anxious about its potentially expansionist incursions into the politics of resource allocation and redistribution drew back. Functionalist logic that supranational action might be timely as states' abilities to satisfy needs waned proved unsustainable given competition over resources and limited progress towards economic integration. Moreover, few states were willing to publicize the extent to which their own employment schemes, for example, were beneficiaries of EC funding, so eroding further the visibility of the construction of a Community with a human face.

Nevertheless, there was some success in the achievement of progress on a number of technical issues ranging from minimum common standards in health and safety, the workplace, environment, transferability of social security benefits, and the principle of equal pay. However, progress in principle was and remains fraught in implementation. It is noteworthy that much of the EC's action in these spheres takes the shape of directives whose implementation has been postponed by governments (notably the UK) or imperfectly met. Indeed, even regulations fail to produce common results (Siedentopf and Ziller, 1988).

This rather piecemeal approach to Social Europe continued into the 1980s. Attention focused mainly on unemployment and workplace matters, including the highly contentious question of relations between the social partners: a relationship which the Commission tried to cement in the Fifth Directive on the harmonization of company law (OJ C240, 9.9.83) and its abortive Vredeling directive on worker consultation and rights to information in 1980 (OJ C297, 11.11.80). The latter's demise was orchestrated largely by the UK and the US. The question of effective relations between the social partners was pursued however, in Val Duchesse meetings after the Tripartite Conference failures.

The so-called Vredeling directive was not revolutionary. It was in line with the Commission's record (COM/80/0423, 23.10.80); however, it met unprecedented opposition from vested employer interests (notably in multinational corporations who were to come within its ambit). By contrast, the various unions in the member states were often ill-informed as to its existence. Similarly, even though '1992' campaigns have had a psychological and a practical impact on employers in the EC, the union response has been truncated. Unions even in multinationals have so far failed to mobilize themselves on a cross-national, national or EC basis. They do not appear for the most part (outside the ETUC) to have a '1992' strategy. Yet, the social dimension to the SEM patently addresses issues central to them: wages, employment, the working environment, social dumping and standards – in short, key topics in industrial relations. In the light of this, Delors's speech to the TUC in 1988 takes on special significance.

Moreover, the SEM's social dimension debate reveals the continuity in social policy and industrial relations. The social dialogue controversy continues to centre on such matters as: the timing, nature, content, frequency and destination of company information to workers' representatives (and the latter's definition – that is whether or not trade union officials should have access to information provided); and the size of the firm (or subsidiary) subject to any EC directive. Particularly contentious is the issue of whether or not workers should be given information about company intentions in advance of decisions affecting workers being taken. In 1989, British EDG MEPs in a display of group cohesion voted against the EP resolution on industrial democracy and social rights.

Social policy towards the 1990s

EC social policy in the latter part of the 1980s ceased to be seen as a separate sector of activity in practice. Awareness of numerous problems associated with labour issues had grown and the problems raised had to be addressed even if the EC itself had few financial resources to alleviate them. Instead, it concentrated on establishing principles of good practice and better standards. Moreover, work and education were also brought into the EC's realm of activities through social policy programmes, especially in the area of health and safety at work, working conditions, employment aids and women's policy. They were also advanced through such provisions as YES (Youth Exchange) and Erasmus (in the field of higher education), the mutual recognition of diplomas and professional qualifications, directives on part-time and temporary workers, medical and biotechnology research programmes, university and industry linkups – as under COMETT, – UETPs and other health, training, information and employment measures designed to boost economic prosperity. Many of these were eligible for special funding from the EC or from the Social Fund and many were orientated towards future needs in the SEM (such as the *Euro-guichets* and EC marriage bureaux for small- and medium-sized enterprises).

However, the main thrust of EC social policy continues to focus on work and employment issues and on the removal of impediments to labour/occupational mobility. In the latter half of the 1980s, the Commission set up a working party to examine the social dimension of the internal market using existing social policy and social dialogue achievements as its starting point. From the outset, the working party considered economic and social issues jointly and saw the establishment of a genuine EC area of occupational mobility as essential to the exercise of one of the four freedoms of movement enshrined in the Rome Treaty. It therefore echoed the 1988 joint opinion of UNICE, ETUC and the European Centre for Public Enterprises (CEEP) in calling for a dynamic application of Article 118 and noted that so far attention had concentrated on the other three freedoms of movement – for capital, goods and services which underpinned the idea of a frontier-free EC. It argued that there was a need for regulation to facilitate the establishment of a European industrial relations area (Social Europe, 1988). Manuel Marin put forward a package of proposals on health and safety, worker participation, training, job mobility and certain guaranteed employment rights (including the right to lifelong training). The most controversial proposals concern worker participation. Even though the Commission stepped back from recommending anything as extensive as the German system of co-determination, the member states proved exceedingly suspicious of what turned out to be a very modest set of recommendations. The Commission suggested a new European company statute to allow company mergers to proceed under EC rather than national law, enabling them to choose between European or national status. However, companies opting for this will not be able to escape the corporate laws of those states that provide for worker participation. Rather, the aim is to further the idea of worker involvement (something that falls far short of 'leading' Dutch practice) in companies.

The need for a European company statute and tougher rules on health and safety, better access to vocational training, the social 'insertion' of migrant workers, pension schemes, industrial democracy and measures to give employees a chance of 'life-long' education and to correct regional imbalances resulting from deregulation in the free movement of goods, services, capital and people were stressed throughout 1988. At the ETUC Stockholm Congress in June, Delors argued that the SEM had to include a guarantee of existing social rights and union freedoms. At the Hanover summit he said that the European

Council should confirm that the social dimension to the SEM has the same priority as other SEA aims. The more moderate response was that action would have to proceed along the lines of Article 118a and that new measures were not to be lower than existing national ones. The incoming Greek Presidency, while broadly sympathetic, was quick to point out that such social policy goals could not be met in view of the inadequacy of the structural funds whose resources were insufficient for realizing social cohesion.

Thus, again it can be seen that as the potential scope of the social policy has widened, greater resources have been made available. But their impact has – as yet – been very limited. This is due to member states underfunding instruments designed to tackle very large problems. Moreover, discrepancies persist even after EC-level micro-sectoral action because uniformity of provision has not resulted from the relevant directives and regulations. Verifying and checking the results of their implementation is haphazard at best in an area where wide divergence exists between the Twelve's practices. Change and upgrading are vital, but progress may continue to be slow given the costs involved and political unwillingness in some states to accept the need for better provision.

The EC does not expect to make a major impact through new social policy regulations in the immediate future. Rather, it is to continue to seek harmonization wherever this is possible and likely to benefit individuals and firms, and convergence between existing provisions in the Twelve. The Commission is amassing data and information on the main practical obstacles to freedom of movement and asking the member states to eliminate discriminatory practices which, it is felt, will worsen unless action is taken. Such measures include those particularly relevant to daily life (for example insurance, moving house, driving licences, frontier workers and so on). It is also examining cases of unequal treatment arising from national laws to assess the possibility of an approval procedure relating to conformity of national laws and regulations within EC law. This is to be bolstered by an energetic policy on certain exemplary cases of infringement by giving a general scope to the ECJ's judgments in requests for preliminary hearings. Obstacles to the freedom of movement of persons (notably professionals) is also being catalogued, with attention focusing on tax and financial matters such as the transferability of acquired rights in supplementary company pension schemes and capital. Furthermore, the Commission intends to promote greater awareness of occupational mobility rights in the EC.

The Commission has already begun action in these fields. Others that will receive attention during the 1990s concern migrant workers, the new poor, rights of residence, training in technology (OJL222, 8.8.86), improved links between national employment offices and employment policies (using the MISEP and SEDOC networks), accelerating the mutual recognition of qualifications including comparability in basic vocational training (OJC143,10.6.86; OJL199,31.7.85) and extending EC social security rules to all insured persons. This type of activity will not have an immediate impact on labour mobility, but the EC is preparing the ground for appropriate future EC intervention (COM(86)410 fin., 24.7.87). The signal to the member governments to put their own house in order is unequivocal (SEC(88)1148 final, 14.9.88).

The second area of concern relates to coping with the changes effected or accelerated by the SEM's completion. To this end the Commission is trying to identify sensitive areas and give effect to the SEM's social dimension. Again, the emphasis is on using and coordinating outside expertise and findings which could then allow the Commission to incorporate social variables in the presentation of its EC industrial outlooks. Thought is being given to the setting up of appropriate mechanisms to facilitate forward planning at the sectoral level, and devising appropriate legislative responses (using the machines directive as a model). Moreover, anticipating the effect of demographic change, attention is also focusing on adult training and on the implementation of a work programme on health, hygiene and safety at work. Finally, the Commission is assessing the coherence between the new assistance instruments of the reformed structural funds and the classic sectoral instruments.

The above areas seem technical and of low political salience. However, measures to mitigate divergent provisions among the Twelve will prove extremely contentious. In the short term, however, it is the third area of the social dimension that has aroused greatest political anxiety: the establishment of a European system of industrial relations. Here concern centres on modest proposals edging towards a European collective agreement as the product of the social dialogue which itself was only revived with some difficulty in early 1989. The Commission wishes to deepen the social dialogue and to direct attention to issues linked to the SEM's completion and its decentralization as well as to occupational mobility (social cover, equal treatment, recognition of qualifications and training). Again, the strategy is to identify and catalogue potential problems in specific areas prior to taking EC-wide action designed to foster a set of minimal social provisions as a starting point for the establishment of a system of European industrial relations. The areas identified concern industrial relations within EC multinationals; the impact of the Val Duchesse agreements on new technologies at multi-sectoral, sectoral and company levels; worker consultation – notably in respect of technological innovation and major changes; minimum social provisions supplementary to existing ones; flexible employment contracts to cover part-time, temporary, fixed contract and subcontracted staff, and the establishment of a standard contract of employment.

The Commission sees cooperation between management and labour as essential to the SEM's success. Its politico-economic justification, it argues, lies in the social progress it is expected to promote. The very modest Marin proposals on aspects of worker consultation did, however, provoke disquiet on both sides of industry. The unions were, understandably, dismayed at their restricted nature. Industry was initially somewhat relieved (though some governments, notably the UK, bitterly rejected the proposals), but some federations affiliated with UNICE (which includes members from EFTA, Turkey and Malta) then tried to acquire additional rights to be consulted by the Commission during the initial pre-publication phases of drafting proposals and preparing impact reports. In December 1988, they issued a Joint Declaration of European Business aimed at maintaining 'the established tradition of dialogue between social partners'. Since the Commission does already consult the ESC (which includes business representatives), there were fears that UNICE was trying to exert undue control over and pressure on the Commission at a time when the Commission was anxious to relaunch the social dialogue and the ESC was preparing the 'Social Charter for Fundamental Rights'.

The Commission's efforts to highlight the EC's social dimension and to relaunch the social dialogue culminated in September 1988 with the issue of a document called the Social Dimension of the Internal Market[5] and Delors's initiative in January 1989. It was agreed to set up a pilot group at political level between the Commission, UNICE and the ETUC entrusted with stimulating the social dialogue which is to be continued at regional and sectoral levels. The pilot group is to analyse the EC labour market during the SEM's creation and to assess education and training and the Commission's role. The Commission is to present an in-depth annual report on employment to the Standing Committee on Employment and then to the Council of Ministers. The Commission is also to consult the social partners, at regional level, on sectoral policies, existing projects on the development of backward regions and the conversion of regions in crisis and rural development. It is to consult them on a European company statute and to seek their opinion on the draft Social Charter.[6] Discussions over a charter or bill of basic rights paralleled the debate about a social charter. The EP's Institutional Affairs Committee outlined the contents of the latter and once again highlighted concern about the EC's 'human face' and the need to ensure that all EC citizens enjoyed comparable rights and freedoms (including the right to life, equality before the law, freedom of thought and expression, protection of the family and so on). In some respects this action, taken together with the Social Charter, complements and applies to the EC many of the rights set down in the Council of Europe's Social Charter (which came into effect in 1965) and its European Convention on Human Rights both of which address social and human rights from welfare to children's rights and those of migrant workers.

By the end of the 1980s, the Commission had set the agenda for the 1990s having identified and listed some eighty individual measures in various social policy fields, and had begun work on the four areas of the EC's social dimension necessary to the SEM's realization: free movement of persons; economic and social cohesion; unemployment; and the social dialogue. However, the impact of its work and the various structural fund programmes cannot be expected to be dramatic given wide discrepancies between the members states, limited financial resources and the member governments' unwillingness to tolerate extensive EC intervention. Growing realization and experience of social dumping, labour shortfalls, inadequate training, demographic change, an ageing population, the needs of the 'new poor', and growing regional disparity may well encourage a change of view. The major impediments are likely to remain political and financial, however, as governments may well want to see the EC's social policy being interpreted in an even more restrictive manner than it has been hitherto. This would damage the credibility of the social dimension. Yet the imperatives of the SEM mean that ideally the Commission will have to monitor and act in order to advance and protect employment, social security, health and safety standards. Its role will inevitably have to expand (as it already has into the education sector broadly conceived (COM(88)192 and 280 final), even if its proposals do not directly impinge upon all aspects of the welfare state. The Commission is likely to need public backing for measures to enhance the lot of EC citizens. Action rather than words will become vital. Moreover, a very narrow interpretation of 'social Europe' that stresses only those issues central to ensuring labour mobility and which is not integrated into the wider panoply of 'human' issues epitomized by the phrase 'a People's Europe' will not impress the public.

The goal of establishing a People's Europe cannot be sustained simply by providing symbols of belonging, no matter how attractive and diverse they may be. There is a need to complement them with tangible benefits that directly affect citizens' living standards and opportunities to benefit from the SEM. If the EC fails in this, the public may become increasingly cynical about People's Europe endeavours such as the EC flag and anthem, Youth Orchestra, sports teams, European Music Year (1985), the 'Europe against Cancer' programme (1987-9), the first Community Games (1989), educational opportunities, programmes to combat aids and smoking, and to regulate and improve aspects of health (through the use of advanced informatics (COM(88)315 fin), the Euro-Link Age project for the elderly, medical research and drug abuse (both human (Stewart-Clark, 1986) and in various points along the food chain), transfrontier civil defence cooperation, voting rights in local elections, passports and driving licences. There's a need for a major public information exercise concerning both measures relevant to people's lives thwarted by member governments and general political information on how the EC functions. The Commission and the European Parliament will have to respond to this and overcome the formidable obstacles in their paths if the SEM's social and 'human' dimensions are to be realized.

Notes

1. Numerous committees were set up during the 1960s, including a Budgetary Policy Committee and a Medium-term Policy Committee. In 1974, these and the short-term policy committee were merged into an Economic Policy Committee.
2. For details see T. Hitiris and A. Zervoyianni in Lodge, J. (ed) Institutions and Politics.
3. France favoured such a move while the FRG resisted it on grounds of anticipated economic and political costs to itself. The Bundesbank's position has since changed.
4. P. Taylor, 1983: 209ff.
5. This was published as SEC(88)1148 which lists the eighty proposals that make up the technical arena of the social dimension.
6. On collective bargaining in the Twelve see European Trade Union Institute, *Collective Bargaining in Western Europe in 1987 and Prospects for 1988*, Brussels, 1988.

References

Cecchini Report (1988), *The European Challenge – 1992: the Benefits of a Single Market*, Aldershot, Gower.
Collins, D. (1983), *The Operations of the European Social Fund*, Kent, Croom Helm.
Collins, D. (1975), *The European Communities: the Social Policy of the First Phase* (Vol. 1), Oxford, Martin Robertson.
— (1975, Vol. 2), *The European Community, 1958-1972*, Oxford, Martin Robertson.
— (1983), 'Social Policy' in J. Lodge, *Institutions and Policies of the European Community*, pp.96-109.
— (1983b), 'The Impact of Social Policy in the United Kingdom' in A. El-Agraa (ed.), *Britain within the European Community*, London, pp.213-36.
Commission of the EC (1974), 'Social Action Programme of the Community', *EC Bulletin*, 2.
— (1988), *Education in the European Community: Medium Term Perspectives: 1989-92*, COM(88)280 final, Brussels.
Cosgrove Twitchett, C. (ed.) (1981), *Harmonisation in the EEC*, London, Macmillan.
Curzon Price, V. (1981), *Industrial Policies in the European Community*, London, Macmillan.

Dennet, J. *et. al.*, (1982), *Europe Against Poverty*, London, Bedford Square Press.

Giavazzi, F. *et. al.*, (1988), *The European Monetary System*, Cambridge, Cambridge Univesity Press.

Hepple, B. (1987), 'The Crisis in EC Labour Law', *Industrial Law Journal*, **16**.

Holloway, J. (1981), *Social Harmonisation in the European Community*, Farnborough, Gower.

Kruse, D. (1980), *Monetary Integration in Western Europe: EMU, EMS and Beyond*, London, Butterworths.

Lodge, J. (1978), 'Towards a Human Union: EEC Social Policy and European Integration', *British Journal of International Studies*, **6**, 107-34.

Ludlow, P. (1982), *The Making of the European Monetary System*, London, Butterworths.

Northup, H. (1988), 'Multinational union-management consultation in Europe: resurgence in the 1980s?', *International Labour Review*, 127.

Padoa-Schioppa, T. *et. al.*, (1987), *Equity, Efficiency and Growth*, Brussels, EC Commission.

Robson, P. (1980), *The Economics of International Integration*, London, Allen & Unwin.

Shanks, M. (1977), *European Social Policy Today and Tomorrow*, Oxford, Pergamon.

Siedentopf, H. and Ziller, J. (eds) (1988), *Making European Policies Work: The Implementation of Community Legislation in the Member States, Vol. 1*, London, Sage.

Stewart-Clark, Sir Jack (1986), *Report on the Results of the Enquiry*. Committee of Inquiry into the Drugs Problem in the Member States of the Community, Luxembourg, European Parliament.

Swann, D. (1988), *The Economics of the Common Market*, London, Penguin.

— (1983), *Competition and Industrial Policy in the European Community*, London, Methuen.

Taylor, P. (1983), *The Limits of European Integration*, Kent, Croom, Helm.

Tsoukalis, L. (1977), *The Politics and Economics of European Monetary Integration*, London, Allen and Unwin.

Vandamme, J. (ed.) (1985), *New Dimensions in European Social Policy*, Kent, Croom Helm.

Vandamme, J. (1986), *Employee Consultation and Information in Multinational Corporations*, London, Croom Helm.

Ypersele, J. van and Koeune, J. (1985), *The European Monetary System*, Luxembourg, Office for Official Publications of the EC.

18 Environment: towards a clean blue-green EC?

Juliet Lodge

The turning point for the environmental lobby is said to have come in 1972: at the United Nations' Stockholm meeting the alarm was raised and cooperation was called for in 'conservation and development'. Two major environmental disasters followed in EC states – Flixborough in 1974, and Seveso in 1976. Daily environmental abuse by petro-chemical and other industries, urban programmes and 'high-tech' agricultural methods grew exponentially. Fears for the ozone layer were voiced but elicited little positive policy response by governments. Major international disasters (Three Mile Island, 1979; Bhopal 1984; and Mexico City's toxic cloud, 1986) heightened public concern. In 1986, two European disasters – Chernobyl and the Rhine's pollution – coincided with the EC's decision to put environmental matters higher on its agenda. As a result, 1987 was designated European Year of the Environment (Fairclough, 1986) and a concerted effort has been made to integrate EC environmental policy into all EC policies.

The problem for the EC in tackling environmental issues on a common basis lies not in the lack of public or government awareness as in the coalition of powerful industrial/political complexes and in the fact that until the SEA, EC action on the environment often was hotly disputed. This can be explained partly in terms of anxiety over the expansive logic of integration and the inevitably comprehensive scope of any EC action in the environmental sectors. It can also be explained in terms of the EC's primary economic orientation and the narrow equation of 'environmental protection' with EC or state intervention to curb industrial pollution (and raise industry's costs).

One of the Rome Treaty's goals is the improvement of the living standards of the people in the EC. Initially construed primarily in economic terms, this has come to be interpreted as referring more generally to the quality of life and the environment. Both have scaled the political agenda of all the member states with the rise of 'Green' parties, ecology and conservation issues. The politicization of environmental issues within the Twelve and in the European Parliament (partly because of the presence of 'Green' parties and the Rainbow Group) highlighted serious discrepancies between the member states. Concern and protests have increased over a range of issues from acid rain, oil pollution, the links between nuclear power stations' emissions and cancer clusters, water pollution (Briggs, 1986; Johnson, 1983), nitrates and pesticide residues entering the food chain, chemical and sewage sludge dumping in the North Sea to radiated food, food additives (including hormones like BST), dangerous labelling and packaging, chlorofluoro-carbons (CFCs), leaded petrol and wide differences in member states' responses to Chernobyl.

For many years, legal opinion was divided over whether or not the EC had competence in environmental matters. Member states have long had powers over industrial pollution and while this is a natural arena for EC involvement given the prevalence of trans-border pollution in the EC, it is only comparatively recently that the wider question of environmental protection has been raised. Moreover, action to safeguard or improve the EC's environment can be 'hidden' under *Euratom* (in the radiation field) and under CAP measures such as set-aside policies which have been developed primarily to deal with an agricultural problem but have incidental beneficial environmental effects. Similarly, environmentally useful decisions may be taken under other headings such as health and energy. Since 1972, environmental action has relied on a liberal interpretation of the Preamble and Articles 2, 100 and 235 of the Rome Treaty and the 'pragmatic legitimacy' derived from its action. Only the SEA, however, provides the EC with an explicit and clear legal base for EC environmental action (Commission, 1984; Davidson, 1987: 259).

The 1972 Paris summit indicated the member states' interest in an EC environmental policy. This was spurred not so much by the upsurge of post-industrial values and the Nine's endeavours to create a 'Human Union' or to give the EC a 'human face' as by the realization that widely differing national rules on industrial pollution could distort competition: 'dirty states' could profit economically by being slack (House of Lords, 1979, Case 92/79). Indeed, in 1988 the United Kingdom's laxness not only earned it the label of Europe's 'dirty man', but its slowness in enforcing EC directives appropriately (for example on water quality (Gameson, 1979; Haigh, 1984; Taylor, *et al.*, 1986)) suggested that it was profiting by being its EC partners' willing dustbin.

In 1972,the Commission was asked to draft a first action programme to form the basis of an environmental policy based on a contentious interpretation of Article 2 (EEC) and Articles 100 (relating to the establishment of a common market and the approximation of national laws that either create barriers to trade or distort competition) and 235 (allowing the Council to take 'appropriate measures' to attain the EC's goals). The action programme was adopted by the Council of Ministers in November 1973 (OJ C 112/1, 1973). This laid down principles, a framework for action and a timetable whose deadlines were often missed. The second action programme elaborated on the first and was adopted in 1977 (OJ C 139/1, 1977). It was confirmed in a third programme in 1981. On each occasion the number of sectors falling within the ambit of the programme was expanded. The fourth action programme (1987-92) was the first to refer to the nuclear industry (COM(86)485, 9.10.86). Central to the current programme is confirmation of the highly contentious issue of the 'polluter pays' principle first raised in 1973 and reasserted in the SEA. The 1973 programme has guided subsequent action.

The 1973 framework action programme guided subsequent legislative activity and established expandable parameters for later action programmes. It comprised three main elements: (i) action to reduce and prevent pollution and nuisances; (ii) action to improve the environment; and (iii) common action at the international level. In 1975 and 1976 respectively, it was decided to set up a common procedure for information exchange among surveillance and monitoring networks on atmospheric pollution (Parry and Dinnage, 1981: 406) and to collate and update an inventory of sources of information on the environment.

The programme also provided for research into pollution by various industries, particularly iron and steel, chemicals, pulp and paper. Later concerted projects examined atmospheric pollutants, sewage sludge and water pollution. The EC continues to attach importance to its monitoring and research activities. In July 1988 it set up a Task Force on the 'greenhouse effect' and charged it also with defining and defending an EC strategy in the international arena. The Commission has also promoted measures designed to prevent environmental damage through its Environmental Impact Assessment (EIA) proposals that seek to evaluate development and land-use projects before planning permission is granted. Developers are, however, adept at circumventing 'red tape' and it remains to be seen how effective the EIA will be.

Ambitious EC environmental goals are frustrated by the reliance on weak vehicles to enforce EC standards: directives, and the even weaker communications and decisions that lack binding effect (for example, the communication on integrated planning of coastal areas, (COM(86)571 30.10.86). Binding action has often needed a nudge from either internal or external environmental disasters. It is significant that the EC itself can become a contracting party to international conventions: for example, it is a member of the International Commission for the Protection of the Rhine against Pollution (ICPR). The ICPR proposed limiting mercury discharges into the Rhine from selected sectors: chemical industries using mercury catalysts, manufacturers using mercury in making vinyl chloride and other compounds and primary batteries containing mercury; non-ferrous metal industries; and plants treating toxic waste containing mercury (COM(86)710) fin 8.12.86). The EC Commission's current dossier on toxic waste in the EC and third states parallels that of the UN Environmental Programme and the OECD in seeking an international convention on the export of wastes.

Since the early 1980s, emphasis has shifted to the control of pollution and potentially dangerous noxious substances including the use of unleaded petrol – mandatory for all new cars from 1993 – fertilizers, sulphur dioxide and nitric oxide emissions and so on. Action has also been taken on air pollution – by fixing, for example, common emission standards for diesel engines (OJ C193, 31.7.86); the disposal of radio-active and chemical waste such as aldrin, dieldrin and endrin into acquatic environments (OJ C309, 3.12.86); 'red mud' (titanium dioxide); the recycling of waste and marine pollution. Noise pollution (known as electromagnetic disturbance) has also been tackled (though ridiculed in the case of lawn mowers (OJ C20, 27.1.87) and tower cranes (OJC 267, 23.10.86). In 1987, in a move regarded as a major breakthrough, money from the ERDF was spent on projects to improve the environment, and the European Investment Bank also helped to finance environmental projects.

Conservation issues assumed a higher profile from the early 1980s. The EC also continued to support measures to protect the environment and endangered species elsewhere (for example the East African coast and desertification in Africa (COM(86)571, 30.10.86). A regulation implementing the Convention on International Trade in Endangered Species of Wild Fauna and Flora in the EC came into effect in 1986 (OJ L201, 21.7.86). An EC-wide ban on the import of numerous whale products came into effect in January 1982; and action on the slaughter of baby seals and on seal imports followed in October 1983. An animal welfare lobby flexed its muscles frequently at the EP.

By the mid-1980s, Commission proposals were informed by the view that environmental protection was an economic and not simply a moral imperative.

The Commission's 'New Directions in Environment Policy' (COM86/76) insists that strict environmental protection measures cannot be divorced from economic policy. It was estimated that some £7,000 million could be saved by recycling waste (Budd, 1985: 121). In 1986, the Council reached agreement on a range of issues including the transfrontier transport of dangerous wastes, and work safety rules. Chernobyl raised awareness of the need for stringent nuclear and health safety measures and led to concern over radiation and the safety of irradiated food (COM(86)607, 7.11.86). It also spurred the December 1986 European Council into a 'Europe Against Cancer Programme' focusing on cancer prevention, education and research (OJ C50, 26.2.87).

The 1988 North Sea seal disaster heightened awareness of the urgent need for EC-wide common action. A future-orientated perspective has resulted in directives on eco-system research, afforestation, the protection of wild life (OJ C 86, 1.4.87), dumping of wastes, use of sewage sludge in farming, industrial hazards, biotechnology, animal experiments, protection of water (*Bulletin of the EC*, 4, 1988, pt, 2.1.110ff). Indeed, action on protecting the aquatic environment (for example by trying to harmonize national legislation to cut water pollution by chromium through the establishment of quality objectives and a common reference method for measurement) has assumed an increasingly high priority. A first directive was made under List II of the basic Directive (76/464/EEC; OJ L129, 18.5.76, 23). The transfrontier implications are highly sensitive given water and airborne pollution from the East bloc.

The aim of the Fourth Environment Action Programme – to integrate environmental protection into social, industrial, agricultural and economic policies – seemed vindicated by developments. Even though this aim demanded coordinated sectoral action on the atmosphere, fresh and sea water, chemicals, biotechnology, noise, nuclear safety, conservation, soil protection and waste management, some governments have tried to re-compartmentalize and limit the scope of EC environmental measures. The UK tried to cut the Commission's nineteen priority areas, for example. However, an informal Council of Ministers' meeting in Delphi in October 1988 reasserted the principle of an integrated approach to environmental issues through the establishment of new financial instruments to ensure the integration of environmental protection across EC policies. This was seen as an integral part of the Single European Market.

It would be wrong to suggest that the EC has had a resounding success on environmental issues. It is true that it has systematically heightened awareness and prompted consideration of critical issues. The weakness of EC action in the environmental field lies with financial constraints and significantly with the instrument chosen for its implementation: the directive. Member states have frequently side-stepped their obligations notably in meeting quality standards in bathing and drinking water, and acid rain for example by contesting the scientific evidence. Industrial and business concerns, moreover, are anxious to see any EC legislation having environmental implications based on environmental articles of the SEA because of the unanimity requirement. The EP, by contrast, has contested the legal base of such measures with a view to their being enacted under the provisions governing the realization of the internal market (whose measures normally can be enacted by qualified majority). In January 1988 the Commission acceded to MEPs' requests that the cooperation procedure be extended to specific research programmes on transport, fisheries and agricultural issues. Governments hoping to delay policies having environmental implications by contesting the legal base of Commission proposals are being publicly challenged.

Commitment to the principle of an integrated approach to environmental protection inevitably means that many proposals will be subject to the cooperation procedure. This gives MEPs plenty of scope to try and amend proposals to raise standards (as in the case of small-car emissions of hydrocarbons, nitrogen oxides and carbon monoxide where MEPs sought amendments to the Commission's proposals in line with the more stringent Swiss, Austrian and Swedish regulations (EPWD, A2-132/88)).

The SEA confirmed the right of the EC's institutions to legislate on environmental issues. It defined the objectives of EC action on the environment as (i) to preserve, protect and improve the quality of the environment; (ii) to contribute towards protecting human health and (iii) to ensure a prudent and rational utilization of natural resources (Article 130R(i)). Such action is to be guided by the principles of preventive action; rectification of environmental damage at source; the 'polluter pays'; and integration of EC environmental policy with other EC policies (a principle established in the Third Environmental Action Programme, 1977). Other EC policies must take into account environmental protection requirements. Article 130R is in the spirit of conservation. It seeks to ensure that the likely environmental effects of policies in other areas are given due regard. It specifies how this is to be attained. The relevant provisions seem rather loose, but they establish important principles and guidelines which must be viewed in the light of the EC's jurisdiction and the ECJ's role in dealing with infringements of treaty obligations. The subsidiary principle means that whereas prior to the SEA, the issue was whether or not the EC had competence to act or not, now measures can be challenged in terms of whether or not the EC or the member states could better deal with the issue. A challenge can also be brought on the grounds that the EC has failed to abide by certain principles set out in Article 130R(2) or failed to make the required assessments under Article 130R(3). Moreover, as Vandenmeersch argues, because the EC's principal environmental instrument seems to be the directive, 'private parties seem severely restricted in their possibilities of bringing a claim for annulment before the European Court of Justice'. They would have to satisfy the 'direct and individual concern' test and persuade the ECJ to ignore Article 173(2)EEC (Vandenmeersch, 1987: 428).

EC environmental action has to have regard to (i) available scientific and technical data; (ii) environmental conditions in the EC's various regions; (iii) the potential benefits and costs of action or of lack of action; (iv) the economic and social development of the EC as a whole and the balanced development of its regions – something that links environmental action into the 'social space' dimension of the SEM. Clearly the potential scope of Commission action on environmental matters is extremely wide and problematic. The acceptance of 'cost-benefit' calculations reveals pragmatism and the need for flexibility. They also raise the spectre of standards being set on the basis of the lowest common denominator. Greece and Ireland at the 1985 Intergovernmental conference made known their wishes to ensure that environmental considerations should not jeopardize industrial development. This in turn raises the matter of the financing of EC environmental action (ACE). The main burden falls on the member states. The EC will finance certain actions only (Kromarek, 1986).

The available instruments to advance environmental goals remain problematic. Apart from the difficulties over the implementation of directives, there is division over market and non-market instruments and disagreement among pragmatists (such as the British who favour low-cost 'practical measures') and the Danish and the Germans who favour measures that exploit the latest technological advances and scientific knowledge. Self-regulation by industrial and agricultural polluters has not proved effective even with government oversight. Problems also arise over measures based on prohibitive taxes, emission standards, certification, chemical measuring and so on. Moreover, the suspicion remains that even EC Commission proposals are too heavily influenced by national interests that already provide possibly biased data to government representatives.

Nevertheless, the EC is committed to acting on environmental matters where it is clear that the specified goals can be better attained at the EC level rather than at the level of the individual member states. This enshrines the principle of subsidiarity advocated by the EUT. The EC and the states must act together to ensure that the environment is improved, but the declaration of the states in the Final Act excludes the EC from taking steps likely to interfere with national policies on the exploitation of energy resources. Confrontation is inevitable here.

Article 130S also provides for decisions on certain environmental issues defined by the Council to be taken by qualified majority as opposed to unanimous vote. The latter is, however, likely to be demanded by those wishing to delay the adoption and implementation of EC standards which are essential in the longer term. Some member states (notably Denmark) remain anxious lest common standards result in lower standards. However, the aim of raising standards is confirmed in the SEA, and member states are to be allowed to introduce or maintain more stringent standards providing they are compatible with the treaty and are not disguised technical barriers to trade which the SEA seeks to eliminate. Article 130T(SEA), recognizing the intent of the Danish Declaration,[1] permits states to maintain or introduce more stringent protective measures.

A further potentially difficult area concerns arrangements with third countries and international organizations. The EC now has the right, under article 228EEC, to make agreements for cooperation with third parties. One of the aims here is to ensure that 'dirty' member states do not profit by having lax, economically profitable, standards which fall below EC minima and which distort competition and/or export pollutants banned elsewhere. This is important where water and windborne transfrontier pollution can easily detrimentally affect other member states' environments. Moreover, eco-system concern means that adverse publicity and increased awareness of one or more states becoming the others' (or an international) dustbin will demand further action. The need to monitor, control and regulate the transportation of noxious and dangerous substances across borders is appreciated. Those along transit routes are highly cynical as to the safety, let alone desirability, of such dirty trade. Indeed, the EP's transport committee has advocated using pipelines to transport wastes, chemicals and refined oil to improve safety, safeguard the environment and reduce border delays (EPWD, A2-131/88).

EC action on environmental issues will grow fast over the next few years. It will prove contentious not just because the legal basis of EC measures will be disputed by the EP but because so many other EC policies (such as the CAP) have clear environmental effects. Moreover, member states will find that their policies (or lack of them) in the area will be challenged with reference to the subsidiarity principle and legal base. The Commission has already decided that questions on the marketing and distribution of dangerous chemicals is a matter of environmental rather than simply internal market policy and should be properly overseen by an 'advisory committee' (rather than the 'regulatory committee' preferred by governments) to give the Commission responsibility for its management (EPWD A2-133/88). The EP has also brought it to heel over proposals that it sees as too weak (for example in October 1988, MEPs threw out the Council's common position on the benzene proposal). Of particular concern to the EC are the management and transport and not simply the labelling of hazardous waste. To this end, the 'Seveso' Directive (OJ L230, 5.8.82) is to be extended to the storage of dangerous chemicals and the type of information to be made public. Moreover, two directives on harmonized procedures on the control of accidents and waste treatment through the deliberate release of genetically modified organisms (available on the market) have been drafted (COM(88)160, final) and attention has turned to civil defence cooperation to manage transborder emergencies, accidents and disasters.

While the EC concentrates on internal measures, it does not take them out of their international context. Article 130S confirms the EC's external competences in environmental matters. It acknowledges the doctrine of parallelism (that is the EC's competence to conclude agreements with third states in areas over which it already has internal competence). Agreements between the EC and third states are subject to Article 228EEC. The EC has concluded numerous agreements on environmental issues (notably marine pollution) with third states and international organizations (Leenan, 1984). More recently, the EC has considered adopting further international agreements including the Vienna Convention for the protection of the ozone layer and the Montreal Protocol on substances that deplete the ozone layer (to be implemented by regulation in the EC). The EC makes its view known internationally, both at the UN and OECD, and on a bilateral basis (*Bulletin of the EC*, 3, 1988, 2.1.130) Two March 1988 Council decisions highlight EC intentions. The first authorized the Commission to negotiate on the EC's behalf, within the OECD, an International Agreement on the control of transfrontier movements of hazardous wastes. This makes mandatory a series of identification, notification, authorization and monitoring measures prior to the movement of hazardous wastes (*Bulletin of the EC*, 3, 1988, 2.1.126). The second authorizes the Commission to negotiate with the US a more limited agreement on monitoring procedures for such wastes. Clearly, the demands of an EC *sans frontières* makes such agreements imperative. However, governments are clearly going to have to cooperate on numerous linked sectoral issues and broader environmental matters under a more centrally regulated regime than hitherto. The 'Greening of the EC' is an integral part of '1992' in a way that has still to be fully appreciated.

Note

1. On the legal status of such Declarations see A. Toth, (1986), 'The Legal Status of the Declarations annexed to the Single European Act', *Common Market Law review*, **23**.

References

Barisich, A. (1987), 'The Protection of the Sea: A European Community Policy', *International Journal of Estuarine and Coastal Law*, 2.

Briggs, D. (1986), 'Environmental problems and policies in the European Community', in C. Parks (ed.), *Environmental Problems: An International Review*, London, Croom Helm.

Budd, S. (1985), *The EEC: A Guide to the Maze*, London, Kogan Page.

Case 92/79 Commission v. Italy (1980), ECR 1115, 1122.

Commission of the EC Report (1987), *The Chernobyl Nuclear Power Plant Accident and its consequences in the Framework of the EC*. COM(86)607,7 November.

Commission of the EC (1987), *Ten Years of Community Environmental Policy*, Brussels.

— (1983), *The European Community's Environmental Policy*, Luxembourg, Office for Official Publications.

Davidson, S. (1987), 'European Communities. Environment', *International Journal of Estuarine and Coastal Law*, 2(4), 257-64.

European Environmental Yearbook, 1987, (1987), London, DocTer UK Ltd.

Fairclough, A.J. (1986), 'The European Year of the Environment', *European Environmental Review*, 1(1), 35-7.

Gameson, A.L.H. (1979), 'EEC Directive on Quality of Bathing Water', *Water Pollution Control*, 78(2), 206-14.

Haigh, N. (1984), EEC *Environmental Policy and Britain*, London, Environmental Data Services.

House of Lords Select Committee on the European Communities (1979), *22nd Report and Minutes of 3 July 1979*, HL 68.

Johnson, S. (1983), *The Pollution Control Policy of the European Communities*, London, Graham & Trotman.

Kromarek, P. (1986), 'The Single European Act and the Environment', *European Environment Review*, 1(1).

Leenen, A. (1984), 'Participation of the EEC in international environmental agreements', *Legal Issues of European Integration*, 6, 93-111.

Parry, A. and Dinnage, J. (1981), *EEC Law*, 2nd ed, Sweet and Maxwell.

Taylor, D. *et. al.* (1986), 'EC Environmental policy and the control of water pollution: the implementation of Directive 76/464 in perspective', *Journal of Common Market Studies*, 24, 225-46.

Vandenmeersch, D. (1987), 'The Single European Act and the Environmental Policy of the European Economic Community', *European Law Review*, 12, 407–29.

Conclusion

It has been shown that contrary to popular misconceptions about the EC, the European Community has undergone rapid change over the past decade. While economic crises and constraints have inhibited the development of policies backed by sufficient resources to ensure that they have the intended impact, new initiatives in the internal and external policy arenas have been launched. While the twelve member states have continued to disagree over major policy issues, consensus has nevertheless emerged on the desirability of maintaining the EC and the system which permits intergovernmental and supranational problem-solving and conflict resolution.

The 1980s have seen a psychological shift among EC elites. In some countries, this psychological shift had to be nudged by instrumental intervention by government officials following the SEA's implementation in July 1987. Realizing the internal market by 1992 was seen as an opportunity for increasing business and states' prosperity and information programmes were launched to ensure that the Euro-dimension to future trade and business was more fully appreciated.

However, realizing the SEM has important implications for a range of other national and EC policies. Indeed, the notion of removing barriers between the EC states and strengthening the EC's external border has far-reaching consequences for individual member states' domestic and international policies. In the UK it was slowly realized that almost all policy areas had a Euro-potential and interfaced with EC objectives. That they did or could mean that the parameters governing policymaking, policy implementation and interdepartmental and intergovernmental coordination had to be reappraised. General awareness of the EC dimension to policymaking grew.

At the international level, protestations that the EC was merely a civilian power, an economic giant but a political dwarf – to borrow clichés of the time – were undermined both by the growing degree of cooperation among EC states on policy areas formerly regarded as the sacred preserve of autonomous foreign ministries and by the need for increased cross-border collaboration between security and customs services. Sensitive issues of high diplomacy were increasingly to come under scrutiny within European Political Cooperation and its various working parties. The EC was increasingly seen as a legitimate and proper forum in which to discuss international issues and to plan cooperative, if not joint, strategies. States like West Germany, which had a tradition of Europeanizing their national foreign policy goals in order to enhance their chances of success, were to see more individualistic states like France and the UK both using EPC in an instrumental manner and appreciating the supranational consequences of such developments. It was no accident that the SEA was to record the member states' interest in cooperating on the highly sensitive area of security.

International developments, the persisting Middle East crises, international terrorism, divergence between the EC and US over major issues (including links with the East bloc) and increased self-confidence among the Twelve over the distinctively different policy priorities and strategies appropriate for the EC, led the EC and its members to become more assertive in the international arena. This policy did not detract from Western Europe's continuing dependence on the US for defence, but it did reopen the question of the extent to which US policy goals were compatible with the perceived priorities of Western Europe (and possibly of an EC expanded to include Norway, Austria and even Turkey) in international affairs.

As the EC enters the 1990s, not only have priorities changed and new policies been developed, but there has been a subtle and significant shift in attitudes towards the EC. This shift is not necessarily marked by increased support for the EC or for the ideal of European unity (indeed, the contrary may be the case). Instead, it is marked by the fact that the EC is regarded, notably by the hesitant Europeans suspicious of how EC membership would diminish their sovereignty, as the parameter within which all manner of policies and initiatives can and should be elaborated. Whether this is conceptualized as a Europeanization of national policies or as the spillover effect of European integration, or both, is less important than the fact that the European dimension is taken as given and is not questioned in terms of its permanence. The British Labour Party's reluctant acceptance of this seems both inevitable and belated. Naturally, anti-marketeers exist almost everywhere in the EC but few really believe that secession from the EC is likely in the foreseeable future. Greenland's withdrawal in 1981 was not interpreted as the great escape blueprint for others.

In conclusion, it can be seen that the EC is still in a period of transition and change. The 1980s established the potency of a majority-based consensus as the driving force behind integration. The 1990s are unlikely to relinquish the gains this brought to a stalling minority. The aim is not the creation of a highly centralized unitary state but a heterogeneous, decentralized community capable of formulating, implementing and overseeing policymaking in a transparent, responsive, effective, efficient and above all democratically legitimate and accountable manner.

While the priority accorded the creation of the SEM inevitably accentuates business and trade issues, the SEM is about much more than a rich man's club. Traditional EC policy sectors are having to be adapted to the increasingly active and complementary social dimension of the EC – to a Citizen's Europe. Environmental, educational and vocational and consumer issues generally will grow in importance. Satellite television, communications policies and cross-national link-ups across a range of activities from sport to policing questions will have a role to play in underlining the European dimension to people's lives and will themselves be subject to a Europeanizing influence. The quiet revolution of the 1980s in the EC will continue well into the 1990s.

Index